GPU Pro⁴

GPU Pro⁴

Advanced Rendering Techniques

Edited by Wolfgang Engel

CRC Press
Taylor & Francis Group
Boca Raton London New York

CRC Press is an imprint of the
Taylor & Francis Group, an **Informa** business

AN A K PETERS BOOK

CRC Press
Taylor & Francis Group
6000 Broken Sound Parkway NW, Suite 300
Boca Raton, FL 33487-2742

© 2013 by Taylor & Francis Group, LLC
CRC Press is an imprint of Taylor & Francis Group, an Informa business

No claim to original U.S. Government works

Printed on acid-free paper
Version Date: 20130204

International Standard Book Number-13: 978-1-4665-6743-6 (Hardback)

Library of Congress Cataloging-in-Publication Data

GPU Pro 4 : advanced rendering techniques / edited by Wolfgang Engel.
  pages cm
  "An A K Peters Book."
  Includes bibliographical references.
  ISBN 978-1-4665-6743-6 (hardback)
  1. Rendering (Computer graphics) 2. Graphics processing units--Programming. 3. Computer graphics. 4. Real-time data processing. I. Engel, Wolfgang.

  T385.G6887 2013
  006.6'93--dc23   2012044435

Visit the Taylor & Francis Web site at
http://www.taylorandfrancis.com

and the CRC Press Web site at
http://www.crcpress.com

Contents

    Markus Billeter, Ola Olsson, and Ulf Assarsson

    4.1   Introduction   99
    4.2   Recap: Forward, Deferred, and Tiled Shading   101
    4.3   Tiled Forward Shading: Why?   104
    4.4   Basic Tiled Forward Shading   104
    4.5   Supporting Transparency   106
    4.6   Support for MSAA   109
    4.7   Supporting Different Shaders   111
    4.8   Conclusion and Further Improvements   111
    Bibliography   113

5   Forward+: A Step Toward Film-Style Shading in Real Time   115
    Takahiro Harada, Jay McKee, and Jason C. Yang

    5.1   Introduction   115
    5.2   Forward+   116
    5.3   Implementation and Optimization   117
    5.4   Results   123
    5.5   Forward+ in the AMD Leo Demo   124
    5.6   Extensions   127
    5.7   Conclusion   133
    5.8   Acknowledgments   134
    Bibliography   134

6   Progressive Screen-Space Multichannel Surface Voxelization   137
    Athanasios Gaitatzes and Georgios Papaioannou

    6.1   Introduction   137
    6.2   Overview of Voxelization Method   138
    6.3   Progressive Voxelization for Lighting   144
    6.4   Implementation   145
    6.5   Performance and Evaluation   145
    6.6   Limitations   151
    6.7   Conclusion   153
    6.8   Acknowledgments   153
    Bibliography   153

7   Rasterized Voxel-Based Dynamic Global Illumination   155
    Hawar Doghramachi

    7.1   Introduction   155
    7.2   Overview   155
    7.3   Implementation   156
    7.4   Handling Large Environments   168

Acknowledgments

The *GPU Pro: Advanced Rendering Techniques* book series covers ready-to-use ideas and procedures that can solve many of your daily graphics-programming challenges.

The fourth book in the series wouldn't have been possible without the help of many people. First, I would like to thank the section editors for the fantastic job they did. The work of Wessam Bahnassi, Sebastien St-Laurent, Carsten Dachsbacher, Michal Valient, and Christopher Oat ensured that the quality of the series meets the expectations of our readers.

The great cover screenshots have been provided courtesy of Sébastien Lagarde. They are from the game *Remember Me* published by Capcom.

The team at Taylor and Francis—formerly A K Peters—made the whole project happen. I want to thank Rick Adams, Sarah Chow, Charlotte Byrnes, and the entire production team, who took the articles and made them into a book. Special thanks go out to our families and friends, who spent many evenings and weekends without us during the long book production cycle.

I hope you have as much fun reading the book as we had creating it.

—Wolfgang Engel

P.S. Plans for an upcoming *GPU Pro 5* are already in progress. Any comments, proposals, and suggestions are highly welcome (wolfgang.engel@gmail.com).

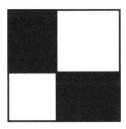

Web Materials

Example programs and source code to accompany some of the chapters are available on the CRC Press website: go to http://www.crcpress.com/product/isbn/9781466567436 and click on the "Downloads" tab.

The directory structure closely follows the book structure by using the chapter number as the name of the subdirectory. You will need to download the DirectX August 2009 software development kit (SDK) or the DirectX June 2010 SDK.

General System Requirements

To use all of the files, you will need

- the DirectX June 2010 SDK;

- a DirectX9, DirectX 10, or even DirectX 11 capable GPU (the articles will mention the exact requirements for their examples);

- Microsoft Windows 7, following the requirement of DirectX 10 or 11 capable GPUs;

- Visual C++ .NET 2008;

- 2 GB RAM or more;

- the latest GPU driver.

Updates

Updates of the example programs will be posted on the website.

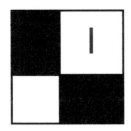

Geometry Manipulation

The "Geometry Manipulation" section of the book focuses on the ability of graphics processing units (GPUs) to process and generate geometry in exciting ways.

The next article "Introducing the Programmable Vertex Pulling Rendering Pipeline" discusses one of the bigger challenges in game development targeting PC platforms: the GPU driver overhead. By moving more tasks onto the quickly evolving GPUs, the number of draw calls per frame can be increased. The article gives also an in-depth view on the latest AMD GPUs.

The first article in this section "GPU Terrain Subdivision and Tessellation" presents a GPU-based algorithm to perform real-time terrain subdivision and rendering of vast detailed landscapes without preprocessing data on the CPU. It also achieves smooth level of detail transitions from any viewpoint.

The last article in the section "A WebGL Globe Rendering Pipeline" describes a globe rendering pipeline that integrates hierarchical levels of detail (HLOD) algorithms used to manage high resolution imagery streamed from standard map servers, such as Esri or OpenStreetMap. All the techniques described in the article are used in Cesium, http://cesium.agi.com, an open source WebGL globe and map engine.

—Wolfgang Engel

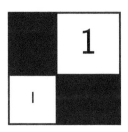

GPU Terrain Subdivision and Tessellation

Benjamin Mistal

This paper presents a GPU-based algorithm to perform real-time terrain subdivision and rendering of vast detailed landscapes. This algorithm achieves smooth level of detail (LOD) transitions from any viewpoint and does not require any preprocessing of data structures on the CPU.

1.1 Introduction

There are a lot of existing terrain rendering and subdivision algorithms that achieve fantastic results, and fast frame rates. Some of these algorithms, however, are limited. They can require the preprocessing of large data sets, constant transferring of large data sets from the CPU to the GPU, limited viewing areas, or complex algorithms to merge together meshes in efforts to avoid cracks and seams as a result of various LOD subdivision techniques.

The GPU-based algorithm we developed addresses all of the above mentioned limitations, and presents a simple alternative to render highly detailed landscapes, without significant impact on the CPU. Figure 1.1 shows an example of this algorithm and also shows the generated underlying wire-frame mesh partially superimposed.

We describe a GPU-based algorithm to create a subdivided mesh with distance-based LOD that can be used for terrain rendering. Data amplification and multiple stream-out hardware capability are utilized to repeatedly subdivide an area to achieve a desired LOD. In addition, culling is also performed at each iteration of the algorithm, therefore avoiding a lot of unnecessary processing or subdivision of areas outside of the viewing frustum. Because the resulting data is retained and refined on the GPU, the CPU is mostly left available to perform other tasks. To show a practical use of this technique, we also utilize a smooth LOD transitioning scheme, and use a procedural terrain generation function to provide real-time rendering of a highly detailed and vast landscape.

Figure 1.1. Rendered terrain, with the underlying wireframe mesh partially superimposed.

Our algorithm was heavily inspired by two existing algorithms. The first inspiration came from the great desire to walk through the procedural mountains created by F. Kenton Musgrave [Ebert et al. 98], in real time. The second inspiration came from the visual beauty of the real-time water created by Claes Johanson, in his introduction of the projected grid concept [Johanson 04]. The concept helped form one of the ideas for the basis of our subdivision algorithm, by showcasing effective and efficient vertex placement to display a vast area of seascape.

1.2   The Algorithm

A few terms are used throughout this paper and are integral to understanding the general algorithm and the related descriptions. Section 1.2.1 will describe these terms and provide related calculations. An algorithm overview is provided in Section 1.2.2, and Sections 1.2.3 to 1.2.5 describe the main separate components of our algorithm.

1.2.1   Terms and Definitions

Viewable region. A *viewable region*, denoted by R, is defined as an axis aligned quadrilateral representing a region that is to be subdivided and/or rendered. This region is defined from a *center position* and an *applied offset* in both the positive and negative directions along each aligning axis (see Figure 1.2). The center position is denoted by R_C. The applied offset is denoted by R_λ. The bounding points of the region are denoted by P_1, P_2, P_3, and P_4.

Viewable region span. To quantify a *viewable region span*, denoted by θ, we defined the following calculation at point P and applied offset λ:

$$\theta(P, \lambda) = |P_{\text{ScreenR}} - P_{\text{ScreenL}}|,$$

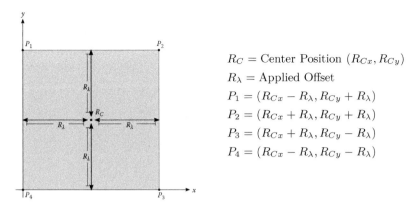

$R_C = \text{Center Position } (R_{Cx}, R_{Cy})$

$R_\lambda = \text{Applied Offset}$

$P_1 = (R_{Cx} - R_\lambda, R_{Cy} + R_\lambda)$

$P_2 = (R_{Cx} + R_\lambda, R_{Cy} + R_\lambda)$

$P_3 = (R_{Cx} + R_\lambda, R_{Cy} - R_\lambda)$

$P_4 = (R_{Cx} - R_\lambda, R_{Cy} - R_\lambda)$

Figure 1.2. Example of a viewable region and its associated properties.

$$P_{\text{ScreenL}} = (P_{\text{VProjL}xy})/P_{\text{ProjLw}},$$
$$P_{\text{ScreenR}} = (P_{\text{ProjR}xy})/P_{\text{ProjRw}},$$
$$P_{\text{ProjL}} = P_{WL} \times \text{matProjection},$$
$$P_{\text{ProjR}} = P_{WR} \times \text{matProjection},$$
$$P_{WL} = (P_{Wx} - \lambda, P_{Wy}),$$
$$P_{WR} = (P_{Wx} + \lambda, P_{Wy}),$$
$$P_W = P \times \text{matWorldView}.$$

The above calculation for the viewable region span can be used at any position P and applied offset λ, and is used extensively within the LOD Transition Algorithm (explained in Section 1.2.4). We use this calculation instead of calculating the actual viewing surface area to avoid inconsistencies when viewable regions are viewed from different angles.

Maximum viewable region span. The *maximum viewable region span*, denoted by $\theta_{\max}$, is the maximum allowable viewable region span. This value, which is set by the user, is one of the main determining factors of the attainable LOD, and it plays a key part in both the Subdivision Algorithm (explained in Section 1.2.3) and the LOD Transition Algorithm (explained in Section 1.2.4).

Relative quadrant code. This code identifies the relative position of a split viewable region in relation to its parent viewable region. This code is utilized by the LOD Transition Algorithm (explained in Section 1.2.4), and calculated in the Subdivision Algorithm (explained in Section 1.2.3). Usually encoded as a 2-bit mask, this code becomes part of the definition of a viewable region.

1.2.2 Algorithm Overview

The algorithm operates in three stages:

Stage 1. Create the initial input stream of one or more viewable regions containing the area(s) to be viewed.

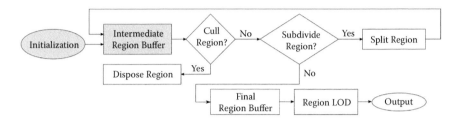

Stage 2. Take the initial input stream of viewable regions from Stage 1 and iteratively process each viewable region utilizing the Subdivision Algorithm (explained in Section 1.2.3).

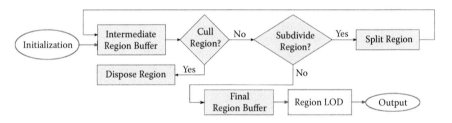

Stage 3. Render the resulting final output stream of viewable regions from Stage 2. At this stage, we utilize an LOD Transition Algorithm (explained in Section 1.2.4), as well as a Procedural Height Generation Algorithm (explained in Section 1.2.5) to render the resulting terrain.

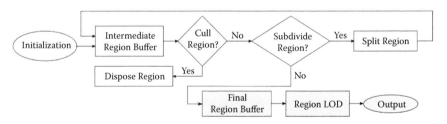

1.2.3 Subdivision Algorithm

In Stage 2 of the algorithm, for each iteration, we feed an input stream of viewable regions into the geometry shader stage of the rendering pipeline. The input stream for the first iteration is the initial input stream that was created in Stage 1. All subsequent iterations use the intermediate output stream from the preceding iteration as the input. Two output streams are utilized in the geometry shader. An intermediate output stream is used to hold viewable regions that are intended for further processing. A final output stream is used to hold viewable regions that require no further processing in the next iteration, and are to be rendered as part of Stage 3 of the algorithm.

Within the geometry shader, each viewable region is processed and one of the following three actions is performed:

Option 1. If the viewable region is determined to not intersect with the view frustum, it is culled. The culled viewable region is not added to either the intermediate or the final output stream.

When determining whether or not the viewable region intersects the view frustum, one must be mindful of any displacements performed during Stage 3 of the algorithm. When using this algorithm for terrain rendering, each viewable region is extruded into a volume, based on the maximum displacement that may be added in Stage 3. It is this extruded volume that is then tested for intersection with the view frustum.

Option 2. If the viewable region span θ, calculated at the viewable region R's center position R_C, and with the applied offset R_λ, written as $\theta(R_C, R_\lambda)$, is greater than the maximum viewable region span $\theta_{\max}$, then the viewable region R is split into four quadrants $(R1, R2, R3, R4)$. The quadrants, each of which become viewable regions themselves, are then added to the intermediate output stream to be reprocessed at the next iteration. A special code, unique to each quadrant, is also added to the output stream to identity the relative location of the split viewable regions to their parent viewable region. This extra piece of information, referred to as a *relative quadrant code*, and usually encoded into a 2-bit mask, is later utilized by the LOD Transition Algorithm (explained in Section 1.2.4) when rendering each viewable region.

To split the viewable region R (see Figure 1.3(a)) into the quadrants (see Figure 1.3(b)), we create four new viewable regions $(R1, R2, R3, R4)$ with their respective center positions $(R1_C, R2_C, R3_C, R4_C)$ and applied offsets $(R1_\lambda, R2_\lambda, R3_\lambda, R4_\lambda)$ defined as follows:

$$R1_C = \left(R_{Cx} - \frac{1}{2}R_\lambda, R_{Cy} + \frac{1}{2}R_\lambda \right),$$

$$R2_C = \left(R_{Cx} + \frac{1}{2}R_\lambda, R_{Cy} + \frac{1}{2}R_\lambda \right),$$

$$R3_C = \left(R_{Cx} + \frac{1}{2}R_\lambda, R_{Cy} - \frac{1}{2}R_\lambda \right),$$

$$R4_C = \left(R_{Cx} - \frac{1}{2}R_\lambda, R_{Cy} - \frac{1}{2}R_\lambda \right),$$

$$R1_\lambda = \frac{1}{2}R_\lambda,$$

$$R2_\lambda = \frac{1}{2}R_\lambda,$$

$$R3_\lambda = \frac{1}{2}R_\lambda,$$

$$R4_\lambda = \frac{1}{2}R_\lambda.$$

Option 3. If the viewable region span θ, calculated at the viewable region R's center position R_C, and with the applied offset R_λ, $\theta(R_C, R_\lambda)$, is less than or equal to the maximum viewable region span $\theta_{\max}$, then the viewable region R is added to final output stream of viewable regions.

Note that for the final iteration in Stage 2 of the algorithm, any viewable region not culled must be added to the final output stream, regardless of the viewable region span. This is to ensure that all remaining viewable regions have a chance

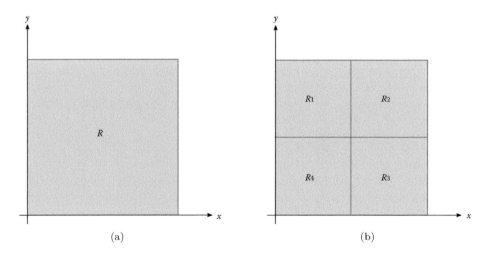

(a)   (b)

Figure 1.3. (a) The viewable region (R). (b) The split viewable regions ($R1, R2, R3, R4$).

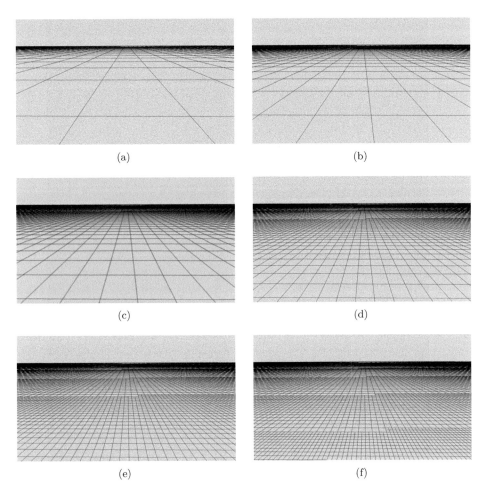

(a)

(b)

(c)

(d)

(e)

(f)

Figure 1.4. Viewable region after (a) N iterations, (b) $N + 1$ iterations, (c) $N + 2$ iterations, (d) $N + 3$ iterations, (e) $N + 4$ iterations, and (f) $N + 5$ iterations.

to be rendered, and are not placed into an intermediate output stream that will not result in any further processing or rendering.

Figures 1.4(a)–1.4(f) show examples of a viewable region after a number of iterations through our subdivision algorithm.

1.2.4 LOD Transition Algorithm

In Stage 3 of the algorithm, a stream of viewable regions are rendered. One viewable region R with an applied offset of R_λ may be adjacent to another viewable

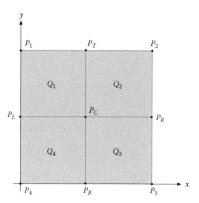

Figure 1.5. Example of the viewable region quadrilateral boundary points.

region with an applied offset that is either half or double the size of R_λ. Without performing a smooth transition between the two differently sized viewable regions, there would be visible discontinuities or other visual anomalies when rendering. We describe a method that offers a smooth transition between differently sized viewable regions. By rendering a viewable region as a set of quadrilaterals, we are able to morph the quadrilaterals in such as way to make the boundary between the larger and smaller viewable regions indistinguishable. This method eliminates seams, T-junctions, and visible boundaries between neighboring viewable regions of different sizes. A similar method was described by Filip Strugar [Strugar 10], although we have extended it to handle various boundary cases to ensure no cracks form anywhere within the mesh.

Each viewable region is rendered by splitting the viewable region into four quadrilaterals, denoted by Q_1, Q_2, Q_3, and Q_4 (see Figure 1.5). The boundary points for each quadrilateral, comprised from the collection of static boundary points (P_1, P_2, P_3, P_4) and the morphing boundary points $(P_L, P_T, P_R, P_B, P_C)$, are defined as follows:

$$Q_1 = \{P_1, P_T, P_C, P_L\},$$
$$Q_2 = \{P_T, P_2, P_R, P_C\},$$
$$Q_3 = \{P_C, P_R, P_3, P_B\},$$
$$Q_4 = \{P_L, P_C, P_B, P_4\}.$$

Collectively, these nonoverlapping quadrilaterals will cover the same surface area as the viewable region they are created from. The boundary points of each quadrilateral are calculated to align with the boundary points of the neighboring viewable region quadrilaterals. The morphing quadrilateral boundary points

$(P_L, P_T, P_R, P_B, P_C)$ are calculated as follows:

$$P_L = \left(P_1 \times \left(1 - \frac{1}{2}T_L\right)\right) + \left(P_4 \times \frac{1}{2}T_L\right),$$

$$P_T = \left(P_1 \times \left(1 - \frac{1}{2}T_T\right)\right) + \left(P_2 \times \frac{1}{2}T_T\right),$$

$$P_R = \left(P_2 \times \left(1 - \frac{1}{2}T_R\right)\right) + \left(P_3 \times \frac{1}{2}T_R\right),$$

$$P_B = \left(P_4 \times \left(1 - \frac{1}{2}T_B\right)\right) + \left(P_3 \times \frac{1}{2}T_B\right),$$

$$P_C = \left(P_1 \times \left(1 - \frac{1}{2}T_C\right)\right) + \left(P_3 \times \frac{1}{2}T_C\right).$$

Given a viewable region span θ at point P and applied offset λ, written as $\theta(P, \lambda)$, we are able to calculate a morphing factor $T(P, \lambda)$, by using the following formula:

$$T(P, \lambda) = \begin{cases} 0, & \theta(P, \lambda) \leq \frac{1}{2}\theta_{\max}, \\ (\theta(P, \lambda)/\theta_{\max}) \times 2 - 1, & \frac{1}{2}\theta_{\max} < \theta(P, \lambda) < \theta_{\max}, \\ 1, & \theta(P, \lambda) \geq \theta_{\max}. \end{cases}$$

We calculate each of the general morphing factors $(T_L, T_T, T_R, T_B, T_C)$ for a viewable region R with a *center position* R_C and applied offset R_λ as follows:

$$T_L = T(\beta_L, R_\lambda),$$
$$T_T = T(\beta_T, R_\lambda),$$
$$T_R = T(\beta_R, R_\lambda),$$
$$T_B = T(\beta_B, R_\lambda),$$
$$T_C = T(R_C, R_\lambda),$$
$$\beta_L = (R_{Cx} - R_\lambda, R_{Cy}),$$
$$\beta_T = (R_{Cx}, R_{Cy} + R_\lambda),$$
$$\beta_R = (R_{Cx} + R_\lambda, R_{Cy}),$$
$$\beta_B = (R_{Cx}, R_{Cy} - R_\lambda).$$

These general morphing factors will be applied when rendering a viewable region, and assumes that the neighboring viewable regions have the same applied offset R_λ. Figure 1.6 provides a diagram of the various positions used when calculating the general morphing factors.

There are two special boundary cases we need to handle when calculating the morphing factors. These special cases arise when one viewable region is adjacent to another viewable region of a larger or smaller applied offset λ. The cases are defined as follows:

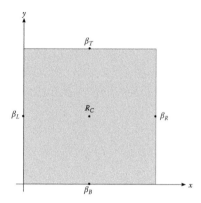

Figure 1.6. Diagram of the various positions used with each viewable region when calculating the general morphing factors.

Boundary Case 1. The viewable region R with applied offset R_λ is adjacent to a smaller viewable region with applied offset of $\frac{1}{2}R_\lambda$.

We will conditionally set the following morphing factors as follows:

- $T_L = 1$, if $\theta(\beta_{NL}, R_\lambda) \geq \theta_{\max}$;
- $T_T = 1$, if $\theta(\beta_{NT}, R_\lambda) \geq \theta_{\max}$;
- $T_R = 1$, if $\theta(\beta_{NR}, R_\lambda) \geq \theta_{\max}$;
- $T_B = 1$, if $\theta(\beta_{NB}, R_\lambda) \geq \theta_{\max}$;
- $\beta_{NL} = (R_{Cx} - (2 \times R_\lambda), R_{Cy})$;
- $\beta_{NT} = (R_{Cx}, R_{Cy} + (2 \times R_\lambda))$;
- $\beta_{NR} = (R_{Cx} + (2 \times R_\lambda), R_{Cy})$;
- $\beta_{NB} = (R_{Cx}, R_{Cy} - (2 \times R_\lambda))$.

The above set of conditionals test for the cases where an adjacent viewable region has been split into smaller viewable regions. We therefore need to lock the affected morphing factors to 1. This is to ensure that all of the overlapping quadrilateral vertices exactly match with those of the smaller adjacent viewable region. Figure 1.7 provides a diagram of the various positions used when calculating the morphing factors for Boundary Case 1.

Boundary Case 2. The viewable region with applied offset R_λ is adjacent to a larger viewable region with applied offset of $(2 \times R_\lambda)$.

In order to be able to test for this case, we need to ensure we have some additional information regarding the current viewable region we are rendering. In Stage 2 of our algorithm (explained in Section 1.2.3), we needed to store

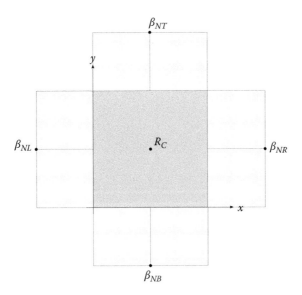

Figure 1.7. Diagram of the various positions used with each viewable region when calculating the morphing factors for Boundary Case 1.

the relative quadrant code for each viewable region. This is so we are able to correctly calculate the center positions for larger neighboring viewable regions. This also allows us to calculate the associated edge of the viewable region that may be adjacent to larger neighboring viewable regions.

We will conditionally set the following morphing factors as follows, based on the relative quadrant code for the viewable region:

$$R1 : T_L = 0, \text{ if } \theta(\beta_{FL}, (2 \times R_\lambda)) < \theta_{\max},$$
$$T_T = 0, \text{ if } \theta(\beta_{FT}, (2 \times R_\lambda)) < \theta_{\max},$$
$$\beta_C = (R_{Cx} + R_\lambda, R_{Cy} - R_\lambda).$$

$$R2 : T_T = 0, \text{ if } \theta(\beta_{FT}, (2 \times R_\lambda)) < \theta_{\max},$$
$$T_R = 0, \text{ if } \theta(\beta_{FR}, (2 \times R_\lambda)) < \theta_{\max},$$
$$\beta_C = (R_{Cx} - R_\lambda, R_{Cy} - R_\lambda).$$

$$R3 : T_R = 0, \text{ if } \theta(\beta_{FR}, (2 \times R_\lambda)) < \theta_{\max},$$
$$T_B = 0, \text{ if } \theta(\beta_{FB}, (2 \times R_\lambda)) < \theta_{\max},$$
$$\beta_C = (R_{Cx} - R_\lambda, R_{Cy} + R_\lambda).$$

$$R4 : T_B = 0, \text{ if } \theta(\beta_{FB}, (2 \times R_\lambda)) < \theta_{\max},$$
$$T_L = 0, \text{ if } \theta(\beta_{FL}, (2 \times R_\lambda)) < \theta_{\max},$$
$$\beta_C = (R_{Cx} + R_\lambda, R_{Cy} + R_\lambda),$$

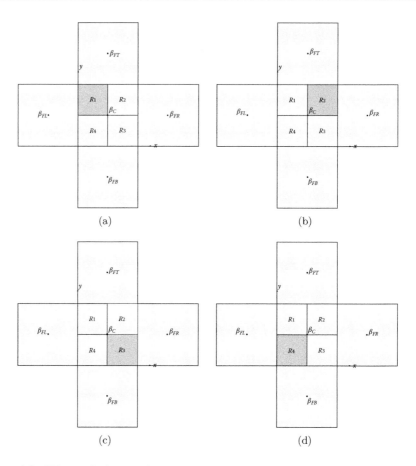

Figure 1.8. When calculating the morphing factors for Boundary Case 2, diagrams of the various positions used with each viewable region with a relative quadrant code of (a) $R1$, (b) $R2$, (c) $R3$, and (d) $R4$.

$$\beta_{FL} = (\beta_{Cx} - (4 \times R_\lambda), \beta_{Cy}),$$
$$\beta_{FT} = (\beta_{Cx}, \beta_{Cy} + (4 \times R_\lambda)),$$
$$\beta_{FR} = (\beta_{Cx} + (4 \times R_\lambda), \beta_{Cy}),$$
$$\beta_{FB} = (\beta_{Cx}, \beta_{Cy} - (4 \times R_\lambda)).$$

The above set of conditionals test for the cases where an adjacent viewable region has not been split to the same size as the current viewable region and instead has an applied offset of $(2 \times R_\lambda)$. We therefore need to lock the affected morphing factors to 0. This is to ensure that all of the overlapping quadrilateral vertices exactly match with those of the larger adjacent viewable region. Figures 1.8(a)–1.8(d) provide diagrams of the various positions

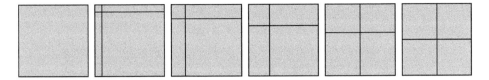

Figure 1.9. Examples of a single viewable region through various stages of the LOD transition. All of the morphing factors $(T_L, T_T, T_R, T_B, T_C)$, for this diagram, are set to 0.0 on the left and increase up to 1.0 on the right in increments of 0.2.

used with each viewable region when calculating the morphing factors for Boundary Case 2, based on the relative quadrant code for the viewable region.

The various morphing stages of a single visible region are shown in Figure 1.9. As a result of how the morphing quadrilateral boundary points are calculated, neighboring visible regions share adjacent boundary points. This results in no cracks or seams when rendering, and smooth transitions when moving through a scene. Figure 1.10 shows examples of rendered viewable regions without (see Figure 1.10(a)) and with (see Figure 1.10(b)) the LOD Transition Algorithm in effect. Notice the T-junctions and visible transition boundaries that are prevalent in Figure 1.10(a).

1.2.5   Procedural Height Generation Algorithm

Any number of methods can be used in conjunction with the subdivision algorithm described in this paper. We chose to base ours on the "Ridged Multifractal Terrain Model" algorithm described by F. Kenton Musgrave [Ebert et al. 98].

The use of this procedural algorithm for us resulted in highly detailed and realistic terrain, as seen in our demo video below. The adaptive nature of the algorithm effectively eliminated high-frequency noise or aliasing and fit quite nicely with our LOD Transition Algorithm. We used a tileable noise texture when the "Ridged Multifractal Terrain Model" algorithm called for a noise value, with several optimizations to speed up the height and surface normal calculations.

The height is calculated at each of the visible region quadrilateral boundary points, resulting in displaced geometry when rendering (see Figure 1.11(c)). We calculate the surface normals on a per pixel basis to achieve even greater surface detail (see Figure 1.11(d)).

This portion of the algorithm quickly became one of the bottlenecks that reduced frame rates. The desire to attain higher levels of detail meant that we needed to come up with some optimizations to facilitate faster rendering. We were able to utilize three main optimizations that enabled us to greatly reduce the cost involved in our use of this algorithm.

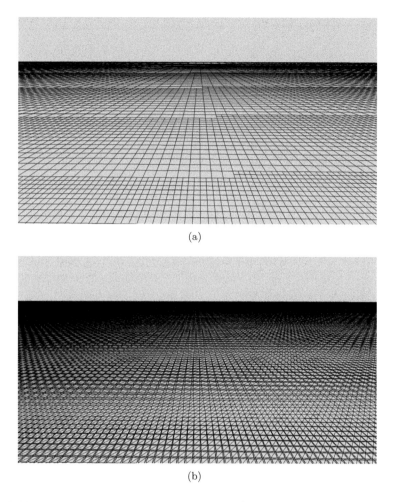

(a)

(b)

Figure 1.10. Example of rendered viewable regions (a) without using and (b) using the LOD Transition Algorithm described in this section.

The first optimization involved us separating the height calculation based on whether we were using the algorithm to displace geometry, or to calculate the surface normal. In the case of geometry displacement, we reduced the number of accumulation iterations (octaves) in the algorithm. This resulted in a less detailed displacement with the benefit of a moderate speed increase. To counteract the loss of displacement detail, we let the surface normal calculation proceed with a higher number of accumulation iterations (octaves). This resulted in greater visual detail. Each application of the algorithm will have its own balance between speed and detail, but the gains when finding the right balance can be significant.

The second optimization involved using a "layering factor" when creating the noise texture used for sampling the height. The original "Ridged Multifractal Terrain Model," in general, accumulates a number of noise octaves (layers) based in part on the distance from the viewer. As described in the algorithm, some processing is performed on each noise value to achieve the desired behavior within the terrain. Using the same noise processing calculations, we embed multiple layers of the noise within a texture. We are calling the number of added layers to the noise texture the "layering factor." The result of this was that we were able to reduce the number of accumulation iterations (octaves) by the same "layering factor," which provided a significant reduction in the total cost of the height calculation. One of the tradeoffs with this optimization was a reduction in the randomness of the resulting heights, although this was hard to detect visually. Another tradeoff was the increase in size of the noise texture in order to preserve the necessary detail of the additional layers.

The third optimization was to embed gradient information within the noise texture itself. Accumulated much like the height values, these gradient values allowed us to attain the surface normal using a variable number of iterations (octaves) without having to take additional samples to calculate a gradient. This also reduced the sharp grid-like "knife edges" that became visually problematic and reduced the overall believability of the terrain model. While this increased the memory footprint of the texture through the use of the additional color channels, the overall speed improvement was significant.

1.3 Results

In our tests, the CPU utilization averaged approximately 1%. Frame rendering times for our demo averaged between 20 to 25 ms, while running at a resolution of $1{,}024 \times 768$. The demo was run on a 2.9 GHz AMD Phenom CPU with 8 GB system memory, and a 512 MB AMD RADEON HD 6450 video card.

A breakdown of the timing for each stage of the algorithm, for a typical frame of our demo, is as follows:

Algorithm Stage	Vertex Shader (ms)	Geometry Shader (ms)	Pixel Shader (ms)	Total (ms)
1	0.005	0.021	0	0.026
2	0.071	0.661	0	0.732
3	0.014	0.955	19.404	20.373

From the timing results listed above, it is interesting to note that the most significant costs involved in the use of the algorithm were not found within the geometry shader, as expected. Both the iterative subdivision in Stage 2, as well as the LOD algorithm used in Stage 3, added comparably marginal costs. The pixel shader, when compositing the resulting subdivided mesh in Stage 3, dominated the incurred costs of the algorithm. Furthermore, when profiling Stage 3,

66% of the time was spent within the GPU Texture Units. This highlights the fact that our choice or implementation of the procedural height algorithm on a per pixel basis, while visually effective, could be improved upon.

Figures 1.11(a)–1.11(e) show some of the various steps taken to create the final rendered scene. In Figure 1.11(e), we added some diffuse lighting from a single directional light source, and modified the color of the terrain based on the calculated surface normal. Greater amounts of realism can be easily added through any number of techniques, such as the use of textures, detail maps, etc.

An example application, as well as the complete source code implementing this algorithm, has been included with this publication.

1.4   Conclusions

The results of our algorithm show promise, and we are continuing our research in this area in an effort to make further gains.

A lot of the speed costs involved in our usage example come from the multi-layered procedural calculation of the terrain height at the specified locations. Swapping our procedural algorithm out and using a simpler method, such as a single texture based height map, results in much faster rendering times. When we swapped out our procedural height calculation for a simpler height map lookup, we were able to achieve frame rendering times of 10 ms or even lower at the same resolution.

One problem with our approach is the visual phenomenon described as "vertex swimming." This can be noticed when moving towards large features that contain a high frequency of detail. The problem can be greatly reduced by increasing the amount of subdivisions created before rendering (i.e., by lowering the θ_{max} value used in the Subdivision Algorithm). When we swapped out our LOD Transition Algorithm and instead added logic to correct the geometry (T-junctions) at the LOD boundaries, we were able to eliminate the "vertex swimming" phenomenon. Unfortunately, this also meant that the LOD boundaries became very noticeable, and in our opinion, were more of a visual distraction than the "vertex swimming" itself. There may be other ways to eliminate this visual distraction, and we are hopeful that this issue will be improved with continued research.

Care must be taken to ensure high precision floating-point calculations are used throughout this algorithm. Artifacts can sometimes appear if care is not taken in this regards, and floating-point errors are inadvertently allowed to compound, which can show up as sporadic pixel noise in the final rendered scene. We solved this problem by using integer based values for our visible region's center positions and applied offsets. Our initial *applied offsets* are set to large factors of two, in order to accommodate the maximum number of iterative subdivisions. By only applying a floating-point conversion factor when we required world space coordinates, we were able to completely eliminate all floating-point difference errors, while also scaling the data appropriately.

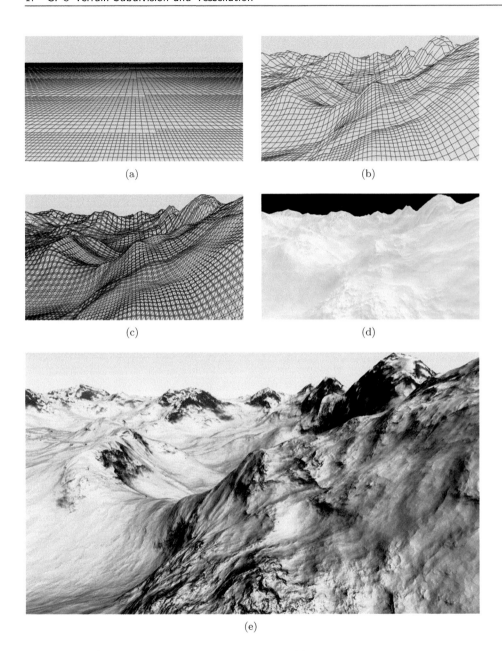

Figure 1.11. (a) The subdivided viewable regions. (b) The subdivided viewable regions shown with the heights added to the viewable region quadrilateral boundary points. (c) The subdivided viewable regions shown with the LOD Transition Algorithm applied. (d) The subdivided viewable regions shown with the per-pixel surface normals. (e) The final scene, with added directional lighting and simple procedural coloring.

Improvements to the subdivision algorithm and resulting data amplification could be made to better utilize hardware depth culling when rendering the resulting mesh. Increasing the subdivision granularity per iteration, and adding the subdivided regions to the output streams in increasing order of average depth (nearest to furthest) would enable the final rendering pass to benefit more from depth culling.

Combining this technique with the built-in hardware tessellation now available in modern graphics hardware could have some benefits, perhaps resulting in increased frame rates. Once a minimally acceptable level of subdivision has been achieved through our iterative process described in Stage 2 of Section 1.2.2, a single additional pass utilizing hardware tessellation may reduce unnecessary computations. Further research into this possibility would be needed to measure possible benefits.

Bibliography

[Ebert et al. 98] D. S. Ebert, F. K. Musgrave, D. Peachey, K. Perlin, and S. Worley. *Texturing and Modeling: A Procedural Approach*, Second Edition. San Diego: Academic Press, 1998.

[Strugar 10] Filip Strugar. "Continuous Distance-Dependent Level of Detail for Rendering Heightmaps (CDLOD)." http://www.vertexasylum.com/downloads/cdlod/cdlod_latest.pdf, 2010.

[Johanson 04] Claes Johanson. "Real-Time Water Rendering Introducing the Projected Grid Concept." Master of Science Thesis, Lund University, 2004. (Available at http://fileadmin.cs.lth.se/graphics/theses/projects/projgrid/projgrid-hq.pdf.)

2

Introducing the Programmable Vertex Pulling Rendering Pipeline

Christophe Riccio and Sean Lilley

2.1 Introduction

We believe that today's GPUs provide us high computing power and enough bandwidth to create scenes with much higher complexity than what is currently found in most real-time applications. Unfortunately, scene complexity is mainly bound by the CPU, which limits the number of draw calls an application can submit per frame.

In this chapter we introduce what we call the *Programmable Vertex Pulling Rendering Pipeline*, which aims to remove the CPU bottleneck by moving more tasks onto the quickly evolving GPU (Figures 2.1 and 2.2). With this design, we show a way to increase the number of draws per frame leading to scenes with a higher level of complexity.

First, we describe the current limitations of existing draw submission designs. Then, we present the Programmable Vertex Pulling Rendering Pipeline. Finally, we propose new API directions we could take advantage of to create real-time scenes with yet unreached levels of complexity.

We base this study on AMD's Southern Islands architecture used for both the AMD Radeon HD 7000 series and the AMD FirePro W series. Though we discuss the hardware design and driver stack details of this architecture, we expect that these concepts would be similar on other post-OpenGL 4 GPUs.

All the performance tests in this chapter have been measured on an AMD FirePro W8000 graphics card with Catalyst 9.01 drivers running on an AMD Phenom X6 1050T and 8 GB of memory.

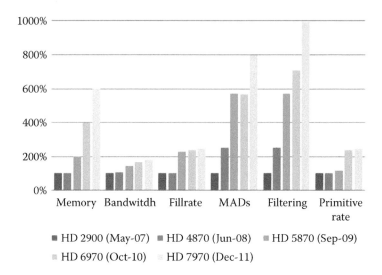

Figure 2.1. Relative evolution of AMD GPU specifications over the last six years.

	Memory MB	Bandwitdh GB/s	Fillrate Gpixels/s	MADs Gflops	Filtering Gtexels/s	Primitive rate Mtriangles/s
HD 2900	512	98.7	11.872	474.9	11.9	742
HD 4870	512	107.3	12	1,200	30	750
HD 5870	1,024	143.1	27.2	2,720	68	850
HD 6970	2,048	163.9	28.2	2,703	84.5	1,760
HD 7970	3,072	179.2	29.6	3,789	118.4	1,850

Figure 2.2. Absolute evolution of AMD GPU specifications over the last six years.

2.2   Draw Submission Limitations and Objectives

It is hard to appreciate how powerful today's GPUs can be. For example, a typical desktop GPU consumes at least two triangles per GPU clock, but if a programmer uses immediate mode to submit these two triangles, then comparatively many more CPU clocks must be expended. While the performance may seem strong, the programmer is still not fully utilizing the hardware.

Extending this discussion to draw calls using vertex buffers, the number of draws an application can submit per frame remains very limited compared to the peak ability of the GPU. Again, this is due to the CPU overhead of draw calls. We believe that this limit for real-time software is about 1,000 to 5,000 draw calls per frame, depending on the state changes and resource switching occurring between them. Another important limitation is the primitive peak rate on the

GPU, which defines the number of primitives that the GPU can render per frame without becoming the bottleneck. Because the draw call limit is so small while the peak primitive rate is proportionally high, programs must aim to render a lot of primitives per draw call.

To tackle this issue, Direct3D 11 introduced the concept of deferred contexts, where multiple contexts can record commands executed later by the main context. Unfortunately, this strategy is not particularly effective and doesn't scale linearly across the number of cores utilized. This is mainly due to the synchronization in the Direct3D 11 runtime and the fact that today's GPUs only have a single graphics ring, which can only process a single command queue at a time.

An earlier solution introduced by OpenGL 3 hardware was instancing. It provides one way to deal with a growing demand for scene complexity without adding CPU overhead. Unfortunately, instancing is nothing but duplicating a mesh multiple times, which limits the complexity we can reach. Another approach is to use batching, which aggregates multiple meshes into a single set of buffer objects and issues a single draw call. This performs well for perfectly static geometry and is relatively practical to use. However, it limits the amount and the granularity of the culling we can perform. It can also waste some memory when padding meshes into fixed-size memory chunks.

To reach a much higher scene complexity, we are looking for a solution where

- we could submit a lot more draws per frame;

- each draw would render meshes with different geometry, number of vertices, and even vertex formats;

- each draw could render a small number of primitives but still hit the GPU primitive rate;

- each draw could access different resources.

2.3 Evaluating Draw Call CPU Overhead and the GPU Draw Submission Limitation

2.3.1 The Performance Test

Due to the complex nature of real-time graphics software, it is difficult to understand the source for the cost of a single draw call: Is the 1,000 to 5,000 draw calls limit a GPU or a CPU limitation?

In this section, we follow our intuition that tells us that the more resource switching we do between draws, the higher the CPU overhead will be. Meanwhile, the GPU has a fixed cost for each draw. To build a relevant test to prove this hypothesis, we define the following criteria:

```
for(size_t i = 0; i <VertexFormat. size (); ++i)
{
    glBindVertexArray( VertexFormat[i]. Name );
    for(size_t j = 0; j <Mesh.size (); ++j)
        glDrawElementBaseVertex(
            Mesh[j].Mode , Mesh[j].Count , Mesh[j].Type ,
            Mesh[j].Offset , Mesh[j].BaseVertex);
}
```

Listing 2.1. Efficient draws submissions.

- The test should not be CPU bound.

- The test should not be primitive limited.

- The test should not be shading limited.

- The test should not be blending limited.

Our tests render a single quad (two triangles) per draw. The quad we render is only 16 pixels to ensure that the GPU or the drivers do not discard the draws. Rendering a slightly larger number of pixels doesn't affect the frame rate, which confirms that shading or blending is not the bottleneck.

We create three tests. The first one uses instancing so that only a single draw call is performed while multiple draws are submitted. Instancing ensures that the GPU command processor [AMD 12] does the draw submission, which guarantees that we are not CPU bound. Hence, we use this test to evaluate the constant GPU cost for a draw submission. In a second test (Listing 2.1), we render different meshes of identical vertex formats using a shared vertex array object (VAO), utilizing the base vertex parameter to avoid state changes [Romanick 08]. In this test we evaluate the constant CPU cost for a draw call. Finally in a third test (Listing 2.2), we bind a different VAO [Koch 09] for every draw call to evaluate the cost of switching a single resource.

We observe from the results of our tests (Figures 2.3 and 2.4) that the GPU is extremely efficient at processing draws. For example, Figure 2.3 shows that

```
for(size_t i = 0; i <Mesh.size(); ++i)
{
glBindVertexArray(Mesh[i].Name);
glDrawElement(Mesh[i].Mode, Mesh[i].Count, Mesh[i].Type, Mesh[i].Offset);
}
```

Listing 2.2. Intensive resource switching approach to submit draws.

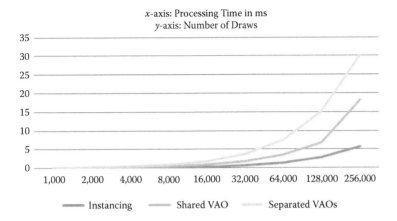

Figure 2.3. Absolute draw submission performance tests comparing instancing against a shared VAO for all draws and separated VAO per draw.

256,000 draws are processed in just above 5 ms when instancing is used in our basic scenario.

As soon as the CPU submits each individual draw (shared VAO), the performance drop is significant, but this impact is much higher with a single resource switching between draws (separated VAOs). Thus, we can expect that this performance cost will rise significantly when we increase the number of resources switching per draw, such as programs, textures, and uniforms. Switching states

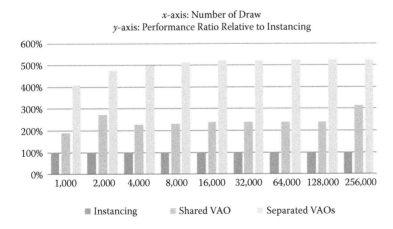

Figure 2.4. Relative draw submission performance tests comparing instancing against a shared VAO for all draws and separated VAO per draw.

and resources between draws actually consumes most of the draw submission performance. From these numbers we can confirm that the number of draw calls per frame is mainly a CPU overhead limitation and that we can reach the GPU submission limit somewhere between the instancing and the shared VAO results. This is the level of performance we are looking for.

2.3.2   Understanding the Nature of the CPU Overhead in Our Test

What is the nature of the CPU overhead in this VAO case? First, there is a validation step where the drivers check that no OpenGL error is generated by the OpenGL commands, as well as checking whether the vertex format and the bound buffers have changed. The second part concerns the vertex setup where the drivers generate a *fetch shader* devoted to building the vertices by indexing the array buffer according to the vertex format. Using a fetch shader allows reusing of the unified arithmetic logic units (ALUs) on the GPU to do the vertex fetching. To avoid increasing the number of VAO validations and vertex setups, the application should sort the rendering by vertex format and pack multiple meshes of identical vertex formats into a single VAO.

2.3.3   Avoiding CPU Overhead by Reducing Resource Switching

In the previous sections we showed that switching resources per draw has a significant impact on performance due to CPU overhead. From a software design point of view, we can avoid this cost by packing multiple resources together and using the GPU to index those resources.

For VAOs, we can pack together multiple meshes sharing the same vertex format and relying on base vertex to access the right data per draw. For textures, we can rely on texture 2D arrays to expose many textures per texture unit. For uniforms, we can pack them into large uniform buffers sorted by update rate and index the uniform blocks in the shader to access the right data per draw. The resource number limits (Figure 2.5) define how many resources we can index inside shaders, hence how much CPU side resource switching we can avoid.

Some resources like uniform blocks are extremely limited but others are generously provided. On AMD Southern Islands the maximum size for a texture 2D array is 16,384 (width) by 16,384 (height) by 8,192 (layers) by 16 (RGBA32F) bytes for a total of 32 TB for a single texture. Obviously we can't store this much memory on a graphics card but we can address it. This is one of the motivations behind the creation of the `AMD_sparse_texture` [Sellers 12a] extension enabling partially resident memory of the GPU resources.

2.3.4   Indexing Resources in Shaders, Dynamically Uniform Expressions

Indexing resources is typically performed by relying on some of the built-in variables provided by OpenGL (Figure 2.6).

Resources	OpenGL 4.3	Southern Islands	Kepler
Max texture units	16	32	32
Max texture 2D layers	2,048	8,192	2,048
Max texture 2D size	16,384	16,384	16,384
Max texture 3D size	2,048	8,192	2,048
Max texture buffer size	64	256	128
Max shader storage buffer binding	8	8	
Max combined shader storage blocks	8		
Max shader buffer size	16 MB		
Max uniform blocks per stage	14	15	14
Max combined uniform blocks	84	90	84
Max uniform block size	64 KB	64 KB	64 KB
Max vertex attributes	16	29	16
Max subroutines	256	4,096	1,024
Max texture image units per stage	16	16	32
Max combined texture image units	96	96	192

Figure 2.5. Some implementation-dependent values used for the count of available resources.

Built-in	Shader Stage	Description
gl_InstanceID	vertex	The instance number of the current draw in an instanced draw call
gl_VertexID	vertex	The integer index i implicitly passed by one of the other drawing commands
gl_PrimitiveID	control, evaluation	The number of primitives processed by the shader since the current set of rendering primitives was started
gl_PrimitiveID	fragment	The value written to the gl_PrimitiveID geometry shader output if a geometry shader is present. Otherwise, it is assigned in the same manner as with tessellation control and evaluation shaders
gl_PrimitiveIDIn	geometry	Filled with the number of primitives processed by the shader since the current set of rendering primitives was started
gl_SampleID	fragment	The sample number of the sample currently being processed
gl_InvocationID	control	The number of the output patch vertex assigned to the tessellation control shader invocation
gl_InvocationID	geometry	The invocation number assigned to the geometry shader invocation
gl_Layer	fragment	Selected framebuffer layer number
gl_ViewportIndex	fragment	Selected viewport number
gl_WorkGroupID	compute	The three dimensional index of the global work group that the current invocation is executing in
gl_LocalInvocationID	compute	The three-dimensional index of the local work group within the global work group that the current invocation is executing in

Figure 2.6. GLSL built-in variables for shader indexing.

Because the constant engine of AMD OpenGL 4 GPUs can only fetch a single resource header per workgroup, indexing an array of resources must be done using what OpenGL calls *dynamically uniform expressions* [Kessenich 12, Section 3.8.3]. All work items in a work group must use the same index to access the same resource. Before OpenGL 4.3 introduced the compute shader stage, OpenGL didn't have the notion of workgroup or work item but we can consider each vertex, primitive or fragment as a work item. If an index is set per primitive, it will be a dynamically uniform expression on the fragment shader stage because all the fragments will belong to the same workgroup. Resources that must be indexed by dynamically uniform expressions are sampler arrays, image arrays, uniform block arrays, atomic counter buffer arrays, shader storage block arrays, and subroutine index arrays. Furthermore, GLSL shaders may access resources through a series of if statements. This is nothing but another embodiment of resource indexing that requires following the same constraints as other dynamically uniform expressions.

2.4   Programmable Vertex Pulling

Relying on resource batching and GPU indexing of resources can significantly reduce the CPU overhead [Hilaire 12]. However, this approach still suffers from several limitations. First, CPU overhead still exists in the form of CPU draw call submissions as shown in the shared VAO case in Figures 2.3 and 2.4. In addition, actual real-time rendering applications don't just submit draws; they need to select the draws that they expect to be visible first, performing culling. This task is not trivial as it often relies on space partitioning techniques to quickly analyze the scene typically consuming a lot of CPU time. To hide this cost, many applications use a dedicated thread for this task, introducing a frame of latency. When the scene increases in complexity, like we are imagining in this chapter, the time consumed by this thread increases until its latency can't be hidden anymore.

One idea is to move the culling and sorting from the CPU to the GPU by relying on OpenCL or the OpenGL compute shader stage so that the GPU selects and submits itself the draws. We call this approach the *Programmable Vertex Pulling Rendering Pipeline* (Figure 2.7). The initial pipeline is composed of two stages. On the one hand, the *Programmable Draw Dispatch* stage uses compute shaders with OpenGL 4.3 multi draw indirect buffers [Sellers 12b]. On the other hand, the *Programmable Vertex Fetching* stage uses the vertex shader stage to index into shader storage buffers or texture buffers to manually compose each vertex instead of using the VAO.

2.4.1   Programmable Draw Dispatch

OpenGL 4.0 introduced the draw indirect functionality that allows storing the parameters of draw commands into a buffer object. Unfortunately, a call to such

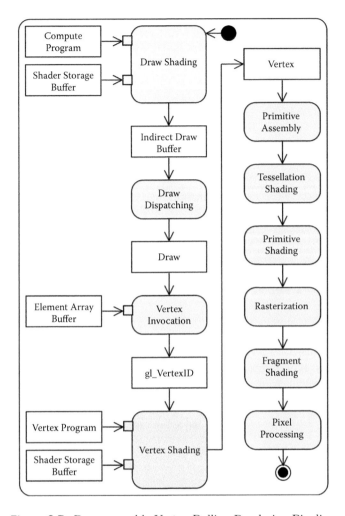

Figure 2.7. Programmable Vertex Pulling Rendering Pipeline.

a draw function is quite expensive on the CPU side, which originally decreased the interest of the draw indirect functionality.

Fortunately, `ARB_multi_draw_indirect`, a version of `AMD_multi_draw_indirect` promoted to the core specification in OpenGL 4.3, extends the draw indirect functionality by packing multiple draw indirect calls into a single call, amortising the high constant cost of the call [Rákos 12a]. With the new functions `glMultiDrawArraysIndi rect` and `glMultiDrawElementsIndirect` the command processor submits the draws in place of the CPU, thus removing nearly all CPU overhead per draw. (See Listing 2.3 and Figure 2.8.)

```
structdrawElementsIndirectCommand
{

 GLuint count;
 GLuintinstanceCount;
 GLuintfirstIndex;
 GLintbaseVertex;
 GLuintbaseInstance;
};
...
// At creation time
glBindBuffer(GL_DRAW_INDIRECT_BUFFER, BufferName);

glBufferData(GL_DRAW_INDIRECT_BUFFER,
    sizeof(drawElementsIndirectCommand) * DrawCount, NULL, GL_STATIC_COPY);
glBindBuffer(GL_DRAW_INDIRECT_BUFFER, 0);
...
// In the rendering loop
glBindBuffer(GL_DRAW_INDIRECT_BUFFER, BufferName);
glMultiDrawElementsIndirect(GL_TRIANGLES,
GL_UNSIGNED_INT, 0, DrawCount, sizeof(drawElementsIndirectCommand));
```

Listing 2.3. Creation and use of a multi draw indirect buffer.

An OpenCL kernel or an OpenGL compute shader is capable of building the multi draw indirect buffer. Just like the CPU visibility culling thread, the GPU processes a batch of object-bounding volumes. When the bounding volumes pass the visibility tests, the corresponding draw parameters for the objects fill the draw

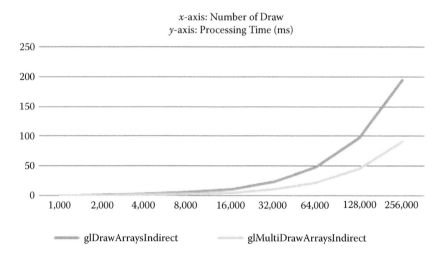

Figure 2.8. Performance comparisons between `glDrawArraysIndirect` and `glMulti DrawArraysIndirect`.

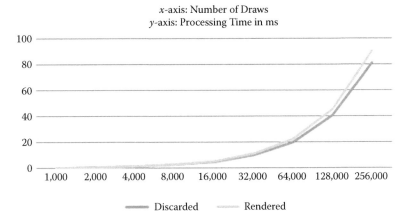

Figure 2.9. Comparing performance between discarded draws and draws rendering a single quad per draw producing 16 pixels on the framebuffer.

indirect buffer. For this chapter we used a brute force OpenCL kernel to check every object in the scene, but nothing prevents us from using space partitioning techniques to continue scaling up the scene complexity.

Taking a closer look at the new draw call functions, it is both interesting and annoying to acknowledge that the `glMultiDrawElementsIndirect` and `glMultiDrawArraysIndirect` parameter `drawcount` is not sourced from the indirect draw buffer. It would be a wrong idea to query the number of draws that the compute program effectively wrote in the indirect draw buffer and use this number for `drawcount`. Such an idea is worse than a CPU draw call overhead as it implies a synchronization point between the CPU and the GPU, preventing them from running in parallel. A better alternative is to use the maximum number of elements in the multi draw indirect buffer for `drawcount` and ask the command processor to discard the draws we don't need by writing 0 for the `primCount` parameter of each draw we want to discard. As Figure 2.9 shows, discarding draws is not free so that the number of draws needs to be carefully chosen.

2.4.2 Programmable Vertex Fetching

Using Programmable Draw Dispatching is an interesting step but it can show some limitations as soon as the scene contains meshes with multiple vertex formats. Sorting the multiple indirect draws per vertex format is not very practical but is necessary. Each vertex format requires a separate CPU call, which increases the CPU overhead. If there are many different vertex formats, then the high CPU cost of indirect draw calls may lead to an overall lower level of performance from the application.

Instead, we propose to no longer rely on the VAO and build the vertices ourselves in the vertex shader stage so that we don't need to sort draws per vertex format. We can group all the meshes into a single set of shader storage buffers, regardless of their vertex format. This allows us to rely on GPU indexing to fetch vertex data, avoiding the CPU overhead of resource switching.

Unfortunately, OpenGL 4.3 doesn't provide a built-in variable `gl_DrawID` that would allow us to identify each draw. One approach that might be considered but is not successful would be to use the expression `gl_VertexID == 0` to detect that a new draw is invoked and to increment an atomic counter each time this case happens. However, the OpenGL specification doesn't specify the order of execution of the atomic operations so we can't identify which DrawID corresponds to which draw.

To generate the DrawID, the proposed solution is to store it in a 32-bit integer vertex attribute. Using `baseInstance` and an attribute equal to one, this attribute is shared with all vertex invocations of a draw. This DrawID is a bit-field where some bits are used to encode the vertex format ID and the rest of the bits are used to index the first vertex of a draw. (See Listing 2.4.)

```
layout(binding = PART_DYNAMIC) buffer partDynamicBuffer
{
    vec4 Kueken[];
} PartDynamicBuffer;

structpartStaticStorage
{
    vec2 Ovtsa;
    vec2 Varken;
};

layout(binding = PART_STATIC) buffer partStaticBuffer
{
    partStaticStorageVertex[];
} PartStaticBuffer;

struct vertex
{
    vec4 Kueken;
    vec2 Ovtsa;
    vec2 Varken;
};

layout(binding = FULL_STATIC) buffer staticBuffer
{
    vertex Vertex[];
} StaticBuffer;

// Only vertex attribute
layout(location = DRAW_OFFSET) in intDrawID;

// The fetch function gathers the vertex data from multiple buffers
vertex vertexFetchPartiallyDynamic(in intDrawOffset, in intVertexID)
{
    intBufferOffset = DrawOffset + VertexID;
```

```
        vertex Vertex;
        Vertex.Kueken = PartDynamicBuffer.Kueken[BufferOffset];
        Vertex.Ovtsa = PartStaticBuffer.Vertex[BufferOffset].Ovtsa;
        Vertex.Varken = PartStaticBuffer.Vertex[BufferOffset].Varken;
        return Vertex;
}

// The fetch function gathers the vertex data from a single static buffer
vertex vertexFetchStatic(in intDrawOffset, in intVertexID)
{
        intBufferOffset = DrawOffset + VertexID;

        return StaticBuffer.Vertex[BufferOffset];
}

// Select the right fetch function per draw according to the vertex format
vertex vertexFetch(in intDrawID, in intVertexID)
{
intDrawOffset = extractDrawOffset(DrawID);
intDrawFormatID = extractDrawFormat(DrawID);

        if(DrawFormatID== PARTIALLY_DYNAMIC)
            return vertexFetchPartiallyDynamic(DrawOffset, gl_VertexID);
        else if(DrawFormatID== FULLY_STATIC)
            return vertexFetchStatic(DrawOffset, gl_VertexID);
        else // ERROR, unknown vertex format
            return vertex();
}

void main()
{
        vertex Vertex = vertexFetch(DrawID, gl_VertexID);
        ...

}
```

Listing 2.4. Code sample of programmable vertex fetching.

Here are a few comments regarding the usage of programmable vertex fetching.

- Many applications rely on *uber-shaders* where all the resources are declared but not necessarily used. When using programmable vertex fetching we can declare a large user-defined **vertex** structure where only the vertex attributes used by the program pipeline would be filled.

- The DrawID is used to index GPU resources; hence, it must be a dynamically uniform expression.

- The more bits we use for vertex format IDs, the less vertices we can store in each shader storage buffer.

- We don't have to create a dedicated buffer for the DrawIDs. We can encode it inside a variable in a custom draw indirect structure (Listing 2.5). This

```
struct drawArraysIndirectCommand
{
    GLuint  Count;
    GLuint  InstanceCount;
    GLuint  First;
    GLuint  BaseInstance;
    GLuint  DrawID;
};
```

Listing 2.5. User-defined draw indirect structure with interleaved DrawID.

way the compute shader stage can write all the draw parameters into a single buffer, but using a `stride` parameter larger than the size of the draw indirect structure will cost performance on AMD hardware.

2.5   Side Effects of the Software Design

2.5.1   Reaching the Primitive Peak Rate

Our quest for higher scene complexity involves performing more draws with less triangles per draw. However, reducing the number of triangles per object too much will have a significant performance hit because the draws wouldn't be able to reach the primitive peak rate of the GPU. To evaluate the minimum number of triangles we should submit per draw, we built a test giving us the performance chart in Figure 2.10.

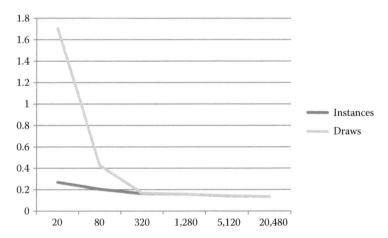

Figure 2.10. Evaluation of the minimum number of primitive to reach the GPU primitive peak rate.

We reach the primitive peak rate with about 320 primitives per draw when using multi draw indirect. This gives us the opportunity to use tessellation where triangle complexity is low, ensuring that we hit the peak primitive rate. Tessellation is not only a great tool to add geometric details; it is also a great tool to ensure that the pixel per primitive rate remains constant.

2.5.2   Memory Repacking

When rendering dynamic scenes, some objects will need to be created and deleted during the lifetime of the program execution. When using the batching approach, meshes must be added and deleted from an existing set of buffers, which typically leads to some level of memory fragmentation. There are multiple approaches to repack the memory and avoid wasting priceless graphics memory:

- The application can rely on `glCopyBufferSubData` and `glCopyImageSubData` to fill empty space in buffers and textures. If the granularity of the data is too thin, then the application would need to make more subdata CPU calls and thus create too much CPU overhead.

- The application can use an OpenCL kernel to move the data around. Such a kernel will probably underutilize the GPU's ALUs. However, because AMD Southern Islands allows us to run one graphics ring and two compute rings in parallel, such kernel execution could be hidden by other shader and kernel executions.

- The application can rely on the virtual memory capability of GPU using `AMD_sparse_buffer` and `AMD_sparse_texture` to manage the memory pages that need to be allocated or not. This relies on memory addressing to avoid moving the data while still effectively using the graphics memory.

2.6   Future Work

At the time of this chapter's writing, the Programmable Vertex Pulling Rendering Pipeline remains a work in progress considering that OpenGL drivers are sub-optimized for this purpose. Many API improvements could strengthen this design for post-OpenGL 4 hardware:

- A built-in `gl_DrawID` would allow us to remove the need for vertex attributes and hence for vertex array objects. All the setup, mostly a CPU overhead and the bandwidth needs, would be avoided and replaced by a simple command processor counter.

- Currently when using programmable vertex fetching, we are basically losing the capabilities of certain draw call parameters: base vertex, base instance, and the offset to the first element or vertex. All those parameters are used to compute the actual index of each vertex. We believe that such parameters are not necessarily useful for all scenarios. The registers used for those parameters should become user-defined variables to store the DrawID, for example.

- The series of if statements required to select the right vertex format inside the vertex fetching function is not very elegant as it introduces a level of indirection. By backing subroutines in buffers, we could select a subroutine per draw and effectively hide this indirection.

- The strategy behind the Programmable Vertex Pulling Rendering Pipeline is to replace CPU resource switching by GPU-based indexing of the resources. For this to be possible, we need to be able to access enough different resources. AMD Southern Islands architecture supports bindless buffers and textures so that an unlimited number of resources could be bound. By working with partially resident memory, we believe that both features would enable rendering of more complex scenes.

Beyond API improvements, we can also consider additional software design research:

- Generating the draw indirect buffer by itself is a complex task that we currently solve by using the brute force performance of the GPU in an OpenCL kernel. Instead, could we rely on GPU-based space partitioning techniques? Octrees, k-d trees, or bounding volume hierarchies (BVHs)? Which space partitioning techniques can be efficiently implemented on the GPU?

- Could we use programmable vertex pulling to bring deferred tile based rendering on immediate rendering GPUs? Is there an efficient GPU-based algorithm to build lists of triangles and dispatch them using separate draws per tile? Could we enable Order Independent Transparency [Knowles 12] in a single pass if we expose a portion of the Local Data Store [AMD 12] in the fragment shader stage?

- Can we use `AMD_query_buffer_object` [Rákos 12b] to build a heuristic to reorganize the memory in a memory management kernel?

2.7 Conclusion

In this chapter we presented the Programmable Vertex Pulling Rendering Pipeline, which can render more complex scenes by significantly reducing the CPU overhead caused by resource switching between draw calls. We detailed the possibilities given by GPU batching and indexing in the two main parts of this approach:

- With Programmable Draw Dispatch we use the GPU to both select the draws necessary to render a frame and to dispatch those draws, releasing the CPU from these tasks.

- With Programmable Vertex Fetching we extend the GPU indexing capability to ensure that each draw submitted by the GPU can render a different mesh with no interference by the CPU.

A special thanks to Arnaud Masserann and Dimitri Kudelski who reviewed this chapter.

Bibliography

[AMD 12] AMD. "AMD Graphics Cores Next (GCN) Architecture." Whitepaper, Radeon Graphics, June 2012.

[Hilaire 12] Sebastien Hillaire. "Improving Performance by Reducing Calls to the Driver." In *OpenGL Insights: OpenGL, Open GL ES, and WebGL Community Experiences*, edited by Patrick Cozzi and Christophe Riccio, Chapter 25. Boca Raton: CRC Press, 2012.

[Kessenich 12] John Kessenich (editor). *The OpenGL Shading Language 4.30.6*. http://www.opengl.org/registry/doc/GLSLangSpec.4.30.6.pdf, 2012.

[Knowles 12] Pyarelal Knowles, Geoff Leach, and Fabio Zambetta. "Efficient Layered Fragment Buffer Techniques." In *OpenGL Insights: OpenGL, Open GL ES, and WebGL Community Experiences*, edited by Patrick Cozzi and Christophe Riccio, Chapter 20. Boca Raton: CRC Press, 2012.

[Koch 09] Daniel Koch. "GL_ARB_draw_elements_base_vertex." http://www.opengl.org/registry/specs/ARB/draw_elements_base_vertex.txt, 2009.

[Rákos 12a] Daniel Rákos. "Programmable Vertex Pulling." In *OpenGL Insights: OpenGL, Open GL ES, and WebGL Community Experiences*, edited by Patrick Cozzi and Christophe Riccio, Chapter 21. Boca Raton: CRC Press, 2012.

[Rákos 12b] Daniel Rákos. "GL_AMD_query_buffer_object." http://www.opengl.org/registry/specs/AMD/query_buffer_object.txt, 2012.

[Romanick 08] Ian Romanick. "GL_ARB_vertex_array_object." http://www.opengl.org/registry/specs/ARB/vertex_array_object.txt, 2008.

[Sellers 12a] Graham Sellers. "GL_AMD_sparse_texture." http://www.opengl.org/registry/specs/AMD/sparse_texture.txt, 2012.

[Sellers 12b] Graham Sellers. "GL_ARB_multi_draw_indirect." http://www.opengl.org/registry/specs/ARB/multi_draw_indirect.txt, 2012.

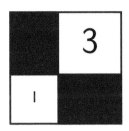

A WebGL Globe
Rendering Pipeline
Patrick Cozzi and Daniel Bagnell

3.1 Introduction

WebGL brings hardware-accelerated graphics based on OpenGL ES 2.0 to the web. Combined with other HTML5 APIs, such as gamepad, fullscreen, and web audio, the web is becoming a viable platform for hardcore game development. However, there are also other killer applications for WebGL; one we are particularly interested in is mapping. The web has a long history of 2D maps such as MapQuest, OpenStreetMap, and Google Maps. WebGL enables web mapping to move from flat 2D maps to immersive 3D globes.

In this chapter, we present a WebGL globe rendering pipeline that integrates with hierarchical levels of detail (HLOD) algorithms used to manage high resolution imagery streamed from standard map servers, such as Esri or OpenStreetMap. Our pipeline uses screen-space techniques, including filling cracks between adjacent tiles with different LODs with a masked Gaussian blur, filling holes in the north and south pole with masking and ray casting, and avoiding depth fighting with vector data overlaid on the globe by rendering a *depth plane*.

We use these techniques in Cesium, http://cesium.agi.com, our open-source WebGL globe and map engine. We found them to be pragmatic, clean, and light on the CPU.

3.2 Rendering Pipeline Overview

Imagery is commonly served from map servers using 256×256 RGB tiles. Tiles are organized hierarchically in a quadtree, where the root node covers the entire globe, $-180°$ to $180°$ longitude and $-90°$ to $90°$ latitude,[1] at a very low resolu-

---

[1] As we'll see in Section 3.4 the latitude bounds are actually $\approx \pm 85°$ for the most common projection.

Figure 3.1. Our globe rendering pipeline.

tion. As we continue down the tree, tiles remain 256 × 256 but cover a smaller longitude-latitude extent, thus increasing their resolution. The extent of one of the root's child tiles is −180° to 0° longitude and 0° to 90°, and the extent of one of its grandchild tiles is −180° to −90° longitude and 45° to 90° latitude.

A 2D map can easily request tiles for rendering based on the visible longitude-latitude extent clipped to the viewport, and the zoom level. In 3D, when tiles are mapped onto a WGS84 ellipsoid representing the globe, more general HLOD algorithms are used to select geometry, i.e., tessellated patches of the ellipsoid at different resolutions, and imagery tiles to render based on the view parameters and a pixel error tolerance. HLOD algorithms produce a set of tiles, both geometry and texture, to be rendered for a given frame.

Our pipeline renders these tiles in the four steps shown in Figure 3.1. First, tiles are rendered to the color buffer only; the depth test is disabled. Next, to fill cracks between adjacent tiles with different geometric LODs, a screen-space Gaussian blur is performed. A fragment is only blurred if it is part of a crack; therefore, most fragments are not changed.

Next, since most map servers do not provide tiles near the poles, two viewport-aligned quads are rendered, and masked and ray-casted to fill the holes in the poles.

Finally, a depth-only pass renders a plane perpendicular to the near plane that slices the globe at the horizon. A ray is traced through each fragment and discarded if it does not intersect the globe's ellipsoid. The remaining fragment's depth values are written, allowing later passes to draw vector data on the globe without z-fighting or tessellation differences between tiles and vector data rendering later.

Let's look these steps in more detail.

3.3   Filling Cracks in Screen Space

Cracks like those in Figure 3.2 occur in HLOD algorithms when two adjacent tiles have different geometric LODs. Since the tile's tessellations are at different resolutions, together they do not form a watertight mesh, and gaps are noticeable.

There are a wide array of geometric techniques for filling cracks. A key observation is that cracking artifacts need to be removed, but adjacent tiles don't necessarily need to line up vertex-to-vertex. For example, in terrain rendering, it is common to drop flanges, ribbons, or skirts vertically or at a slight angle to minimize noticeable artifacts [Ulrich 02]. This, of course, requires creating extra geometry and determining its length and orientation. Other geometric

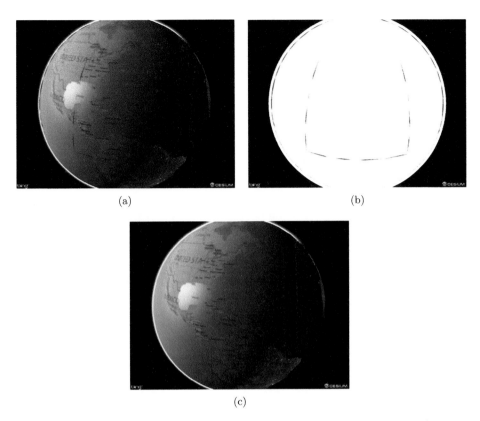

(a)

(b)

(c)

Figure 3.2. (a) Cracking between adjacent tiles with different geometric LODs (exaggerated for clarity). (b) An alpha mask that is white where tiles are rendered. (c) Cracks are detected using the alpha mask, and filled using a Gaussian blur.

techniques involve matching vertices in adjacent tiles by marking triangles that overlap a boundary as restricted during decimation [Erikson et al. 01].

Instead of filling cracks geometrically, we fill them in screen space. Cracks need to be filled with something plausible, but not necessarily extra geometry. To shade a fragment in a crack, we use a Gaussian blur that only includes samples from surrounding fragments not in the crack. The result is visually plausible, simple to implement, and well-suited to WebGL since it requires no extra geometry and is light on the CPU.

In the first rendering pass, each tile's color is rendered, and the alpha channel is set to 1.0. As shown in Figure 3.2(b), the alpha mask is 1.0 where tiles were rendered, and 0.0 in cracks and the sky.

To fill the cracks, a bounding sphere encompassing the ellipsoid is projected into screen space, and the bounding rectangle is found to reduce fragment workload. A viewport-aligned quad is rendered in two passes, one vertical and one horizontal, to perform a masked Gaussian blur. Using two passes instead of one reduces the number of texture reads from n^2 to $n + n$ for an $n \times n$ kernel [Rákos 10].

The fragment shader first reads the alpha mask. If the alpha is 1.0, the color is passed through since the fragment is part of a tile. Otherwise, two other values are read from the alpha mask. For the vertical pass, these are the topmost and bottommost texels in the kernel's column for this fragment. For example, for a 7×7 kernel, the texels are $(0, \pm 3)$ texels. If the alpha for both texels is 0.0, sky is detected, and the color is passed through. Otherwise, the blur is performed including only texels in the kernel with an alpha of 1.0. Essentially, pixels surrounding cracks are bled into the cracks to fill them.

Kernel size selection presents an important tradeoff. An $n \times n$ kernel can only fill cracks up to $n - 2 \times n - 2$ pixels because of the sky check. We found that a 7×7 kernel works well in practice for our engine. However, we do not restrict geometry such that cracks will never exceed five pixels. It is possible cracks will not be completely filled, but we have found these cases to be quite rare.

3.4 Filling Poles in Screen Space

Most standard map servers provide tiles in the Web Mercator projection. Due to the projection, tiles are not available above $85.05112878°$ latitude and below $-85.05112878°$. Not rendering these tiles results in holes in the poles as shown in Figures 3.3(a) and 3.4(a). For many zoomed-in views, the holes are not visible. However, for global views, they are obvious.

There are several geometric solutions to fill the holes. Tiles can be created above and below the latitude bounds, essentially creating the same geometry as if image tiles were available. This is simple but can lead to over-tessellation at the poles. To avoid this, a projection tailored to the poles can be used similar to Miller and Gaskins [Miller and Gaskins 09]. However, this requires a good bit of code, and cracking between the two different tessellation methods needs to addressed. Alternatively, a coarsely tessellated globe can be rendered after the imagery tiles, but tessellation and lighting discontinuities can be noticeable.

Instead of a geometric solution, holes can be filled in screen space, avoiding any concerns about over-tessellation or cracking. We render viewport-aligned quads covering the poles, and detect and shade the holes in a fragment shader.

For each pole, first compute a bounding sphere around the pole's longitude-latitude extent; for example, the north pole extent is $-180°$ to $180°$ longitude, and $85.05112878°$ to $90°$ latitude. The sphere can be frustum and occlusion culled like any other geometry. If visible, the bounding rectangle of the sphere projected into screen space is computed, and a viewport-aligned quad is rendered as shown in Figure 3.3(b).

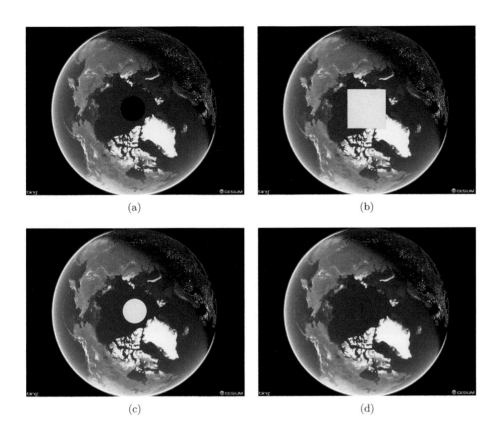

(a)

(b)

(c)

(d)

Figure 3.3. (a) A hole at the north pole since tiles are not available outside of $\approx \pm 85°$ latitude. (b) A rectangle covering the hole in screen space. (c) Masking and ray casting to detect the hole. (d) Shading the hole.

The quad is larger than the hole behind it. For horizon views, it extends high above the ground. The fragment shader discards fragments that are not in front of the hole by first checking the alpha mask; if it is 1.0, a tile was rendered to this fragment, and it is not a hole. To discard fragments above ground, a ray is cast from the eye through the fragment to the ellipsoid. If the ray doesn't hit the ellipsoid, the fragment is above the ground, and discarded. At this point, if the fragment was not discarded, it covers the hole as in Figure 3.3(c).

We shade the fragment by computing the geodetic surface normal on the ellipsoid where the ray intersects, and use that for lighting with a solid diffuse color. Texture coordinates can also be computed and used for specular maps and other effects. Given that the poles are mostly uniform color, a solid diffuse color looks acceptable as shown in Figures 3.3(d) and 3.4(b).

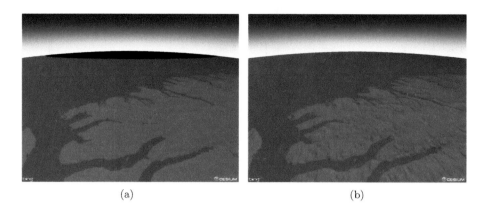

(a)   (b)

Figure 3.4. Horizon views. (a) A hole at the north pole. (b) The filled hole.

Compared to geometric solutions, our screen-space approach has excellent visual quality with no tessellation or geometric cracking artifacts, uses very little memory, and is light on the CPU, requiring only the bounding rectangle computations, culling, and two draw calls. However, its fragment load can be higher given that many fragments are discarded from extreme horizon views,[2] early-z and hierarchical-z are disabled due to using `discard`, and that a ray/fragment intersection test is used. Given the speed difference between JavaScript and C++, and CPUs and GPUs, we believe this is a good tradeoff.

3.5   Overlaying Vector Data

Maps often overlay vector data, i.e., points, polylines, and polygons, on top of the globe. For example, points may represent cities, polylines may represent driving directions, and polygons may represent countries. Either raster or vector techniques can be used to render this data [Cozzi and Ring 11]. Raster techniques burn vector data into image tiles with an alpha channel. These tiles are then overlaid on top of the base map imagery. This is widely used; it keeps the rendering code simple. However, as the viewer zooms in, aliasing can become apparent, it is slow for dynamic data, and does not support points as viewport-aligned labels and billboards.

To overcome these limitations, we render vector data using point, line, and triangle primitives, which requires subdividing polylines and polygons to approximate the curvature of the globe. Given that these polygonal representations only represent the true globe surface when infinitely subdivided, the primitives are

---

[2]This could be reduced by using a screen-space rectangle that is the intersection of the pole's projected rectangle and the ellipsoid's projected rectangle.

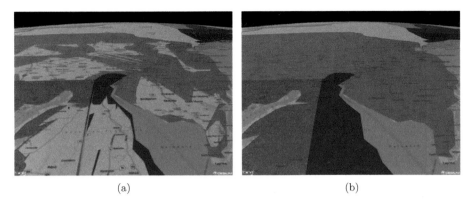

(a)   (b)

Figure 3.5. (a) Vector data drawn without the depth plane result in artifacts. (b) With the depth plane.

actually under the true globe, which itself is approximated by triangles. With standard depth testing, parts of the vector data will fail the depth test and z-fight with the globe as shown in Figure 3.5.

We solve this using a method that is well-suited for JavaScript and WebGL; it uses very little CPU and does not rely on being able to write `gl_FragDepth`.[3] The key observation is that objects on or above the backside of the globe should fail the depth test, while objects on—but actually under—the front side of the globe should pass. We achieve this by rendering a *depth plane*, shown in Figure 3.6(a),

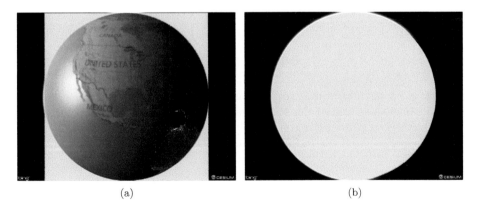

(a)   (b)

Figure 3.6. (a) The depth plane intersects the globe at the horizon. (b) A ray is sent through each fragment in the plane to determine which fragments intersect the globe, and, therefore, need to write depth.

---

[3]We expect an extension for writing depth in the future.

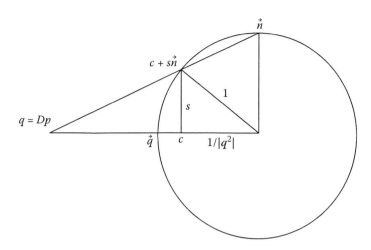

Figure 3.7. Computing the depth plane: a cross section of the ellipsoid scaled to a sphere as viewed from east of the camera.

in a depth-only pass that is perpendicular to the near plane and intersects the globe at the horizon. This plane is computed by determining the visible longitude and latitude extents given the camera position.

Following Figure 3.7, for an ellipsoid, $\frac{x^2}{a^2} + \frac{y^2}{b^2} + \frac{z^2}{c^2} = 1$, and camera position in WGS84 coordinates, p, we compute

$$D = \begin{pmatrix} \frac{1}{a} & 0 & 0 \\ 0 & \frac{1}{b} & 0 \\ 0 & 0 & \frac{1}{c} \end{pmatrix},$$

$$q = Dp,$$

where D is a scale matrix that transforms from the ellipsoid to a unit sphere and q is the camera position in the scaled space. Next, we compute the east vector, $\vec{e}$; the north vector, $\vec{n}$; the center of the circle where the depth plane intersects the unit sphere, c; and the radius of that circle, s:

$$\vec{e} = (0, 0, 1) \times \vec{q},$$
$$\vec{n} = \vec{q} \times \vec{e},$$
$$c = \frac{q}{|q|^2},$$
$$s = \sin \arccos \frac{1}{|q|^2}.$$

Finally, we compute the corners of the visible extent in WGS84 coordinates.

$$\text{upper left} = D^{-1}\left(c + s\left(\vec{n} - \vec{e}\right)\right)$$
$$\text{upper right} = D^{-1}\left(c + s\left(\vec{n} + \vec{e}\right)\right)$$
$$\text{lower left} = D^{-1}\left(c + s\left(-\vec{n} - \vec{e}\right)\right)$$
$$\text{lower right} = D^{-1}\left(c + s\left(-\vec{n} + \vec{e}\right)\right)$$

In the fragment shader, a ray is cast from the eye through each fragment in the depth plane. If the fragment does not intersect the ellipsoid, the fragment is discarded as shown in Figure 3.6(b). The result is the globe's depth is replaced with the depth plane's depth, which allows objects on the front side of the globe to pass the depth test and those on the backside to fail without z-fighting or tessellation differences between image tiles and vector data. This is like backface culling, except it doesn't require the primitives to be backfacing; for example, a model of a satellite works with the depth plane but does not work with backface culling alone.

We originally used a technique based on backface culling. First, we rendered the tiles without depth. Next, we rendered polygons and polylines on the ellipsoid's surface without depth, and with backface culling implemented by discarding in the fragment shader based on the ellipsoid's geodetic surface normal. Finally, we rendered the tile's depth. Like the depth plane, this did not require writing `gl_FragDepth`; however, it had created a shortcoming in our API. Users needed to specify if a polygon or polyline was on the surface or in space. The depth plane works in both cases except for the rare exception of polylines normal to and intersecting the ellipsoid. The backface-culling technique also relies on two passes over the tiles, which increases the number of draw calls. This is a major WebGL bottleneck.

3.6 Conclusion

As long-time C++ and desktop OpenGL developers, we have found JavaScript and WebGL to be a viable platform for serious graphics development. We hope this chapter provided both inspiration for what is possible with WebGL, and concrete techniques for globe rendering that are well-suited to WebGL. To see these techniques in action, see our live demos at http://cesium.agi.com.

3.7 Acknowledgments

We thank Matt Amato, Norm Badler, Wolfgang Engel, Scott Hunter, and Kevin Ring for reviewing this chapter. We especially thank Frank Stoner for deriving the equations for the depth plane.

Bibliography

[Cozzi and Ring 11] Patrick Cozzi and Kevin Ring. *3D Engine Design for Virtual Globes*. Boca Raton: CRC Press, 2011. (Information at http://www.virtualglobebook.com.)

[Erikson et al. 01] Carl Erikson, Dinesh Manocha, and William V. Baxter III. "HLODs for Faster Display of Large Static and Dynamic Environments." In *Proceedings of the 2001 Symposium on Interactive 3D Graphics*, pp. 111–120. New York: ACM, 2001. (Available at http://gamma.cs.unc.edu/POWERPLANT/papers/erikson2001.pdf.)

[Miller and Gaskins 09] James R. Miller and Tom Gaskins. "Computations on an Ellipsoid for GIS." *Computer-Aided Design* 6:4 (2009), 575–583. (Available at http://people.eecs.ku.edu/~miller/Papers/CAD_6_4_575-583.pdf.)

[Rákos 10] Daniel Rákos. "Efficient Gaussian Blur with Linear Sampling." *RasterGrid Blogosphere*, http://rastergrid.com/blog/2010/09/efficient-gaussian-blur-with-linear-sampling/, 2010.

[Ulrich 02] Thatcher Ulrich. "Rendering Massive Terrains Using Chunked Level of Detail Control." *SIGGRAPH 2002 Super-Size It! Scaling Up to Massive Virtual Worlds Course Notes.* http://tulrich.com/geekstuff/sig-notes.pdf, 2002.

II

Rendering

Real-time rendering is an exciting field in part because of how rapidly it evolves and advances to meet the ever-rising demands of game developers and game players. In this section we introduce new techniques that will be interesting and beneficial to both hobbyists and experts alike—these are technologies you can expect to find in the very latest real-time rendering engines.

The first article in the rendering section is "Practical Planar Reflections Using Cubemaps and Image Proxies," by Sébastien Lagarde and Antoine Zanuttini. This article discusses a very fast and efficient system for approximating dynamic glossy and specular reflections on planar surfaces. The authors discuss the art tools, strategies, and runtime requirements for the their system and provide code snippets to help readers integrate a similar system into their own engine. The authors also provide a video of their techniques on the accompanying DVD.

Our next article is "Real-Time Ptex and Vector Displacement," by Karl Hillesland. This article discusses a technique for overcoming issues introduced by texture seams particularly in the application of displacement maps where small texturing errors can result in very noticeable surface artifacts and cracks. An additional benefit of this system is that it eliminates the need for an explicit UV space.

In "Decoupled Deferred Shading on the GPU," Gábor Liktor and Carsten Dachsbacher describe a technique that leverages a unique G-Buffer structure to reduce the amount of shading computation and memory footprint of an antialiasing deferred renderer that matches the quality of hardware multisample antialiasing (MSAA). The authors discuss an implementation that includes a stochastic rasterization framework.

Our fourth article, "Tiled Forward Shading," is by Markus Billeter, Ola Olsson and Ulf Assarsson. The authors describe a new and powerful rendering system that combines the flexibility of forward shading with the efficiency of deferred rendering. In addition to greater flexibility this system also natively supports hardware MSAA, transparency and heterogeneous materials. The authors provide a detailed description of their implementation (full demo source code available on the DVD) as well as a very thorough performance analysis.

Next is, "Forward+: A Step Toward Film-style Shading in Real Time," by Takahiro Harada, Jay McKee, and Jason C. Yang. This article builds on the previous article in this section by discussing an advanced tiled forward renderer that was used in a full production environment. The authors go on to describe many extensions to tiled forward rendering such as exploiting the latest GPU hardware features, indirect lighting, advanced tile culling, and hybrid raytraced shadows.

"Progressive Screen-Space Multichannel Surface Voxelization," by Athanasios Gaitatzes and Georgios Papaioannou, describes a new technique for computing scene voxelizations that can be used for real-time global illumination computation. The key idea of their article is that a voxelization is built incrementally across frames from geometry present in the depth buffer, combining the performance of screen-space approaches with improved volume coverage comparable to full-scene voxelization.

Finally we present, "Rasterized Voxel-Based Dynamic Global Illumination," by Hawar Doghramachi. This article presents an approximate global illumination technique, again building on a voxel representation: the scene is rendered into a 3D read-write buffer using atomic functions. Next, the illumination of each voxel is computed and it is then treated as an indirect (virtual) light source. After propagating its contribution through the grid (similar to light propagation volumes (LDVs)), the scene can be indirectly lit.

We would like to thank all our authors for sharing their exciting new work with the graphics community. We hope that these ideas encourage readers to further extend the state-of-the-art in real-time rendering and we look forward to the new advances that these ideas inspire.

—Christopher Oat and Carsten Dachsbacher

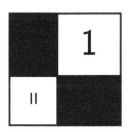

Practical Planar Reflections Using Cubemaps and Image Proxies

Sébastien Lagarde and Antoine Zanuttini

1.1 Introduction

Rendering scenes with glossy and specular reflections has always been a challenge in the field of real-time rendering. Due to their importance in assessing image quality, many techniques have been developed to simulate reflections. These techniques can be classified in four categories:

1. Real-time techniques, such as dynamic environment mapping, with all kinds of parameterization: cubemaps, 2D mirror planes, dual paraboloid. Dynamic reflections of this type are accurate but costly because they require resending the whole scene to the graphics pipeline. Many optimizations have been devised to speed up the process, such as mesh or shader simplifications, but it still induces a significant overhead.

2. Precomputed techniques, such as static environment mapping with all kinds of parameterization: cube maps, sphere maps, dual paraboloid, etc. Static reflections lack the accuracy of dynamic reflection but are far cheaper to use.

3. Screen-space techniques, such as screen-space local reflection [Tiago et al. 12], often come at a manageable cost for pleasant localized results, but fail where on-screen information is missing.

4. Real-time ray-tracing techniques such as the image-based reflections found in Epic's Samaritan demo [Mittring and Dudash 11] are promising techniques, but they require support for features not available on older graphics hardware.

For our game *Remember Me*, targeting current generation console hardware (DX9/PS3/Xbox 360), we tried to find a reflection technique similar in cost to precomputed techniques, but with improved accuracy and realism.

This chapter introduces a new algorithm with a set of artist tools that allow simulating planar glossy/specular reflections. The goal of our method is to replace the accurate but costly real-time planar reflection with a cheaper approximation that does not require re-rendering the scene geometry. In our game, we mostly use these tools for ground reflections.

The principle of the algorithm is to render an approximation of the reflected scene into a 2D reflection texture, then use this texture during the scene rendering. In order to build the approximated reflected scene, we provide our artists with several tools that let them combine the reflected scene with offline-generated elements: environment maps and image proxies. To increase quality, we parallax-correct elements of the reflected scene for the current view when they are rendered in the reflection texture. In order to update the parallax-correction, the reflection texture is updated for each frame.

We will start the description of our algorithm and tools with the generation of the reflection texture. We will describe how our algorithm fits within a local image-based lighting (IBL) strategy, following the work we presented in [Lagarde and Zanuttini 12]. We will conclude with the processing and usage of this 2D reflection texture for the scene rendering.

1.2 Generating Reflection Textures

1.2.1 Cubemap Reflection Environment

Our algorithm begins by generating an approximation of the reflected scene. We are trying to avoid the cost of re-rendering the scene geometry at runtime. In this case, the common technique for approximating reflections is to create an environment map, such as a cubemap, that is the parameterization of choice due to its hardware efficiency. However, the reflection stored in the cubemap is correct only from a single point in space. Applying a cubemap onto a planar geometry such as a ground surface creates visual issues in part due to lack of parallax (Figure 1.3). The graphics literature proposes several algorithms to fix this problem. All these algorithms share the requirement of a geometry proxy to represent the reflection environment: simple sphere volumes [Bjorke 04], box volumes [Czuba 10] or cube depth buffers [Szirmay-Kalos et al. 05]. The reflected view vector by the surface normal is used to intersect the proxy geometry. A corrected reflected view vector is created from the pixel's world position, which can then be used to fetch the right cubemap sample. Cost and quality increase with the geometry proxy's complexity. For completeness, we note that other cheap parallax correction methods without a geometry proxy are available [Geiss 05, Brennan 02], but they require manual tuning for each object. Our solution to the parallax problem

Figure 1.1. Cubemap with a box volume (white) and reflection plane (red) matching a rectangular room environment.

is unique in that we don't use the scene's geometry since we cannot access the pixel's world position when we render into the 2D reflection texture. Moreover, we limit ourselves to planar reflections.

We developed tools for our artists to allow placing cubemaps in levels and associating them with a geometry proxy: a convex volume approximating the reflection environment. For example, in a rectangular room an artist can place a cubemap in the center of the room and define a box volume to approximate the room boundaries. The center of the box volume doesn't need to match the position of the cubemap. As we target planar reflections, we also require having a reflection plane for the cubemap (Figure 1.1). The reflection plane could be specified as a distance from the cubemap position and oriented by the cubemap's up axis or extracted from a game's entity.

In order to correct for parallax, we make the following observation (see Figure 1.2):

Consider a scene with a ground surface (hashed line), a reflection environment (yellow) approximated by a proxy geometry (box volume in green) and a camera. The camera looks at a position on the ground. The reflected view vector $\vec{R}$ is used to get the intersection P with the proxy geometry. P is then used with the cubemap that was captured at center C to recover the cubemap's sample direction $\vec{D}$. If we reflect the camera about the reflection plane, the new view vector $\vec{V}$ of the reflected camera matches the previous $\vec{R}$ vector and intersects the same point P. From this observation, we deduce that in order to fix the parallax issue we could simply project the cubemap onto its geometry proxy, and then render the geometry from the point of view of the reflected camera.

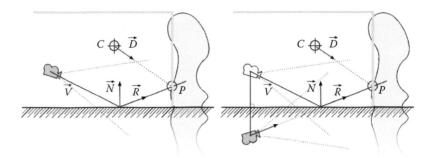

Figure 1.2. The view vector of the reflected camera equals the reflected view vector of the camera.

The rendering process is similar to standard real-time planar reflection rendering. We build a `ViewProjection` matrix by mirroring the `View` matrix by the reflection plane and compose it with an oblique near clipping plane matrix [Lengyel 07]. We then render the back face of the geometry proxy with this ViewProjection matrix. As we reflect the camera, we must inverse the winding order. C++ pseudocode and shader code are provided in Listing 1.1.

```
// C++ pseudocode
Matrix Mirror = CreateMirrorMatrix(ReflectionPlaneWS);
Matrix ReflectView = Mirror * View;
Matrix ClipProjection = NearObliqueMatrix(ReflectionPlaneVS);
Matrix ViewProjection = View * ClipProjection;
// Render back face but remember to inverse culling order
SetInverseFrontFaceCulling();
DrawConvexVolume();


// Shader code
float4x4 LocalToWorld;
float4x4 ViewProjection;

VertexMain() {

  float4 PositionWS = mul(LocalToWorld, InPositionOS);
  float4 PositionSS = mul(ViewProjection, PositionWS);
  OutPosition = PositionSS;
  // Current direction sampling direction
  OutDirection = PositionWS.xyz - CubeCenterWS.xyz;
}

PixelMain() {
  OutColor = texCUBE(CubeTexture, OutDirection);
}
```

Listing 1.1. Pseudocode of parallax-corrected cubemap.

Figure 1.3. Box (top) and convex (bottom) room with a specular ground reflecting the environment with a cubemap. With parallax issue (left) and with correction (right).

Our algorithm allows for the rendering of accurate reflections for any space matching the convex volume used as a geometry proxy (Figure 1.3). It is possible to use concave volumes as geometry proxies but it will result in artifacts because we don't use the Z-buffer during the drawing. Additionally, some information will not be captured in the cubemap. In the next section, we will present a technique to add information into the 2D reflection texture to complete the cubemap that can be used to hide these artifacts.

1.2.2 Image Proxies

The previous section described the projection of a parallax-corrected cubemap onto a 2D reflection texture to approximate the reflected scene. This kind of rendering has its limits because it can miss or lose information: dynamic elements may disappear, the 2D texture resolution can be too low, causing flickering or the disappearance of bright small elements, and concave volumes used as geometry proxies will occlude details. It is possible to enhance the cubemap's contribution to the rendering of the reflected scene with image proxies in the spirit of the light cards used in the AMD's Whiteout demo [Wiley and Scheuermann 07] or the billboards from Epic's Samaritan demo [Mittring and Dudash 11]. The addition of image proxies to our algorithm is easy. We use a quad as a geometry proxy for an image representing a part of the reflected scene, then we render the quad as in the previous section. A detailed description of the creation, rendering and usage of image proxies follows.

Figure 1.4. Editor view showing the link between an image proxy and a cubemap (left) and the orthogonal frustum for a 2D scene capture (right).

Creating image proxies. An image proxy is a quad textured with an authored image or a 2D capture from the scene. The quad is used as a geometric approximation of the reflection environment a.k.a. the geometry proxy.

We developed tools for our artists to allow placing image proxies in levels, customizing the quad size, customizing the texture resolution and performing 2D scene captures (Figure 1.4). The 2D capture is done with an orthogonal frustum set up inside our game editor. The capture considers empty areas (pixels that have not been touched during rendering) as transparent.

Image proxies are very similar to sprite particles and they can share many properties. We decided to take a subset of sprite particles functionality. Image proxies can

- always face the camera, resulting in a spherical billboard;

- define a constraint axis and try to face the camera but rotate along that axis, resulting in a cylindrical billboard;

- use different blending modes (interpolative, additive).

Note that we restrict ourselves to quad image proxies for efficiency, but other plane shapes could apply here.

Rendering image proxies. All image proxies are transparent objects (this choice will be explained later in this section) and thus need to be sorted back to front before rendering since we do not use a Z-buffer. We use the distance from the camera to the image proxies as a criterion for sorting. For an accurate rendering, particularly in the case of overlapping image proxies, we should perform a binary space partitioning (BSP) of the quads but we found out that using a priority system to force the rendering order was sufficient in our case. Rendering image proxies is similar to cubemap rendering. We also allow image proxies to be two sided. C++ pseudocode and shader code are provided in Listing 1.2.

```
// C++ pseudocode
Matrix Mirror = CreateMirrorMatrix(ReflectionPlaneWS);
Matrix ReflectView = Mirror * View;
Matrix ClipProjection = NearObliqueMatrix(ReflectionPlaneVS);
Matrix ViewProjection = View * ClipProjection;

// Image proxy specific
Vector ReflectViewOrigin = Mirror * ViewOrigin;
Matrix InverseReflectView = ReflectView.Inverse();
Vector ViewUp = -InverseReflectView * Vector(0,1,0);

// Following is done for each IP (Image proxy)
// Calc X and Y sprite vector based on option.
Vector YVector = IP->LocalToWorld * Vector(0, 1, 0);
if(IP->bCameraFacing) {
  float ScaleFactor = YVector.Length();
  YVector = CameraUp.Normalize() * ScaleFactor;
}

Vector CameraDirWS = (CameraWS - IP->Location).Normalize();

Vector XVector = IP->LocalToWorld * Vector(1, 0, 0);
if(IP->bCameraFacing || IP->bCameraFacingReflectionAxis) {
  float ScaleFactor = XVector.Lenght();
  XVector = CameraDir ^ YVector;
  XVector = XVector.Normalize() * ScaleFactor;
}


// Shader code
float4x4 LocalToWorld;
float4x4 ViewProjection;
float3 IPPosition;

VertexMain() {
  float3 VPosition = IPPosition + InPosition.x * XVector -
InPosition.y * YVector;
  float4 PositionSS = mul(ViewProjection, float4(VPosition, 1));
  OutPosition = PositionSS;
  UVOut = UV;
}

float4 IPColor;

PixelMain() {}
  OutColor = IPColor * tex2D(SpriteTexture, InUV);
}
```

Listing 1.2. Pseudocode for parallax-corrected rendering of image proxies.

A disturbing problem of naively rendering image proxies as presented here is temporal aliasing. The low resolution of our textures (both 2D reflection textures and image proxy textures) causes severe aliasing along the edges of image proxies, especially when the camera moves near the boundaries of the geometry proxy. To minimize aliasing we set the alpha value of image proxy texture borders to be fully translucent, forcing us to render the image proxies as transparent objects (Figure 1.5). It would also be possible to set this value from within the shader.

Figure 1.5. An image proxy of a door rendered with aliasing (left). The floor is flat and specular to highlight the aliasing issue. The same with fully transparent texture borders (right).

It should be noted that the choice of a quad geometry simplifies this step: a more complex geometry would require more efforts in order to deal with aliasing.

Using image proxies for dynamic reflections. An image proxy is not restricted to a static quad. By dynamically updating its position (for instance by attaching it to a game entity), it is possible to handle gameplay events such as an opening door (Figure 1.6). In this case the cubemap must not contain the scene geometry represented by the image proxies, i.e., the door must not be present when generating the cubemap. We provide flags to our artists to specify the scene object visibility based on the type of rendering (2D capture, cubemap, or scene).

We also use dynamic updates of image proxies to simulate character reflections. Character image proxies are just image proxies linked to the character's main bones with a constraint along each bone's axis. In this case we use an authored texture that consists in just a white sphere that can be tinted by characters. During gameplay we update the character's image proxies based on the transformation of their attached bones and link them to the current cubemap (Figure 1.7).

Figure 1.6. Image proxies can be moved in real-time to match the action.

Best practices. Image proxies are powerful tools, but they require production time from the artists. There are plenty of creative ways to use them to enhance reflections and we present some best practices here. Figure 1.8 shows screenshots of typical use cases with only the cubemap applied and with the contribution of the image proxies:

Figure 1.7. Character proxies (left), the texture used for the main bones (center), and the character proxies on a flat mirror, highlighting the coarse approximation (right).

1. Rendering small light sources inside small resolution cubemap is problematic. They can flicker or completely drop out. Image proxies can compensate for the low resolution.

2. Control the brightness strength of the cubemap: As a cubemap is a single texture generated in the engine, it is painful to boost the brightness in only a part of it. Image proxies can control their brightness individually.

3. Enhance lights: in order to emulate a stretch highlight on a wet ground similar to the Blinn-Phong lighting model, artists can create a cylinder billboard image proxy with an authored texture instead of a capture of that part of the scene.

4. Hide undesirable reflections: by placing a 2D scene capture proxy at the appropriate position, it is possible to hide reflection elements either in the cubemap or in another image proxy.

5. Handle multiple reflection planes: Standard real-time reflection can only reflect for one plane at a time. By settings image proxies at different height with their quad geometries parallel to the reflection plane, we could simulate multiple plane reflections inside one texture.

6. Hide concave geometry proxy artifacts: if the cubemap captures a corner corridor, image proxies can be used to hide the missing information caused by occlusions.

Another useful property of image proxies arises when dealing with multiple cubemaps at the same time, as will be shown in the next section.

1.2.3 Local Image-Based Lighting

Our game uses a local image-based lighting (IBL) system. Our local IBL provides accurate environment lighting information that can be used for glossy and/or specular reflections and has the additional advantage of smooth lighting transitions between objects. The system has been covered in detail in the authors' SIGGRAPH 2012 talk [Lagarde and Zanuttini 12] and personal blog [Lagarde 12]. It consists of blending multiple cubemaps in the neighborhood of a point of interest (the camera, the player...) and using the blended cubemap for indirect lighting on scene objects. The blending weights are authored by artists as influence regions around a cubemap. We extend the previous work by blending cubemaps inside a 2D reflection texture instead of a cubemap and by adding image proxies to the mix. The move from a cubemap to a 2D texture is motivated by performance requirements since we need to handle only one view instead of six.

Figure 1.8. Examples of best practices. Top to bottom: cases 2, 3, and 4. On the left, the scene with only the cubemap reflection and the image proxy capture frustum (red box). on the right, the enhancement resulting from image proxy use.

Rendering multiple cubemaps and image proxies. In order to render multiple cubemaps correctly, we should render each cubemap and its linked image proxy separately and then blend the result. This is because of the reflection plane, the sorting order and the blending mode of the image proxies. This has both a memory and a computational cost. As a performance optimization, we chose to first render all cubemaps sorted by increasing blend weight with additive blending, then render all sorted image proxies. This can cause trouble when mixing cubemaps with different reflection planes but we let artists manage this case. Other artifacts are less noticeable.

Extra care needs to be taken for character image proxies as these are dynamically linked to the cubemaps. In the blending case, they must be linked to all the gathered cubemaps in order to be fully visible (the sum of their blending weights will equal 100%). We render them in each cubemap rather than at the end to get smoother transitions when a cubemap with a different reflection plane comes into the mix.

Similarly to character proxies, other image proxies may be shared by multiple cubemaps. If the image proxy uses interpolative blending, this could result in a final image intensity that is lower than expected because of repeated interpolation. This can be fixed in the shader by tweaking the alpha value according to the blending weight.

Image proxy best practices with local IBL. Our local IBL approach provides seamless transitions between lighting environments represented by cubemaps. A simple example of a corridor environment has been presented in our SIGGRAPH talk. This still applies to our planar reflection. We set up three cubemaps in the corridor with overlapping influence regions and identical geometry proxies. For clarity, only the geometry proxies (the box volumes in red, green, and blue) are shown, with a small scale so that they are all visible. This setup and our planar reflection technique provide detailed reflections and smooth transitions (Figure 1.9). There is a video on the CD accompanying this article showing the result when the camera moves.

Image proxies are of great help in more complex cases. Again, artists must be creative, and we help by presenting some best practices. Figure 1.9 shows the setup of geometry proxies and screenshots of typical usage (refer to the video for better visualization). Purple lines are image proxies; red, green and blue boxes are geometry proxies of cubemaps:

1. Corner corridor: The set of geometry proxies include a concave volume. Artists use image proxies to hide the artifacts. The image proxies are captures of the walls.

2. Two successive rooms, separated by an opening door: The geometry proxies overlap and include the two rooms. The image proxies are captures of the separating walls. Walls should not be included in the cubemap generation.

Figure 1.9. Top view of the scene's cubemap setup (left) and the resulting rendition (right). From top to bottom: corridor case from the SIGGRAPH talk, best case 1, and best case 2.

1.3 Using Reflection Textures

1.3.1 Glossy Material Support

We saw how to generate a 2D reflection texture to approximate a reflected scene. This texture is better suited for specular materials like perfect mirrors. In order to support glossy material we store preconvolved versions of the base texture in the mipmaps (Figure 1.10). This is similar to a preconvolved cubemap [Kautz et al. 00]. Each mipmap level maps to a different glossiness. A highly glossy reflection (more detailed) will look up a lower mipmap level, a less glossy reflection (more blurred) will look up the average of a large number of pixels. We experimented with two ways of generating the mipmaps: by rendering the reflected scene for each mipmap, and by successively blurring base mipmaps.

Rendering the reflected scene in each mipmap. We first try to re-render the approximated reflected scene for each mipmap. For better results, we should use both preconvolved cubemaps and preconvolved image proxies. At rendering time, the current mipmap level to render is used to sample the current mipmap level of the texture applied on the cubemap or image proxies. The difficulty of this

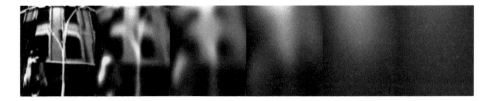

Figure 1.10. Different mipmap levels matching different roughness strengths.

approach lies in the generation of accurate preconvolved image proxies, which is impossible because of the lack of information outside of the 2D texture. The low resolution of the mipmap is also problematic: small image proxies will contribute too few pixels. Finally, if there are several characters in a scene then the number of draw calls can increase significantly. Since we know we cannot achieve sufficient accuracy anyway, we choose a cheaper approach.

Convolving base mipmaps. A simpler approach consists of recursively blurring mipmap textures. Each mipmap stores the result of convolving the previous lower mipmap level with a specified blurring kernel. We use a Gaussian blur that we found to be sufficient for our needs.

Aliasing. Aliasing is an important issue that our method must address. The reader may notice that in Listing 1.1 a `texCUBE` instruction is used instead of `texCUBElod` that would force a fetch from the base cubemap. This reduces aliasing even if mipmaps are generated in a subsequent step. For completeness, it should be added that a better way would be to use the `texCUBElod` instruction and, at scene rendering time, compute the required hardware mipmap level and the desired mipmap level based on roughness, then chose the larger of the two values [Scheuermann and Isidoro 05]. We decided against this approach for performance reasons.

1.3.2 Applying the 2D Reflection Texture

The preconvolved 2D reflection texture can now be used on any planar objects lying at the same height as the reflection plane used to generate the texture. The rendering process for our texture is similar to the mirror surface case. We use the texture to provide the reflection value by performing a texture lookup with the actual screen coordinates as the texture coordinates. We approximate rough surfaces by offsetting the texture coordinates along the XY components of the surface normal with an artist-controlled parameter for the distortion strength. We also use the glossiness of the surface to select the right mipmap level to use (Listing 1.3). It is possible to divide the distortion value by the post-perspective Z-coordinate. The distortion will vary with distance but we did not find it to

```
float2 ScreenUV = ScreenPosition.xy / ScreenPosition.w *
float2(0.5f, -0.5f) + 0.5f;
float2 R = ScreenUV + TangentNormal.xy * DistortionStrenght;
return tex2Dlod(ReflectionTexture, float4(R, 0.0f, ScaleBias.x *
Glossiness + ScaleBias.y)).rgb;
```

Listing 1.3. High-level shading language (HLSL) pseudocode to use a 2D reflection texture.

improve the final quality in our case. Note that for performance reasons, we do not transform the normal to view-space but keep it in tangent space, implying that we could not distort in the correct direction. In practice the result is good enough and the correct result would still be an approximation anyway (Figure 1.11).

1.3.3 Cost

We provide some performance measurements of our implementation with a $128 \times 128 \times 6$ cubemap stored using DXT1 compression, 128×128 image proxies using DXT5, and a 256×256 2D reflection texture. Image proxies use DXT5 to support the alpha pixel border we add for antialiasing. We provide our performance measurements as ranges since timings vary with the number of cubemaps, image proxies and pixels clipped by the reflection plane. The typical case includes two cubemaps and 10 to 15 image proxies. The whole process is in HDR format.

Figure 1.11. The influence of the distortion strength on the reflection.

On the PlayStation 3, we generate the reflection texture in the RGBA half16 format. The texture generation costs between 0.10 ms and 0.33 ms, with an average of 0.17 ms. The mipmap generation costs 0.16 ms. The process is render-output-bound due to the use of RGBA half16.

On the Xbox 360 we use the 10-bit float 7e3 format. The texture generation costs between 0.06 ms and 0.24 ms with an average of 0.1 ms. The mipmap generation costs 0.09 ms.

1.4   Conclusion and Future Work

We have presented a good alternative to real-time 2D reflections applied to planar objects to simulate specular and/or glossy materials. Our approach is fast and practical and can be used in conjunction with other techniques such as local IBL. It has been used in production in our game targeting current generation consoles. A video showing various best practices and use cases of our technique is available on the accompanying CD.

The technique is satisfying but could be improved in a number of ways:

First, using a cubemap reflection texture instead of a 2D reflection texture will improve the accuracy of the reflection distortion with rough surfaces at the cost of doing the process six times and requiring more time to generate mipmap. It should be highlighted that this still does not provide the correct result because we are generating the cubemap reflection texture only for normals perpendicular to the reflection plane. Using it for shifted normals introduces a distortion that increases with the angle between the normal and the plane normal (Figure 1.12) [Lagarde and Zanuttini 12]. Another parameterization, more efficient but with the same benefits, could be a dual paraboloid map [Scherzer et al. 12]. This will require tessellating our geometry proxies to limit the projection warping artifacts and rotating the lighting to local space aligned on the reflection plane's normal.

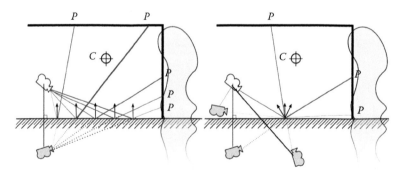

Figure 1.12. Our cubemap reflection is only valid for pixels with a normal vector perpendicular to the ground (left). For perturbed normals, the intersection requires moving the reflected camera's position (right).

Second, anisotropic reflections could be emulated by stretching image proxies based on some physical properties. A more physically based approach could be developed for the mipmap generation step.

Finally, image reflections as used in Epic's Samaritan demo [Mittring and Dudash 11] also are an interesting future development.

1.5 Acknowledgments

The screenshots in Figures 1.1, 1.4, 1.5, 1.6, 1.8, and 1.11 are *Remember Me* gameplay images from the game demo at Gamescom 2012. Images courtesy of Capcom U.S.A., Inc., © Capcom Co. Ltd. 2013, all rights reserved.

Bibliography

[Bjorke 04] Kevin Bjorke. "Image base lighting." In *GPU Gems*, edited by Randima Fernando, pp. 307–321. Reading, MA: Addison-Wesley, 2004.

[Brennan 02] Chris Brennan. "Accurate Environment Mapped Reflections and Refractions by Adjusting for Object Distance." In *ShaderX*, edited by Wolfgang Engel, pp. 290–294. Plano, TX: Wordware Inc., 2002.

[Czuba 10] Bartosz Czuba. "Box Projected Cubemap Environment Mapping." *Gamedev.net.* http://www.gamedev.net/topic/568829-box-projected-cubemap-environment-mapping/, April 20, 2010.

[Geiss 05] Ryan Geiss. "The Naked Truth Behind NVIDIA's Demos." Exhibitor Tech Talk, ACM SIGGRAPH 2005, Los Angeles, CA, 2005.

[Kautz et al. 00] Jan Kautz, Pere-Pau Vázquez, Wolfgang Heidrich, and Hans-Peter Seidel. "Unified Approach to Prefiltered Environment Maps." In *Proceedings of the Eurographics Workshop on Rendering Techniques 2000*, pp. 185–196. London: Springer-Verlag, 2000.

[Lagarde 12] Sébastien Lagarde. "Image-Based Lighting Approaches and Parallax-Corrected Cubemap." *Random Thoughts about Graphics in Games.* http://seblagarde.wordpress.com/2012/09/29/image-based-lighting-approaches-and-parallax-corrected-cubemap/, September 29, 2012.

[Lagarde and Zanuttini 12] Sébastien Lagarde and Antoine Zanuttini. "Local Image-Based Lighting with Parallax-Corrected Cubemap." In *ACM SIGGRAPH 2012 Talks*, article no. 36. New York: ACM, 2012.

[Lengyel 07] Eric Lengyel. "Projection Matrix Tricks." Presentation, Game Developers Conference 2007, San Francisco, CA, 2007.

[Mittring and Dudash 11] Martin Mittring and Bryan Dudash. "The Technology Behind the DirectX 11 Unreal Engine 'Samaritan' Demo." Presentation, Game Developers Coneference 2001, San Francisco, CA, 2011.

[Scherzer et al. 12] Daniel Scherzer, Chuong H. Nguyen, Tobias Ritschel, and Hans-Peter Seidel. "Pre-convolved Radiance Caching." Eurographics Symposium on Rendering: *Computer Graphics Forum* 31:4 (2012), 1391–1397.

[Scheuermann and Isidoro 05] Thorsten Scheuermann and John Isidoro. "Cubemap filtering with CubeMapGen." Presentation, Game Developers Conference, San Francisco, CA, 2005.

[Szirmay-Kalos et al. 05] László Szirmay-Kalos, Barnabás Aszódi, István Lazányi, and Mátyás Premecz. "Approximate Ray-Tracing on the GPU with Distance Impostors." *Computer Graphics Forum* 24:3 (2005), 695–704.

[Tiago et al. 12] Tiago Sousa, Nickolay Kasyan, and Nicolas Schulz. "CryENGINE 3: Three Years of Work in Review." In *GPU Pro 3*, edited by Wolfgang Engel, pp. 133–168. Boca Raton, FL: CRC Press, 2012.

[Wiley and Scheuermann 07] Abe Wiley and Thorsten Scheuermann. "The Art and Technology of Whiteout." Presentation, ACM SIGGRAPH 2007, San Diego, CA, 2007.

2

Real-Time Ptex and Vector Displacement

Karl Hillesland

2.1 Introduction

A fundamental texture authoring problem is that it's difficult to unwrap a mesh with arbitrary topology onto a continuous 2D rectangular texture domain. Meshes are broken into pieces that are unwrapped into "charts" and packed into a rectangular texture domain as an "atlas" as shown in Figure 2.4(b). Artists spend time setting up UVs to minimize distortion and wasted space in the texture when they should ideally be focusing on the actual painting and modeling.

Another problem is that edges of each chart in the atlas introduce seam artifacts. This seam problem becomes much worse when the texture is a displacement map used for hardware tessellation, as any discrepancy manifests as a crack in the surface.

This chapter describes an implicit texture parametrization system to solve these problems that we call *packed Ptex*. It builds on the Ptex method developed by Disney Animation Studios for production rendering [Burley and Lacewell 08]. Ptex associates a small independent texture map with each face of the mesh. Each texture map has its own mip chain. In the original Ptex method, adjacency information is used for filtering across the edge of one face texture and into the next.

There are two main advantages of Ptex relative to conventional texture atlasing. First, there is no need for explicit UV. Second, there are no seaming issues arising from unwrapping a complete mesh of arbitrary topology onto a single-texture domain. These are the two main advantages of the original Ptex method that we preserve in our adaptation.

The drawbacks of packed Ptex relative to conventional texture atlasing are additional runtime computation, additional texture filtering expense, and changes in asset production. The main change in asset production is that our method currently targets meshes consisting of quads. There can either be additional memory cost or savings relative to conventional texture atlasing methods depending on the particular circumstances.

Although this approach works for many texture types, it works particularly well for vector displacement mapping. The lack of seam issues is particularly valuable for this application, while many of the drawbacks of the approach are irrelevant.

There are two barriers to real-time performance in the original Ptex method. First, it's typically not practical to have an individual texture for each primitive. Second, the indirection required when a filter kernel crosses from one face to another is costly in performance, and precludes the use of any hardware texture filtering. The next section describes the offline process to address these issues. Then we follow up with how to use this at runtime and some details related to displacement mapping. We finish by discussing the tradeoffs of this method as well as some possible alternatives.

2.2 Packed Ptex

To reduce the number of textures required, we pack all face textures and their mip chains into a single texture atlas (Figure 2.1). The atlas is divided into blocks of the same resolution. Within the block, the face textures are packed one after another in rows. Because the atlas width generally is not a multiple of the face-texture width, there will be unused texels at the end of each row. There will be additional empty space at the end of the last row, because it generally will not be filled to capacity.

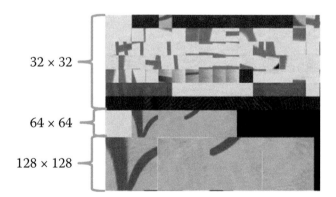

Figure 2.1. This is a portion of a packed Ptex atlas. There are four faces that have 128×128 base (level 0) resolution and one with 64×64 base resolution. The block of 64×64 contains both the one level 0 for the 64×64 face texture, and the four level 1 mips from the 128×128 face textures.

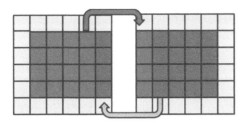

Figure 2.2. Faces that are adjacent in model space are not generally adjacent in texture space. A filter kernel that spills over the edge of a face must pick up texels from the adjacent face, which will generally be somewhere else in the texture atlas. We copy border texels from adjacent face textures to handle this case.

Just as in the original Ptex system, each face texture has its own mip chain. We sort the faces by their base (level 0) resolution to create the packing we describe here, and for runtime as described in Section 2.3.2. Since we are including face textures with different base resolutions, a given block will include different mip levels (Figure 2.1).

2.2.1 Borders for Filtering

Texture filtering hardware assumes that neighbors in texture space are also neighbors in model space. Generally, this is not true either for conventional texture atlasing methods nor for Ptex. It's the reason conventional texture atlasing methods often come with seam artifacts.

For our method, we copy texels from the border of a neighboring face to solve this problem (Figure 2.2). That way, there will be data available when the texture filter crosses the edge of the face texture. The padding on each side will be equal to at least half the filter width. This is a common solution to the problem, particularly for situations like tile-based textures for terrain. However, the memory overhead for this solution is generally much higher for Ptex than for conventional texture atlasing methods. This is one disadvantage in using Ptex; anisotropic filtering quickly becomes too expensive in terms of memory cost.

2.2.2 Texture Compression

Current GPUs have hardware support for texture compression. The compression relies on coherency within 4×4 texel blocks. For this reason, it is best not to have a 4×4 block span face textures. We have already discussed adding a single-texel border to support hardware bilinear filtering. To get good results with compression, we add an additional border to get to a multiple of 4×4. Generally, this means two-texel borders for compressed textures.

2.3   Runtime Implementation

In the original Ptex system, texture lookups were done by first finding which face you are in and then finding where you are within the face. The real-time version essentially starts with the same steps, but with an additional mapping into the texture atlas space. This section walks through each of these steps in detail. For trilinear filtered lookups, the basic outline is the following:

1. Select the texture level of detail (LOD) (Section 2.3.1).

2. Compute the location within atlas for each LOD level and perform a hard-ware, bilinear lookup for each (Section 2.3.2).

3. Lerp in the shader for a final trilinear value.

For nonfiltered lookups, the sequence is easier; all that's required is to find the location in the atlas and do a single lookup. We will discuss the first two steps in detail.

2.3.1   Texture LOD Selection

The first step in a trilinear filtered, packed Ptex lookup is to determine which res-olution of face texture is desired. In conventional hardware trilinear filtering, this is done for you automatically by the GPU. However, hardware trilinear filtering assumes the derivative of texture space with respect to screen space is continuous everywhere. This is not the case for a texture atlas in general, although it's often "good enough" for conventional texture atlasing with some tweaking. However, tiled textures like real-time Ptex often require manual texture LOD selection. The code for this is given in Listing 2.1.

2.3.2   Packed Ptex Lookup

Once we know which resolution we want, we clamp it to the maximum resolution available for that face (i.e., mip level 0). Table 2.1 demonstrates how to look up the maximum resolution for a face texture without having to resort to any per-face information. The method uses a sorted ordering according to face texture resolution and prefix sums.

The next step is to find the location of the resolution block within the atlas. This is possible by lookup into a table indexed by resolution.

The sorted ordering and prefix sum are used again to find the index of the face within the block. In general, not all faces will have a representation in the resolution block, as some face-texture base resolutions will be higher than others. Again, Table 2.1 describes the procedure.

We can find the face texture origin within the block using the index of the face within the resolution block. If the texture width is W and the face texture

```
float ComputeLOD( float2 vUV, float nMipLevels )
{
    float2 vDx = ddx(vUV);
    float2 vDy = ddy(vUV);

    // Compute du and dv magnitude across quad
    float2 vDCoords;
    vDCoords = vDx * vDx;
    vDCoords += vDy * vDy;

    // Standard mip mapping uses max here
    float fMaxTexCoordDelta = max(vDCoords.x, vDCoords.y);
    float fMipLevelPower;

    if (fMaxTexCoordDelta == 0)
        fMipLevelPower = nMipLevels - 1;
    else
    {
        // 0.5 is for the square root
        fMipLevelPower = 0.5 * log2(1.0 / fMaxTexCoordDelta);
    }

    float mipLevel = clamp(fMipLevelPower, 0, nMipLevels - 1);
    return nMipLevels - 1 - mipLevel;
}
```

Listing 2.1. Texture LOD Selection. Allowing for nonsquare textures simply requires a scale by aspect ratio on one of the directions.

width including borders is w, then the number of faces in a row is $n = \lfloor W/w \rfloor$. Using i as the index within the block, we can compute the row as $\lfloor i/n \rfloor$ and the column as $i \% n$.

Each face has its own implicit UV parametrization. We adopt a convention with respect to the order of the vertices in the quad. For example, we choose the first index to be (0,0), the next is (1,0) and the last as (0,1). These can be assigned in the hull-shader stage. The pixel shader will receive the interpolated coordinate, which we call the "face UV." We also need the primitive ID, which is also defined in the hull-shader stage.

Max Resolution	Face Count	Prefix Sum
16×16	5	5
32×32	5	10
64×64	3	13

Table 2.1. If faces are sorted by resolution, and you have the prefix sum of face count for each resolution bin, you can look up the resolution for any given face from the index in the sorting. In this example, a face of index 7 would have a maximum resolution of 32×32 because it is greater than 5 and less than 10. If we want the index of that face within that bin, it is $7 - 5 = 2$.

```
float2 ComputeUV(
    uint faceID, // From SV_PrimitiveID
    float2 faceUV, // Position within the face
    uint nLog2, // Log2 of the resolution we want
    int texWidth, // Atlas texture width
    int resOffset, // Prefix sum for this resolution
    int rowOffset, // Start of resolution block in atlas
    int borderSize ) // Texel thickness of border on each face
{
    // Here we assume a square aspect ratio.
    // A non-square aspect would simply scale the height
    // relative to width accordingly.
    float faceWidth = 1 << nLog2;
    float faceHeight = faceWidth;
    float borderedFaceWidth = faceWidth + 2*borderSize;
    float borderedFaceHeight = borderedFaceWidth;

    int nFacesEachRow = (int)texWidth / (int)borderedFaceWidth;
    int iFaceWithinBlock = faceID - resOffset;

    float2 faceOrigin = float2(
        (iFaceWithinBlock % nFacesEachRow) * borderedFaceWidth,
        (iFaceWithinBlock / nFacesEachRow) * borderedFaceHeight
        + rowOffset );


    // Take face UV into account.
    // Still in texel units, but generally not
    // an integer value for bilinear filtering purposes.
    float2 uv = float2(faceWidth, faceHeight) * faceUV;
    uv += float2(nBorderSize, nBorderSize);
    uv += faceOrigin;

    // Finally scale by texture width and height to get
    // value in [0,1].
    return float2(uv) / float2(texWidth, texHeight);
}
```

Listing 2.2. Go from face UV to atlas UV.

Scale and offsets are applied to get the face UV range of [0,1] mapped into the atlas UV, including an offset to get to the right resolution block and another to put the face texture origin (0,0) inside the face border. Listing 2.2 details the process of computing a UV within the packed Ptex atlas.

The last steps are to do the bilinear filtered lookup for each LOD we need, and the final trilinear lerp between them.

2.3.3 Resolution Discrepancies

There are discrepancies in resolution that translate to discontinuities when approaching a polygon edge from either side. This is illustrated in Figure 2.3. This can happen when the gradient used for mip selection changes as the edge of a polygon is crossed. However, this is not particular to packed Ptex and is fur-

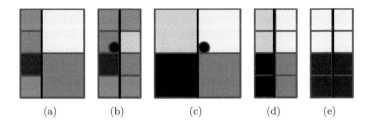

Figure 2.3. (a) Resolution discrepency (b) Bilinear lookup into border from view of left face. (c) Bilinear lookup into border from view of right face. (d) Changing the border on the left face to resolve resolution discrepancy by downsampling. (e) The solution for displacement when values must match exactly is to replicate at the lower resolution.

ther mitigated by the final lerp of trilinear filtering. In cases when we have used packed Ptex with trilinear filtering we have not seen any problems yet; therefore we have not pursued more sophisticated solutions.

The second cause for resolution discrepancy is capping to different resolutions due to different maximum (mip level 0) resolutions. The problem of max resolution discrepancy is mitigated by effectively clamping borders to the lower resolution when padding (Figure 2.3).

2.4 Adding Displacement

Displacement mapping adds geometric detail to a coarser mesh. Each polygon of the coarse mesh is tessellated further at runtime, and the vertices are displaced according to values stored in a displacement texture map. Displacement mapping provides a method of geometric LOD. The model can be rendered without the displacement for the lowest poly model, and different tessellations can be applied for higher quality models.

In classical displacement mapping, there is just a single scalar per texel. However, we have pursued vector displacement, which uses a 3D vector to specify displacement. This technique is much more expressive, but at greater memory cost on a per texel basis.

Authoring displacement maps in a conventional texture atlas without cracks can be quite difficult. If a shirt, for example, is unwrapped onto a texture, the edges where the charts meet on the model must match in value at every location. This is why games typically only apply displacement maps to flat objects like terrain, and why even Pixar's RenderMan, which is considered well engineered for displacement mapping, still performs a messy procedural crack-fill step during rendering [Apodaca and Gritz 99]. By contrast, you can export Ptex vector displacement maps from Autodesk Mudbox, and apply them without the need for manual fixup or runtime crack patching.

For displacement maps, we treat the borders and corners a little differently than described in Section 2.2.1. First of all, we do not need an extra border for filtering, as we use point sampling. However, adjacent faces must have identical values along their shared border to avoid cracks when using hardware tessellation. So instead of copying in a border from an adjacent face, we change the original borders by averaging them as shown in Figure 2.3.

Corners of a face texture correspond to a vertex in the model. Similar to how we handle borders, we walk the mesh around the vertex, gathering all corner values and average them. This value is then written back to all corners that share this vertex so that they are consistent and do not produce cracks. Note that it's necessary that this value is exactly the same. If you recompute this average for each quad, remember you are using floating-point math, and therefore must accumulate in the same order for each quad.

Displacement mapping is done in object space in the domain shader. In our implementation, we point sample from the highest resolution displacement map regardless of tessellation level. Because we are not filtering, the filter-related issues of packed Ptex are not relevant, and there is both less compute and bandwidth cost than for the typical texture map application in a pixel shader.

2.5   Performance Costs

To give a general idea of the cost difference between packed Ptex and conventional texturing, we measured the difference between a packed-Ptex and a conventionally textured version of the character shown in Figure 2.4(a). The AO, specular, albedo, normal and displacement maps are packed Ptex. GPU render time is 3.6 ms on an AMD Radeon HD 7970. If we change the AO, specular, albedo and normal maps to conventional texture lookups (all but displacement) we find the time goes down by an average of 0.6 ms.

The main cost is the search for maximum resolution in this implementation, for which there are plenty of opportunities for optimization we have not yet explored. We could, for example, move the computation as far up as the hull constant shader. There is also a cost due to reduced texture cache efficiency, as packed Ptex will generally not have as good locality of reference relative to conventional texturing. The entire UV computation was repeated for each texture, which should also not generally be necessary in practice.

Given the difficulty in authoring a valid displacement map for a model like the character in Figure 2.4(a) we measured packed Ptex displacement mapping against no displacement mapping at all. This model is made from 5,504 quads and tessellated up to 99,072 triangles. The cost of vector displacement with packed Ptex on this model is 0.14 ms. This is with 16-bit floats for each component, which is on the high end of what should normally be necessary in practice.

(a)

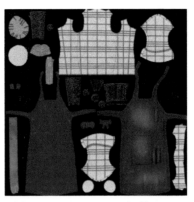

(b) Conventional atlas: 37% black.

(c) Packed Ptex atlas: 7% black

Figure 2.4. All textures for the model in (a) are in the packed Ptex format: Albedo, AO, specular, normal, and vector displacement: (b) an example of a conventional texture map and (c) an equivalent packed Ptex texture map.

We have a second model, shown in Figure 2.5, that uses packed Ptex only for vector displacement. It has a total of 86,954 quads in the base mesh and is animated with both skinning and blend shapes. When tessellated up to 1.6 million triangles, the cost of displacement lookup is 2.7 ms out of a total of 14.2 ms with our current implementation.

Figure 2.5. Model with vector displacement.

2.6   Memory Costs

Conventional texture atlases are often difficult to author without wasting texture space between the charts. In Figure 2.4(b) we see a typical example where 37% of the space is wasted. Ptex, by contrast, is built completely from rectangular pieces and is therefore much easier to pack into a rectangular domain. We make no special effort to find the optimal resolution to pack the face textures into, and yet the waste in our experience has been only around 7% (Figure 2.4(c)).

The greater memory overhead for packed Ptex is in the use of borders. Fundamentally, the border cost goes up proportional to the square root of the area. Here we give some formulas and concrete numbers to give an idea of what the overhead is. Each face of square resolution r and border size n_B wastes $(2n_B + r)^2 - r^2$ texels. Table 2.2 shows example costs as a percentage of waste due to borders in packed Ptex. Two items are worth mentioning here. First, we can see more concretely how high the per-face resolution should be to keep memory overhead down. Second, we also see why borders beyond a couple texels, as would be required for anisotropic filtering, is too expensive in memory cost.

Resolution	Border Size		
	1	2	4
4×4	56/56%	75/75%	89/89%
8×8	36/41%	56/62%	75/80%
16×16	21/24%	36/41%	56/62%
32×32	11/13%	21/23%	36/40%
64×64	6.0/6.4%	11/12%	21/23%
128×128	3.1/3.2%	6.0/6.2%	11/12%

Table 2.2. This table shows memory overhead for borders. The first percentage in each pair is for a single resolution, and the second is for mip chains down to 4×4. These values should be weighed against the waste inherent in a conventional texture atlas, such as the 37% illustrated in Figure 2.4(b).

2.7   Alternatives and Future Work

One way to avoid having a separate texture per face is to put each per-face texture in its own texture array slice [McDonald and Burley 11, McDonald 12]. This simplifies the texture addressing to some extent. However, there are limitations in the number of texture array slices, and resolutions cannot be mixed within a single texture array. Therefore, what would be a single texture in the conventional or packed Ptex approach would be split into multiple textures, one for each resolution, with further splitting as required for texture array limits. The amount of texture data used in the shader does not increase, excepting perhaps due to alignment or other per-texture costs, but the amount of conditional reads is significantly higher.

Rather than computing per-face texture information, we could store it in a resource indexed by face ID, and possibly by mip level [McDonald and Burley 11, McDonald 12].

Ptex takes the extreme approach of assigning an individual texture map to each primitive. The paper by B. Purnomo, et al. describes similar solutions to what is described here, but they group multiple primitives into rectangular patches in texture space for packing and handling seams [Purnomo et al. 04]. This reduces the overhead for borders, which would make larger filter kernels feasible. A next step might be to integrate some of the ideas from that paper.

2.8   Conclusion

Packed Ptex enables the main advantages of the original Ptex method while enabling real-time use. Authoring effort is saved first by eliminating the need for explicit UV assignment and second by naturally avoiding seaming issues that normally arise when trying to unwrap a 3D surface into at 2D rectangular domain. It does, however, require modeling with quads in its current implementation.

Packed Ptex also incurs higher runtime cost than conventional texture mapping. Memory costs can actually be lower relative to conventional texturing, depending primarily on the per-face texture resolution, filter kernel width, and the savings relative to the waste inherent with conventional texture atlases. Although packed Ptex can be applied to many different texture types, the most promising is probably displacement mapping, where the relative overhead is lower and the benefit of seamlessness is greatest.

2.9 Acknowledgments

The techniques described here were developed in collaboration with Sujeong Kim and Justin Hensley. Tim Heath, Abe Wiley, Exigent and Zoic helped on the art side. This work was done under the management and support of Jason Yang and David Hoff. Sujeong Kim, Takahiro Harada and Christopher Oat all provided valuable feedback in writing this article.

Bibliography

[Apodaca and Gritz 99] Anthony A. Apodaca and Larry Gritz. *Advanced RenderMan: Creating CGI for Motion Picture*, First edition. San Francisco: Morgan Kaufmann Publishers Inc., 1999.

[Burley and Lacewell 08] Brent Burley and Dylan Lacewell. "Ptex: Per-Face Texture Mapping for Production Rendering." In *Proceedings of the Nineteenth Eurographics conference on Rendering*, pp. 1155–1164. Aire-la-Ville, Switzerland: Eurographics Association, 2008.

[McDonald 12] John McDonald. "Practical Ptex for Games." *Game Developer Magazine* 19:1 (2012), 39–44.

[McDonald and Burley 11] John McDonald, Jr and Brent Burley. "Per-face Texture Mapping for Real-Time Rendering." In *ACM SIGGRAPH 2011 Talks*, article no. 10. New York: ACM, 2011.

[Purnomo et al. 04] Budirijanto Purnomo, Jonathan D. Cohen, and Subodh Kumar. "Seamless Texture Atlases." In *Proceedings of the 2004 Eurographics/ACM SIGGRAPH Symposium on Geometry Processing*, pp. 65–74. New York: ACM, 2004.

3

Decoupled Deferred Shading on the GPU

Gábor Liktor and Carsten Dachsbacher

Deferred shading provides an efficient solution to reduce the complexity of image synthesis by separating the shading process itself from the visibility computations. This technique is widely used in real-time rendering pipelines to evaluate complex lighting, and recently gained increasing focus of research with the advent of computational rendering.

The core idea of the technique is to presample visible surfaces into a *G-buffer* prior to shading. However, antialiasing is complicated with deferred shading, as supersampling the G-buffer leads to tremendous growth in memory bandwidth and shading cost. There are several post-processing methods that are mostly based on smoothing discontinuities in the G-buffer [Reshetov 09, Chajdas et al. 11], but these result in inferior antialiasing quality compared to forward rendering with multisample antialiasing (MSAA) or do not address the problem of memory requirements.

3.1 Introduction

In this article we discuss decoupled deferred shading, a technique that uses a novel G-buffer structure to reduce the number of shading computations while keeping the antialiasing quality high. Our edge antialiasing is an exact match of hardware MSAA, while shading is evaluated at a per-pixel (or application-controlled) frequency, as shown in Figure 3.1.

Our G-buffer implementation stores visibility samples and shading samples in independent memory locations, where a visibility sample corresponds to a subsample tested by the rasterizer, while shading samples contain surface information, which has been previously stored on a subsample level. Using decoupled sampling, several visibility samples can refer to a single shading sample. We do not seek to skip the shading of G-buffer samples in order to reduce shading costs,

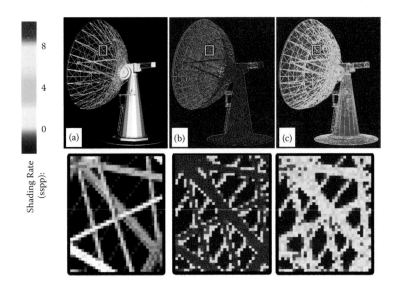

Figure 3.1. In this example our deferred shading method (a) achieves equivalent antialiasing quality to 8× MSAA, but (c) significantly reduces the number of shader evaluations. (b) To the same antialiasing quality, classic deferred shading needs a supersampled G-buffer.

instead we *deduplicate* the data itself, ensuring that a visible surface is shaded only once, regardless of the number of subsamples it covers.

This article is based on our recent research paper, presented at the 2012 ACM Symposium on Interactive 3D Graphics and Games [Liktor and Dachsbacher 12]. We cover the basic theory of decoupled sampling, and then focus on the implementation details of our new G-buffer in the OpenGL pipeline.

3.2 Decoupled Sampling in a Rasterization Pipeline

3.2.1 The Nature of Aliasing

To understand the motivation of decoupled sampling, let us consider the rendering of a 2D image as a signal-processing problem. Rasterization uses point sampling to capture visible surfaces that causes problems if the sampled signal is not band-limited: frequencies higher than the sampling frequency lead to aliasing in the rendered image. Antialiasing methods can prefilter the signal to eliminate frequencies above the sampling limit, increase the frequency of sampling, or alternatively apply reconstruction filters to supress aliasing artifacts.

Any rendering method using point sampling must first solve the *visibility problem* to find the surface points that determine the colors at each sample.

Discontinuities, such as surface silhouettes, are the primary sources of aliasing. The second type of aliasing is the possible undersampling of surface shading. Unlike visibility, shading is often treated as a continuous signal on a given surface, thus it can be prefiltered (e.g., by using texture mipmaps). It is therefore a tempting idea to save computations by sampling visibility and shading information at different granularities.

3.2.2 Decoupled Sampling

In a modern rasterization pipeline this problem is addressed by MSAA. The rasterizer invokes a single fragment shader for each covered pixel; however, there are multiple subsample locations per pixel, which are tested for primitive coverage. Shading results are then copied into covered locations. This is an elegant solution for supersampling visibility without increasing the shading cost.

Decoupled sampling [Ragan-Kelley et al. 11] is a generalization of this idea. Shading and visibility are sampled in separate domains. In rasterization, the *visibility domain* is equivalent to subsamples used for coverage testing, while the *shading domain* can be any parameterization over the sampled primitive itself, such as screen-space coordinates, 2D patch-parameters, or even texture coordinates. A *decoupling map* assigns each visibility sample to a coordinate in the shading domain. If this mapping is a many-to-one projection, the shading can be reused over visibility samples.

Case study: stochastic rasterization. Using stochastic sampling, rasterization can be extended to accurately render effects such as depth of field and motion blur. Each coverage sample is augmented with temporal and lens parameters. Defocused or motion blurred triangles are bounded in screen space according to their maximum circle of confusion and motion vectors. A deeper introduction of this method is outside the scope of this article, but we would like to refer the interested reader to [McGuire et al. 10] for implementation details. In short, the geometry shader is used to determine the potentially covered screen region, the fragment shader then generates a ray corresponding to each stochastic sample, and intersects the triangle.

We now illustrate decoupled sampling using the example of motion blur: if the camera samples over a finite shutter interval, a moving surface is visible at several different locations on the screen. A naïve rendering algorithm would first determine the barycentics of each stochastic sample covered by a triangle, and evaluate the shading accordingly. In many cases, we can assume that the observed color of a surface does not change significantly over time (even offline renderers often do this). MSAA or post-processing methods cannot solve this issue, as corresponding coverage samples might be scattered over several pixels of the noisy image. We can, however, rasterize a sharp image of the triangle at a fixed *shading time*, and we can find corresponding shading for each visibility sample by projecting them into the pixels of this image.

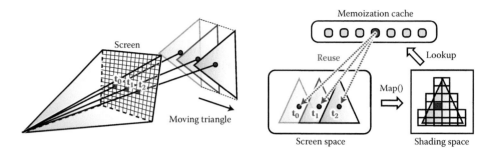

Figure 3.2. The idea of the memoization cache. Decoupled sampling uses visibility and shading samples in separate domains. Assuming constant shading over a short exposure time, multiple visibility samples can refer to the identical shading sample. Recently computed shading samples are cached during rasterization, to avoid redundant shader execution.

Memoization cache. This concept is illustrated in Figure 3.2. Note that the second rasterization step mentioned above does not actually happen, it is only used to define a *shading grid* on the triangle, a discretization of the shading domain. A shading sample corresponds to one cell of the shading grid, and we can then assign a linear index to each shading sample. Using this indexing, Ragan-Kelley et al. augmented the conventional rasterization pipeline with a *memoization cache* [Ragan-Kelley et al. 11]. In their extended pipeline, each visibility sample requests its shading sample from the cache using the decoupling map, and fragment shaders are only executed on a cache miss. Unfortunately, this method is not directly applicable to the current hardware architecture.

3.3   Shading Reuse for Deferred Shading

Conventional deferred shading methods couple visibility and surface data in the G-buffer. After the geometry sampling pass it is no longer trivial to determine which samples in the G-buffer belong to the same surface. Stochastic rasterization further increases the complexity of the problem by adding significant noise to visibility samples, preventing the use of any edge-based reconstruction.

The memory footprint is one of the most severe problems of deferred shading. As all shading data must be stored for each subsample in the G-buffer, even if one could save computation by reusing shading among these samples, the supersampling quality would still be bounded by memory limitations. Current real-time applications typically limit their deferred multisampling resolution to $2\times/4\times$ MSAA, then apply reconstruction filters. It has been demonstrated that accurate rendering of motion blur or depth of field would require an order of magnitude larger sample count with stochastic sampling [McGuire et al. 10].

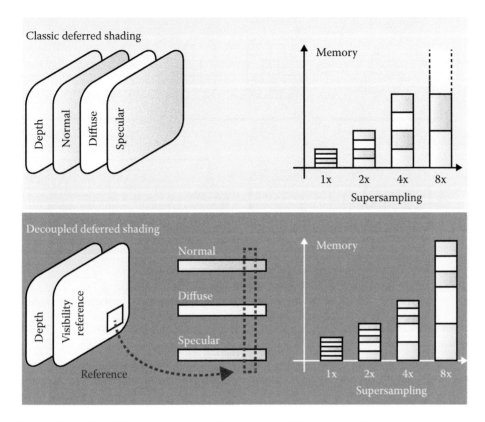

Figure 3.3. The G-buffer stores shading data at full supersampled resolution before shading and resolving. We introduce a visibility buffer that references shading data in compact linear buffers. Due to our shading reuse scheme, the size of the compact buffers does not scale with the supersampling density.

Compact geometry buffer. Instead of trying to use reconstruction filters or sparse shading of the supersampled G-buffer, we can avoid any shading and memory consumption overhead by not storing redundant shading data in the first place. We address this problem with a novel data structure, the *compact G-buffer*, a decoupled storage for deferred shading. It has the same functionality as the G-buffer, storing the inputs of shaders for delayed evaluation. However, instead of storing this information in the framebuffer, we collect *shading samples* in compact linear buffers. The contents of the framebuffer are purely *visibility samples*, each sample storing its depth value and a reference to a shading sample in the linear buffers. We compare this data layout to the conventional G-buffer in Figure 3.3. Akin to classic deferred shading, our methods can render images in three main stages.

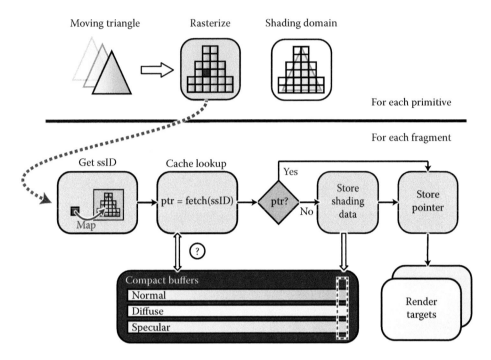

Figure 3.4. The outline of decoupled deferred shading in a rasterization pipeline. Prior to rasterization, each primitive is bound and projected to a shading grid. During fragment processing, the fragments are mapped to their corresponding cells on the shading grid. Shading reuse is implemented by referencing the same data from multiple samples in the render targets.

3.3.1 Algorithm Outline

Sampling stage. We rasterize all surfaces into the compact geometry buffer (*CG-buffer*). Figure 3.4 shows the outline of this sampling stage. During rasterization each fragment is assigned to a shading sample ID (*ssID*), which is searched in the cache. If the shading data was found, we only store a pointer to its address in the memory. In case of a miss, we also need to allocate a new slot in the compact buffers and store the data in addition to referencing it.

In Section 3.2.2 we have already introduced the concept of a shading grid. In our pipeline, we use this grid to allocate an ssID range for each primitive. This virtual address space ensures that shading sample keys of concurrently rasterized primitives do not overlap, and the sampler can use these ssIDs to uniquely reference a cached shading sample entry.

We provide further implementation details in the next section. In fact, we only made a small modification in the decoupled sampling pipeline. While the

CG-buffer itself could be directly used as a global memoization cache, it would be very inefficient to search for shading samples directly in it, especially that a cached entry is only relevant for the currently rasterized primitives in flight.

Shading and resolving stages. The collected samples in the compact buffers are then shaded using GPU compute kernels. These kernels only execute for shading samples that are marked visible (see the next section). Finally each visibility sample can gather its final color value in a full-screen pass. This method trivially extends to an arbitrary number of render targets, supporting efficient shading reuse for multiview rasterization as well.

3.4   Implementation

In this section we focus on how to implement decoupled deferred shading on a modern GPU. In our examples we provide OpenGL Shading Language (GLSL) source code snippets. We use global atomics and scatter operations, therefore a minimum version of OpenGL 4.2 is required for our application. The implementation could also be done in DirectX 11.1, which supports unordered access binding to all shader stages.

The primary problem for our example is the lack of hardware support for decoupled shading reuse, which is an architectural limitation. The hardware version of the memoization cache, as described in Section 3.2.2, is a fast on-chip least recently used (LRU) cache assigned to each rasterizer unit. Of course, every component of the pipeline (ultimately even rasterization) can be implemented in software, but only with reduced performance compared to dedicated hardware. From now on we assume that our renderer still uses the hardware rasterizer, though this technique could be also integrated into a full software implementation, such as [Laine and Karras 11].

3.4.1   Architectural Considerations

Note that the implementation of decoupled sampling for a forward renderer would be very inefficient on current GPUs. First, using hardware rasterization, we can only simulate the caching behavior from fragment shaders. Unfortunately we cannot prevent the execution of redundant shaders, like the proposed architecture of [Ragan-Kelley et al. 11] does. The rasterizer will launch fragment shaders for each covered pixel or subsample and we can only terminate redundant instances afterwards. This introduces at least one new code path into the shading code, breaking its coherency.

The second problem is how to avoid redundant shading. Shading reuse can be regarded as an *election problem*: shader instances corresponding to the same shading sample must elect one instance that will evaluate the shading, the others need to wait for the result. This can only be solved using global synchronization, as current hardware does not allow local on-chip memory usage in rasterization mode, and the execution of fragment shaders is nondeterministic. Furthermore, waiting for the result would mean a significant delay for a complex shader.

With our modification we can move the shader evaluation into a deferred stage, which results in a more coherent fragment shader execution. While we cannot avoid using the global memory to simulate the memoization cache, the overhead of decoupled sampling is independent from the shading complexity. This is the key difference that makes our algorithm feasible even for current GPUs: if the shading computation is "expensive enough," the constant overhead of our caching implementation will be less than the performance gain of reduced shading. Furthermore, we can utilize our CG-buffer to keep the memory footprint of the shading data minimal.

3.4.2 Decoupling Shading Samples

We now discuss a method that implements the sampling stage of decoupled deferred shading in a single rasterization pass. The first problem we need to solve is how to assign shading samples to fragments. Prior to rasterization, each primitive needs to be processed to determine its shading domain (see Section 3.3.1

```
in vec2 in_scrPos[]; // screen-space positions
flat out ivec4 domain; // shading grid of the triangle
flat out uint startID; // ID of the first sample in the sh. grid

uniform float shadingRate;

// global SSID counter array
layout(size1x32) uniform uimageBuffer uCtrSSID;

void main(){
    // project screen position to the shading grid
    vec2 gridPos0 = scrPos[0] * shadingRate; [...]

    vec2 minCorner = min(gridPos0, min(gridPos1, gridPos2));
    vec2 maxCorner = max(gridPos0, max(gridPos1, gridPos2));

    // shading grid: xy-top left corner, zw-grid size
    domain.x = int(minCorner.x) - 1;
    domain.y = int(minCorner.y) - 1;
    domain.z = int((maxCorner.x)) - domain.x + 1;
    domain.w = int((maxCorner.y)) - domain.y + 1;

    // we allocate the ssID range with an atomic counter.
    uint reserved = uint((domain.z) * (domain.w));
    startID = imageAtomicAdd(uCtrSSID, 0, reserved);
}
```

Listing 3.1. The geometry shader generates a shading grid for each triangle, and ensures globally unique ssIDs using an atomic counter

for details). As we only consider triangles, we can conveniently implement this functionality in a geometry shader.

Listing 3.1 is an extract from the geometry shader code that assigns a shading grid for each rasterized triangle. In our implementation, the geometry shader might also set up conservative bounds for stochastically rasterized triangles.

Listing 3.2 shows the pseudocode of the fragment shader, implementing the remainder of our pipeline. As we described before, the output of this shader is only a pointer to the corresponding shader data. Note that due to driver limitations on integer multisampling, we need to store the references in floating point, using the `intBitsToFloat` GLSL function. The shading samples are stored using image buffers.

We omit the details of visibility testing, which might be standard multi-sampled rasterization, or the implementation of stochastic rasterization, which casts randomly distributed rays inside the conservative screen space bounds of the triangles. We only assume that the visibility method returned the barycentrics of the intersection point. The visibility sample is then assigned to a shading sample, using the grid provided by the geometry shader.

```
layout(location = 0, index = 0) out float FragPtr;

// shader inputs: position, normal, texcoords
flat in vec3 vpos0...

// packed CG-buffer data
layout(rg32ui) uniform uimageBuffer uColorNormalBuffer;
layout(rgba32f) uniform uimageBuffer uViewPosBuffer;

void main(){
    // hw-interpolation or stochastic ray casting...
    vec3 baryCoords = getViewSamplePos();

    // get nearest shading sample
    uint localID = projectToGrid(baryCoords, shadingRate);
    uint globalID = startID + localID;
    bool needStore = false;

    int address = getCachedAddress(globalID, needStore);
    FragPtr = intBitsToFloat(address);

    if(needStore){
        // for each texture...
        textureGradsInShadingSpace(localID, dx, dy);
        vec4 diffuse = textureGrad(texDiffuse, texCoord, dx, dy);
        [...]
        // pack color, normal, view positions into the CGbuffer
        imageStore(uColorNormalBuffer, address, ...);
    }
}
```

Listing 3.2. The fragment shader implements the decoupling map and the chaching mechanism for shading samples.

```
uint projectToGrid(vec3 baryCoords, float shadingRate){
    vec3 vpos = coords.x * vpos0 + coords.y * vpos1 + coords.z * vpos2;
    vec2 screenPos = projToScreen(vpos);
    ivec2 gridPos = ivec2(screenPos * shadingRate + vec2(0.5f)) - domain
        .xy;
    return uint(domain.z * gridPos.y + gridPos.x);
}
```

Listing 3.3. The decoupling map is a simple projection to a regular grid. The density of this grid is determined by the shading rate.

The method `projectToGrid` assigns the fragment to a shading sample, as we show in Listing 3.3. The local index of the shading sample is the linearized index of the closest shading grid cell to the visibility sample. Later, when the shading data is interpolated, some shading samples might fall outside the triangle. These are snapped to the edges (by clamping the barycentrics to 0 or 1, respectively), otherwise some shading values would be extrapolated.

The computation of the texture mip levels also needs special attention. Normally, this is done by the hardware, generating texture gradients of 2×2 fragment blocks. Depending on the shading rate, the shading space gradients can be different. For example, a shading rate of 0.5 would mean that 2×2 fragments might use the same shading sample, which would be detected (incorrectly) as the most detailed mip level by the hardware. Therefore we manually compute the mip level, using the `textureGrad` function.

In Listing 3.2 we have also tried to minimize the divergence of fragment shader threads. The method `getCachedAddress` returns the location of a shading sample in the global memory. In case of a cache miss, a new slot is reserved in the CG-buffer (see below), but the shading data is only written later, if the `needStore` boolean was set.

3.4.3 Global Shading Cache

For a moment let us consider the cache as a "black box" and focus on the implementation of the CG-buffer. If a shading sample is not found in the cache, we need to append a new entry to the compact linear buffers, as shown in Figure 3.4. The CG-buffer linearly grows as more samples are being stored. We can implement this behavior using an atomic counter that references the last shading data element:

```
address = int(atomicCounterIncrement(bufferTail));
```

The streaming nature of the GPU suggests that even a simple first-in, first-out (FIFO) cache could be quite efficient as only the recently touched shading samples are "interesting" for the fragments. We therefore did not attempt to simulate an LRU cache, as suggested by Ragan-Kelley et al. On a current GPU there can be several thousand fragments rasterized in parallel, thus the global cache should also be able to hold a similar magnitude of samples to achieve a good hit rate. In a naïve implementation, a thread could query the buffer tail, and check the last N items in the CG-buffer. Of course the latency of the iterative memory accesses would be prohibitively high. We now show a cache implementation that performs cache lookups *with only one buffer load* and an atomic lock.

The concept of the shading grid already creates indices for shading samples that are growing approximately linearly with the rasterized fragments. Thus the FIFO cache could also be implemented by simply storing the last N *ssID* values. Consequently, instead of linearly searching in a global buffer, we could introduce a bucketed hash array. The full implementation of our optimized algorithm is shown in Listing 3.4.

The hash function (hashSSID) is a simple modulo operation with the number of buckets. This evenly distributes queries from rasterized fragments over the buckets, which is important to minimize cache collisions (when threads with different ssIDs compete for the same bucket). In case of a cache miss, multiple threads compete for storing the shading samples in the same bucket, therefore we use a per-bucket locking mechanism (uBucketLocks). Note that we try to minimize the number of instructions between obtaining and releasing a lock: the computation of a shading sample does not happen inside the critical section, but we only set the needStore flag to perform the storage later.

As the execution order of fragments is nondeterministic, there is no guarantee that all threads obtain the lock in a given number of steps. In practice we have very rarely experienced cases when the fragment shader execution froze for starving fragment shaders. While we hope this will change on future architectures, we have limited the spinlock iterations, and in case of failure the fragment shader falls back to storing the shading sample without shading reuse. In our experiments this only happened to a negligible fraction of fragments.

One other interesting observation was that if the number of cache buckets is high enough, we can really severely limit the bucket size. As the reader can see in the source code, a bucket stores only a single uvec4 element, which corresponds to two shading samples: a cache entry is a tuple of an ssID and a memory address. This is a very important optimization, because instead of searching inside the cache, we can look up any shading sample with a single load operation using its hash value.

In our first implementation, each bucket in the cache has been stored as a linked list of shading sample addresses, similarly to the per-pixel linked list algorithm of [Yang et al. 10]. When we have made experiments to measure the necessary length of this list, we have found that in most cases even a single element per bucket is sufficient, and we did not have any cache misses when we considered only two elements per bucket. This is why we could discard the expensive linked

```
layout(rgba32ui) uniform uimageBuffer uShaderCache;
layout(r32ui) uniform volatile uimageBuffer uBucketLocks;

int getCachedAddress(uint ssID, inout bool needStore){
    int hash = hashSSID(ssID);
    uvec4 bucket = imageLoad(uShaderCache, hash);
    int address = searchBucket(ssID, bucket);

    // cache miss
    while(address < 0 && iAttempt++ < MAX_ATTEMPTS){
        // this thread is competing for storing a sample
        uint lock = imageAtomicCompSwap(uBucketLocks, hash, FREE, LOCKED
            );
        if(lock == FREE){
            address = int(atomicCounterIncrement(bufferTail));

            // update the cache
            bucket = storeBucket(ssID, hash, bucket);
            imageStore(uShaderCache, hash, bucket);
            needStore = true;

            memoryBarrier(); // release the lock
            imageStore(uBucketLocks, hash, FREE);
        }

        if(lock == LOCKED){
            while(lock == LOCKED && lockAttempt++ < MAX_LOCK_ATTEMPTS)
                lock = imageLoad(uBucketLocks, hash).x;

            // now try to get the address again
            bucket = imageLoad(uShaderCache, hash);
            address = searchBucket(ssID, bucket);
        }

        // if everything failed, store a the data redundantly
        if(address < 0){
            address = int(atomicCounterIncrement(bufferTail));
            needStore = true;
        }
    }
}
```

Listing 3.4. Implementation of the global shading cache.

list behavior and pack all buffers in a single vector. However, this optimization only works if the hash function uniformly distributes cache requests (like ours), and the number of buckets is high. In our examples we use a bucket count of 32,768.

3.4.4 Shading and Resolving

While the sampling stage described above successfully eliminates all duplicate shading samples, the resulting CG-buffer might still hold redundant information. Depending on the rasterization order of triangles, several samples in the compact buffers might not belong to any visible surfaces. Even filling up the z-buffer in a depth prepass might not solve the problem: if early z-testing is disabled a z-culled fragment can still write data into a uniform image buffer. We therefore execute another pass that marks visible shading samples, and optionally removes invisible data from the CG-buffer.

Visibility. Marking visible samples is surprisingly easy. After the sampling stage is finished, we render a full-screen quad with subsample fragment shader execution, and each fragment shader stores a visibility flag corresponding to its shading sample. There is no synchronization needed, as each thread stores the same value. To evaluate the quality of shading reuse, we used a variant of this technique, which counts visibility samples per-shading sample. In the diagnostics code we atomically increment a per-shading sample counter for each subsample in the framebuffer. The heatmap visualizations in this article were generated using this method.

Compaction. Because of the rasterization order, there is no explicit bound on the size of the compact buffers. Using the visibility flags, we can perform a stream compaction on the shading data before shading. Besides efficient memory footprint this also increases the execution coherence during the shading process.

In this article we do not provide implementation details for shading, as it is orthogonal to our decoupling method. The final pixel colors are evaluated by rendering a full-screen quad and gathering all shaded colors for each visibility sample. This is the same behavior as the resolve pass of a standard multisampled framebuffer, except for the location of subsample colors.

3.5   Results

In this section we discuss possible application of our method in deferred rendering. While current GPU architectures do not have hardware support for decoupled sampling, the overhead of our global cache management can be amortized by the reduction of shader evaluations. We focus on stochastic sampling, a rendering problem especially challenging for deferred shading.

While the software overhead of decoupled sampling makes our method rather interactive than real time, we demonstrate significant speedup for scenes with complex shading. All images in this article were rendered at $1{,}280 \times 720$ pixels on an Nvidia GTX580 GPU and Intel Core i7 920 CPU.

Adaptive shading. We have computed the average shading rate of these images, to roughly estimate the shading speedup compared to supersampled deferred shading. We save further computation by reducing the density of the shading grid of blurry surfaces. Our adaptive shading rate implementation is only a proof-of-concept based entirely on empirically chosen factors. For better quality,

Figure 3.5. Focusing from the background (left column) to a foreground object (right column), our adaptive method concentrates shading samples on sharp surfaces. The motivation is to prefilter shading more agressively, as defocus is similar to a low-pass filter over the image. The middle row visualizes the shading rate. In the bottom row we show how the same surface shading would appear from a pinhole camera. The texture filtering matches the shading resolution.

our method could be easily extended with the recent results of [Vaidyanathan et al. 12], who presented a novel anisotropic sampling algorithm, based on image space frequency analysis.

Depth of field. Figure 3.5 shows two renderings of the Crytek Sponza Atrium scene from the same viewing angle, but different focusing distance. In this example the most expensive component of rendering is the computation of the single-bounce global illumination, using 256 virtual point lights (VPLs), generated from a reflective shadow map (RSM) [Dachsbacher and Stamminger 05].

We do not only avoid supersampling the G-buffer, but also reduce the shading frequency of surfaces using the minimum circle of confusion inside each primitive. This approach prefilters shading of defocused triangles, causing slight overblurring of textures, however, we found this effect even desirable if the number of visibility

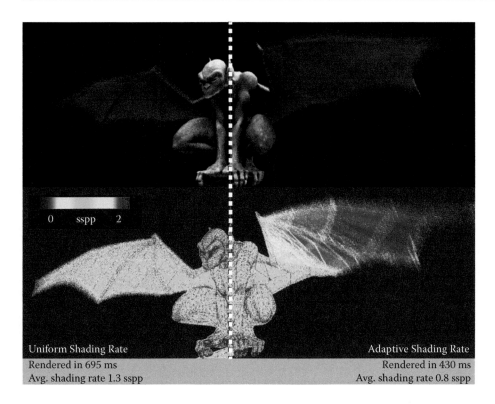

Figure 3.6. A motion blurred character rendered with eight times stochastic supersampling. Deferred shading is computed using 36 ambient occlusion samples per shading sample. The shading rate stays close to one shading sample per pixel (sspp) despite the supersampling density (left side). We can save further ~30% of the rendering time by adaptively reducing sampling of fast-moving surfaces (right side).

samples is small (it effectively reduces the apparent noise of surfaces). The images were rendered using four times supersampling, the stochastic sampling stage took 90 ms, and the shading with 256 VPLs took 160 ms.

Motion blur. Figure 3.6 presents an animated character, rendered with motion blur. This example features ray-traced ambient occlusion and image-based lighting, using the Nvidia OptiX raytracing engine. When using hardware rasterization, high-performance ray tracing is only possible in a deferred computational shading pass. Here we demonstrate adaptive shading again, by reducing the shading rate of fast-moving triangles. We scale the shading grid based on the x and y component of the triangle motion vectors. Our results (and the reduction of shading) can be significantly improved by using the anisotropic shading grid of [Vaidyanathan et al. 12].

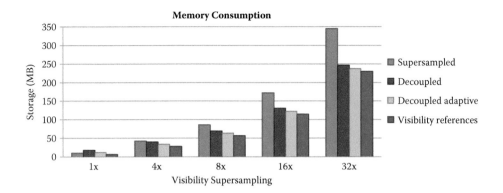

Figure 3.7. Storage requirements of the CG-buffer compared to a standard deferred G-buffer. Only the size of the visibility data grows with supersampling. We rendered the Sponza scene at $1{,}280 \times 720$ pixels.

3.5.1 Memory Consumption

We have analyzed the memory consumption of our method, compared to supersampled deferred shading. We save storage by essentially deduplicating shading data in the G-buffer. However, as a shading sample might not coincide with any visibility samples on the surface, we cannot reconstruct the surface positions based on a subpixel depth value. While other solutions are possible, we assume that we are forced to store the view space position of each shading sample.

We assume that the ground truth deferred method uses 12 bytes per subsample in the G-buffer: 32 bits for depth-stencil and two RGBA8 textures for normals and material information. In fact, most modern deferred renderers use typically more bytes per subsample. The memory footprint of our CG-buffer can be divided into per-visibility and per-shading sample costs. In the former we need to store an integer pointer besides the 32-bit depth-stencil. We need 16 bytes per shading sample: the view positions are packed into 8 bytes (16 bits for $x - y$ and 32 bits for z), and we store the same normal and material information.

If the shading rate is one and there is no multisampling, our method uses twice as much memory as conventional techniques. However, the number of shading samples does not scale with the supersampling resolution. At $4\times$ MSAA, our memory consumption matches the supersampled G-buffer's, and we save significant storage above this sample count. Our measurements on the Sponza scene are summarized in Figure 3.7.

3.5.2 Conclusion

In this chapter we presented a decoupled deferred shading method for high-quality antialiased rendering. To our knowledge this is the first deferred shading method designed for stochastic rasterization. Unfortunately on current GPUs we need to implement stochastic rasterization and the shading cache using shaders, to overcome the limitations of the hardware pipeline. We consider our results beneficial for interactive applications, where shading cost dominates the rendering, however, the overhead of the global cache implementation is generally too high for real-time rendering.

We expect that the major synchronization bottleneck will disappear in future rendering architectures. While we cannot predict whether future GPUs would have a hardware-accelerated version of the memoization cache, some way of local synchronization among fragment shaders would already remove most of the overhead. Using a tile-based rendering architecture instead of sort-last-fragment would allow us to use a more efficient, per-tile on-chip shading cache.

In our examples we have assumed that the visible color of surfaces remains constant in a single frame, and shading can be prefiltered. This might cause artifacts on fast-moving surfaces, therefore we could extend our method to support interpolation among temporal shading samples. In the future it will be interesting to separate the frequency content of shading itself: a hard shadow edge in fact cannot be prefiltered, but there are low-frequency components of shading, e.g., diffuse indirect illumination, where sparse shading can bring relevant speedup.

3.6 Acknowledgments

We would like to thank Anton Kaplanyan and Balázs Tóth for the helpful discussions during the development of this project. Gabor Liktor is funded by Crytek GmbH.

Bibliography

[Chajdas et al. 11] Matthäus G. Chajdas, Morgan McGuire, and David Luebke. "Subpixel Reconstruction Antialiasing for Deferred Shading." In *Proceedings of Symposium on Interactive 3D Graphics and Games*, pp. 15–22. New York: ACM, 2011.

[Dachsbacher and Stamminger 05] Carsten Dachsbacher and Marc Stamminger. "Reflective Shadow Maps." In *Proceedings of the 2005 Symposium on Interactive 3D Graphics and Games*, pp. 203–231. New York: ACM, 2005.

[Laine and Karras 11] Samuli Laine and Tero Karras. "High-Performance Software Rasterization on GPUs." In *Proceedings of the ACM SIGGRAPH Symposium on High Performance Graphics*, pp. 79–88. New York: ACM, 2011.

[Liktor and Dachsbacher 12] Gábor Liktor and Carsten Dachsbacher. "Decoupled Deferred Shading for Hardware Rasterization." In *Proceedings of the*

ACM Symposium on Interactive 3D Graphics and Games, pp. 143–150. New York: ACM, 2012.

[McGuire et al. 10] M. McGuire, E. Enderton, P. Shirley, and D. Luebke. "Real-Time Stochastic Rasterization on Conventional GPU Architectures." In *Proceedings of the Conference on High Performance Graphics*, pp. 173–182. Aire-la-Ville, Switzerland: Eurographics Association, 2010.

[Ragan-Kelley et al. 11] J. Ragan-Kelley, J. Lehtinen, J. Chen, M. Doggett, and F. Durand. "Decoupled Sampling for Graphics Pipelines." *ACM Transactions on Graphics* 30:3 (2011), article no. 17.

[Reshetov 09] Alexander Reshetov. "Morphological Antialiasing." In *Proceedings of the Conference on High Performance Graphics 2009*, pp. 109–116. New York: ACM, 2009.

[Vaidyanathan et al. 12] Karthik Vaidyanathan, Robert Toth, Marco Salvi, Solomon Boulos, and Aaron E. Lefohn. "Adaptive Image Space Shading for Motion and Defocus Blur." In *Proceedings of the Fourth ACM SIGGRAPH/Eurographics COnference on High Performance Graphics*, pp. 13–21. Aire-la-Ville, Switzerland: Eurographics Association, 2012.

[Yang et al. 10] Jason C. Yang, Justin Hensley, Holger Grün, and Nicolas Thibieroz. "Real-Time Concurrent Linked List Construction on the GPU." *Computer Graphics Forum* 29:4 (2010), 1297–1304.

4

Tiled Forward Shading

Markus Billeter, Ola Olsson, and Ulf Assarsson

4.1 Introduction

We will explore the *tiled forward shading* algorithm in this chapter. Tiled forward shading is an extension or modification of *tiled deferred shading* [Balestra and Engstad 08, Swoboda 09, Andersson 09, Lauritzen 10, Olsson and Assarsson 11], which itself improves upon traditional deferred shading methods [Hargreaves and Harris 04, Engel 09].

Deferred shading has two main features: decoupling of lighting and shading from geometry management and minimization of the number of lighting computations performed [Hargreaves and Harris 04]. The former allows for more efficient geometry submission and management [Shishkovtsov 05] and simplifies shaders and management of shader resources. However the latter is becoming less of an issue on modern GPUs, which allow complex flow control in shaders, and support uniform buffers and more complex data structures in GPU memory.

Traditional forward pipelines typically render objects one by one and consider each light for each rasterized fragment. In deferred shading, one would instead render a representation of the geometry into a screen-sized G-buffer [Saito and Takahashi 90], which contains shading data for each pixel, such as normal and depth/position. Then, in a separate pass, the lighting and shading is computed by, for example, rendering light sources one by one (where each light source is represented by a bounding volume enclosing the light's influence region). For each generated fragment during this pass, data for the corresponding pixel is fetched from the G-buffer, shading is computed, and the results are blended into an output buffer. The number of lighting computations performed comes very close to the optimum of one per light per visible sample (somewhat depending on the bounding volumes used to represent light sources).

Deferred shading thereby succeeds in reducing the amount of computations needed for lighting, but at the cost of increased memory requirements (the G-buffer is much larger than a color buffer) and much higher memory bandwidth usage. Tiled deferred shading fixes the latter (Section 4.2), but still requires large G-buffers.

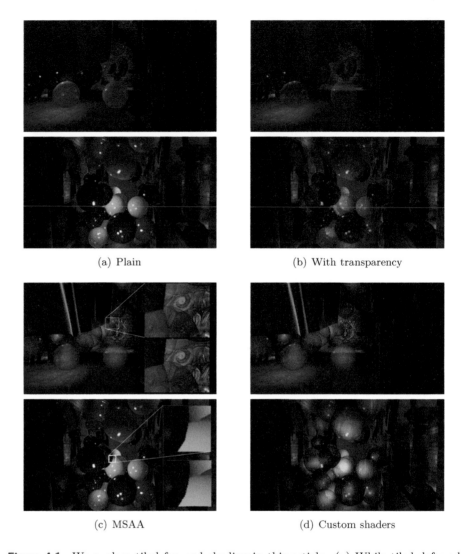

(a) Plain   (b) With transparency

(c) MSAA   (d) Custom shaders

Figure 4.1. We explore tiled forward shading in this article. (a) While tiled deferred shading outperforms tiled forward shading in the plain (no transparency, no multisample antialiasing (MSAA)) case by approximately 25%, (b) tiled forward shading enables use of transparency. Additionally, (c) we can use hardware supported MSAA, which, when emulated in deferred shading requires large amounts of memory. Furthermore, at 4× MSAA, tiled forward shading outperforms deferred with equal quality by 1.5 to 2 times. The image shows 8× MSAA, which we were unable to emulate for deferred rendering due to memory constraints. (d) Finally, we discuss custom shaders. As with standard forward rendering, shaders can be attached to geometry chunks. The scene contains 1,024 randomly placed lights, and the demo is run on an NVIDIA GTX480 GPU.

Tiled forward shading attempts to combine one of the main advantages of (tiled) deferred rendering, i.e., the reduced amount of lighting computations done, with the advantages of forward rendering. Besides reduced memory requirements (forward rendering does not need a large G-buffer), it also enables transparency [Kircher and Lawrance 09, Enderton et al. 10] (Section 4.5), enables multisampling schemes [Swoboda 09, Lauritzen 10] (Section 4.6), and does not force the use of übershaders if different shading models must be supported (Section 4.7). See the images in Figure 4.1 for a demonstration of these different aspects.

4.2   Recap: Forward, Deferred, and Tiled Shading

The terms *forward, deferred,* and *tiled shading* will be appearing quite frequently in this chapter. Therefore, let us define what we mean, since usage of these terms sometimes varies slightly in the community. The definitions we show here are identical to the ones used by [Olsson and Assarsson 11].

With *forward shading*, we refer to the process of rendering where lighting and shading computations are performed in the same pass as the geometry is rasterized. This corresponds to the standard setup consisting of a vertex shader that transforms geometry and a fragment shader that computes a resulting color for each rasterized fragment.

Deferred shading splits this process into two passes. First, geometry is rasterized, but, in contrast to forward shading, geometry attributes are output into a set of geometry buffers (G-buffers). After all geometry has been processed this way, an additional pass that computes the lighting or full shading is performed using the data stored in the G-buffers.

In its very simplest form, the second pass (the lighting pass) may look something like following:

```
for each G-buffer sample {
  sample_attr = load attributes from G-buffer

  for each light {
    color += shade(sample_attr, light)
  }

  output pixel color;
}
```

Sometimes, the order of the loops is reversed. The deferred algorithm described in Section 4.1 is an example of this.

The light pass shown above requires $\mathcal{O}\left(N_{\text{lights}} \cdot N_{\text{samples}}\right)$ lighting computations. If we somehow know which lights were affecting what samples, we could reduce this number significantly [Trebilco 09].

Tiled deferred shading does this by dividing samples into tiles of $N \times N$ samples. (We have had particularly good successes with $N = 32$, but this should be somewhat hardware and application dependent.) Lights are then assigned to these tiles. We may optionally compute the minimum and maximum Z-bounds of each tile, which allows us to further reduce the number of lights affecting each tile (more discussion on this in Section 4.4).

Benefits of tiled deferred shading [Olsson and Assarsson 11] are the following:

- The G-buffers are read only once for each lit sample.

- The framebuffer is written to once.

- Common terms of the rendering equation can be factored out and computed once instead of recomputing them for each light.

- The work becomes coherent within each tile; i.e., each sample in a tile requires the same amount of work (iterates over the same lights), which allows for efficient implementation on SIMD-like architectures (unless, of course, the shader code contains many branches).

For tiled deferred shading (and most deferred techniques) to be worthwhile, most lights must have a limited range. If all lights potentially affect all of the scene, there is obviously no benefit to the tiling (Figure 4.2(a)).

Tiled deferred shading can be generalized into *Tiled Shading*, which includes both the deferred and forward variants. The basic tiled shading algorithm looks like the following:

1. Subdivide screen into tiles.

2. Optional: find minimum and maximum Z-bounds for each tile.

3. Assign lights to each tile.

4. For each sample: process all lights affecting the current sample's tile.

Step 1 is basically free; if we use regular $N \times N$ tiles, the subdivision is implicit. Finding minimum and maximum Z-bounds for each tile is optional (Step 2). For instance, a top-down view on a scene with low depth complexity may not allow for additional culling of lights in the Z-direction. Other cases, however, can benefit from tighter tile Z-bounds, since fewer lights are found to influence that tile (Figure 4.2(b)).

In tiled *deferred* shading, the samples in Step 4 are fetched from the G-buffers. In tiled *forward* shading, the samples are generated during rasterization. We will explore the latter in the rest of the article.

We recently presented an extension to tiled shading, called *clustered shading* [Olsson et al. 12b]. Clustered shading is an extension of tiled shading that

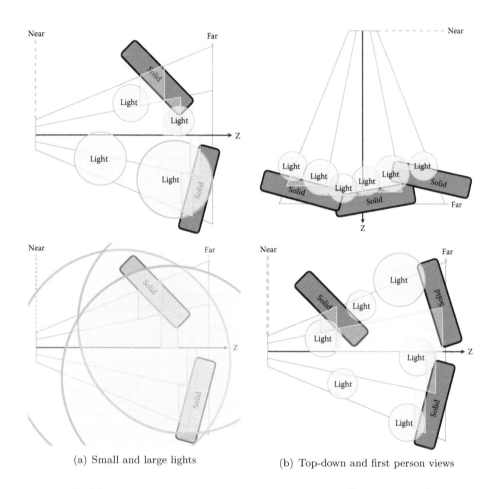

(a) Small and large lights   (b) Top-down and first person views

Figure 4.2. (a) The effect of having lights that are too large (bottom image): there is
no gain from the tiling, as all light sources affect all tiles (drawn in yellow), compared
to the top image, where there is one light per tile on average. (b) Comparison of a
top-down view and a first-person view. In the top-down view (top), all lights are close
to the ground, which has only small variations in the Z-direction. In this case, not much
is gained from computing minimum and maximum Z-bounds. In the first-person view
(bottom), the bounds help (three lights in the image affect no tiles at all).

handles complex light and geometry configurations more robustly with respect
to performance. However, tiled forward shading is significantly simpler to implement, and works on a much broader range of hardware. We will discuss the
clustered shading extension and how it interacts with the tiled forward shading
presented here in Section 4.8.

4.3   Tiled Forward Shading: Why?

The main strength of deferred techniques, including tiled deferred shading, is that
over-shading due to over-draw is eliminated. However, most deferred techniques
suffer from the following weaknesses when compared to forward rendering:

- Transparency/blending is tricky, since traditional G-buffers only allow storage of a single sample at each position in the buffer.

- The memory storage and bandwidth requirements are higher and become even worse with MSAA and related techniques (Section 4.6).

Forward rendering, on the other hand, has good support for

- transparency via alpha blending,

- MSAA and related techniques through hardware features (much less memory storage is required).

In addition, forward rendering trivially supports different shaders and materials
for different geometries. Deferred techniques would generally need to fall back to
übershaders (or perform multiple shading passes).

A special advantage for tiled forward shading is its low requirements on GPU
hardware. It is possible to implement a tiled forward renderer without compute
shaders and other (relatively) recent hardware features. In fact, it is possible
to implement a tiled forward renderer on any hardware that supports dependent texture lookups in the fragment shader. On the other hand, if compute
shaders are available, we can take advantage of this during, say, light assignment
(Section 4.4).

In the following sections, we first present a tiled forward shading renderer
to which we add support for transparency, MSAA and finally experiment with
having a few different shaders for different objects. We compare performance
and resource consumption to a reference tiled deferred shading renderer and show
where the tiled forward renderer wins.

4.4   Basic Tiled Forward Shading

We listed the basic algorithm for all tiled shading variants in Section 4.2. For
clarity, it is repeated here including any specifics for the forward variant.

1. Subdivide screen into tiles

2. Optional: pre-Z pass—render geometry and store depth values for each sample in the standard Z-buffer.

3. Optional: find minimum and/or maximum Z-bounds for each tile.

4. Assign lights to each tile.

5. Render geometry and compute shading for each generated fragment.

Subdivision of screen. We use regular $N \times N$ pixel tiles (e.g., $N = 32$). Having very large tiles creates a worse light assignment; each tile will be affected by more light sources that affect a smaller subset of samples in the tile. Creating very small tiles makes the light assignment more expensive and increases the required memory storage—especially when the tiles are small enough that many adjacent tiles are found to be affected by the same light sources.

Optional pre-Z pass. An optional pre-Z pass can help in two ways. First, it is required if we wish to find the Z-bounds for each tile in the next step. Secondly, in the final rendering pass it can reduce the number of samples that need to be shaded through early-Z tests and similar hardware features.

The pre-Z pass should, of course, only include opaque geometry. Transparent geometry is discussed in Section 4.5.

Though a pre-Z pass is scene and view dependent, in our tests we have found that adding it improves performance significantly. For instance, for the images in Figure 4.1(a), rendering time is reduced from 22.4 ms (upper view) and 37.9 ms (lower view) to 15.6 ms and 18.7 ms, respectively.

Optional minimum or maximum Z-bounds. If a depth buffer exists, e.g., from the pre-Z pass described above, we can use this information to find (reduce) the extents of each tile in the Z-direction (depth). This yields smaller per-tile bounding volumes, reducing the number of lights that affect a tile during light assignment.

Depending on the application, finding only either the minimum or the maximum bounds can be sufficient (if bounds are required at all). Again, transparency (Section 4.5) interacts with this, as do various multisampling schemes (Section 4.6).

In conjunction with the pre-Z test above, the minimum or maximum reduction yields a further significant improvement for the views in Figure 4.1(a). Rendering time with both pre-Z and minimum or maximum reduction is 10.9 ms (upper) and 13.8 ms (lower), respectively—which is quite comparable to the performance of tiled deferred shading (8.5 ms and 10.9 ms). The reduction itself is implemented using a loop in a fragment shader (for simplicity) and currently takes about 0.75 ms (for $1{,}920 \times 1{,}080$ resolution).

Light assignment. Next, we must assign lights to tiles. Basically, we want to efficiently find which lights affect samples in which tiles. This requires a few choices and considerations.

In tiled shading, where the number of tiles is relatively small (for instance, a resolution of $1{,}920 \times 1{,}080$ with 32×32 tiles yields just about 2,040 tiles), it can be feasible to do the assignment on the CPU. This is especially true if the number of lights is relatively small (e.g., a few thousand). On the CPU, a simple implementation is to find the screen-space axis-aligned bounding boxes (AABBs) for each light source and loop over all the tiles that are contained in the 2D region of the AABB. If we have computed the minimum and maximum depths for each tile, we need to perform an additional test to discard lights that are outside of the tile in the Z-direction.

On the GPU, a simple brute-force variant works for moderate amounts of lights (up to around 10,000 lights). In the brute-force variant, each tile is checked against all light sources. If each tile gets its own thread group, the implementation is fairly simple and performs relatively well. Obviously, the brute-force algorithm does not scale very well. In our clustered shading implementation [Olsson et al. 12b], we build a simple light hierarchy (a BVH) each frame and test the tiles (clusters) against this hierarchy. We show that this approach can scale up to at least one million lights in real time. The same approach is applicable for tiled shading as well.

Rendering and shading. The final step is to render all geometry. The pipeline for this looks almost like a standard forward rendering pipeline; different shaders and related resources may be attached to different chunks of geometry. There are no changes to the stages other than the fragment shader.

The fragment shader will, for each generated sample, look up which lights affect that sample by checking what lights are assigned to the sample's tile (Listing 4.1).

4.5 Supporting Transparency

As mentioned in the beginning of this article, deferred techniques have some difficulty dealing with transparency since traditional G-buffers only can store attributes from a single sample at each buffer location [Thibieroz and Grün 10]. However, with forward rendering, we never need to store attributes for samples. Instead we can simply blend the resulting colors using standard alpha-blending.

Note that we are not solving the order-dependent transparency problem. Rather, we support, unlike many deferred techniques, standard alpha-blending where each layer is lit correctly. The application must, however, ensure that transparent objects are drawn in the correct back-to-front order.

We need to make the following changes, compared to the basic tiled forward shading algorithm (Section 4.4).

Optional minimum or maximum Z-bounds. We need to consider transparent geometry here, as nonoccluded transparent objects will affect a tile's bounds inasmuch that it moves a tile's minimum Z-bound ("near plane") closer to the camera.

We ended up using two different sets of tiles for opaque and transparent geometries, rather than extending a single set of tiles to include both opaque and

```glsl
// 1D texture holding per-tile light lists
uniform isampleBuffer tex_tileLightLists;

// uniform buffer holding each tile's light count and
// start offset of the tile's light list (in
// tex_tileLightIndices)
uniform TileLightListRanges
{
  ivec2 u_lightListRange[MAX_NUM_TILES];
}

void shading_function( inout FragmentData aFragData )
{
  // ...

  // find fragment's tile using gl_FragCoord
  ivec2 tileCoord = ivec2(gl_FragCoord.xy)
    / ivec2(TILE_SIZE_X, TILE_SIZE_Y);
  int tileIdx = tileCoord.x
    + tileCoord.y * LIGHT_GRID_SIZE_X;

  // fetch tile's light data start offset (.y) and
  // number of lights (.x)
  ivec2 lightListRange = u_lightListRange[tileIdx].xy;

  // iterate over lights affecting this tile
  for( int i = 0; i < lightListRange.x; ++i )
  {
    int lightIndex = lightListRange.y + i;

    // fetch global light ID
    int globalLightId = texelFetch(
      tex_tileLightLists, lightIndex ).x;

    // get the light's data (position, colors, ...)
    LightData lightData;
    light_get_data( lightData, globalLightId );

    // compute shading from the light
    shade( aFragData, lightData );
  }

  // ...
}
```

Listing 4.1. GLSL pseudocode that demonstrates how lights affecting a given sample are fetched. First, we find the fragment's associated tile (tileIdx) based on its position in the framebuffer. For each tile we store two integers (u_lightListRange array), one indicating the number of lights affecting the tile, and the other describes the offset into the global per-tile light list buffer (tex_tileLightLists). The light list buffer stores a number of integers per tile, each integer identifying a globally unique light that is affecting the tile.

transparent geometries. The Z-bounds for tiles used with opaque geometry are computed as described in Section 4.4, which gives a good light assignment for the opaque geometry (Figure 4.3(a)).

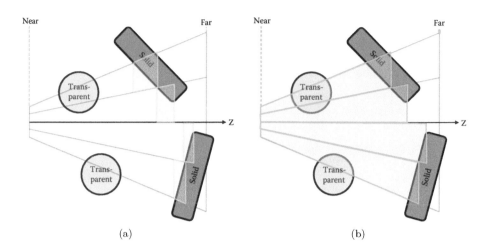

Figure 4.3. Z-bounds used for (a) opaque and (b) transparent geometries.

For transparent geometry, we would like to find the transparent objects' minimum Z-value and the minimum of the transparent objects' and opaque objects' respective maximum Z-values. However, this is somewhat cumbersome, requiring several passes over the transparent geometry; therefore, we simply use the maximum Z-value from the opaque geometry to cap the tiles in the far direction. This discards lights that are hidden by opaque geometry. In the near direction, we extend the tiles to the camera's near plane, as shown in Figure 4.3(b).

Using separate bounds turned out to be slightly faster than using the same tile bounds for both opaque and transparent geometry; in Figure 4.1(b), when using separate bounds, rendering takes 15.1 ms (upper) and 21.9 ms (lower), compared to 16.1 ms and 23.5 ms when using the extended bounds for both opaque and transparent geometries.

We would like to note that this is, again, scene dependent. Regardless of whether we use the approximate variant or the exact one, we can still use the depth buffer from the opaque geometry during the final render in order to enable early-Z and similar optimizations. If we do not use the minimum or maximum reduction to learn a tile's actual bounds, no modifications are required to support transparency.

Light assignment. If separate sets of tiles are used, light assignment must be done twice. In our case, a special optimization is possible: we can first assign lights in two dimensions and then discard lights that lie behind opaque geometry (use the maximum Z-bound from the tiles only). This yields the light lists for transparent geometry. For opaque geometry, we additionally discard lights based on the minimum Z-bound information (Listing 4.2).

```
// assign lights to 2D tiles
tiles2D = build_2d_tiles();
lightLists2D = assign_lights_to_2d_tiles( tiles2D );

// draw opaque geometry in pre-Z pass and find tiles'
// extents in the Z-direction
depthBuffer = render_preZ_pass();
tileZBounds = reduce_z_bounds( tiles2D, depthBuffer );

// for transparent geometry, prune lights against maximum Z-direction
lightListsTrans
  = prune_lights_max( lightLists2D, tileZBounds );

// for opaque geometry additionally prune lights against
// minimum Z-direction
lightListsOpaque
  = prune_lights_min( lightListsTrans, tileZBounds );

// ...

// later: rendering
draw( opaque geometry, lightListsOpaque );
draw( trasparent geometry, lightListsTrans );
```

Listing 4.2. Pseudocode describing the rendering algorithm used to support transparency, as shown in Figure 4.1(b). We perform the additional optimization where we first prune lights based on the maximum Z-direction, which gives the light assignment for transparent geometry. Then, we prune lights in the minimum Z-direction, which gives us light lists for opaque geometry.

Rendering and shading. No special modifications are required here, other than using the appropriate set of light lists for opaque and transparent geometries, respectively. First, all opaque geometry should be rendered. Then the transparent geometry is rendered back to front.[1]

4.6 Support for MSAA

Supporting MSAA and similar schemes is very simple with tiled forward shading. We mainly need to ensure that all render targets are created with MSAA enabled. Additionally, we need to consider all (multi)samples during the optional minimum or maximum Z-reduction step.

   We show the effect of MSAA on render time in Figure 4.4. As we compare to tiled deferred shading, which does not support transparency, Figure 4.4 includes timings for tiled forward both with (Figure 4.1(b)) and without (Figure 4.1(a)) transparency. Additionally, we compare memory usage between our forward and deferred implementations.

---

[1]In our demo, we sort on a per-object basis, which obviously causes some artifacts when transparent objects overlap. This is not a limitation in the technique but rather one in our implementation.

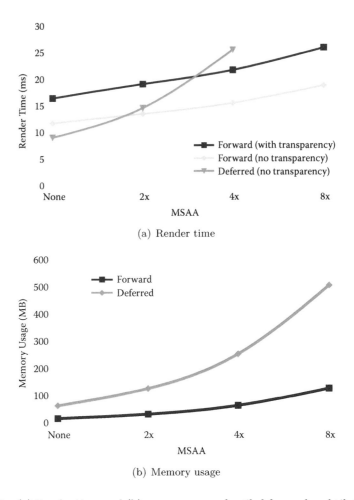

Figure 4.4. (a) Render time and (b) memory usage for tiled forward and tiled deferred shading with varying MSAA settings. We were unable to allocate the 8× MSAA frame-buffer for deferred, which is why no timing results are available for that configuration. Memory usage estimates are based on a G-buffer with 32-bit depth, 32-bit ambient, and 64-bit normal, diffuse, and specular components (using the RGBA16F format).

One interesting note is that our unoptimized Z-reduction scales almost linearly with the number of samples: from 0.75 ms when using one sample to 5.1 ms with 8× MSAA. At that point, the contribution of the Z-reduction is quite significant with respect to the total frame time. However, it still provides a speedup in our tests. It is also likely possible to optimize the Z-reduction step further, for instance, by using compute shaders instead of a fragment shader.

4.7   Supporting Different Shaders

Like all forward rendering, we can attach different shaders and resources (textures, uniforms, etc.) to different chunks of geometry. Of course, if desired, we can still use the übershader approach in the forward rendering.

We have implemented three different shader types to test this, as seen in Figure 4.1(d): a default diffuse-specular shader, a shader emulating two-color car paint (see transparent bubbles and lion), and a rim-light shader (see large fabric in the middle of the scene).

The forward renderer uses the different shaders, compiled as different shader programs, with different chunks of geometry. For comparison, we implemented this as an übershader for deferred rendering. An integer identifying which shader should be used is stored in the G-buffer for each sample. (There were some unused bits available in the G-buffer, so we did not have to allocate additional storage.) The deferred shading code selects the appropriate shader at runtime using runtime branches in GLSL.

Performance degradation for using different shaders seems to be slightly smaller for the forward renderer; switching from diffuse-specular shading only to using the different shaders described above caused performance to drop by 1.4 ms on average. For the deferred shader, the drop was around 2.2 ms. However, the variations in rendering time for different views are in the same order of magnitude.

4.8   Conclusion and Further Improvements

We have explored *tiled forward shading* in this chapter. Tiled forward shading combines advantages from both tiled deferred shading and standard forward rendering. It is quite adaptable to different conditions, by, for instance, omitting steps in the algorithm made unnecessary by application-specific knowledge. An example is the optional computation of minimum and/or maximum Z-bounds for top-down views.

An extension that we have been exploring recently is *clustered shading*. Tiled shading (both forward and deferred) mainly considers 2D groupings of samples, which, while simple, cause performance and robustness issues in some scene and view configurations. One example of this is in scenes with first-person-like cameras where many discontinuities occur in the Z-direction (Figure 4.5). In clustered shading, we instead consider 3D groupings of samples, which handle this case much more gracefully.

Clustered shading's main advantage is a much lower view dependency, delivering more predictable performance in scenes with high or unpredictable complexity in the Z-direction. The disadvantages are increased complexity, requirements on hardware (we rely heavily on compute shaders/CUDA), and several new constant costs. For instance, with tiled shading, the subdivision of the screen into tiles is basically free. In clustered shading, this step becomes much more expensive—in

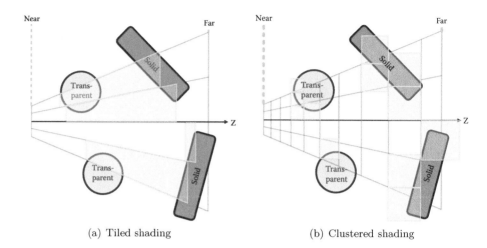

(a) Tiled shading   (b) Clustered shading

Figure 4.5. Comparison between volumes created by (a) the tiling explored in this article and (b) clustering, as described in [Olsson et al. 12b]. Finding the tiled volumes is relatively simple and can be done in standard fragment shaders. Clustering is implemented with compute shaders, as is the light assignment to clusters.

fact, in some cases it offsets time won in the shading from the better light-to-sample mapping offered by clustering (Figure 4.6). We are also further exploring clustered forward shading [Olsson et al. 12a], which shows good promise on modern high-end GPUs with compute shader capabilities. Tiled forward shading, on the other hand, is implementable on a much wider range of hardware.

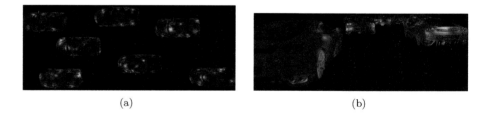

(a)   (b)

Figure 4.6. Comparison between tiled forward shading and clustered forward shading. (a) In the top-down view, tiled forward outperforms our current clustered forward implementation (6.6 ms versus 9.3 ms). (b) In the first-person-like view, tiled forward becomes slightly slower (9.4 ms versus 9.1 ms). While somewhat slower in the first view, one of the main features of clustered shading is its robust performance. There are 1,024 randomly placed light sources.

Bibliography

[Andersson 09] Johan Andersson. "Parallel Graphics in Frostbite - Current & Future." SIGGRAPH Course: Beyond Programmable Shading, New Orleans, LA, August 6, 2009. (Available at http://s09.idav.ucdavis.edu/talks/04-JAndersson-ParallelFrostbite-Siggraph09.pdf.)

[Balestra and Engstad 08] Christophe Balestra and Pål-Kristian Engstad. "The Technology of Uncharted: Drake's Fortune." Presentation, Game Developer Conference, San Francisco, CA, 2008. (Available at http://www.naughtydog.com/docs/Naughty-Dog-GDC08-UNCHARTED-Tech.pdf.)

[Enderton et al. 10] Eric Enderton, Erik Sintorn, Peter Shirley, and David Luebke. "Stochastic Transparency." In *I3D '10: Proceedings of the 2010 ACM SIGGRAPH Symposium on Interactive 3D Graphics and Games*, pp. 157–164. New York: ACM, 2010.

[Engel 09] Wolfgang Engel. "The Light Pre-Pass Renderer: Renderer Design for Efficient Support of Multiple Lights." SIGGRAPH Course: Advances in Real-Time Rendering in 3D Graphics and Games, New Orleans, LA, August 3, 2009. (Available at http://www.bungie.net/News/content.aspx?type=topnews&link=Siggraph_09.)

[Hargreaves and Harris 04] Shawn Hargreaves and Mark Harris. "Deferred Shading." Presentation, NVIDIA Developer Conference: 6800 Leagues Under the Sea, London, UK, June 29, 2004. (Available at http://http.download.nvidia.com/developer/presentations/2004/6800_Leagues/6800_Leagues_Deferred_Shading.pdf.)

[Kircher and Lawrance 09] Scott Kircher and Alan Lawrance. "Inferred Lighting: Fast Dynamic Lighting and Shadows for Opaque and Translucent Objects." In *Sandbox '09: Proceedings of the 2009 ACM SIGGRAPH Symposium on Video Games*, pp. 39–45. New York: ACM, 2009.

[Lauritzen 10] Andrew Lauritzen. "Deferred Rendering for Current and Future Rendering Pipelines." SIGGRAPH Course: Beyond Programmable Shading, Los Angeles, CA, July 29, 2010. (Available at http://bps10.idav.ucdavis.edu/talks/12-lauritzen_DeferredShading_BPS_SIGGRAPH2010.pdf.)

[Olsson and Assarsson 11] Ola Olsson and Ulf Assarsson. "Tiled Shading." *Journal of Graphics, GPU, and Game Tools* 15:4 (2011), 235–251. (Available at http://www.tandfonline.com/doi/abs/10.1080/2151237X.2011.621761.)

[Olsson et al. 12a] Ola Olsson, Markus Billeter, and Ulf Assarsson. "Clustered and Tiled Forward Shading: Supporting Transparency and MSAA." In *SIGGRAPH '12: ACM SIGGRAPH 2012 Talks*, article no. 37. New York: ACM, 2012.

[Olsson et al. 12b] Ola Olsson, Markus Billeter, and Ulf Assarsson. "Clustered Deferred and Forward Shading." In *HPG '12: Proceedings of the Fourth ACD SIGGRPAH/Eurographics Conference on High Performance Graphics*, pp. 87–96. Aire-la-Ville, Switzerland: Eurogaphics, 2012.

[Saito and Takahashi 90] Takafumi Saito and Tokiichiro Takahashi. "Comprehensible Rendering of 3D Shapes." *SIGGRAPH Comput. Graph.* 24:4 (1990), 197–206.

[Shishkovtsov 05] Oles Shishkovtsov. "Deferred Shading in S.T.A.L.K.E.R." In *GPU Gems 2*, edited by Matt Pharr and Randima Fernando, pp. 143–166. Reading, MA: Addison-Wesley, 2005.

[Swoboda 09] Matt Swoboda. "Deferred Lighting and Post Processing on PLAYSTATION 3." Presentation, Game Developer Conference, San Francisco, 2009. (Available at http://www.technology.scee.net/files/presentations/gdc2009/DeferredLightingandPostProcessingonPS3.ppt.)

[Thibieroz and Grün 10] Nick Thibieroz and Holger Grün. "OIT and GI Using DX11 Linked Lists." Presentation, Game Developer Conference, San Francisco, CA, 2010. (Available at http://developer.amd.com/gpu_assets/OIT%20and%20Indirect%20Illumination%20using%20DX11%20Linked%20Lists_forweb.ppsx.)

[Trebilco 09] Damian Trebilco. "Light Indexed Deferred Rendering." In *ShaderX7: Advanced Rendering Techniques*, edited by Wolfgang Engel, pp. 243–256. Hingham, MA: Charles River Media, 2009.

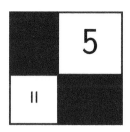

5

Forward+: A Step Toward Film-Style Shading in Real Time

Takahiro Harada, Jay McKee, and Jason C. Yang

5.1 Introduction

Modern GPU hardware along with the feature set provided by the DirectX 11 API provides developers more flexibility to choose among a variety of rendering pipelines. In order to exploit the performance of modern GPUs, we believe it is important to choose a pipeline that takes advantage of GPU hardware features, scales well, and provides flexibility for artists, tech artists, and programmers to achieve high-quality rendering with unique visuals. The ability to differentiate a game's visual look from today's games, which modern computer-generated (CG) films are extremely good at doing, likely will be a key for game graphics in the future. However, the ability to produce high-quality renderings that approach the styling in CG films will require great flexibility to support arbitrary data formats and shaders for more sophisticated rendering of surface materials and special effects.

Our goal was to find a rendering pipeline that would best meet these objectives. We boiled things down to a few specific requirements:

- Materials may need to be both physically and nonphysically based. Tech artists will want to build large trees of materials made of arbitrary complexity. Material types will likely be similar to those found in offline renderers such as RenderMan, mental ray, and Maxwell Render shading systems.

- Artists want complete freedom regarding the number of lights that can be placed in a scene at once.

- Rendering data should be decoupled from the underlying rendering engine. Artists and programmers should be able to write shaders and new materials freely at runtime for quick turnaround—going from concept to seeing results

115

should be fast and easy. The architecture should be simple and not get in the way of creative expression.

We have devised a rendering pipeline that we believe meets these objectives well and is a good match for modern GPU hardware going into the foreseeable future. We refer to it as the Forward+ rendering pipeline [Harada et al. 11].

5.2   Forward+

The Forward+ rendering pipeline requires three stages:

- **Z prepass**. Z prepass is an option for forward rendering, but it is essential for Forward+ to reduce the pixel overdraws of the final shading step. This is especially expensive for Forward+ due to the possible traversal of many lights per pixel, which we will detail later in this section.

- **Light culling**. Light culling is a stage that calculates the list of lights affecting a pixel.

- **Final shading**. Final shading, which is an extension to the shading pass in forward rendering, shades the entire surface. A required change is the way to pass lights to shaders. In Forward+, any lights in a scene have to be accessible from shaders rather than binding some subset of lights for each objects as is typical of traditional forward rendering.

5.2.1   Light Culling

The light-culling stage is similar to the light-accumulation step of deferred lighting. Instead of calculating lighting components, light culling calculates a list of light indices overlapping a pixel. The list of lights can be calculated for each pixel, which is a better choice for final shading.

However, storing a per-pixel light list requires a large memory footprint and significant computation at the light-culling stage. Instead, the screen is split into tiles and light indices are calculated on a per-tile basis (Figure 5.1). Although tiling can add false positives to the list for a pixel in a tile, it reduces the overall memory footprint and computation time necessary for generating the light lists. Thus we are making a tradeoff between light-index buffer memory and final shader efficiency.

By utilizing the computing capability of modern GPUs, light culling can be implemented entirely on the GPU as detailed in Section 5.3. Therefore, the whole lighting pipeline can be executed entirely on the GPU.

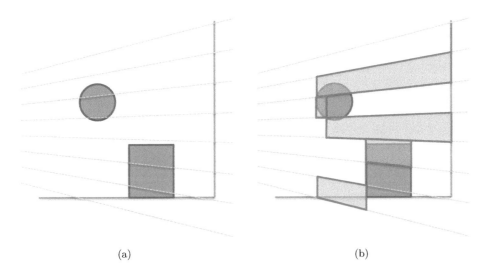

(a)   (b)

Figure 5.1. Illustration of light culling in 2D. (a) A camera is placed on the left, and green lines indicate tile borders. (b) Light culling creates a frustum for each tile bounded by minimum and maximum depth of pixels in a tile.

5.2.2 Shading

Whereas light culling creates the list of lights overlapping each pixel, final shading loops through the list of lights and evaluates materials using material parameters describing the surface properties of the rendered object along with information stored for each light. With unordered access view (UAV) support, per-material instance information can be stored and accessed in linear structured buffers passed to material shaders. Therefore, at least in theory, the full render equation can be satisfied without limitation because light accumulation and shading happen simultaneously in one place with complete material and light information.

Use of complex materials and more accurate lighting models to improve visual quality is not constrained other than by the GPU computational cost, which is largely determined by the average number of overlapping lights on each pixel multiplied by the average cost for material calculation.

With this method, high pixel overdraw can kill performance; therefore, a Z prepass is critical to minimize the cost of final shading.

5.3 Implementation and Optimization

A standard forward rendering pipeline can be converted to a Forward+ rendering pipeline by adding the light-culling stage and modifying existing pixel shaders to make them implement Forward+'s final shading stage as described in Section 5.2.

No modification is necessary for the Z prepass, so we do not describe its implementation. The light-culling stage can be implemented in several ways thanks to the flexibility of current GPUs. Specifically, direct compute and read-writable structure data buffers or UAVs are the key features to utilizing Forward+. In this section, we first describe which features of DirectX 11 are essential to making Forward+ work well on modern GPUs. Then we explain a light-culling implementation that works well for a scene with thousands of lights. If there are more lights, we might be better off considering other implementations such as those described in [Harada et al. 11]. This section concludes by describing modifications for final shading.

5.3.1 Gather-Based Light Culling

During light culling, the computation is done on a by-tile basis. Therefore, it is natural to execute a thread group for a tile. A thread group can share data using thread group shared memory (called shared memory from now on), which can reduce a lot of redundant computation in a thread group. The computation is identical for each tile; therefore, we explain the computation for a single tile.

The compute shader for light culling is executed as a two-dimensional (2D) work group. A thread group is assigned a unique 2D index, and a thread in a thread group is assigned a unique 2D index in the group.

In the pseudocode in this subsection, the following macros are used for these variables:

- GET_GROUP_IDX: thread group index in X direction (SV_GroupID);

- GET_GROUP_IDY: thread group index in Y direction (SV_GroupID);

- GET_GLOBAL_IDX: global thread index in X direction (SV_DispatchThreadID);

- GET_GLOBAL_IDY: global thread index in Y direction (SV_DispatchThreadID);

- GET_LOCAL_IDX: local thread index in X direction (SV_GroupThreadID);

- GET_LOCAL_IDY: local thread index in Y direction (SV_GroupThreadID).

The first step is computation of the frustum of a tile in view space. To reconstruct four side faces, we need to calculate the view-space coordinates of the four corner points of the tile. With these four points and the origin, four side planes can be constructed.

```
float4 frustum[4];
{  // construct frustum
  float4 v[4];
  v[0]=projToView(8*GET_GROUP_IDX , 8*GET_GROUP_IDY ,1.f) );
  v[1]=projToView(8*(GET_GROUP_IDX+1), 8*GET_GROUP_IDY ,1.f) );
  v[2]=projToView(8*(GET_GROUP_IDX+1),8*(GET_GROUP_IDY+1),1.f));
```

```
  v[3]=projToView(8*GET_GROUP_IDX , 8*(GET_GROUP_IDY+1),1.f) );
  float4 o = make_float4(0.f,0.f,0.f,0.f);
  for(int i=0; i<4; i++)
    frustum[i] = createEquation( o, v[i], v[(i+1)&3] );
}
```

projToView() is a function that takes screen-space pixel indices and depth value
and returns coordinates in view space. createEquation() creates a plane equation
from three vertex positions.

The frustum at this point has infinite length in the depth direction; however,
we can clip the frustum by using the maximum and minimum depth values of the
pixels in the tile. To obtain the depth extent, a thread first reads the depth value
of the assigned pixel from the depth buffer, which is created in the depth prepass.
Then it is converted to the coordinate in view space. To select the maximum and
minimum values among threads in a group, we used atomic operations to shared
memory. We cannot use this feature if we do not launch a thread group for
computation of a tile.

```
float depth = depthIn.Load(
uint3(GET_GLOBAL_IDX ,GET_GLOBAL_IDY ,0) );

float4 viewPos = projToView(GET_GLOBAL_IDX , GET_GLOBAL_IDY ,
depth);

int lIdx = GET_LOCAL_IDX + GET_LOCAL_IDY*8;
{// calculate bound
  if( lIdx == 0 )// initialize
  {
    ldsZMax = 0;
    ldsZMin = 0xffffffff;
  }
  GroupMemoryBarrierWithGroupSync();
  u32 z = asuint( viewPos.z );
  if( depth != 1.f )
  {
    AtomMax( ldsZMax, z );
    AtomMin( ldsZMin, z );
  }
  GroupMemoryBarrierWithGroupSync();
  maxZ = asfloat( ldsZMax );
  minZ = asfloat( ldsZMin );
}
```

ldsZMax and ldsZMin store maximum and minimum z coordinates, which are
bounds of a frustum in the z direction, in shared memory. Once a frustum is
constructed, we are ready to go through all the lights in the scene. Because there
are several threads executed per tile, we can cull several lights at the same time.
We used 8×8 for the size of a thread group; thus, 64 lights are processed in
parallel. The code for the test is as follows:

```
for(int i=0; i<nBodies; i+=64)
{
  int il = lIdx + i;
  if( il < nBodies )
  {
    if(overlaps(frustum, gLightGeometry[il]))
    {
      appendLightToList(il);
    }
  }
}
```

In overlaps(), a light-geometry overlap is checked against a frustum using the separating axis theorem [Ericson 04]. If a light is overlapping the frustum, the light index is stored to the list of the overlapping lights in appendLightToList(). There are several data structures we can use to store the light list. The obvious way would be to build a linked list using a few atomic operations [Yang et al. 10].

However, this approach is relatively expensive: we need to use a few global atomic operations to insert a light, and a global memory write is necessary whenever an overlapping light is found. Therefore, we took another approach in which a memory write is performed in two steps. A tile is computed by a thread group, and so we can use shared memory for the first level storage. Light index storage and counter for the storage is allocated as follows:

```
groupshared u32 ldsLightIdx[LIGHT_CAPACITY];
groupshared u32 ldsLightIdxCounter;
```

In our implementation, we set LIGHT_CAPACITY to 256. The appendLightToList() is implemented as follows:

```
void appendLightToList( int i )
{
  u32 dstIdx = 0;
  InterlockedAdd( ldsLightIdxCounter, 1, dstIdx );
  if( dstIdx < LIGHT_CAPACITY )
    ldsLightIdx[dstIdx] = i;
}
```

With this implementation, no global memory write is necessary until all the lights are tested.

After testing all the lights against a frustum, indices of lights overlapping that frustum are collected in the shared memory. The last step of the kernel is to write these to the global memory.

For the storage of light indices in the global memory, we allocated two buffers: gLightIdx, which is a memory pool for the indices, and gLightIdxCounter, which is a memory counter for the memory pool. Memory sections for light indices for a tile are not allocated in advance. Thus, we first need to reserve memory in gLightIdx. This is done by an atomic operation to gLightIdxCounter using a thread in the thread group.

Once a memory offset is obtained, we just fill the light indices to the assigned contiguous memory of gLightIdx using all the threads in a thread group. The code for doing this memory write is as follows:

```
{  // write back
  u32 startOffset = 0;
  if( lIdx == 0 )
  {// reserve memory
    if( ldsLightIdxCounter != 0 )
      InterlockedAdd( gLightIdxCounter , ldsLightIdxCounter,
startOffset );

    ptLowerBound[tileIdx] = startOffset;
    ldsLightIdxStart = startOffset;
  }
  GroupMemoryBarrierWithGroupSync();
  startOffset = ldsLightIdxStart;

  for(int i=lIdx; i<ldsLightIdxCounter; i+=64)
  {
    gLightIdx[startOffset+i] = ldsLightIdx[i];
  }
}
```

This light-culling kernel reads light geometry (for spherical lights, that includes the location of the light and its radius). There are several options for the structure of the light buffer. Of course, we can pack light geometry and lighting properties, such as intensity and falloff, to a single structure. However, this is not a good idea for our light-culling approach because all the necessary data for the light culling is padded with light properties, which are not used in the light culling. A GPU usually reads data by page. Therefore, it is likely to transfer lighting properties as well as light geometry although they are not read by the kernel when this data structure is employed for the lights.

A better choice for the data structure is to separate the light geometry and lighting properties into two separate buffers. The light-culling kernel only touches the light geometry buffer, increasing the performance because we do not have to read unnecessary data.

5.3.2 Final Shading

For final shading, all objects in the camera frustum are rendered with their authored materials. This is different than forward rendering because we need to iterate through the lights overlapping each tile.

To write a pixel shader, we created "building blocks" of common operations for different shaders. This design makes it easy to write shaders, as we will show now. The most important building blocks are the following two, implemented as macros:

```
#define LIGHT_LOOP_BEGIN
  int tileIndex = GetTileIndex(screenPos);
  uint startIndex, endIndex;
  GetTileOffsets( tileIndex, startIndex, endIndex );

  for( uint lightListIdx = startIdx;
       lightListIdx < endIdx;
       lightListIdx++ )
  {
    int lightIdx = LightIndexBuffer[lightListIdx];
    LightParams directLight;
    LightParams indirectLight;

    if( isIndirectLight( lightIdx ) )
    {
      FetchIndirectLight(lightIdx , indirectLight);
    }
    else
    {
      FetchDirectLight( lightIndex, directLight );
    }
#define LIGHT_LOOP_END
  }
```

`LIGHT_LOOP_BEGIN` first calculates the tile index of the pixel using its screen-space position. Then it opens a loop to iterate all the lights overlapping the tile and fills light parameters for direct and indirect light. `LIGHT_LOOP_END` is a macro to close the loop.

By using these building blocks, an implementation of a pixel shader is simple and looks almost the same as a pixel shader used in forward rendering. For example, a shader for a microfacet surface is implemented as follows:

```
float4 PS ( PSInput i ) : SV_TARGET
{
  float3 colorOut = 0;
#LIGHT_LOOP_BEGIN
  colorOut += EvaluateMicrofacet ( directLight, indirectLight );
#LIGHT_LOOP_END
  return float4(colorOut, 1.f );
}
```

Other shaders can be implemented by just changing the lines between the two macros. This building block also allows us to change the implementation easily based on performance needs. For instance, we can change `LIGHT_LOOP_BEGIN` to iterate a few lights on a slower platform.

An optimization we can do for the host side is to sort all render draw calls by material type and render all triangles that belong to each unique material at the same time. This reduces GPU state change and makes good use of the cache because all pixels needing the same data will be rendered together.

5.4 Results

We implemented Forward+ using DirectX 11 and benchmarked using the scene shown in Figure 5.2 to compare the performance of Forward+ to compute-based deferred lighting [Andersson 11].

In short, Forward+ was faster on both the AMD Radeon HD 6970 and HD 7970 (Figure 5.3). Once we compare the memory transfer size and the amount of computing, it makes sense. Three timers are placed in a frame of the benchmark to measure time for prepass, light processing, and final shading. In Forward+, these three are depth prepass, light culling, and final shading. In compute-based deferred, they are geometry pass (or G-pass), which exports geometry information to full screen buffers, light culling, screen-space light accumulation, and final shading.

Prepass. Forward+ writes a screen-sized depth buffer while deferred writes a depth buffer and another `float4` buffer that packs the normal vector of the visible pixel. The specular coefficient can be stored in the W component of the buffer, too. Therefore, Forward+ writes less than deferred and is faster on prepass.

(a)   (b)

Figure 5.2. A scene with 3,072 dynamic lights rendered in 1,280 × 720 resolution. (a) Using diffuse lighting. (b) Visualization of number of lights overlapping each tile. Blue, green and red tiles have 0, 25, and 50 lights, respectively. The numbers in between are shown as interpolated colors. The maximum number is clamped to 50.

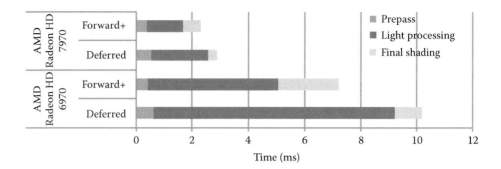

Figure 5.3. Breakdown of the computation time for three stages of Forward+ and deferred on an AMD Radeon HD 6970 GPU and an AMD Radeon HD 7970 GPU.

Light processing. Forward+ reads the depth and light geometry buffers. Deferred also reads them, but the `float4` buffer storing normal vectors and lighting properties has to be read as well because lighting is done at this stage. Therefore, Forward+ has less memory read compared to deferred.

As for the amount of the computation, Forward+ culls lights. On the other hand, deferred not only culls lights but also performs lighting computation. Forward+ has less computation.

For the memory write, Forward+ writes light indices, the sizes of which depend on the scene and tile size. If 8×8 tiles are used, deferred has to write $8 \times 8 \times 4$ bytes if a `float4` data is written for each pixel. With this data size, Forward+ can write 256 ($8 \times 8 \times 4$) light indices for a tile; if the number of lights is less than 256 per tile, Forward+ writes less. In our test scene, there was no tile overlapped with more than 256 lights.

To summarize this stage, Forward+ is reading, computing, and writing less than deferred. This is why Forward+ is so fast at this stage.

Final shading. It is obvious that Forward+ takes more time compared to deferred at shading because it has to iterate through all the lights in the pixel shader. This is a disadvantage in terms of the performance, but it is designed this way to get more freedom.

5.5   Forward+ in the AMD Leo Demo

We created the AMD Leo demo to show an implementation of Forward+ in real-time in a real-world setting. A screenshot from the demo is shown in Figure 5.4. We chose scene geometry on the order of what can be found in current PC-based video games (one to two million polygons). We also had the objective of rendering with a unique stylized look that could be characterized as "CGish" in that it uses material types that resemble those found in an offline renderer. There are more

Figure 5.4. A screenshot from the AMD Leo Demo.

than 150 lights in the scenes. Artists created about 50 lights by hand. Other lights are dynamically spawned at runtime for one-bounce indirect illumination lighting using the technique described in this section. Although Forward+ is capable of using thousands of dynamic lights, a few hundred lights were more than enough for our artists to achieve their lighting goals, especially for a single-room indoor scene.

We use a material system in which a material consists of N layers where each layer can have M weighted BRDF models along with other physically based constants like those involving transmission, absorption, refraction, and reflections of incoming light.

Material parameters for a single layer include physical properties for lighting such as coefficients for a microfacet surface and a refractive index as well as many modifiers for standard lighting parameters. We deliberately allow numeric ranges to go beyond the "physically correct" values to give artists freedom to bend the rules for a given desired effect.

For lighting, artists can dynamically create and place any number of omnidi-rectional lights and spotlights into a scene. The light data structure contains a material index mask. This variable is used to filter lights to only effect specific material types. While not physically correct, this greatly helps artists fine-tune lighting without unwanted side effects.

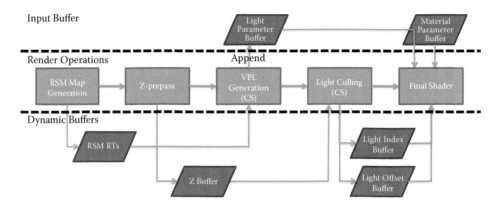

Figure 5.5. Forward+ render passes and GPU buffers in the AMD Leo Demo.

5.5.1   One-Bounce Indirect Illumination

As a unique extension of the light-culling system, lights can be used as what we call an indirect light to generate one-bounce indirect illumination in the scene. If a given light is tagged to be an indirect light, the following will occur for that light before any rendering passes at runtime:

- Generate a reflective shadow map (RSM) of the scene from the point of view of the light [Dachsbacher and Stamminger 05]. Normal buffer, color buffer, and world-space buffers are generated.

- A compute shader is executed to create spotlights at the location captured in the RSM. The generated spotlights are appended to the main light list. The direction of the spotlight will be the reflection of the vector from the world position to the original indirect light around the normal. Set other parameters for the new spotlight that conforms to the settings for the indirect light. We added art-driven parameters to control the effect of indirect lighting.

This new "indirect" light type is used by artists to spawn virtual spotlights that represent one-bounce lighting from the environment. This method seems to give artists good control over all aspects of lighting without requiring them to hand-place thousands or millions of lights or prebake lightmaps. Each indirect light can spawn $N \times N$ virtual spotlights, so it takes only a handful to create a nice indirect lighting effect. Once virtual lights are spawned in the compute shader, they go through the same light-culling process as all the other lights in the system. Thus, we could keep the entire rendering pipeline simple. Figure 5.5 illustrates the rendering pipeline used in the AMD Leo demo.

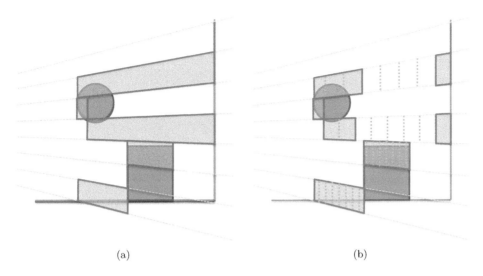

(a)   (b)

Figure 5.6. Illustration of 2.5D culling. (a) Frustum culling creates a long frustum for a tile with foreground and background. (b) 2.5D culling—splitting depth into eight cells—does not capture lights falling between foreground and background.

5.6 Extensions

5.6.1 2.5D Culling

At the light-culling stage of Forward+, light geometries are tested against a frustum of each tile that is clipped by the maximum and minimum depth values of a tile. This light culling works well if there is little variance in the depth in a tile. Otherwise, it can create a long frustum for a tile. This results in capturing a lot of lights for a tile, as we can see at the edge of geometries in Figure 5.3(b), although some lights have no influence on any of the pixels in a tile if they fall at the void space in the frustum.

As the number of lights reported for a tile increases, the computational cost of final shading increases. This is critical especially when the shading computation for a light is expensive. This is often the case because one of the motivations of employing Forward+ is its ability to use sophisticated BRDFs for shading.

One obvious way to improve the efficiency of culling is to cull the lights using a 3D grid. However, this increases the computation as well as the size of the data to be exported. It is possible to develop sophisticated and expensive culling, but it shouldn't be overkill. Our proposed 2.5D culling constructs a nonuniform 3D grid without adding a lot of computation or stressing the memory bandwidth.

The idea is illustrated in Figure 5.6. This approach first constructs a frustum for a tile in the same way as the screen-space culling described in Section 5.3.

Then the extent of a frustum is split into cells; for each pixel in a tile, we flag a cell to which the pixel belongs. We call the data we construct for a tile a frustum and an array of occupancy flags a depth mask.

To check overlap of light geometry on the tile, the light geometry first is checked against the frustum. If the light overlaps, a depth mask is created for the light. This is done by calculating the extent of the light geometry in the depth direction of the frustum and flagging the cells to that extent. By comparing the depth mask for a light to the depth mask for the tile, we can cull the light in the depth direction. Overlap of the light is reported only if there is at least one cell flagged by both depth masks.

If a tile has a foreground and background, the 2.5D culling can detect and drop lights that fall between these two surfaces, thus reducing the number of lights to be processed at the final shading.

Implementation. The 2.5D culling splits a frustum into 32 cells, and so the occupancy information is stored in a 32-bit value. This cell data is allocated in shared memory to make it available to all threads in a group. The first modification to the light-culling kernel is the construction of an occupancy mask of the surface. This is performed after calculating the frustum extent in the depth direction. The pitch of a cell is calculated from the extent.

Once the pitch and the minimum depth value are obtained, any depth value can be converted to a cell index. To create the depth mask for a tile, we iterate through all the pixels in the tile and calculate a cell index for each pixel. Then a flag for the occupied cell is created by a bit shift, which is used to mark the depth mask in shared memory using an atomic logical-or operation.

Once we find a light overlapping the frustum, a depth mask is created for the light. The minimum and maximum depth values of the geometry are calculated and converted to cell indices. Once the cell indices are calculated, two bit-shift operations and a bit-and operation are necessary to create the depth mask for the light. If the light and surface occupy the same cell, both have the same flag at the cell. Thus taking logical and operation between these two masks is enough to check the overlap.

Results. We took several scenes and counted the number of lights per tile with the original Forward+ and Forward+ with our proposed 2.5D culling. The first benchmark is performed against the scene in Figure 5.7(a), which has a large variance in the depth. Figures 5.7(b) and 5.7(c) visualize the number of lights overlapping each tile using Forward+ with frustum culling and the proposed 2.5D culling.

Figure 5.7(b) makes clear that tiles that contain an object's edge capture a large number of lights. The number of overlapping lights is reduced dramatically when 2.5D culling is used (Figure 5.7(c)). We also counted the number of lights overlapping each tile and quantitatively compared these two culling methods

Figure 5.7. (a) A scene with a large depth variance that the original Forward+ could not process efficiently. (b) Visualization of the number of lights per tile using frustum culled with maximum and minimum depth values in a tile. (c) Visualization of the number of lights per tile using the proposed 2.5D culling.

(Figure 5.9(a)). Without the proposed method, there are a lot of tiles with more than 200 lights overlapping. However, by using the 2.5D culling, a tile has at most 120 overlapping lights. The benefit we can get from final shading depends on the implementation of shader, but culling eliminates a lot of unnecessary memory reads and computation for the final shader.

We also performed a test on the scene shown in Figure 5.8(a), which does not have as much depth variance as the scene in Figure 5.7(a). Because the depth difference is not large in these scenes, the number of lights overlapping a tile, including an edge of an object, is less than in the previous scene. However, color temperature is low when the 2.5D culling is used. A quantitative comparison is shown in Figure 5.9(b). Although the improvement is not as large as the

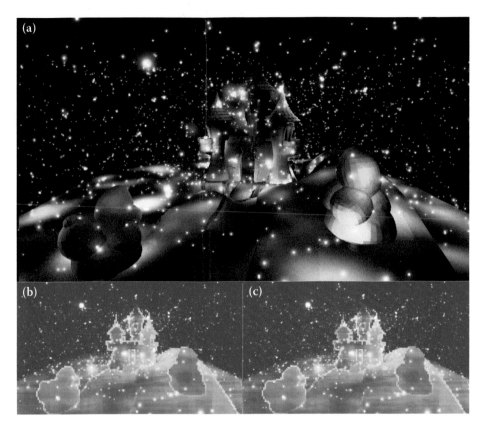

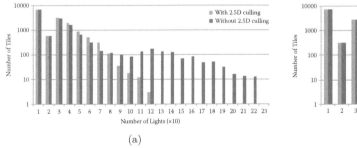

Figure 5.8. (a) A scene without a large depth variance. (b) Visualization of the number of lights per tile using frustum culled with maximum and minimum depth values in a tile. (c) Visualization of the number of lights per tile using the proposed 2.5D culling.

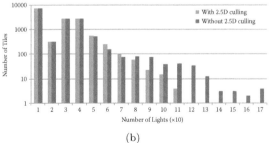

Figure 5.9. The count of tiles in terms of the number of lights for the scenes shown in Figures 5.7(a) and 5.8(a), respectively.

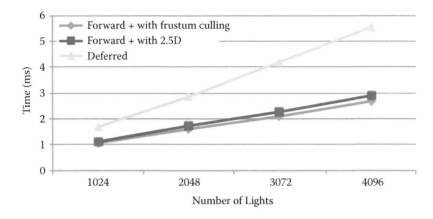

Figure 5.10. Comparison of computation time for the light-culling stage of Forward+ using frustum culling only and frustum culling plus 2.5D culling by changing the number of lights in the scene shown in Figure 5.7(a). Computation time for the light accumulation in compute-based deferred lighting is also shown.

previous scene, the proposed method could reduce the number of overlapping lights on tiles.

Figure 5.10 compares the computation time for the light-culling stage for the scene of Figure 5.1(a) as measured on an AMD Radeon HD 7970 GPU. This comparison indicates the overhead of additional computation in 2.5D culling is less than 10% of the time without the culling; when there are 1,024 lights, the overhead is about 5%. The 2.5D culling is effective regardless of the number of the light in the scene.

Figure 5.10 also contains the light accumulation time of the compute-based deferred lighting. We can see that the light-culling stage with the 2.5D culling in Forward+ is much faster than its counterpart in deferred lighting.

5.6.2 Shadowing from Many Lights

Shadows from a light can be calculated by a shadow map, with which we can get occlusion from the light in the pixel shader when the forward-rendering pipeline is used. We can calculate shadows in the same way for Forward+.

Because Forward+ is capable of using hundreds of lights for lighting, it is natural to wonder how we can use all of those lights in the scene as shadow-casting lights. One option is use a shadow map for each light. This solution is not practical because shadow map creation—the cost of which is linear to scene complexity—can be prohibitively expensive.

We can reduce the shadow map resolution, but this results in low-quality shadows.

Another option relies on rasterization and also borrows an idea from ray tracing. To check the visibility to a light, we can cast a ray to the light. If the light is local, the length of the ray is short. This means we do not have to traverse much in the scene; the cost is not as high as the cost of ray casting a long ray in full ray tracing.

In this subsection, we describe how ray casting can be integrated in Forward+ to add shadows from hundreds of lights and show that a perfect shadow from hundreds of lights can be obtained in real time. After adding this feature, Forward+ is not just an extension of forward-rendering pipeline but a hybrid of forward, deferred-rendering pipelines and ray tracing.

Implementation. To ray cast against the scene, we need the position and normal vector of a primary ray hit and the acceleration data structure for ray casting. The position of a primary ray hit can be reconstructed from the depth buffer by applying inverse projection. The normal vector of the entire visible surface, which is used to avoid casting rays to a light that is at the back of the surface and to offset the ray origin, can be written at the depth prepass. The prepass is no longer writing only the depth value, and so it is essentially identical to a G-pass in the deferred-rendering pipeline. The acceleration structure has to be updated every frame for a dynamic scene; however, this is a more extensive research topic and we do not explore it in this chapter. Instead, we just assume that the data structure is built already.

After the prepass, implementing a ray-cast shadow is straightforward. In a pixel shader, we have access to all the information about lights, which includes light position. A shadow ray can be created by the light position and surface location. Then we can cast the ray against the acceleration structure for an intersection test. If the ray is intersecting, contribution from the light is masked.

Although this naive implementation is easy to implement, it is far from practical in terms of performance. The issue is a legacy of the forward-rendering pipeline. The number of rays to be cast for each pixel is not constant, which means the computational load or time can vary considerably among pixels even if they belong to the same surface. This results in a poor utilization of the GPU.

An alternative is to separate ray casting from pixel shading for better performance. After separating ray casting from pixel shading, the pipeline looks like this:

- G-pass,

- light culling,

- ray-cast job creation,

- ray casting,

- final shading.

After indices of lights overlapping each tile are calculated in the light-culling stage, ray-cast jobs are created and accumulated in a job buffer by iterating through all the screen pixels. This is a screen-space computation in which a thread is executed for a pixel and goes through the list of lights. If a pixel overlaps a light, a ray-cast job is created. To create a ray in the ray-casting stage, we need a pixel index to obtain surface position and normal, and a light index against which the ray is cast. These two indices are packed into a 32-bit value and stored in the job buffer.

After creating all the ray-cast jobs in a buffer, we dispatch a thread for each ray-cast job. Then it does not have the issue of uneven load balancing we experience when rays are cast in a pixel shader. Each thread is casting a ray. After identifying whether a shadow ray is blocked, the information has to be stored somewhere to pass to a pixel shader. We focused only on a hard shadow, which means the output from a ray cast is a binary value. Therefore, we have packed results from 32 rays into one 32-bit value.

But in a scene with hundreds of lights, storing a mask for all of them takes too much space even after the compression. We took advantage of the fact that we have a list of lights per tile; masks for lights in the list of a tile are only stored. We limit the number of rays to be cast per pixel to 128, which means the mask can be encoded as an int4 value. At the ray-casting stage, the result is written to the mask of the pixel using an atomic OR operation to flip the assigned bit.

After separating ray casting from pixel shading, we can keep the final shading almost the same in Forward+. We only need to read the shadow mask for each pixel; whenever a light is processed, the mask is read to get the occlusion.

Results. Figure 5.11 is a screenshot of a scene with 512 shadow-casting lights. We can see legs of chairs are casting shadows from many dynamic lights in the scene. The screen resolution was 1,280 × 720. The number of rays cast for this scene was more than 7 million. A frame computation time is about 32 ms on an AMD Radeon HD 7970 GPU. G-pass and light culling took negligible time compared to ray-cast job creation and ray casting, each of which took 11.57 ms and 19.91 ms for this frame. This is another example of hybrid ray-traced and rasterized graphics.

5.7 Conclusion

We have presented Forward+, a rendering pipeline that adds a GPU compute-based light-culling stage to the traditional forward-rendering pipeline to handle many lights while keeping the flexibility for material usage. We also presented the implementation detail of Forward+ using DirectX 11, and its performance. We described how the Forward+ rendering pipeline is extended to use an indirect illumination technique in the AMD Leo Demo.

Figure 5.11. Dynamic shadowing from 512 lights in a scene with 282,755 triangles.

Because of its simplicity and flexibility, there are many avenues to extend Forward+. We have described two extensions in this chapter: a 2.5D culling, which improves the light-culling efficiency, and dynamic shadowing from many lights.

5.8   Acknowledgments

We would like to thank to members of AMD GPU Tech initiatives and other people who worked on the AMD Leo demo.

Bibliography

[Andersson 11] J. Andersson. "DirectX 11 Rendering in Battlefield 3." Presentation, Game Developers Conference, San Francisco, CA, 2011.

[Dachsbacher and Stamminger 05] C. Dachsbacher and M. Stamminger. "Reflective Shadow Maps." In *Symposium on Interactive 3D Graphics and Games (I3D)*, pp. 203–231. New York: ACM, 2005.

[Ericson 04] C. Ericson. *Real-Time Collision Detection*. San Francisco: Morgan Kaufmann, 2004.

[Harada et al. 11] T. Harada, J. McKee, and J. C. Yang. "Forward+: Bringing Deferred Lighting to the Next Level," Eurographics Short Paper, Cagliari, Italy, May 15, 2012.

[Yang et al. 10] J. C. Yang, J. Hensley, H. Grun, and N. Thibieroz. "Real-Time Concurrent Linked List Construction on the GPU." *Computer Graphics Forum* 29:4 (2010), 1297–1304.

6

II

Progressive Screen-Space Multichannel Surface Voxelization

Athanasios Gaitatzes and Georgios Papaioannou

6.1 Introduction

An increasing number of techniques for real-time global illumination effects rely on volume data. Such representations allow the fast, out-of-order access to spatial data from any deferred shading graphics pipeline stage as in [Thiedemann et al. 11, Mavridis and Papaioannou 11, Kaplanyan and Dachsbacher 10]. For dynamic environments where both the geometry of the scene and the illumination can arbitrarily change between frames, these calculations must be performed in real time. However, when the per frame time budget is limited due to other, more important operations that must take place while maintaining a high frame rate, the fidelity of full-scene voxelization has to be traded for less accurate but faster techniques. This is especially true for video games, where many hundreds of thousands of triangles must be processed in less than 2–3 ms. In this chapter we present the novel concept of *progressive voxelization*, an incremental image-based volume generation scheme for fully dynamic scenes that addresses the view-dependency issues of image-based voxelization within the above time constraints.

Screen-space volume generation methods provide very fast and guaranteed response times compared to geometry-based techniques but suffer from view-dependency. More specifically, any technique that is performed entirely in screen space (as in deferred shading) considers only geometry that has been rendered into the depth buffer and thus has the following strong limitations: First, it ignores geometry located outside the field of view. Second, it ignores geometry that is inside the view frustum but occluded by other objects. Yet these geometry parts may have a significant influence on the desired final result (see our indirect illumination case study in this article).

In single-frame screen-space voxelization, volume attributes already available as fragment data in view-dependent image buffers are transformed and rasterized (*injected*) into the volume buffer to form a partial volume of the observed space. These commonly include the view camera G-buffers like depth, albedo, normals, and the light sources' *reflective shadow maps* (RSMs) [Dachsbacher and Stamminger 05]. The injection procedure is explained in more detail in [Kaplanyan 09] and Section 6.2.2. Since the only volume samples that can be produced in each frame are the ones that are visible in at least one of the images available in the rendering pipeline, each time the (camera or light) view changes, a new set of sample points becomes available and the corresponding voxels are generated from scratch to reflect the newly available image samples. Thus the generated volume will never contain a complete voxelization of the scene. This leads to significant frame-to-frame inconsistencies and potentially inadequate volume representations for the desired volume-based effect, especially when the coverage of the scene in the available image buffers is limited.

To alleviate the problems of screen-space voxelization techniques, but maintain their benefit of predictable, controllable, and bound execution time relative to full-scene volume generation methods, we introduce the concept of *progressive voxelization* (PV). The volume representation is incrementally updated to include the newly discovered voxels and discard the set of invalid voxels, which are not present in any of the current image buffers. Using the already available camera and light source buffers, a combination of volume injection and voxel-to-depth-buffer reprojection scheme continuously updates the volume buffer and discards invalid voxels, progressively constructing the final voxelization.

The algorithm is lightweight and operates on complex dynamic environments where geometry, materials, and lighting can change arbitrarily. Compared to single-frame screen-space voxelization, our method provides improved volume coverage (completeness) over nonprogressive methods while maintaining its high performance merits.

We demonstrate our technique by applying it as an alternative voxelization scheme for the *light propagation volumes* (LPV) diffuse global illumination method of [Kaplanyan and Dachsbacher 10]. However, being a generic multiattribute scalar voxelization method, it can be used in any other real-time volume generation problem.

6.2   Overview of Voxelization Method

Our progressive voxelization scheme is able to produce stable and valid volume data in a geometry-independent manner. As the user interacts with the environment and dynamic objects move or light information changes, new voxel data are accumulated into the initial volume and old voxels are invalidated or updated if their projection in any of the image buffers (camera or light) proves inconsistent with the respective available recorded depth. For a schematic overview see Figure 6.1, and for a resulting voxelization see Figures 6.4 and 6.5.

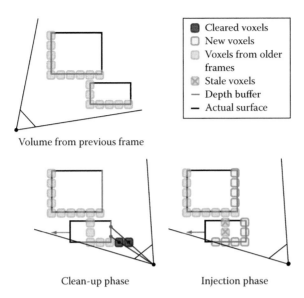

Volume from previous frame

Clean-up phase   Injection phase

Figure 6.1. Schematic overview of the algorithm. During the cleanup phase each voxel is tested against the available depth images. If the projected voxel center lies in front of the recorded depth, it is cleared; otherwise it is retained. During the injection phase, voxels are "turned-on" based on the RSM-buffers and the camera-based depth buffer.

In each frame, two steps are performed: First, in a *cleanup* stage, the volume is swept voxel-by-voxel and the center of each voxel is transformed to the eye-space coordinate system of the buffer and tested against the available depth image value, which is also projected to eye-space coordinates. If the voxel lies closer to the image buffer viewpoint than the recorded depth, the voxel is invalidated and removed. Otherwise, the current voxel attributes are maintained. The update of the volume is performed by writing the cleared or retained values into a separate volume in order to avoid any atomic write operations and thus make the method fast and a very broadly applicable one. At the end of each cleanup cycle, the two volume buffers are swapped. After the cleanup phase, samples from all the available image buffers are injected into the volume (similar to the LPV method [Kaplanyan 09]).

When multiple image buffers are available, the cleanup stage is repeated for each image buffer, using the corresponding depth buffer as input for voxel invalidation. Each time, the currently updated (read) and output (written) buffers are swapped. The current image buffer attributes are then successively injected in the currently updated volume. The whole process is summarized in Figure 6.1.

```
in vec3 voxel_position , voxel_tex_coord;
uniform float voxel_r; // voxel radius
uniform sampler3D vol_shR, vol_shG, vol_shB, vol_normals;

void main (void)
{
  vec4 voxel_pos_wcs = vec4 (voxel_position , 1.0);
  vec3 voxel_pos_css = PointWCS2CSS (voxel_pos_wcs.xyz);
  vec3 voxel_pos_ecs = PointWCS2ECS (voxel_pos_wcs.xyz);
  vec3 zbuffer_ss = MAP_-1To1_0To1 (voxel_pos_css);
  float depth = SampleBuf (zbuffer, zbuffer_ss.xy).x;
  vec3 zbuffer_css = vec3 (voxel_pos_css.xy, 2.0*depth-1.0);
  vec3 zbuffer_ecs = PointCSS2ECS (zbuffer_css);

  vec3 voxel_mf_wcs = voxel_pos_wcs.xyz + voxel_r * vec3(1.0);
  voxel_mf_wcs = max (voxel_mf_wcs ,
                      voxel_pos_wcs.xyz + voxel_half_size);
  vec3 voxel_mb_wcs = voxel_pos_wcs.xyz + voxel_r * vec3(-1.0);
  voxel_mb_wcs = min (voxel_mb_wcs ,
                      voxel_pos_wcs.xyz - voxel_half_size);
  vec3 voxel_mf_ecs = PointWCS2ECS (voxel_mf_wcs);
  vec3 voxel_mb_ecs = PointWCS2ECS (voxel_mb_wcs);
  float bias = distance (voxel_mf_ecs , voxel_mb_ecs);

  vec4 shR_value = SampleBuf (vol_shR, voxel_tex_coord);
  vec4 shG_value = SampleBuf (vol_shG, voxel_tex_coord);
  vec4 shB_value = SampleBuf (vol_shB, voxel_tex_coord);
  vec4 normal_value = SampleBuf (vol_normals, voxel_tex_coord);

  if (voxel_pos_ecs.z > zbuffer_ecs.z + bias) { // discard
    normal_value = vec4 (0,0,0,0);
    shR_value = shG_value = shB_value = vec4 (0,0,0,0);
  }

  // keep
  gl_FragData[0] = normal_value;
  gl_FragData[1] = shR_value;
  gl_FragData[2] = shG_value;
  gl_FragData[3] = shB_value;
}
```

Listing 6.1. Cleanup phase fragment shader.

6.2.1   Cleanup Phase

Throughout the entire voxelization process, each voxel goes through three state transitions: "turn-on," "turn-off," and "keep" (see Listing 6.1). The "turn-on" state change is determined during the injection phase. During the cleanup stage we need to be able to determine if the state of the voxel will be retained or turned off (cleared). For each one of the available depth buffers, each voxel center $\mathbf{p}_v$ is transformed to eye-space coordinates $\mathbf{p}'_v$; accordingly the corresponding image buffer depth $Z(\mathbf{p}')$ is transformed to eye-space coordinates z_e.

Expressing the coordinates in the eye reference frame (Figure 6.2), if $\mathbf{p}'_{v,z} > z_e$ the voxel must be cleared, as it lies in front of the recorded depth boundary in the

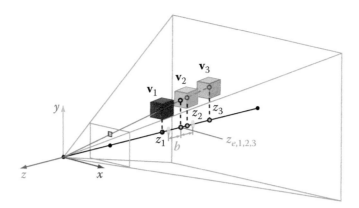

Figure 6.2. Cleanup stage: Voxels beyond the boundary depth zone are retained (orange), while voxels closer to the buffer center of projection are rejected (red). Voxels that correspond to the depth value registered in the buffer must be updated (green).

image buffer. However, the spatial data are quantized according to the volume resolution and therefore a bias b has to be introduced in order to avoid rejecting boundary samples. Since the depth comparison is performed in eye-space, b is equal to the voxel's $\mathbf{p}_v$ radius (half diagonal) clamped by the voxel boundaries in each direction. Therefore the rejection condition becomes

$$\mathbf{p}'_{v,z} > z_e + b.$$

The example in Figure 6.2 explains the cleanup and update state changes of a voxel with respect to the available depth information in an image buffer. All voxels in the figure correspond to the same image buffer sample with eye-space value $z_{e,1,2,3}$. Voxel $\mathbf{v}_1$ is rejected (cleared) because z_1 is greater than $z_{e,1,2,3} + b$. Voxel $\mathbf{v}_2$ must be updated since it lies within the boundary depth zone $[z_{e,1,2,3} - b, z_{e,1,2,3} + b]$. Finally, voxel $\mathbf{v}_3$ is retained, since it lies beyond the registered depth value.

6.2.2   Injection Phase

In the injection phase, a rectangular grid of point primitives corresponding to each depth image buffer is sent to a vertex shader that offsets the points according to the stored depth. The points are subsequently transformed to world space and finally to volume-clip space. If world-space or volume clip-space coordinates are already available in the buffers, they are directly assigned to the corresponding injected points. The volume clip-space depth is finally used to determine the slice in the volume where the point sample attributes are accumulated (see Listing 6.2). At the end of this stage, the previous version of the scene's voxel representation has been updated to include a partial voxelization of the scene based on the newly

```
// Vertex-Shader Stage

flat out vec2 tex_coord;
uniform sampler2D zbuffer;

void main (void)
{
  tex_coord = gl_Vertex.xy;
  float depth = SampleBuf (zbuffer, tex_coord).x;

  // screen space --> canonical screen space
  vec3 pos_css = MAP_0To1_-1To1 (vec3 (gl_Vertex.xy, depth));

  // canonical screen space --> object space
  vec3 pos_wcs = PointCSS2WCS (zbuffer_css);

  // world space --> clip space
  gl_Position = gl_ModelViewProjectionMatrix *
                vec4 (pos_wcs, 1.0);
}

// Geometry-Shader Stage

layout(points) in;
layout(points, max_vertices = 1) out;

uniform int vol_depth;
flat in vec2 tex_coord[];
flat out vec2 gtex_coord;

void main (void)
{
  gtex_coord = tex_coord[0];
  gl_Position = gl_PositionIn[0];
  gl_Layer = int (vol_depth * MAP_-1To1_0To1 (gl_Position.z));

  EmitVertex();
}
```

Listing 6.2. Injection phase using a geometry shader to select the destination slice of the volume for the point samples.

injected point samples. The resolution of the grid of 2D points determines how much detail of the surfaces represented by the depth buffer is transferred into the volume and whether or not the geometry is sparsely sampled. If too few points are injected, the resulting volume will have gaps. This may be undesirable for certain application cases, such as the LPV method [Kaplanyan 09] or algorithms based on ray marching.

6.2.3   Single-Pass Progressive Algorithm

In order to transfer the geometric detail present in the G-buffers to the volume representation and ensure a dense population of the resulting volume, a large resolution for the grid of injected points must be used. However, the injection stage involves rendering the point grid using an equal number of texture lookups and, in some implementations, a geometry shader. This has a potentially serious impact on performance (see Figure 6.8), especially for multiple injection viewpoints.

We can totally forgo the injection phase of the algorithm and do both operations in one stage. Using the same notation as before, the logic of the algorithm remains practically the same. If the projected voxel center lies in front of the recorded depth (i.e., $\mathbf{p}'_{v,z} > z_e + b$), it is still cleared. If the projected voxel center lies behind the recorded depth (i.e., $\mathbf{p}'_{v,z} < z_e - b$), the voxel is retained; otherwise it is turned-on (or updated) using the attribute buffers information. The last operation practically replaces the injection stage.

As we are effectively sampling the geometry at the volume resolution instead of doing so at higher, image-size-dependent rate and then down-sampling to volume resolution, the resulting voxelization is expected to degrade. However, since usually depth buffers are recorded from multiple views, missing details are gradually added. A comparison of the method variations and analysis of their respective running times is given in Section 6.5.

6.3   Progressive Voxelization for Lighting

As a case study, we applied progressive voxelization to the problem of computing indirect illumination for real-time rendering. When using the technique for lighting effects, as in the case of the LPV algorithm of [Kaplanyan 09] or the ray marching techniques of [Thiedemann et al. 11, Mavridis and Papaioannou 11], the volume attributes must include occlusion information (referred to as *geometry volume* in [Kaplanyan 09]), sampled normal vectors, direct lighting (VPLs), and optionally surface albedo in the case of secondary indirect light bounces. Direct illumination and other accumulated directional data are usually encoded and stored as low-frequency spherical harmonic coefficients (see [Sloan et al. 02]).

Virtual point lights (VPLs) are points in space that act as light sources and encapsulate light reflected off a surface at a given location. In order to correctly accumulate VPLs in the volume, during the injection phase, a separate volume buffer is used that is cleared in every frame in order to avoid erroneous accumulation of lighting. For each RSM, all VPLs are injected and additively blended. Finally, the camera attribute buffers are injected to provide view-dependent dense samples of the volume. If lighting from the camera is also exploited (as in our implementation), the injected VPLs must replace the corresponding values in the volume, since the camera direct lighting buffer provides cumulative illumination. After the cleanup has been performed on the previous version of the attribute volume V_{prev}, nonempty voxels from the separate injection buffer replace corresponding values in V_{curr}. This ensures that potentially stale illumination on valid volume cells from previous frames is not retained in the final volume buffer. In Figure 6.3 we can see the results of progressive voxelization and its application to diffuse indirect lighting.

Figure 6.3. (a–f) As the camera moves left to right, we observe correct indirect illumination. (g) Final rendering of the room.

6.4 Implementation

The progressive voxelization method runs entirely on the GPU and has been implemented in a deferred shading renderer using basic OpenGL 3.0 operations on a NVIDIA GTX 285 card with 1 GB of memory. We have implemented two versions of the buffer storage mechanism in order to test their respective speed. The first uses 3D volume textures along with a geometry shader that sorts injected fragments to the correct volume slice. The second unwraps the volume buffers into 2D textures and dispenses with the expensive geometry processing (respective performance can be seen in Figure 6.8).

In the texture requirements are two volume buffers for ping-pong rendering (V_{prev}, V_{curr}). Each volume buffer stores N-dimensional attribute vectors $\mathbf{a}$ and corresponds to a number of textures (2D or 3D) equal to $\lceil N/4 \rceil$, for 4-channel textures. For the reasons explained in Section 6.3 an additional N-dimensional volume buffer is required for lighting applications. In our implementation we need to store surface normals and full color spherical harmonics coefficients for incident flux in each volume buffer, which translates to 3×4 textures in total.

In terms of volume generation engine design, the user has the option to request several attributes to be computed and stored into floating-point buffers for later use. Among them are surface attributes like albedo and normals, but also dynamic lighting information and radiance values in the form of low-order spherical harmonics (SH) coefficients representation (either monochrome radiance or full color encoding, i.e., separate radiance values per color band). In our implementation the radiance of the corresponding scene location is calculated and stored as a second-order spherical harmonic representation for each voxel. For each color band, four SH coefficients are computed and encoded as RGBA float values.

6.5 Performance and Evaluation

In terms of voxelization robustness, our algorithm complements single-frame screen-space voxelization and supports both moving image viewpoints and fully dynamic geometry and lighting. This is demonstrated in Figures 6.4 and 6.5. In addition, in Figure 6.6, a partial volume representation of the Crytek Sponza II Atrium model is generated at a 64^3 resolution and a 128^2-point injection grid using single-frame and progressive voxelization. Figures 6.6(a) and (b) are the single-frame volumes from two distinct viewpoints. Figure 6.6(c) is the progressive voxelization after the viewpoint moves across several frames. Using the partial single-frame volumes for global illumination calculation, we observe abrupt changes in lighting as the camera reveals more occluding geometry (e.g., left arcade wall and floor in Figures 6.6(d) and (e)). However, the situation is gradually remedied in the case of progressive voxelization, since newly discovered volume data are retained for use in following frames (Figures 6.6(f) and (g)).

Figure 6.4. Left: Screen-space voxelization after one step of the process having injected the camera and light buffers (top), and voxelization of the scene after the camera has moved for several frames (bottom). Right: Example of resulting indirect illumination (top) and final illumination (bottom).

Figure 6.5. Progressive voxelization of a scene. Red voxels correspond to screen-space voxelization using image buffers from the current frame only, while other colors refer to voxels generated during previous frames using PV. On the right, volume-based global illumination results using the corresponding volumes. PV (top) achieves more correct occlusion and stable lighting.

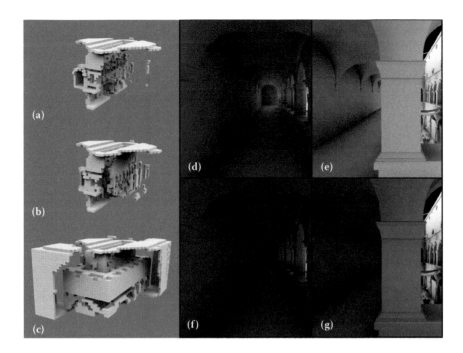

Figure 6.6. Comparison of the voxelization of the Crytek Sponza II Atrium. (a, b) Single-frame screen-space voxelization from two distinct viewpoints where it is not possible to capture all environment details as no information exists in the buffers. (c) Progressive voxelization produced over several frames. (d, e) Indirect lighting buffers corresponding to the single frame voxelization of (a) and (b). (f, g) PV indirect lighting buffers (of the voxelization in (c)).

Figure 6.7 demonstrates progressive voxelization in a dynamic environment in real time. In particular, it shows an animated sequence of a scene with moving and deformable objects, as well as the corresponding voxelization from the camera viewpoint. Observe how the wall behind the closed door is not initially present in the volume, but after the door opens, it is gradually added to the volume and remains there even after the door swings back. The same holds true for the geometry behind the character. Notice also how the voxels representing the articulated figure correctly change state as the figure moves.

Figure 6.8 shows a decomposition of the total algorithm running time into the cleanup and injection stage times respectively versus different volume buffer resolutions for three different injection grid sizes using the 3D volume textures implementation (left) and the 2D textures implementation (center). For fixed injection grid resolutions, we have observed that injection times are not monotonically increasing with respect to volume size as one would expect. The performance also decreases when the buffer viewpoint moves close to geometry.

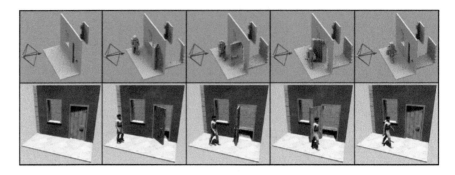

Figure 6.7. Screen-space voxelization of a dynamic scene containing an articulated object using only camera-based injection.

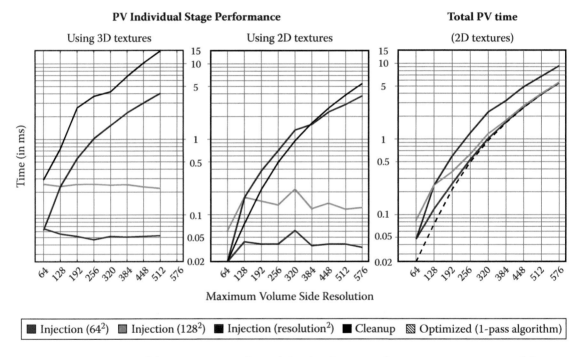

Figure 6.8. Running time (in ms) for the cleanup and injection stages against different volume resolutions for the Crytek Sponza II Atrium model using the 3D volume textures implementation (left) and the 2D textures implementation (center). We used a single G-buffer (camera) as input and one multiple render target (four floats) as output. Injection is measured for three different grid sizes, one being proportional to the volume side. We also show the total progressive voxelization times (right). Note that the performance of the optimized progressive voxelization is identical to that of the cleanup stage.

We attribute this to the common denominator of both cases, namely the fact that pixel overdraw is induced, as points are rasterized in the same voxel locations. This is particularly evident in the blue curve of the 64^2 injection stage graph of Figure 6.8 (left). Note that this behavior is an inherent attribute of injection techniques in general; screen-space voxelization methods depend heavily on the sampling rate used. When this rate is incompatible with the voxel space resolution, holes might appear (undersampling). To ensure adequate coverage of the voxel grid, dense screen-space point samples are drawn, which in turn leads to overdraw problems in many cases. One can use an injection grid proportional to the volume resolution, which partially alleviates the overdraw issue but in turn decreases performance as can be seen in the red curve of the injection graph of Figure 6.8 (left and center).

The time required for a single-frame screen-space voxelization (one G-buffer) equals the time of our injection stage plus a very small overhead to clear the volume buffer, since the two operations are equivalent. Thus, the only difference in the execution time of progressive voxelization is the cleanup stage time. With regard to the quality of the two methods, PV offers more stable and accurate results as new viewpoints gradually improve the volume.

The total voxelization time (Figure 6.8, right) is the sum of the cleanup and injection stages. As the cleanup stage performance depends only on the volume resolution and not on the injection grid size, it vastly improves the voxelization quality compared to using only screen-space injection from isolated frames, at a constant overhead per frame. Especially when applied to global illumination calculations, where small volumes are typically used, the version of the algorithm that uses 2D textures (Figure 6.8, center) has a significantly lower execution footprint. This is because it is not influenced by the geometry shader execution of the 3D textures version (Figure 6.8, left), though both methods are affected by pixel overdraw during injection.

The performance of the optimized progressive voxelization is identical to that of the cleanup stage as expected, since it is essentially a modified cleanup stage. It follows that the dual stage version performance will always be slower than the optimized one.

The maximum volume resolution reported is due to hardware resource limitations on the number and size of the allocated buffers and not algorithm bounds.

In Table 6.1 we report the voxelization performance results for several scenes using our method and the geometry-based multichannel full scene voxelization method of [Gaitatzes et al. 11], which, as ours, is based on the rendering pipeline (GPU). We show a big speed improvement even when adding to the whole process the G-buffers creation time.

In Table 6.2 we report on the quality of our voxelization method. The camera was moved around the mesh for several frames, in order for the algorithm to *progressively* compute the best possible voxelization. For several models and resolutions we show the Hausdorff distance between the original mesh and the

Scene	Grid	GS	G-buffers	PV
	Size	4-floats	Creation	4-floats
Conference	128^3	31.73		0.28
(282K tris)	512^3	64.67	3.2	4.93
Dragon	128^3	198.33		0.18
(871K tris)	512^3	–	59	6.98
Turbine Blade	128^3	265.7		0.14
(1.76M tris)	512^3	–	121	5.37
Hairball	128^3	436.2		0.33
(2.88M tris)	320^3	–	–	4.04

Table 6.1. Voxelization timings (in ms) of various scenes using progressive voxelization (PV) and the geometry slicing (GS) method of [Gaitatzes et al. 11] with 11 output vertices. We present the total (injection + cleanup) performance values of our 2D textures implementation using an injection grid proportional to the volume size, which is our algorithm's worst case as can be seen from the red plot of Figure 6.8.

Scene	Grid	Hausdorff	
	Size	% d_H	(X, Y)
Bunny	64^3	0.3289	0.2168
	128^3	0.1694	0.1091
(69.5K tris)	256^3	0.1064	–
Dragon	64^3	0.3621	0.2565
	128^3	0.1878	0.1289
(871K tris)	256^3	0.1256	0.0645
Turbine Blade	64^3	0.3457	0.2763
	128^3	0.1821	0.1424
(1.76M tris)	256^3	0.1232	0.0697

Table 6.2. Comparison of a full voxelization. We record the normalized (with respect to the mesh bounding box diagonal) average Hausdorff distance (percent). Mesh X is the original mesh to be voxelized and Y is the point cloud consisting of the voxel centers of the voxelization using PV (column 3) and a geometry-based full scene voxelization (column 4).

resulting voxelization using the PV method (see column 3). We notice that our voxelized object (voxel centers) is on average 0.1% different from the original mesh. In addition, we report the Hausdorff distance between the original mesh and the geometry-based full scene voxelization of [Gaitatzes et al. 11] (see col-

Figure 6.9. A series of voxelizations of the dragon model at 128^3 resolution showing the normal vectors. The voxelization is incrementally updated over several frames as the camera moves around the model.

umn 4). We observe that the difference between the corresponding volumes is in the 0.01% range.

In Figure 6.9 we show a series of voxelizations of the dragon model using only the camera G-buffers. In addition, we show the respective Hausdorff distance between the original dragon model and the computed voxel centers (see plot in Figure 6.10). The voxelization is incrementally updated and improved over

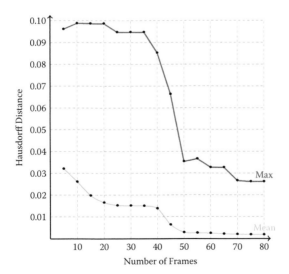

Figure 6.10. The decreasing Hausdorff distance between the original dragon model and the computed progressive voxelizations of Figure 6.9.

several frames as the camera does a complete rotation around each of the principal axis for an equal amount of frames. As the animation progresses, we observe that the Hausdorff distance decreases as the process converges to a full voxelization.

6.6   Limitations

One limitation of our method is that the cleanup phase will only remove invalid voxels that are visible in any of the current image buffers (camera multiple render targets and light RSMs). The visible invalid voxels will be removed from the voxelization the next time they appear in the image buffers. However, the correctness of the voxelization cannot be guaranteed for existing voxels that are not visible in any buffer. For moving geometry, some progressively generated voxels may become stale, as shown in the case of the bottom right of Figure 6.1. Nevertheless, in typical dynamic scenes, the stale voxels are often eliminated either in subsequent frames due to their invalidation in the moving camera buffer or due to their invalidation in other views in the same frame (see Figure 6.11).

Another limitation is that the extents of the voxelization region must remain constant throughout volume updates; otherwise computations are performed with stale buffer boundaries. When the bounding box of the scene is modified or the scene changes abruptly or it is reloaded, the attribute volumes must be deleted and progressively populated again. This is also the reason why the cascaded light propagation volumes method of [Kaplanyan and Dachsbacher 10] could not take advantage of progressive voxelization for the cascades near the user, as the method assumes that they follow the user around, constantly modifying the current volume extents.

Figure 6.11. Correct indirect shadowing effects and color bleeding: Stale voxels from one view (behind the tank) are effectively invalidated in other views (reflective shadow map).

6.7 Conclusion

We have presented a novel screen-space method to progressively build a voxelization data structure on the GPU. Our method achieves improved quality over nonprogressive methods, while it maintains the high performance merits of screen-space techniques.

6.8 Acknowledgments

The Atrium Sponza II Palace in Dubrovnik model was remodeled by Frank Meinl at Crytek. The original Sponza model was created by Marko Dabrovic in early 2002. The Bunny and Dragon models are provided courtesy of the Stanford University Computer Graphics Laboratory.

Bibliography

[Dachsbacher and Stamminger 05] Carsten Dachsbacher and Marc Stamminger. "Reflective Shadow Maps." In *Symposium on Interactive 3D Graphics and Games (I3D)*, pp. 203–231. New York: ACM, 2005.

[Gaitatzes et al. 11] Athanasios Gaitatzes, Pavlos Mavridis, and Georgios Papaioannou. "Two Simple Single-Pass GPU Methods for Multi-channel Surface Voxelization of Dynamic Scenes." In *Pacific Conference on Computer Graphics and Applications—Short Papers (PG)*, pp. 31–36. Aire-la-Ville, Switzerland: Eurographics Association, 2011.

[Kaplanyan 09] Anton Kaplanyan. "Light Propagation Volumes in CryEngine 3." SIGGRAPH Course: Advances in Real-Time Rendering in 3D Graphics and Games, SIGGRAPH 2009, New Orleans, LA, August 3, 2009.

[Kaplanyan and Dachsbacher 10] Anton Kaplanyan and Carsten Dachsbacher. "Cascaded Light Propagation Volumes for Real-Time Indirect Illumination." In *Symposium on Interactive 3D Graphics and Games (I3D)*, pp. 99–107. New York: ACM, 2010.

[Mavridis and Papaioannou 11] Pavlos Mavridis and Georgios Papaioannou. "Global Illumination Using Imperfect Volumes." Presentation, International Conference on Computer Graphics Theory and Applications (GRAPP), Algarve, Portugal, 2011.

[Sloan et al. 02] Peter-Pike Sloan, Jan Kautz, and John Snyder. "Precomputed Radiance Transfer for Real-Time Rendering in Dynamic, Low-Frequency Lighting Environments." In *29th Conference on Computer Graphics and Interactive Techniques (SIGGRAPH)*, pp. 527–536. New York: ACM, 2002.

[Thiedemann et al. 11] Sinje Thiedemann, Niklas Henrich, Thorsten Grosch, and Stefan Müller. "Voxel-Based Global Illumination." In *Symposium on Interactive 3D Graphics and Games (I3D)*, pp. 103–110. New York: ACM, 2011.

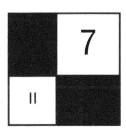

Rasterized Voxel-Based
Dynamic Global Illumination
Hawar Doghramachi

7.1 Introduction

For modern games it becomes more and more important to offer a realistic environment, where a convincing illumination plays a central role. Therefor, not only direct illumination but also indirect illumination has to be taken into account. At the same time modern games increasingly offer the player the possibility to interact with the game world, i.e., move objects around, destroy buildings, or change the lighting dynamically. This is where *dynamic global illumination* comes into play; in contrast to static precalculated solutions, it does account for highly dynamic environments.

Rasterized voxel-based dynamic global illumination takes into consideration that scenes, especially indoor, can contain a large number of light sources of different types (e.g., point, spot, and directional lights). At the same time it produces visually good and stable results while maintaining high interactive frame rates.

7.2 Overview

This technique efficiently utilizes features, which were introduced by DirectX 11 hardware, to accomplish the above stated results.

In the first step a voxel grid representation is created for the scene by using the hardware rasterizer. Here the scene is rendered without depth testing into a small 2D render-target, but instead of outputting the results into the bound render-target, the rasterized pixels are written into a 3D read-write buffer by using atomic functions. In this way the rasterizer is turned into a "voxelizer," creating efficiently a highly populated 3D grid representation of the scene. This voxel grid contains the diffuse albedo and normal information of the geometry

155

and is used later to generate the indirect illumination and to test for geometry occlusion. Since the voxel grid is recreated each frame, the proposed technique is fully dynamic and does not rely on any precalculations.

In the second step, the voxels inside the grid are illuminated by each light source. The illumination is then converted into virtual point lights (VPLs), stored as second-order spherical harmonics coefficients (SH-coefficients). The graphics hardware is utilized again by using the built in blending stage, in order to combine the results of each light source. Later the generated VPLs are propagated within the grid, in order to generate the indirect illumination. In contrast to the light propagation volume (LPV) technique, as proposed by [Kaplanyan and Dachsbacher 10], it is required neither to create a reflective shadow map for each light source nor to inject VPLs into a grid afterwards. Furthermore, there is no need to generate occlusion information separately. Yet the obtained information will be more precise than, e.g., information obtained from depth peeling.

7.3   Implementation

The proposed technique can be subdivided into five distinct steps.

7.3.1   Create Voxel Grid Representation of the Scene

We first need to define the properties of a cubic voxel grid, i.e., its extents, position, and view-/projection-matrices. The grid is moved synchronously with the viewer camera and snapped permanently to the grid cell boundaries to avoid flickering due to the discrete voxel grid representation of the scene. To correctly map our scene to a voxel grid, we need to use an orthographic projection; thus, we will use three view-matrices to get a higher coverage of the scene: one matrix for the back-to-front view, one matrix for the right-to-left view, and one for the top-to-down view. All other calculations will be done entirely on the GPU.

Next we render the scene geometry that is located inside the grid boundaries with disabled color writing and without depth testing into a small 2D render-target. We will use a $32 \times 32 \times 32$ grid; for this it is entirely enough to use a 64×64 pixel render-target with the smallest available pixel format, since we will output the results into a read-write buffer anyway. Basically we pass the triangle vertices through the vertex shader to the geometry shader. In the geometry shader the view-matrix is chosen at which the triangle is most visible, in order to achieve the highest number of rasterized pixels for the primitive. Additionally the triangle size in normalized device coordinates is increased by the texel size of the currently bound render-target. In this way, pixels that would have been discarded due to the low resolution of the currently bound render-target will still be rasterized. The rasterized pixels are written atomically into a 3D read-write structured buffer in the pixel shader. In this way, in contrast to [Mavridis and Papaioannou 11], there is no need to amplify geometry within the geometry shader in order to obtain a highly populated 3D grid representation of the scene. Listing 7.1 shows how this is done for DirectX 11 in HLSL.

```
// vertex shader

VS_OUTPUT main(VS_INPUT input)
{
  VS_OUTPUT output;
  output.position = float4(input.position,1.0f);
  output.texCoords = input.texCoords;
  output.normal = input.normal;
  return output;
}

// geometry shader

static float3 viewDirections[3] =
{
  float3(0.0f,0.0f,-1.0f), // back to front
  float3(-1.0f,0.0f,0.0f), // right to left
  float3(0.0f,-1.0f,0.0f) // top to down
};

int GetViewIndex(in float3 normal)
{
  float3x3 directionMatrix;
  directionMatrix[0] = -viewDirections[0];
  directionMatrix[1] = -viewDirections[1];
  directionMatrix[2] = -viewDirections[2];
  float3 dotProducts = abs(mul(directionMatrix,normal));
  float maximum = max (max(dotProducts.x,dotProducts.y), dotProducts.z);
  int index;
  if(maximum==dotProducts.x)
    index = 0;
  else if(maximum==dotProducts.y)
    index = 1;
  else
    index = 2;
  return index;
}

[maxvertexcount(3)]
void main(triangle VS_OUTPUT input[3],inout TriangleStream<GS_OUTPUT>
          outputStream)
{
  float3 faceNormal = normalize(input[0].normal+input[1].normal+
                                input[2].normal);
  // Get view, at which the current triangle is most visible, in order to
  // achieve highest possible rasterization of the primitive.
  int viewIndex = GetViewIndex(faceNormal);

  GS_OUTPUT output[3];
  [unroll]
  for(int i=0;i<3;i++)
  {
    output[i].position = mul(constBuffer.gridViewProjMatrices[viewIndex],
                             input[i].position);
    output[i].positionWS = input[i].position.xyz; // world-space position
    output[i].texCoords = input[i].texCoords;
    output[i].normal = input[i].normal;
  }
```

```
  // Increase size of triangle in normalized device coordinates by the
  // texel size of the currently bound render-target.
  float2 side0N = normalize(output[1].position.xy-output[0].position.xy);
  float2 side1N = normalize(output[2].position.xy-output[1].position.xy);
  float2 side2N = normalize(output[0].position.xy-output[2].position.xy);
  float texelSize = 1.0f/64.0f;
  output[0].position.xy += normalize(-side0N+side2N)*texelSize;
  output[1].position.xy += normalize(side0N-side1N)*texelSize;
  output[2].position.xy += normalize(side1N-side2N)*texelSize;

  [unroll]
  for(int j=0;j<3;j++)
    outputStream.Append(output[j]);

  outputStream.RestartStrip();
}

// pixel shader
struct VOXEL
{
  uint colorMask; // encoded color
  uint4 normalMasks; // encoded normals
  uint occlusion; // voxel only contains geometry info if occlusion > 0
};
RWStructuredBuffer<VOXEL> gridBuffer: register(u1);

// normalized directions of four faces of a tetrahedron
static float3 faceVectors[4] =
{
  float3(0.0f,-0.57735026f,0.81649661f),
  float3(0.0f,-0.57735026f,-0.81649661f),
  float3(-0.81649661f,0.57735026f,0.0f),
  float3(0.81649661f,0.57735026f,0.0f)
};

int GetNormalIndex(in float3 normal,out float dotProduct)
{
  float4x3 faceMatrix;
  faceMatrix[0] = faceVectors[0];
  faceMatrix[1] = faceVectors[1];
  faceMatrix[2] = faceVectors[2];
  faceMatrix[3] = faceVectors[3];
  float4 dotProducts = mul(faceMatrix,normal);
  float maximum = max (max(dotProducts.x,dotProducts.y),
                       max(dotProducts.z,dotProducts.w));
  int index;
  if(maximum==dotProducts.x)
    index = 0;
  else if(maximum==dotProducts.y)
    index = 1;
  else if(maximum==dotProducts.z)
    index = 2;
  else
    index = 3;

  dotProduct = dotProducts[index];
  return index;
}

void main(GS_OUTPUT input)
{
  float3 base = colorMap.Sample(colorMapSampler,input.texCoords).rgb;
```

```
// Encode color into the lower 24 bit of an unsigned integer, using
// 8 bit for each color channel.
uint colorMask = EncodeColor(base.rgb);

// Calculate color-channel contrast of color and write value into the
// highest 8 bit of the color mask.
float contrast = length(base.rrg-base.gbb)/
                 (sqrt(2.0f)+base.r+base.g+base.b);
int iContrast = int(contrast*255.0f);
colorMask |= iContrast<<24;

// Encode normal into the lower 27 bit of an unsigned integer, using
// for each axis 8 bit for the value and 1 bit for the sign.
float3 normal = normalize(input.normal);
uint normalMask = EncodeNormal(normal.xyz);

// Calculate to which face of a tetrahedron current normal is closest
// and write corresponding dot product into the highest 5 bit of the
// normal mask.
float dotProduct;
int normalIndex = GetNormalIndex(normal,dotProduct);
int iDotProduct = int(saturate(dotProduct)*31.0f);
normalMask |= iDotProduct<<27;

// Get offset into voxel grid.
float3 offset = (input.positionWS-constBuffer.snappedGridCenter)*
                constBuffer.invGridCellSize;
offset = round(offset);

// Get position in voxel grid.
int3 voxelPos = int3(16,16,16)+int3(offset);

// Only output voxels that are inside the boundaries of the grid.
if((voxelPos.x>-1)&&(voxelPos.x<32)&&(voxelPos.y>-1)&&
   (voxelPos.y<32)&&(voxelPos.z>-1)&&(voxelPos.z<32))
{
   // Get index into voxel grid.
   int gridIndex = (voxelPos.z*1024)+(voxelPos.y*32)+voxelPos.x;

   // Output color.
   InterlockedMax(gridBuffer[gridIndex].colorMask,colorMask);

   // Output normal according to normal index.
   InterlockedMax(gridBuffer[gridIndex].normalMasks[normalIndex],
                  normalMask);

   // Mark voxel that contains geometry information.
   InterlockedMax(gridBuffer[gridIndex].occlusion,1);
}
}
```

Listing 7.1. Generation of the voxel grid.

To avoid race conditions between multiple threads that write into the same location, atomic functions have to be used. Since atomic operations are only supported in DirectX 11 for integer types, all values have to be converted into integers. Among the variety of DirectX 11 buffers, the `RWStructuredBuffer` is chosen, since this is the only way to hold multiple integer variables in one single buffer and at the same time perform atomic operations on them.

Since voxels are a simplified representation of the actual scene, detailed geometric information is lost. In order to amplify color bleeding in the final global
illumination output, colors with high difference in their color channels ("contrast") are preferred. By writing the contrast value into the highest 8 bit of the
integer color mask, colors with the highest contrast will dominate automatically,
since we write the results with an `InterlockedMax()` into the voxel grid. Since,
e.g., thin geometry can have opposite normals in one single voxel, not only the
color but also the normal has to be carefully written into the voxels. Therefore
it is determined to which face of a tetrahedron the current normal is closest. By
writing the corresponding dot product into the highest 5 bit of the integer normal
mask, the closest normal to each tetrahedron face is selected automatically since
we again write the results with an `InterlockedMax()`. According to the retrieved
tetrahedron face, the normal is written into the corresponding normal channel of
the voxel. Later on, when the voxels are illuminated, the closest normal to the
light vector is chosen so that the best illumination can be obtained. In this way
sometimes it is possible that the normal is taken from a different geometry face
as the color. However, since voxels condense information from the actual geometry within its boundaries, this is completely fine and will not have any negative
impact on the global illumination result.

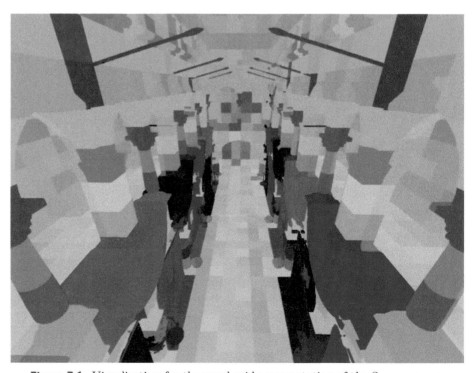

Figure 7.1. Visualization for the voxel grid representation of the Sponza scene.

Since all operations are performed using a very small render-target (64×64 pixels), this generation step is surprisingly fast. Figure 7.1 shows a screenshot in which the voxel grid representation of the Sponza scene is visualized. To create this image for each visible pixel of the rendered scene, the word-space position is reconstructed. With the help of the reconstructed position, we can determine the location of the corresponding voxel inside the grid. Finally, each visible pixel will be colored with the diffuse albedo information that is stored inside the corresponding voxel. In order to cover the entire scene, two nested voxel grids have been used: a fine-resolution grid for the area near to the viewer and a coarse-resolution grid for the distant area.

7.3.2 Create VPLs in Voxel Space

In this step we create VPLs entirely from the previously generated voxel grid. For each light source that is located inside the boundaries of the grid, we render a small quad of 32×32 pixels. By using hardware instancing, for each quad we are able to render 32 instances with a single draw call. After passing the vertices through the vertex shader, the geometry shader will choose the corresponding render-target slice in the currently bound 2D texture arrays. The pixel shader will then illuminate all voxels that contain geometry information according to the type of the current light source. Finally, the illuminated voxels are converted into a second-order spherical harmonic representation of VPLs. By using additive hardware blending, the results of all light sources are automatically combined. Listing 7.2 generically shows how this is done for DirectX 11 in HLSL.

```
// vertex shader

VS_OUTPUT main(VS_INPUT input,uint instanceID: SV_InstanceID)
{
  VS_OUTPUT output;
  output.position = float4(input.position,1.0f);
  output.instanceID = instanceID;
  return output;
}

// geometry shader

struct GS_OUTPUT

{

  float4 position: SV_POSITION;
  uint rtIndex: SV_RenderTargetArrayIndex;
};

[maxvertexcount(4)]
void main(line VS_OUTPUT input[2],inout TriangleStream<GS_OUTPUT>
          outputStream)
{
  // Generate a quad from two corner vertices.
  GS_OUTPUT output[4];
```

```
  // lower-left vertex
  output[0].position = float4(input[0].position.x,input[0].position.y,
                              input[0].position.z,1.0f);

  // lower-right vertex
  output[1].position = float4(input[1].position.x,input[0].position.y,
                              input[0].position.z,1.0f);

  // upper-left vertex
  output[2].position = float4(input[0].position.x,input[1].position.y,
                              input[0].position.z,1.0f);

  // upper-right vertex
  output[3].position = float4(input[1].position.x,input[1].position.y,
                              input[0].position.z,1.0f);
  // By using hardware instancing, the geometry shader will be invoked 32
  // times with the corresponding instance ID. For each invocation the
  // instance ID is used to determine into which slice of a 2D texture
  // array the current quad should be rasterized.
  [unroll]
  for(int i=0;i<4;i++)
  {
    output[i].rtIndex = input[0].instanceID;
    outputStream.Append(output[i]);
    }
    outputStream.RestartStrip();
}

// pixel shader

StructuredBuffer<VOXEL> gridBuffer: register(t0);

struct FS_OUTPUT
{
  float4 fragColor0: SV_TARGET0; // red SH-coefficients
  float4 fragColor1: SV_TARGET1; // blue SH-coefficients
  float4 fragColor2: SV_TARGET2; // green SH-coefficients
};
// Calculate second-order SH-coefficients for clamped cosine lobe function.
float4 ClampedCosineSHCoeffs(in float3 dir)
{
  float4 coeffs;
  coeffs.x = PI/(2.0f*sqrt(PI));
  coeffs.y = -((2.0f*PI)/3.0f)*sqrt(3.0f/(4.0f*PI));
  coeffs.z = ((2.0f*PI)/3.0f)*sqrt(3.0f/(4.0f*PI));
  coeffs.w = -((2.0f*PI)/3.0f)*sqrt(3.0f/(4.0f*PI));
  coeffs.wyz *= dir;
  return coeffs;
}
// Determine which of the four specified normals is closest to the
// specified direction. The function returns the closest normal and as
// output parameter the corresponding dot product.
float3 GetClosestNormal(in uint4 normalMasks,in float3 direction,out float
                        dotProduct)
{
  float4x3 normalMatrix;
  normalMatrix[0] = DecodeNormal(normalMasks.x);
  normalMatrix[1] = DecodeNormal(normalMasks.y);
  normalMatrix[2] = DecodeNormal(normalMasks.z);
  normalMatrix[3] = DecodeNormal(normalMasks.w);
  float4 dotProducts = mul(normalMatrix,direction);

  float maximum = max (max(dotProducts.x,dotProducts.y),
                       max(dotProducts.z,dotProducts.w));
```

```
    int index;
    if(maximum==dotProducts.x)
      index = 0;
    else if(maximum==dotProducts.y)
      index = 1;
    else if(maximum==dotProducts.z)
      index = 2;
    else
      index = 3;

    dotProduct = dotProducts[index];
    return normalMatrix[index];
}

PS_OUTPUT main(GS_OUTPUT input)
{
  PS_OUTPUT output;

  // Get index of current voxel.
  int3 voxelPos = int3(input.position.xy,input.rtIndex);
  int gridIndex = (voxelPos.z*1024)+(voxelPos.y*32)+voxelPos.x;

  // Get voxel data and early out, if voxel has no geometry information.
  VOXEL voxel = gridBuffer[gridIndex];
  if(voxel.occlusion==0)
    discard;

  // Get world-space position of voxel.
  int3 offset = samplePos-int3(16,16,16);
  float3 position = (float3(offset)*constBuffer.gridCellSize)+
                     constBuffer.snappedGridCenter;

  // Decode color of voxel.
  float3 albedo = DecodeColor(voxel.colorMask);

  // Get normal of voxel that is closest to the light direction.
  float nDotL;
  float3 normal = GetClosestNormal(voxel.normalMasks,lightVecN,nDotL);

  // Calculate diffuse lighting according to current light type.
  float3 diffuse = CalcDiffuseLighting(albedo,nDotL);

#ifdef USE_SHADOWS

  // Calculate shadow term according to current light type with the help
  // of a shadow map.
  float shadowTerm = ComputeShadowTerm(position);
  diffuse *= shadowTerm;
#endif

  // Calculate clamped cosine lobe SH-coefficients for VPL.
  float4 coeffs = ClampedCosineSHCoeffs(normal);

  // Output SH-coefficients for each color channel.
  output.fragColor0 = coeffs*diffues.r;
  output.fragColor1 = coeffs*diffuse.g;
  output.fragColor2 = coeffs*diffuse.b;

  return output;
}
```

Listing 7.2. VPL creation.

To output the second-order SH-coefficients for all three color channels, we render this time into three 2D texture arrays with half floating-point precision. Since all calculations are done entirely in voxel space and are limited to voxels, which actually contain geometry information, this technique scales very well with an increasing number of light sources of all different types.

In many situations we can even abandon the use of shadow maps for point lights and spotlights without noticeably affecting the final render output. However, for large point lights, spotlights, and directional lights, we do need to use shadow maps to avoid light leaking. Here we can simply reuse the shadow maps that have already been created for the direct illumination step.

7.3.3 Propagate VPLs

In this step the previously created VPLs are propagated iteratively across the grid according to the LPV technique proposed by [Kaplanyan and Dachsbacher 10]. Basically each VPL cell propagates its light along the three axes of a Cartesian coordinate system to its surrounding six neighbor cells. While doing this propagation, the voxel grid from the first step is used to determine how strongly the light transport to the neighbor cells is occluded. The results from the first propagation step are then used to perform a second propagation step. This is done iteratively until we get a visually satisfying light distribution. In the first iteration no occlusion is used, in order to initially let the light distribute; from the second iteration on, we use the geometry occlusion in order to avoid light leaking.

The iterative propagation is performed in DirectX 11 by utilizing a compute shader since we do not need the rasterization pipeline for this job. Listing 7.3 demonstrates this.

```
// compute shader
Texture2DArray inputRedSHTexture: register(t0);
Texture2DArray inputGreenSHTexture: register(t1);
Texture2DArray inputBlueSHTexture: register(t2);
StructuredBuffer<VOXEL> gridBuffer: register(t3);
RWTexture2DArray<float4> outputRedSHTexture: register(u0);
RWTexture2DArray<float4> outputGreenSHTexture: register(u1);
RWTexture2DArray<float4> outputBlueSHTexture: register(u2);

// directions to six neighbor cell centers
static float3 directions[6] =
{
  float3(0.0f,0.0f,1.0f), float3(1.0f,0.0f,0.0f), float3(0.0f,0.0f,-1.0f),
  float3(-1.0f,0.0f,0.0f), float3(0.0f,1.0f,0.0f), float3(0.0f,-1.0f,0.0f)
};

// SH-coefficients for six faces (ClampedCosineSHCoeffs(directions[0-5])
static float4 faceCoeffs[6] =
{
  float4(PI/(2*sqrt(PI)),0.0f,((2*PI)/3.0f)*sqrt(3.0f/(4*PI)),0.0f),
  float4(PI/(2*sqrt(PI)),0.0f,0.0f,-((2*PI)/3.0f)*sqrt(3.0f/(4*PI))),
  float4(PI/(2*sqrt(PI)),0.0f,-((2*PI)/3.0f)*sqrt(3.0f/(4*PI)),0.0f),
  float4(PI/(2*sqrt(PI)),0.0f,0.0f,((2*PI)/3.0f)*sqrt(3.0f/(4*PI))),
```

```
    float4(PI/(2*sqrt(PI)),-((2*PI)/3.0f)*sqrt(3.0f/(4*PI)),0.0f,0.0f),
    float4(PI/(2*sqrt(PI)),((2*PI)/3.0f)*sqrt(3.0f/(4*PI)),0.0f,0.0f)
};

// offsets to six neighbor cell centers
static int3 offsets[6] =
{
  int3(0,0,1), int3(1,0,0), int3(0,0,-1),
  int3(-1,0,0), int3(0,1,0), int3(0,-1,0)
};

[numthreads(8,8,8)]
void main(uint3 GroupID: SV_GroupID,uint3 DispatchThreadID:
          SV_DispatchThreadID,uint3 GroupThreadID: SV_GroupThreadID,
          uint GroupIndex: SV_GroupIndex)
{
  // Get grid position of current cell.
  int3 elementPos = DispatchThreadID.xyz;

  // Initialize SH-coefficients with values from current cell.
  float4 sumRedSHCoeffs = inputRedSHTexture.Load(int4(elementPos,0));
  float4 sumGreenSHCoeffs = inputGreenSHTexture.Load(int4(elementPos,0));
  float4 sumBlueSHCoeffs = inputBlueSHTexture.Load(int4(elementPos,0));

  [unroll]
  for(int i=0;i<6;i++)
  {
    // Get grid position of six neighbor cells.
    int3 samplePos = elementPos+offsets[i];
    // continue, if cell is out of bounds
    if((samplePos.x<0)||(samplePos.x>31)||(samplePos.y<0)||
       (samplePos.y>31)||(samplePos.z<0)||(samplePos.z>31))
      continue;

    // Load SH-coefficients for neighbor cell.
    float4 redSHCoeffs = inputRedSHTexture.Load(int4(samplePos,0));
    float4 greenSHCoeffs = inputGreenSHTexture.Load(int4(samplePos,0));
    float4 blueSHCoeffs = inputBlueSHTexture.Load(int4(samplePos,0));

#ifdef USE_OCCLUSION
    float4 occlusionCoeffs = float4(0.0f,0.0f,0.0f,0.0f);

    // Get index of corresponding voxel.
    int gridIndex = (samplePos.z*1024)+(samplePos.y*32)+samplePos.x;
    VOXEL voxel = gridBuffer[gridIndex];

    // If voxel contains geometry information, find closest normal to
    // current direction. In this way the highest occlusion can be
    // generated. Then calculate SH-coefficients for retrieved normal.
    if(voxel.occlusion > 0)
    {
      float dotProduct;
      float3 occlusionNormal = GetClosestNormal(voxel.normalMasks,
                              -directions[i],dotProduct);
      occlusionCoeffs = ClampedCosineSHCoeffs(occlusionNormal);
    }
#endif

    [unroll]
    for(int j=0;j<6;j++)
    {
      // Get direction for face of current cell to current neighbor
      // cell center.
      float3 neighborCellCenter = directions[i];
```

```
      float3 facePosition = directions[j]*0.5f;
      float3 dir = facePosition-neighborCellCenter;
      float fLength = length(dir);
      dir /= fLength;

      // Get corresponding solid angle.
      float solidAngle = 0.0f;
      if(fLength>0.5f)
        solidAngle = (fLength>=1.5f) ? (22.95668f/(4*180.0f)) :
                                       (24.26083f/(4*180.0f));
      // Calculate SH-coefficients for direction.
      float4 dirSH;
      result.x = 1.0f/(2*sqrt(PI));
      result.y = -sqrt(3.0f/(4*PI));
      result.z = sqrt(3.0f/(4*PI));
      result.w = -sqrt(3.0f/(4*PI));
      result.wyz *= dir;

      // Calculate flux from neighbor cell to face of current cell.
      float3 flux;
      flux.r = dot(redSHCoeffs,dirSH);
      flux.g = dot(greenSHCoeffs,dirSH);
      flux.b = dot(blueSHCoeffs,dirSH);
      flux = max(0.0f,flux)*solidAngle;
#ifdef USE_OCCLUSION
      // apply occlusion
      float occlusion = 1.0f-saturate(dot(occlusionCoeffs,dirSH));
      flux *= occlusion;
#endif
      // Add contribution to SH-coefficients sums.
      float4 coeffs = faceCoeffs[j];
      sumRedSHCoeffs += coeffs*flux.r;
      sumGreenSHCoeffs += coeffs*flux.g;
      sumBlueSHCoeffs += coeffs*flux.b;
    }
  }
  // Write out generated red, green, and blue SH-coefficients.
  outputRedSHTexture[elementPos] = sumRedSHCoeffs;
  outputGreenSHTexture[elementPos] = sumGreenSHCoeffs;
  outputBlueSHTexture[elementPos] = sumBlueSHCoeffs;
}
```

Listing 7.3. Propagation of VPLs.

For each propagation step the compute shader is dispatched with $4 \times 4 \times 4$ thread groups so that altogether $32 \times 32 \times 32$ threads are utilized, which corresponds to the total cell count of the grid.

7.3.4 Apply Indirect Lighting

In this step the previously propagated VPLs are finally applied to the scene. For this we need a depth buffer from which the world-space position of the visible pixels can be reconstructed, as well as a normal buffer that contains the perturbed normal information for each pixel. Obviously, deferred rendering as a direct illumination approach is perfectly fitted for our case since both pieces of information are already available and no extra work has to be done.

While rendering a full-screen quad, the pixel shader reconstructs the world-space position and the normal for each pixel. According to the world-space position, the previously generated grid (in the form of three 2D texture arrays) is sampled with linear hardware filtering. Therefore we manually only have to perform a filtering in the third dimension so that we retrieve smooth results. With the help of the sampled SH-coefficients and the surface normal, we can perform an SH-lighting for each pixel. See Listing 7.4 for details.

```
// pixel shader

Texture2DArray inputRedSHTexture: register(t0);
Texture2DArray inputGreenSHTexture: register(t1);
Texture2DArray inputBlueSHTexture: register(t2);

PS_OUTPUT main(GS_OUTPUT input)
{
  PS_OUTPUT output;
  float depth = depthBuffer.Sample(depthBufferSampler,input.texCoords).r;
  float4 position = ReconstructPositionFromDepth(depth);


  float3 albedo = colorMap.Sample(colorMapSampler,input.texCoords).rgb;
  float3 normal =
    normalBuffer.Sample(normalBufferSampler,input.texCoords).xyz;

  // Get offset into grid.
  float3 offset = (position.xyz-constBuffer.snappedGridCenter)*
                  constBuffer.invGridCellSize;

  // Get texCoords into Texture2DArray.
  float3 texCoords = float3(16.5f,16.5f,16.0f)+offset;
  texCoords.xy /= 32.0f;

  // Get texCoords for trilinear sampling.
  int lowZ = floor(texCoords.z);
  int highZ = min(lowZ+1,32-1);
  float highZWeight = texCoords.z-lowZ;
  float lowZWeight = 1.0f-highZWeight;
  float3 tcLow = float3(texCoords.xy,lowZ);
  float3 tcHigh = float3(texCoords.xy,highZ);

  // Perform trilinear sampling of red, green, and blue SH-coefficients
  // from Texture2DArray.
  float4 redSHCoeffs =
    lowZWeight*inputRedSHTexture.Sample(linearSampler,tcLow)+
    highZWeight*inputRedSHTexture.Sample(linearSampler,tcHigh);
  float4 greenSHCoeffs =
    lowZWeight*inputGreenSHTexture.Sample(linearSampler,tcLow)+
    highZWeight*inputGreenSHTexture.Sample(linearSampler,tcHigh);
  float4 blueSHCoeffs =
    lowZWeight*inputBlueSHTexture.Sample(linearSampler,tcLow)+
    highZWeight* inputBlueSHTexture.Sample(linearSampler,tcHigh);

  // Calculate clamped cosine lobe SH-coefficients for surface normal.
  float4 surfaceNormalLobe = ClampedCosineSHCoeffs(normal);

  // Perform diffuse SH-lighting.
  float3 diffuseGlobalIllum;
  diffuseGlobalIllum.r = dot(redSHCoeffs,surfaceNormalLobe);
```

```
diffuseGlobalIllum.g = dot(greenSHCoeffs,surfaceNormalLobe);
diffuseGlobalIllum.b = dot(blueSHCoeffs,surfaceNormalLobe);
diffuseIllum = max(diffuseIllum,float3(0.0f,0.0f,0.0f));
diffuseGlobalIllum /= PI;


output.fragColor = float4(diffuseGlobalIllum*albedo,1.0f);
return output;
}
```

Listing 7.4. Indirect lighting.

As can be seen in the above listing, only the diffuse indirect illumination is calculated. However there is the possibility to extract a dominant light source from SH-coefficients [Sloan 08]. With the help of this extracted light source, a conventional specular lighting can be performed. This gives us the possibility to add a fast, but coarse, approximation of specular indirect lighting.

7.3.5 Clear the Voxel Grid

In this final step the `RWStructuredBuffer` used for the voxel grid is cleared by using a simple compute shader. Just like for the propagation step, the compute shader is dispatched with $4 \times 4 \times 4$ thread groups, whereby each thread group runs $8 \times 8 \times 8$ threads, so that $32 \times 32 \times 32$ threads are utilized, which corresponds to the total voxel count of the grid.

7.4 Handling Large Environments

Since we are using a $32 \times 32 \times 32$ voxel grid, it is quite obvious that this alone cannot deal with realistic large game environments. According to the use of multiple cascades in the LPV technique proposed by [Kaplanyan and Dachsbacher 10], several nested voxel grids can be used. Each grid will have the same number of cells, but the size of the grid cells will increase. In this way detailed indirect lighting can be maintained in the vicinity of the viewer, while in the distance still sufficient coarse indirect lighting is used. However, a linear interpolation should be performed between the grids to avoid a harsh transition at the borders between them. This can be done in the step when indirect lighting is applied to each visible pixel. Therefor across the border area the global illumination value is calculated for both adjoining grids. The distance of the world-space position of the current pixel to the center of the higher-resolution grid can be used to linearly interpolate between both global illumination values.

7.5 Results

Table 7.1 shows the performance results using the proposed technique in the Sponza scene. All lights were fully dynamic and contributed to the indirect illumination.

	Min fps	Max fps	Average fps
1 directional light	63	90	71
1 directional light + 12 medium-sized moving point lights	61	89	70

Table 7.1. Performance results in the Sponza scene (~280,000 triangles) using two grid cascades (on a Nvidia Geforce 485 GTX Mobile with 1,280 × 720 resolution).

Figure 7.2. Sponza scene with direct illumination only.

Figures 7.2–7.4 show how this technique can improve the appearance of a scene. For the screenshots the same Sponza scene has been used as for the previous performance results.

7.6 Conclusion

By utilizing new DirectX 11 features, this technique is capable of producing visually good and stable results for a high number of light sources contained in realistic game environments while maintaining high interactive frame rates. Moreover the video memory consumption is kept at a low level.

Figure 7.3. Sponza scene with indirect illumination only.

Figure 7.4. Final combined output of the Sponza scene.

However, besides the fact that this approach will only run on DirectX 11 or higher hardware, it requires also a depth and a normal buffer for reconstructing the position and normal of the visible pixels. Therefore it is best fitted for direct illumination approaches such as deferred rendering.

Bibliography

[Kaplanyan and Dachsbacher 10] Anton Kaplanyan and Carsten Dachsbacher. "Cascaded Light Propagation Volumes for Real-Time Indirect Illumination." In *Symposium on Interactive 3D Graphics and Games (I3D)*, pp. 99–107. New York: ACM, 2010.

[Mavridis and Papaioannou 11] Pavlos Mavridis and Georgios Papaioannou. "Global Illumination Using Imperfect Volumes." Presentation, International Conference on Computer Graphics Theory and Applications (GRAPP), Algarve, Portugal, 2011.

[Sloan 08] Peter-Pike Sloan. "Stupid Spherical Harmonics (SH) Tricks." Companion to Game Developers Conference 2008 lecture, http://www.ppsloan.org/publications/StupidSH36.pdf, February 2008.

Image Space

The effective image space algorithms are becoming a more and more important way of achieving more realism or higher quality of the final image.

We start the section with two articles improving the depth-of-field effect used in many modern games. The first article is "The Skylanders SWAP Force Depth-of-Field Shader," by Michael Bukowski, Padraic Hennessy, Brian Osman, and Morgan McGuire. It describes the depth-of-field shader used in production at Vicarious Visions for the *Skylanders* series of games. Their technique generates very convincing near and far out of focus areas completely in image space without any additional scene rendering.

The second article "Simulating Partial Occlusion in Post-Processing Depth-of-Field Methods," by David C. Schedl and Michael Wimmer uses the ideas similar to order independent transparency methods to store multiple depth layers of the rendered scene. Having the multiple depth layers allows for more realistic rendering of the out of focus areas of the scene.

"Second-Depth Antialiasing," by Emil Persson discusses novel semi-analytical antialiasing method that uses the regular depth buffer and a new second-depth depth buffer to precisely identify the geometry edges and the amount of antialiasing they need. The author provides detailed implementation information, performance analysis and full source code on the accompanying DVD.

The next article is "Practical Frame Buffer Compression," by Pavlos Mavridis and Georgios Papaioannou. Authors describe a lossy buffer compression method based on the principles chrominance subsampling. The method provides a practical way of reducing bandwidth and improving associated performance, which are required in the modern high-resolution games. It allows for direct rendering into two channel render targets including alpha blending. The authors discuss multiple methods of reconstruction of the regular RGB data.

The last article, "Coherence-Enhancing Filtering on the GPU," by Jan Eric Kyprianidis and Henry Kang, shows CUDA implementation of a fully automatic image filter, which aggressively smoothes out the less important image regions while preserving the important features. The authors provide extensive background for the filtering along with very detailed implementation guidelines.

I would like to thank all authors for the effort they put into their articles and for the novel, inspiring ideas that go beyond regular polygon rendering.

—Michal Valient

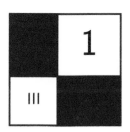

The Skylanders SWAP Force Depth-of-Field Shader

Michael Bukowski, Padraic Hennessy, Brian Osman, and Morgan McGuire

1.1 Introduction

This chapter describes the depth-of-field (DoF) shader used in production at Vicarious Visions for the *Skylanders SWAP Force* game on multiple console platforms.

DoF is an important rendering effect. A real camera lens focuses on a single plane in the scene. Images of objects in that plane are perfectly sharp. Images of objects closer to or farther from the camera are blurry. Of course, most objects are typically outside the exact plane of focus. Photographers recognize that each point on an out-of-focus object blurs into the shape of the camera aperture, which is usually a disk, octagon, or hexagon. They call the bounding circle of a blurred point the *circle of confusion* (CoC) of that point. They say that an object is in focus (for a digital image) when the *radius* of the CoC is half a pixel or less. In that case, the object does not appear blurred because the blur falls below the image resolution. Photographers refer to the depth range over which the CoC radius is less than half a pixel as the *focus field*. They refer to the extent of this range as the *depth of field*. In computer graphics, that phrase is now associated with the effect of blurring images of objects outside of the field.

In a game, a DoF effect serves both gameplay and aesthetics. It allows the art director to control the player's attention by de-emphasizing background objects or those that are merely in the foreground to frame the shot. Rack-focus (Figure 1.1) in on a specific object can emphasize goals and powerups during gameplay without resorting to floating arrows or halos. In cut-scenes, DoF is a powerful cinematic tool. DoF also conceals many rendering limitations. Defocusing the background conceals aliasing and low level of detail. Defocusing the extreme foreground conceals texture magnification and tessellation limits.

Figure 1.1. Three frames from a cinematic "rack focus" transition designed to move the player's attention from the background to the extreme foreground. In each shot, the yellow dot shows the location of camera focus.

True DoF arises because each point on the camera lens has a slightly different viewpoint and the final image is a composite of images from all of them. Research papers have simulated this brute-force rendering of multiple viewpoints to an accumulation buffer, sampling viewpoints with distribution ray tracing [Cook et al. 84], and sampling with stochastic rasterization [McGuire et al. 10]. These methods are all too expensive to be practical today and are overkill for achieving a convincing effect. Since the goal is to blur parts of the image, we need not render a perfect result. It should be enough to selectively apply some post-processing blur filters to a typical frame. Like many other game engines, ours follows this approach. There's a good argument for this approximation over physically correct solutions: it is what Photoshop's Lens Blur and many film editing packages do. The DoF seen in advertisements and feature films is certainly of sufficient quality for game graphics.

We distinguish three depth ranges of interest: the *far field* in which objects are blurry because they are too far away, the *focus field* where objects are in focus, and the *near field* in which objects are blurry because they are too close to the camera.

A post-processing DoF shader is essentially a blur filter with a spatially varying kernel. The way that the kernel varies poses three challenges. First, unlike a typical Gaussian or box blur, DoF blur must respect depth edges. For example, the effect should not let a blurry distant object bleed over a nearer sharp object. We observe that it is most critical that the far-focus-near ordering of occlusion be preserved. However, incorrect blurring of images of neighboring objects *within* a field is often undetectable.

Second, when preventing bleeding, the effect must also not create sharp silhouettes on blurry objects in the near field. These sharp silhouettes are the primary visual artifact in previous methods.

Third, foreground objects have to be able to blur fairly far (up to 10% of the screen width) without compromising performance. The naïve approaches of scattering each pixel as a disk and the inverse of performing the equivalent gather operation are too slow—those methods require $O(r^2)$ operations for blur radius r and thrash the texture/L1 cache.

The DoF post-process in our engine is fast and produces good-quality near- and far-field blurring with little perceptible color bleeding. It reads a color buffer with a specially encoded alpha channel and produces a convincing DoF effect in three "full-screen" 2D passes over various size buffers. It uses 1.9 ms of GPU time running at 720p on the Xbox 360. On a PC it uses 1.0 ms of GPU time running at 1080p on a GeForce GTX 680.

We developed our DoF effect from Gillham's *ShaderX^5* one [Gillham 07]. Like his and other similar techniques [Riguer et al. 03, Scheuermann 04, Hammon 07, Kaplanyan 10, Kasyan et al. 11], we work with low-resolution buffers when they are blurry and lerp between blurred and sharp versions of the screen. The elements of our improvements to previous methods are

- treating near field separately to produce blurry silhouettes on the near field,

- inpainting behind blurry near-field objects,

- a selective background blur kernel,

- using CoC instead of depth to resolve occlusion and blur simultaneously,

- processing multiple blurs in parallel with dual render targets.

1.2 Algorithm

Figure 1.3 shows the structure of our algorithm. The input is a color buffer with the (scaled and biased) *signed CoC radius* stored in the alpha channel. Two passes blur horizontally and then vertically in a typical separated blur pattern, and a final pass composites the blurred image over the sharp input. Each blur pass processes two textures: one that represents the focus and far field, and one that represents objects in the near field (with an alpha channel for coverage).

1.2.1 Input

The radius in the alpha channel of the color input buffer is signed, meaning that radius r at each pixel is on the range [−maximum blur, +maximum blur]. Far-field objects have a negative radius, near-field objects have a positive one, and $0.5 < r < 0.5$ in the focus field. Under a physically correct CoC model, this signed radius naturally arises. There, it models the fact that the silhouette of the aperture appears inverted in the far field. That inversion is irrelevant for the disc

Figure 1.2. Extreme near- and far-field defocus with smooth transitions rendered by our algorithm. Note the blurry silhouettes on near-field objects and detail inpainted behind them.

aperture that we model, but we depend on the signed radius for another reason. Signed radius decreases monotonically with depth, so if $r_A < r_B$, then point A is closer to the camera than point B. Thus the single signed radius value at each pixel avoids the need for separate values to encode the field, radius, and depth of a point.

Our demo supports two methods to compute the signed radius. The first is the physically correct model derived from Figure 1.4. Let a be the radius of the lens, $z_\mathrm{F} < 0$ be the depth of the focus plane, and R be the world-space (versus screen-space) radius. By similar triangles, the screen-space radius r for a point at depth z is

$$\frac{R}{|z_\mathrm{F} - z|} = \frac{a}{|z_\mathrm{F}|}, \quad r \propto a\frac{|z_\mathrm{F} - z|}{z_\mathrm{F} \cdot z}.$$

The proportionality constant depends on screen resolution and field of view. Our art team felt that this physical model gave poor control over the specific kinds of shots that they were trying to direct. They preferred the second model, in which the artists manually place four planes (near-blurry, near-sharp, far-sharp, far-blurry). For the near- and far-blurry planes, the artists specify the CoC radius explicitly. At the near-sharp and far-sharp planes, the radius is $1/2$ pixel. The CoC at depths between the planes is then linearly interpolated. Depths closer than the near-blurry and farther than the far-blurry have radii clamped to the values at those planes.

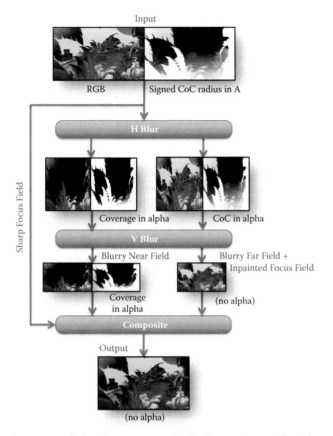

Figure 1.3. Diagram of shading passes with buffers shown. See the supplemental material for high-resolution images.

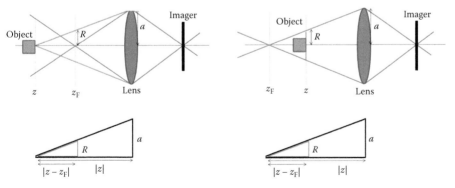

Figure 1.4. The geometry of lens blur. Left: the orange cube is in the far field and out of focus. Right: the orange cube in the near field and out of focus. The radius of the CoC (in camera space) is given by using similar triangles to find R in each case.

1.2.2 Blur Passes

The two blur passes are similar to one another. Each reads a fixed-length set of adjacent samples, either horizontal or vertical, and computes two weighted sums. The key outer loop section of the code is shown below.

```
// Accumulates the blurry image color
blurResult.rgb = float3(0.0f);
float blurWeightSum = 0.0f;

// Accumulates the near-field color and coverage
nearResult = float4(0.0f);
float nearWeightSum = 0.0f;

// Location of the central filter tap (i.e., "this" pixel's location)
// Account for the scaling down by 50% during blur
int2 A = int2(gl_FragCoord.xy) * (direction + ivec2(1));

float packedA = texelFetch(blurSourceBuffer, A, 0).a;
float r_A = (packedA * 2.0 - 1.0) * maxCoCRadiusPixels;

// Map large negative r_A to 0.0 and large positive r_A to 1.0
float nearFieldness_A = saturate(r_A * 4.0);

for (int delta = -maxCoCRadiusPixels; delta <= maxCoCRadiusPixels;
                                      ++delta) {
    // Tap location near A
    int2 B = A + (direction * delta);

    // Packed values
    float4 blurInput = texelFetch(blurSourceBuffer, clamp(B, int2(0),
                    textureSize(blurSourceBuffer, 0)
                    - int2(1)), 0);

    // Signed kernel radius at this tap, in pixels
    float r_B = (blurInput.a * 2.0 - 1.0) * float(maxCoCRadiusPixels);

    // [Compute blurry buffer]
    ...

    // [Compute near-field super blurry buffer and coverage]
    ....
}

blurResult.a = packedA;
blurResult.rgb /= blurWeightSum;
nearResult /= nearWeightSum;
```

The details of the two blur kernel sections follow. See also our demo source code, which contains extensive comments explaining optimizations and alternative implementations.

Let A be the center sample of the kernel and B be a nearby sample (note that $B = A$ is included in the set of samples that we consider). We compute the weight of sample B as follows.

```
If A is in the near field:
    // Inpaint behind A using some arbitrary constant weight k ≈ 1.
    w_B = k
else if B is not in the near field:
    // Obey occlusion; note that both r values are always negative in this case.
    w_B = max(0, min(1, |r_A - r_B + 1.5|))· Gaussian (BA)
else:
    // Avoid divide-by-zero if every sample pair hits this case.
    w_B = ε
```

In practice, we smooth the transitions by implementing the branches with lerps. The relevant section of VVDoF_blur.glsl in our demo source code is

```
float weight = 0.0;

float wNormal =
    // Only consider mid- or background pixels (allows inpainting of the
    // near field).
    float(! inNearField(r_B)) *

    // Only blur B over A if B is closer to the viewer (allow 0.5 pixels
    // of slop and smooth the transition).
    saturate(abs(r_A) - abs(r_B) + 1.5) *

    // Stretch the Gaussian extent to the radius at pixel B.
    gaussian[clamp(int(float(abs(delta) * (GAUSSIAN_TAPS - 1)) /
            (0.001 + abs(r_B * 0.5))), 0, GAUSSIAN_TAPS)];

weight = lerp(wNormal, 1.0, nearFieldness_A);
// far- + mid-field output
blurWeightSum += weight;
blurResult.rgb += blurInput.rgb * weight;
```

We compute the coverage value (alpha) for the separate near-field buffer in the horizontal pass as

$$\alpha_B = \begin{cases} \min\left(1, \dfrac{r_B}{\text{maximum near-field blur}}\right)^4 & \text{if } |A - B| < r_B, \\ 0 & \text{otherwise}; \end{cases}$$

in code, this is somewhat more verbose:

```
float4 nearInput;
#if HORIZONTAL
    nearInput.a = float(abs(delta) <= r_B) *
        saturate(r_B * invNearBlurRadiusPixels * 4.0);
    nearInput.a *= nearInput.a; nearInput.a *= nearInput.a;

    // Compute premultiplied-alpha color.
    nearInput.rgb = blurInput.rgb * nearInput.a;

#else
```

```
    // On the second pass, use the already-available alpha values.
    nearInput = texelFetch(nearSourceBuffer, clamp(B, int2(0),
            textureSize(nearSourceBuffer, 0) - int2(1)), 0);
#endif

    weight = float(abs(delta) < nearBlurRadiusPixels);
    nearResult += nearInput * weight;
    nearWeightSum += weight;
}
```

We empirically tuned this coverage falloff curve to provide good coverage when the near field is extremely blurry and to fade smoothly into the focus field. For example, in Figure 1.5, the out-of-focus fence in the near field must have sufficient coverage to smear white pixels over a large region, while we still want the transition of the ground plane into the focus field to look like gradual focusing and not simply a lerp between separate blurry and sharp images. This is an extremely hard case for a post-processing DoF algorithm that previous real-time methods do not handle well.

The near-field buffer is written with premultiplied alpha values for the color channel, and the color and alpha are both blurred during the subsequent vertical pass.

1.2.3 Compositing

The compositing pass (shown below) reads the original input buffer along with the low-resolution blurry near- and far-field buffers. It interpolates pixels between the original input and the blurred, inpainted far-field buffer based on the CoC at each

Figure 1.5. Input image with a chain-link fence very close to the camera (left), and near field under extreme blur with inpainted details visible through the "solid" parts of the fence and a smooth ground-plane transition between depth regions (right).

pixel. It then blends the near-field buffer over that result with premultiplied alpha blending. Near-field pixels exhibit inpainted detail from the far-field buffer and existing detail from the input buffer, both of which then receive the significantly blurred near-field content over them. Far-field pixels are blurry from the far-field image, the focus field is sharp and from the original image, and all transition regions are smooth because of the lerp.

```
uniform sampler2D packedBuffer;
uniform sampler2D blurBuffer;
uniform sampler2D nearBuffer;

out vec3 result;

const float coverageBoost = 1.5;

float grayscale(float3 c) {
    return (c.r + c.g + c.b) / 3.0;
}

void main() {
  int2 A = int2(gl_FragCoord.xy);

  float4 pack = texelFetch(packedBuffer, A, 0);
  float3 sharp = pack.rgb;
  float3 blurred = texture(blurBuffer,
          gl_FragCoord.xy / textureSize(packedBuffer, 0));
  float4 near = texture(nearBuffer,
          gl_FragCoord.xy / textureSize(packedBuffer, 0));

  // Normalize radius.
  float normRadius = (pack.a * 2.0 - 1.0);

  if (coverageBoost != 1.0) {\{}
      float a = saturate(coverageBoost * near.a);
      near.rgb = near.rgb * (a / max(near.a, 0.001f));
      near.a = a;
  }

  // Decrease sharp image's contribution rapidly in the near field.
  if (normRadius > 0.1) {\{}
      normRadius = min(normRadius * 1.5, 1.0);
  }

  result = lerp(sharp, blurred, abs(normRadius)) * (1.0 - near.a)
        + near.rgb;
}
```

The effect is extremely robust to camera and object movement and varying blur radii, independent of the scene. It should be tuned for two application-specific cases: transitions from mid to near depending on the field of view, and objects that don't write the depth buffer.

A compile-time constant, coverageBoost, allows increasing the partial coverage (alpha) of the near field to make it feel more substantial. This should always be greater than or equal to 1. If the near-field objects seem too transparent, then increase `coverageBoost`. If an obvious transition line is visible between the blurred near-field region and the sharp mid-field, then decrease the `coverageBoost`. Which of these cases an application is in largely depends on whether the field of view makes the ground plane visible within this transition region. For example, a first-person camera typically cannot see the ground plane in this region but a third-person camera often can. The third-person camera benefits from a smaller `coverageBoost` setting.

Because the effect assumes a single depth at each pixel in the input, we process particle systems separately by MIP-biasing their textures during a forward rendering pass rather than relying on the post-processing. For non-particle, translucent and reflective objects such as glass, we simply choose to use the depth of the translucent object or the background depending on the amount of translucency.

1.3   Conclusion

We knew that depth of field was an essential effect for the art direction of *Skylanders SWAP Force*, where the visuals resemble a CG animated film more than a traditional video game. By addressing the perception of the phenomenon of blurring instead of the underlying physics, we were able to achieve both high quality and high performance on a range of target platforms.

The primary limitations of previous real-time depth-of-field approaches are poor near-field blur and poor transitions between blurred and sharp regions. Figure 1.2 shows that even under a narrow depth of field, our effect overcomes both of those limitations. The interaction of depth of field with translucent surfaces remains problematic in the general case; however, we've described the forward-rendering techniques that we applied successfully to such surfaces in this specific game.

It is important for game graphics to serve game design for engagement as well as to please the eye. In this game, we've found depth of field to be a powerful tool for both gameplay and cinematic expression. Designers employ it for controlling attention and indicating gameplay elements as well as the artists using it to enhance visuals and mitigate certain artifacts. We hold this effect as an example of a technological advance serving to enhance all aspects of the player's experience.

Bibliography

[Cook et al. 84] Robert L. Cook, Thomas Porter, and Loren Carpenter. "Distributed Ray Tracing." In *SIGGRAPH '84: Proceedings of the 11th Annual Conference on Computer Graphics and Interactive Techniques*, pp. 137–145. New York: ACM, 1984.

[Gillham 07] David Gillham. "Real-Time Depth-of-Field Implemented with a Postprocessing-Only Technique. In *ShaderX⁵: Advanced Rendering Techniques*, edited by Wolfgang Engel, pp. 163–175. Boston: Charles River Media, 2007.

[Hammon 07] Earl Hammon, Jr. "Practical Post-Process Depth of Field." In *GPU Gems 3*, edited by Hubert Nguyen, Chapter 28. Upper Saddle River, NJ: Addison-Wesley, 2007.

[Kaplanyan 10] Anon Kaplanyan. "CryENGINE 3: Reaching the Speed of Light." Talk, SIGGRAPH 2010, Los Angeles, CA, July 28, 2010. (Available at http://www.crytek.com/sites/default/files/AdvRTRend_crytek_0.ppt.)

[Kasyan et al. 11] Nickolay Kasyan, Nicolas Schulz, and Tiago Sousa. "Secrets of CryENGINE 3 Graphics Technology." SIGGRAPH Course, Vancouver, Canada, August 8, 2011. (Available at http://www.crytek.com/sites/default/files/S2011_SecretsCryENGINE3Tech_0.ppt.)

[McGuire et al. 10] Morgan McGuire, Eric Enderton, Peter Shirley, and David Luebke. "Real-Time Stochastic Rasterization on Conventional GPU Architectures." In *Proceedings of teh Converence on High Performance Graphics*, pp. 173–182. Aire-la-Ville, Switzerland: Eurographics, 2010.

[Riguer et al. 03] Guennadi Riguer, Natalya Tatarchuk, and John Isidoro. "Real-Time Depth-of-Field Simulation." In *ShaderX²: Shader Programming Tips and Tricks with DirectX 9.0*, edited by Wolfgang Engel, pp. 529–556. Plano, TX: Wordware Publishing, Inc., 2003

[Scheuermann 04] Thorsten Scheuermann. "Advanced Depth of Field." Presentation, Game Developers Conference 2004, San Francisco, CA, 2004. (Available at http://www.amddevcentral.com/media/gpu_assets/Scheuermann_DepthOfField.pdf.)

2

Simulating Partial Occlusion
in Post-Processing
Depth-of-Field Methods
David C. Schedl and Michael Wimmer

2.1 Introduction

This chapter describes a method for simulating depth of field (DoF). In particular, we investigate the so-called *partial occlusion* effect: objects near the camera blurred due to DoF are actually *semitransparent* and therefore result in partially visible background objects (Figure 2.1). This effect is strongly apparent in miniature and macro photography and in film making. Games and interactive applications are nowadays becoming more cinematic, including strong DoF effects, and therefore it is important to be able to convincingly approximate the partial-occlusion effect. We show how to do so in this chapter, with the proposed optimizations even in real time.

2.2 Depth of Field

Before we discuss the technique in detail, let us first revisit the theory. DoF is an effect caused by the fact that optical lenses in camera systems refract light rays onto the image sensor, but different light paths representing the same object point only converge exactly if the object is at the focus distance. For other distances, objects appear blurred. This imperfection is not reproduced by the standard pinhole camera model used in rendering and needs to be simulated. Object-space methods like ray tracing can do so at high quality but are too slow for interactive rates.

Faster methods are based on the idea of using rasterized images and simulating DoF via post-processing. The first to discuss such an approach were Potmesil and Chakravarty in 1981. Based on the parameters of an optical lens, the diameter of

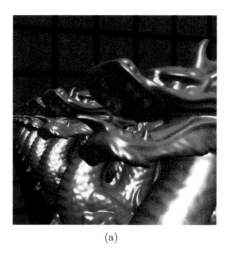 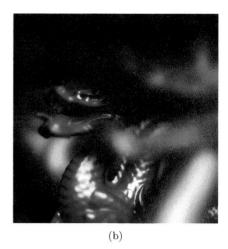

(a)   (b)

Figure 2.1. (a) A pinhole rendering resulting in a crisp image. (b) Simulating shallow DoF with the proposed method partly reveals occluded scene content. Note how the tongue of the dragon almost vanishes. This effect can be explained by partial occlusion.

the blurriness, the so-called *circle of confusion* (CoC) for an out-of-focus fragment at depth z can be calculated as

$$d_{\text{coc}}(z, f, N, z_{\text{focus}}) = \left| \frac{f^2 \, (z - z_{\text{focus}})}{z \, N \, (z_{\text{focus}} - f)} \right|, \qquad (2.1)$$

where f is the focal length of the lens, N is the f-stop number, and z_{focus} is the distance to the focus plane [Potmesil and Chakravarty 81]. Note that Equation (2.1) is based on a thin lens model, which is sufficient for simulating DoF. To simulate DoF, each fragment in the rasterized image is blurred according to its CoC in a post-process.

However, if the blurriness of an out-of-focus object increases, fragments are strongly smeared and become transparent, thus revealing background information, as shown in Figure 2.1 (b). Current rasterization renderings do not store occluded fragments, therefore it is not possible to accurately simulate this transparency. To do so, occluded information has to be either stored or interpolated. Most DoF methods that correctly simulate partial occlusion (such as [Lee et al. 10, Schedl and Wimmer 12]) store the scene content in depth layers. One way of assigning fragments into layers can be based on depth, which has the advantage that it is possible to uniformly blur each depth layer. Prominent artifacts in layered DoF methods are discretization artifacts: Layers are blurred and therefore object borders are smeared out. When this smeared-out layer is blended with the other layers, the smeared border region appears as a ringing artifact at object borders due to the reduced opacity [Barsky et al. 03].

One method to avoid that, from [Lee et al. 10], is to first render the scene content into layers and then use ray traversal to combine these layers, which is a costly operation but avoids the previously mentioned discretization artifacts and allows the simulation of additional lens effects (e.g., chromatic aberration and lens distortion).

2.3 Algorithm Overview

The approach presented in the following sections is a layered DoF method and is based on [Schedl and Wimmer 12]. We first decompose the scene into *depth layers*, where each layer contains pixels of a certain depth range. The resulting layers are then blurred with a filter that is sized according to the depth layer's CoC and then composited. This approach handles partial occlusion, because hidden objects are represented in more distant depth layers and contribute to the compositing.

In order to avoid rendering the scene K times, we use an A-buffer to generate *input buffers*. Note that each input buffer can contain fragments from the full depth range of the scene, while a depth layer is bound by its associated depth range. We then generate the depth layers by decomposing the input buffers into the depth ranges, which is much faster than rendering each depth layer separately.

To avoid discretization artifacts, we do not use hard boundaries for each depth layer, but a smooth transition between the layers, given by *matting functions*. Furthermore, we also show a method for efficiently computing both the blur and the layer composition in one step.

The algorithm consists of the following steps:

1. Render the scene into an A-buffer, containing the color and depth from front fragments and occluded fragments in an unsorted way. Sorting the fragments produces the input buffers I_0 to I_{M-1}.

2. Decompose the fragments of the input buffers into K depth layers L_0 to L_{K-1}, based on a matting function and the fragments' depth. Thus the rendered scene is now stored in a layered form, where each layer holds fragments of a certain depth range.

3. Blur every layer according to its CoC (computed by the layer's depth range) and alpha-blend them starting with the layer furthest away. We apply an optimization for this step where we blend and blur recursively: each layer L_k is blended onto the *composition buffers* I'_{front} (containing layers in front of the focus layer) or I'_{back} (holds layers behind the focus layer), where the composition buffers are blurred after each blending step. Finally the composition buffers are blended together.

We now describe the individual steps.

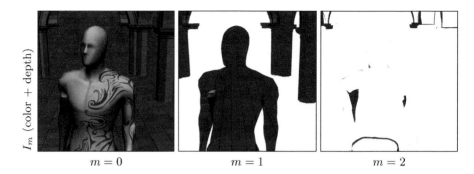

I_m (color + depth)

$m = 0$ $m = 1$ $m = 2$

Figure 2.2. The input buffers (color and depth) of the *Homunculus* scene, where m represents the mth fragment sorted by depth. The depth of the fragments is stored in the alpha channel, which is not represented in this figure. Note that white represents empty fragments and that there can be M input buffers.

2.4   Rendering

In [Schedl and Wimmer 12], rendering is done by the well-known depth-peeling technique, which needs to render the scene several times. Therefore, in our implementation we use an A-buffer [Carpenter 84] to avoid rerendering the scene. Our A-buffer consists of a 3D texture (A_0 to A_{M-1}) of depth M and a second texture for counting fragments, C. While the scene is rendered, each processed fragment increases the counting texture at the fragment's screen coordinate. Note that the increasing of the counter has to be atomic, which means that a value in the texture should not be altered in parallel. Based on the counter, the computed color of the fragment is written into the texture position A_c, where c is the value of the increased counter. Thus, all fragments processed by the graphics card are stored, in an unsorted way, in the 3D texture A. The counter is initially set to 0, therefore empty fragments have the counter value 0.

Next, all fragments in A are sorted by depth and written into the *input buffers* (I_0 to I_{M-1} for color and Z_0 to Z_{M-1} for depth), thus allowing up to M fragments per screen position, as shown in Figure 2.2. Note that only C fragments have to be sorted. Therefore the sorting effort depends on the scene complexity. We use the bubble sort algorithm to sort the fragments. Our implementation of the A-buffer is inspired by the implementation in [Crassin 10] and needs OpenGL 4.2 for atomic operations, and for image load and image store functionality. A pseudocode on how to render into an A-buffer is shown in Listing 2.1.

2.5   Scene Decomposition

The input buffers I_0 to I_{M-1} are decomposed into K *depth layers* L_0 to $L_{(K-1)}$. Only C fragments have to be matted, which reduces the matting costs for simpler

```
coherent uniform layout(size4x32) image2DArray abufferImg;
coherent uniform layout(size1x32) uimage2D abufferCounterImg

void main(void) {
  // atomic increment of the counter
  int c = int(imageAtomicInc(abufferCounterImg, coord.xy));

  vec4 val = ShadeFragment(); // compute shading color
  val.w = coord.z; // depth used for sorting

  // store fragment into A-buffer
  imageStore(abufferImg, ivec3(coord.xy, c), val);
}
```

Listing 2.1. Pseudocode for the fragment shader rendering fragments into the A-buffer. First the fragment counter C is increased to the value c. Then the shading color of the processed fragment is written into the 3D texture at position A_c.

scenes. For each depth layer, there are splitting depths (called *anchor points*) that specify which layer fragments will be sorted into. The decomposition is done by multiplying the fragments with a *matting function* (ω_k and $\dot{\omega}_k$), where the matting function differs for each depth layer L_k:

$$L_k = \Big(I_0 \cdot \omega_k(Z_0)\Big) \oplus \Big(I_1 \cdot \dot{\omega}_k(Z_1)\Big) \oplus \ldots \oplus \Big(I_{C-1} \cdot \dot{\omega}_k(Z_{C-1})\Big). \qquad (2.2)$$

The notation $A \oplus B$ denotes alpha-blending of A over B. In Figure 2.3, a schematics of this algorithm is shown for an example layer L_k. Equation (2.2) is applied K times to produce K depth layers. (See Figure 2.5.)

2.5.1 Matting Functions

The matting function ω_k (Figure 2.4 (a)) was introduced in [Kraus and Strengert 07] and guarantees a smooth transition of objects between layers. The special matting function $\dot{\omega}_k$ (Figure 2.4 (b)) retains a hard cut at the back layer boundaries to avoid situations where background fragments would be blended over foreground layers. The formulas are

$$\omega_k(z) = \begin{cases} \frac{z_k - z}{z_k - z_{k+1}} & \text{for} \quad z_k < z < z_{k+1}, \\ \dot{\omega}_k(z) & \text{otherwise}, \end{cases} \qquad (2.3)$$

and

$$\dot{\omega}_k(z) = \begin{cases} \frac{z - z_{k-2}}{z_{k-1} - z_{k-2}} & \text{for} \quad z_{k-2} < z < z_{k-1}, \\ 1 & \text{for} \quad z_{k-1} \leq z \leq z_k, \\ 0 & \text{otherwise}, \end{cases} \qquad (2.4)$$

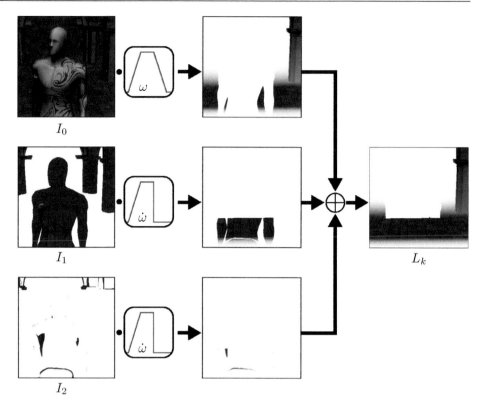

Figure 2.3. A flowchart showing how the input buffers get decomposed into a depth layer: First, the fragments in the input buffers get weighted by ω and $\dot{\omega}$. The resulting subdepth layers get alpha-blended to compose the depth layer L_k. The formula for this schematics can be found in Equation (2.2).

where z_{k-2} to z_{k+1} defines anchor points for the layer boundaries. Pseudocode for how to do matting in a fragment shader is shown in Listing 2.2.

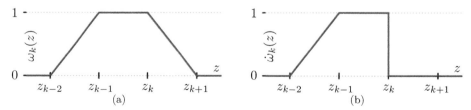

Figure 2.4. The matting functions (a) ω_k and (b) $\dot{\omega}_k$ with exemplary anchor points z_{k-2} to z_{k+1}.

```
uniform float anchor[4]; // anchor points array
// fragment counter and input buffer textures
uniform layout(size1x32) uimage2D abufferCounterImg;
uniform layout(size4x32) image2DArray inputBufferImg;

void main(void) {
  int C = int(imageLoad(abufferCounterImg, coord.xy).r);
  vec4 finalColor = vec4(0, 0, 0, 0);
  for(int c = 0; c < C; ++ c) {
    vec4 val = imageLoad(inputBufferImg, vec3(coord.xy, c));
    vec4 color = vec4(val.rgb,1.0);
    float depth = val.z; // depth is stored in alpha channel

    // check if fragment is within z_{k-2} and z_{k+1},
    // or z_{k} if (c!=0)
    if(anchor[3] <= depth && depth < anchor[(c==0)?0:1]) {
      float w = 1.0; // weight
      // z_{k} < z
      if(anchor[1] < depth) {
        w = (anchor[0] - depth) / (anchor[0] - anchor[1]);
      }
      // z < z_{k-1}
      else if (depth < anchor[2]) {
        w = (depth - anchor[3]) / (anchor[2] - anchor[3]);
      }

      // alpha blending
      finalColor += (1.0f - finalColor.a) * color * w;
} } }
```

Listing 2.2. Pseudocode for matting fragments into a depth layer with a shader (Equation (2.2)). The anchor points are computed on the CPU and handed in as a uniform array. Depending on which input buffer is processed, either ω or $\dot{\omega}$ is used.

2.5.2 Anchor Points

The layer matting relies on anchor points, which are spaced according to the filter size of the blurring method, similar to [Kraus and Strengert 07]. This means that the positions of the layer boundaries for a depth layer L_k are determined by the filter size (approximating d_k, the CoC for this layer) of the chosen blurring method. Since all fragments in the depth layer will be uniformly blurred, the anchor points should be evenly spaced with respect to the filter sizes. Therefore, we use the average CoC of a depth layer and its adjacent layer:

$$\bar{d}_k = \frac{d_k + d_{k+1}}{2}.$$

If we neglect the absolute value computation in Equation (2.1), we can invert the formula and calculate approximate depth values based on the filter size:

$$z_k = d_{\text{coc}}^{-1}(\bar{d}_k) = \frac{z_{\text{focus}} \cdot f^2}{f^2 + \bar{d}_k \cdot N \cdot (z_{\text{focus}} - f)}. \tag{2.5}$$

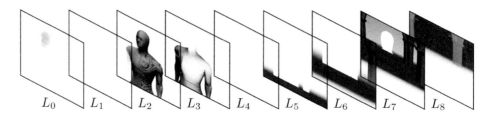

L_0 L_1 L_2 L_3 L_4 L_5 L_6 L_7 L_8

Figure 2.5. The depth layers produced after matting the input buffers.

Note that the CoCs (d_k) for depth layers located behind the focus plane $(k > k_{\text{focus}})$ will be negative and that Equation (2.5) is only applicable as long as

$$\bar{d}_{K-1} > \frac{f^2}{N \cdot (z_{\text{focus}} - f)}.$$

The anchor point furthest away from the camera, z_{K-1}, is limited by this constraint. Special care has to be taken when matting the foremost layer (L_0) and the back layer (L_{K-1}), shown in Figure 2.5, where all fragments with a depth smaller than the foremost anchor point (z_0) are matted into L_0 and fragments with depths beyond the back anchor point (z_{K-1}) are matted into L_{K-1}.

To simulate DoF, a sufficient number of depth layers spanning the whole depth range of the scene have to be generated.

Simply using the near and far clipping planes would produce empty depth layers, at the front and the back, if the rendered scene's depth range is smaller. Therefore, a better method is to use a dynamically adapted frustum, either by looking at bounding-box depth or by calculating a minimum-maximum mipmap on the framebuffer.

2.6   Blurring and Composition

Each depth layer L_k has a CoC d_k that determines the width of the blur filter. We use Gaussian filters, because they are separable, can be recursively applied, and produce smooth results. The mapping from CoC to the standard deviation σ of a Gaussian kernel H is chosen empirically as

$$d_{\text{pix}} = 4\sigma.$$

Note that d_{pix} is the d_{coc} in screen coordinates and has to be transformed into the world coordinate system.

One could convolve each layer separately, but this would require large and thus expensive filter widths farther away from the focus plane. Instead, we use a recursive filtering approach, where we start with the farthest layers and filter after each composition step. Thus, the further away from the focus plane a layer is, the more often it gets blurred.

```
GLuint pDepthLayer[K]; // storing the depth layers
GLuint bufferFront, bufferFocus, bufferBack; // composition b

// do front buffer compositing
bindAndClearFbo( bufferFront );
for( uint k = 0 ; k < kFocus ; ++ k ) {
   glBlendFunc( GL_ONE_MINUS_DST_ALPHA, GL_ONE );
   blendLayer( pDepthLayer[k] );
   blurBuffer( bufferFront, computeSigmaForLayer( k ) );
}

// do focus buffer compositing
bindAndClearFbo( bufferFocus );
blendLayer( pDepthLayer[kFocus] );

// do back buffer compositing
bindAndClearFbo( bufferBack );
for( uint k = K-1 ; k > kFocus ; -- k ) {
   glBlendFunc( GL_ONE, GL_ONE_MINUS_SRC_ALPHA );
   blendLayer( pDepthLayer[k] );
   blurBuffer( bufferBack, computeSigmaForLayer( k ) );
}
```

Listing 2.3. OpenGL pseudocode for blending and blurring the depth layers onto the composition buffers: front, focus, and back.

In particular, depth layers are blended onto one of three so-called *composition buffers* for the front, back, and focus parts of the scene. (I'_{front}, I'_{back}, and I'_{focus}). While the latter is only filled with the in-focus depth layer ($L_{k_{\text{focus}}}$), the other depth layers are composed iteratively onto the front and back composition buffers, starting from the foremost and the furthest depth layer (L_0 and L_{K-1}), respectively. The two composition buffers have to be used because otherwise it is not possible to keep the correct depth ordering of the layers. Between each composition iteration, the composition buffers are blurred with a Gaussian filter $\hat{H}_k$, where the index k is the same as the recently composed depth layer L_k. Composition is done by alpha blending, where the front composition buffer is blended over the next depth layer and for the back composition buffer the depth layer is blended over the composition buffer ($I'_{\text{front}} \oplus L_k$ and $L_k \oplus I'_{\text{back}}$, respectively). Pseudocode for this operation is shown in Listing 2.3.

As desired, stronger blurs can be achieved with smaller filter kernel sizes. For example, a depth layer L_0 will be blurred $k_{\text{focus}} - 1$ times with the Gaussian kernels $\hat{H}_0$ to $\hat{H}_{k_{\text{focus}}-1}$. Blurring recursively has a similar result to blurring with a Gaussian kernel H_k, where the filter width (in σ) is the Euclidean distance of all applied recursive filter sizes:

$$\sigma_k = \sqrt{\sum_{i=k}^{k_{\text{focus}}} \hat{\sigma}_i^2}, \tag{2.6}$$

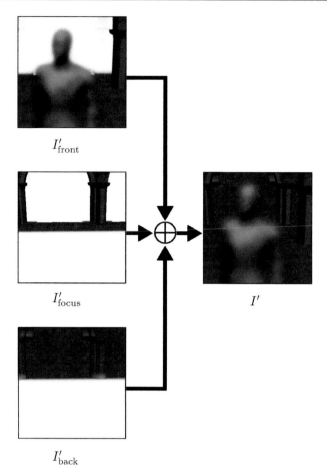

I'_{front}

I'_{focus}

I'

I'_{back}

Figure 2.6. Final composition of the three composition buffers (front, focus, and back) as in Equation (2.7). The focus point is the pillar in the back, which is different to results shown in Figure 2.7.

where $\hat{\sigma}_{k_{\text{focus}}} = 0$. In the previous example, this means that layer L_0 is as strongly blurred as it would have been if a bigger filter H_0 (σ_0 calculated by Equation (2.6)) has been used for blurring. Although the filtering results are not exactly the same, due to occlusions that are avoided if each layer is blurred separately, the results are sufficient for approximating DoF. In our implementation, we use a standard deviation of $\hat{\sigma}_k = |k - k_{\text{focus}}|$ for the recursive Gaussians, thus there are smaller kernel-size changes around the focal plane, which results in less visible grading.

The final composition I' is calculated by alpha-blending the composition buffers from front to back (Figure 2.6):

$$I' = I'_{\text{front}} \oplus I'_{\text{focus}} \oplus I'_{\text{back}}. \tag{2.7}$$

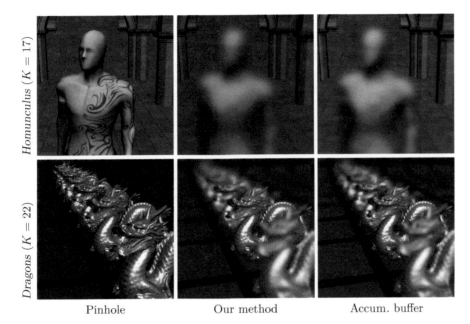

Pinhole   Our method   Accum. buffer

Figure 2.7. A pinhole rendering and DoF effects produced with our algorithm and the accumulation-buffer method (256 views). The first row shows the scene *Homunculus* (74,000 faces), and the second shows *Dragons* (6,000,000 faces). Renderings have the resolution $1,024 \times 1,024$, and 17 and 22 depth layers, respectively, have been used for our algorithm. The lens settings are $f = 0.1$, $N = 1.4$, and it is focused at the stone wall in the back ($z_{\text{focus}} = 18.5$) for *Homunculus* and at the foremost blue dragon ($z_{\text{focus}} = 3$) for *Dragons*.

2.6.1 Normalization

Due to the usage of matting functions ω and $\dot{\omega}$, resulting in expanded depth layers, and the usage of depth peeling, discretization artifacts as discussed in [Barsky et al. 03] are mostly avoided. However, in some circumstances (e.g., almost perpendicular planes), such artifacts may still appear, but they can be further minimized by normalizing the result (divide color by alpha). Note that for matting and blurring, premultiplied colors (color multiplied by alpha) are used.

2.7 Results

We show some results of the method, rendered on an Intel Core i7 920 CPU with a Geforce GTX 480 graphics card and implemented in GLSL. To avoid depth imprecisions when storing and sorting the fragments in the A-buffer, we

| | Our method | | Accum. buffer |
	A-buffer	Depth peeling	256 views
Homunculus ($K = 17$)	(3/6/36)45	(6/22/36)64	4,809
Dragons ($K = 22$)	(14/6/53)73	(114/28/52)194	4,163

Table 2.1. Performance comparisons, in ms, of our method using the A-buffer, with depth peeling (as in [Schedl and Wimmer 12]), and with the accumulation-buffer method for the scenes *Homunculus* (74k faces) and *Dragons* (6M faces). Renderings have the resolution 1024×1024 and $M = 8$. Note that the rendering times in brackets represent the costs for (scene rendering/matting/blurring).

use 32-bit float textures (GL_RGBA32F for color and depth and GL_R32F for the counter).

We compare our method to the accumulation buffer method and to an implementation of our method with depth peeling (as implemented in [Schedl and Wimmer 12]). The methods are applied to the scenes *Homunculus* (74,000 triangles) and *Dragons* (6,000,000 triangles), shown in Figure 2.7, next to a pinhole rendering of the scenes. In Table 2.1 the rendering times are shown. The retrieval of $M = 8$ hidden fragments is very costly with the previously used depth peeling, especially in complex scenes such as *Dragons*. Although simpler scenes (e.g., *Homunculus*) can be rendered several times with less impact, the latter might be less practical for applications with a constrained rendering budget. Our optimized A-buffer method also does more efficient layer matting, because with the counter texture we don't have to process empty input buffer fragments. The costs for blurring one depth layer are quite similar in both scenes.

The reference accumulation-buffer technique is implemented in OpenGL and uses a 32-bit-per-channel float texture for accumulation. The lens samples are positioned with a Gaussian distribution.

In [Schedl and Wimmer 12] we also compare our method to a ray-traversal technique, and we show that the rendering costs for [Lee et al. 10] are higher ($>$ $5\times$) at comparable settings. Note that for the scenes in [Schedl and Wimmer 12], only $M = 4$ input buffers are used, which is often sufficient.

2.8   Conclusion

We have shown an algorithm to render high-quality DoF effects, in particular including the partial occlusion effect. We use an A-buffer to avoid having to rerender the scene, which would be a costly operation. With recursive Gaussian filters, high-blur radii can be simulated efficiently, while previous methods produce sampling artifacts when too few rays are used. However, since blurring is the most costly operation, if higher frame rates are needed and visual quality can be sacrificed, faster methods (e.g., box and pyramid filters) can be used. With the usage of faster blurring methods, our method could be used in real-time applications such as games. Notice that altering the blurring method also changes the number of depth layers and the spacing between them. At the moment, our method produces practically artifact-free images at reasonable frame rates, making high-quality DoF with partial occlusion available for high-quality rendering applications at interactive rates. Furthermore, our method can be used to preview the impact of camera settings (i.e., focus and aperture) in scenes that later will be rendered with great computational costs, e.g., ray tracing.

The A-buffer uses the space of M screen-sized buffers on the GPU, although the A-buffer might not be filled completely. Therefore, one optimization to reduce memory demand is to use fragment-linked lists instead of an A-buffer (rendering costs might increase). To avoid allocating the A-buffer memory twice, we reuse the allocated A-buffer (unsorted fragments) for later storing the sorted input buffers.

Our implementation uses a texture for each depth layer simply for debugging reasons. However, memory consumption for depth layers can be easily reduced, if matting directly writes into the composition buffers.

2.9 Acknowledgments

Thanks to Juergen Koller for providing the Homunculus model. The Dragon and Sponza models are courtesy of Stanford Computer Graphics Laboratory and Marko Dabrovic.

Bibliography

[Barsky et al. 03] Brian A. Barsky, Daniel R. Tobias, Michael J. Horn, and Derrick P. Chu. "Investigating Occlusion and Discretization Problems in Image Space Blurring Techniques." In *First International Conference on Vision, Video, and Graphics*, pp. 97–102. Bath, UK: University of Bath, 2003.

[Carpenter 84] Loren Carpenter. "The A-buffer, an Antialiased Hidden Surface Method." *SIGGRAPH Computer Graphics* 18 (1984), 103–108.

[Crassin 10] Cyril Crassin. "Fast and Accurate Single-Pass A-Buffer Using OpenGL 4.0+." *Icare3D Blog*, http://blog.icare3d.org/2010/06/fast-and-accurate-single-pass-buffer.html, June 9, 2010.

[Kraus and Strengert 07] Martin Kraus and Magnus Strengert. "Depth-of-Field Rendering by Pyramidal Image Processing." *Computer Graphics Forum* 26:3 (2007), 645–654.

[Lee et al. 10] Sungkil Lee, Elmar Eisemann, and Hans-Peter Seidel. "Real-Time Lens Blur Effects and Focus Control." *ACM Transactions on Graphics* 29:4 (2010), 65:1–65:7.

[Potmesil and Chakravarty 81] Michael Potmesil and Indranil Chakravarty. "A Lens and Aperture Camera Model for Synthetic Image Generation." In *Proceedings of the 8th Annual Conference on Computer Graphics and Interactive Techniques*, SIGGRAPH '81, pp. 297–305. Dallas, TX: ACM, 1981.

[Schedl and Wimmer 12] David Schedl and Michael Wimmer. "A Layered Depth-of-Field Method for Solving Partial Occlusion." *Journal of WSCG* 20:3 (2012), 239–246.

Second-Depth Antialiasing

Emil Persson

3.1 Introduction and Previous Work

For nearly a decade multisampling was the one and only antialiasing solution for real-time rendering. For most of this time, multisampling was never challenged because it worked relatively well. As rendering technology has developed and engines become more advanced, multisampling has become an increasingly bigger stumbling block and maintenance problem when developing new rendering techniques. With the recent popularization of deferred shading, the memory inefficiency of multisample antialiasing (MSAA) has further been magnified to a point where it becomes impractical, in particular on current generation consoles, and the inherent weaknesses of this technique become much more apparent.

In recent years a number of interesting alternatives to multisampling has emerged. In 2009 morphological antialiasing (MLAA) [Reshetov 09] was introduced, starting off a wave of new techniques. The fundamental difference between MLAA and MSAA is that the former is entirely a post-process operation. This means that the algorithm is provided a finished rendered image, which it then analyzes and antialiases. This works by first detecting edges in the image (defined, for instance, by a certain difference in luminance between neighboring pixels) and then classifying those edges into a set of shapes. From these shapes it reconstructs what the original edge might have been and uses that to compute a coverage value used for blending with neighboring pixels. MLAA was initially a CPU-based technique for ray tracers but was later expanded to GPU implementations by others [Jimenez et al. 11]. At the point of this writing, several games have shipped with MLAA in some form as their antialiasing solution. Another very popular technique is fast approximate antialiasing (FXAA) [Lottes 11] that, due to its simple single-pass implementation with optimized targets for all important platforms, is a very convenient alternative.

The above and several other approaches can be described as post-process antialiasing techniques, because they require no particular knowledge about how the image was generated. Being decoupled from scene rendering is a great advantage, allowing for a more modular engine design. On the downside the heuristics on which these methods are based are not accurate and may fail or cause artifacts. There are also a number of analytical techniques emerging. These techniques do not try to recover information from buffers but instead take advantage of a priori knowledge of the scene. Examples of this include distance-to-edge antialiasing (DEAA) [Malan 10] and geometry buffer antialiasing (GBAA) [Persson 12]. By using available information about the underlying geometry, these methods can provide much more accurate results. The downside is that they require more engine support and consequently are not as modular and may require a greater amount of maintenance effort in an engine.

This article will introduce a semianalytical method that requires very little in terms of data from the game engine to do its job.

3.2   Algorithm

3.2.1   Overview

This technique uses the regular depth buffer and a buffer containing the second layer of depth. The former should already be available; however, the latter is not something an engine normally has and thus is something the engine will have to provide. Fortunately it is relatively straightforward to generate, and should the engine already be using a pre-Z pass, only a trivial change is required.

The underlying idea of this technique is to use the slope of depth to compute where the original edge is located. If we draw a line through the depth samples and find the intersection point, this is where the original edge was. This assumes that there is an adjacent triangle on the other side of an edge, which normally ought to be the case (with some exceptions). To understand how this works, we must first understand the basic properties of depth. If you already have a thorough understanding of depth, you may skip the next section.

3.2.2   Understanding depth

A depth buffer can contain a surprising amount of useful information. For instance, in deferred shading it is common to extract the world position for a pixel from a depth buffer value and its screen-space position alone. The depth buffer also has some interesting properties that are crucial for this technique. The key insight we need to bring before heading into the details of this technique is that a depth buffer is in fact linear.

It is commonly stated that Z is nonlinear. This claim is usually done in the context of Z-buffering and refers to the distribution of depth values in the depth buffer in regards to view distance. There is indeed a nonlinear distribution of depth values in depth buffers, at least with a perspective projection. In a traditional depth buffer ranging from 0 at the near plane to 1 at the far plane,

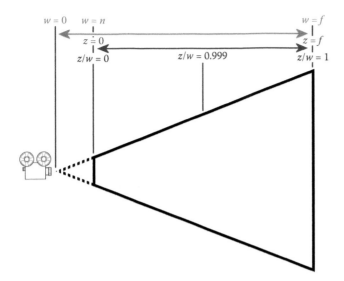

Figure 3.1. Distribution of z, w, and z/w. Both z and w are linear in view depth and differ only by a scale and bias; z/w is highly nonlinear.

the value 0.5 is absolutely not anywhere close to the middle of the frustum. It is in fact very close to the near plane. The vast majority of the values in the depth buffer will land somewhere very close to 1. The value in the middle of the frustum will be something like 0.999. This of course results in a significant loss of a precision, which is a problem. In the past the solution to this was a W-buffer, which some hardware supported, offering linear distribution of depth values. The difference between z and w is not that big, actually; z is essentially w with a slightly larger scale factor, and z starts at near plane whereas w starts at the eye position. So both z and w are linear, but it is z/w that is stored in a Z-buffer, which is not linearly distributed. Refer to Figure 3.1 for a visualization of z, w, and z/w.

While z/w has nonlinear distribution of values, it is on the other hand linear in the gradients pixel-to-pixel in screen space. If you have three neighboring pixels belonging to the same surface, or coplanar surfaces, you can expect the difference in depth values from the first pixel to the second to be equal to that of the second to the third pixel, ignoring precision issues of course. In other words, the screen-space gradients are constant. This is visualized in Figure 3.2.

Constant gradients are a highly desirable property for the hardware, because the z/w values can simply be computed at the triangle vertices and then linearly interpolated across the triangle. In addition to simplifying the rasterizer, this property also facilitates some newer hardware features such a Z-compression. In the relatively likely event that some screen-space tile—for instance, 8×8 pixels—

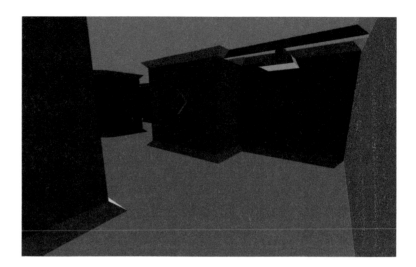

Figure 3.2. The screen-space linearity of z/w visualized by outputting the Z gradients. Notice the flat shading, indicating constant gradients within planar surfaces.

is completely covered by the same primitive, all of the entire tile's depth values can be encoded with three values, the two gradients and an offset, or essentially a plane equation. Assuming that the value is stored as three 32-bit floats,[1] this would represent a bandwidth reduction of no less than 95% for reading and writing depth.

The linearity in screen space is also a property that is very useful on the software side of things. It makes it easy to write an accurate edge-detection routine. Given that the gradients within a primitive are constant, if we detect that the depth delta to the left and to the right of a pixel is different, we know there is an edge there, and similarly in the vertical direction. We can also use this information to find where the original geometrical edge that generated the depth values is. This is the foundation upon which this technique is based.

3.2.3   Method

This technique extracts the original geometrical edges analytically from the depth buffer values. There are two types of edges that need to be handled separately, creases and silhouette edges. A *crease* is where a primitive meets an adjacent primitive—for instance, corners between walls—and a *silhouette edge* is where there is no adjacent primitive on the other side of the edge and instead you have

---

[1]The hardware is likely using a custom format that matches whatever precision the rasterizer has. The hardware also needs to allocate at least one bit to signal whether the tile is compressed or not.

```
bool edge_x = (abs(dx1 + dx2 - 2 * dc) > 0.00001f * dc);
bool edge_y = (abs(dy1 + dy2 - 2 * dc) > 0.00001f * dc);
```

Listing 3.1. Horizontal and vertical edge detection.

some sort of background there. The algorithm will first detect whether there is a discontinuity in the depth buffer. If not, we are in the middle of a primitive and no antialiasing is necessary. If a discontinuity is present, it will first attempt to resolve it as a crease. If that fails, it assumes it is dealing with a silhouette instead and resolves it as such.

Edge detection. Detecting a discontinuity in the depth buffer is fairly straightforward. For pixels from the same primitive we expect the delta to the left and to the right to be equal, or $left + right - 2 \times center = 0$. Of course, due to limited precision and such, we need some sort of epsilon there. An epsilon relative to the center sample works quite well. Listing 3.1 has the edge detection part of the shader. Note that we are detecting both horizontal and vertical discontinuities here. To simplify understanding, for the rest of this article only the horizontal case will be covered, but the same operations are done in both directions. In the case that we detect a valid edge in both directions, we will decide with which direction to go depending on in which direction the edge is closer.

Creases. Once it has been established that we have an edge, we try to resolve it as a crease. If we have a crease, the original geometry would have the two primitives meet at some point. In Figure 3.3, the blue and green primitives meet at the purple dot. The red dots represent our depth buffer samples. Provided the constant gradients in the screen space, finding this edge point is simply about computing the intersection between the lines passing through the samples.

Figure 3.3. Finding the original geometric edge in the crease case.

```
if (edge_x)
{
    float k0 = dx1 - dx0; // Left slope
    float k1 = dx3 - dx2; // Right slope
    float m0 = dx1 + k0; // Left offset
    float m1 = dx2 - k1; // Right offset
    offset.x = (m1 - m0) / (k0 - k1); // Intersection point

    is_silhouette = (abs(offset.x) > 1.0f);
    offset.x = (abs(offset.x) < 0.5f)? offset.x : 0.5f;
}
```

Listing 3.2. Computing horizontal crease intersection point.

In Listing 3.2 we are computing the intersection point horizontally. The math is relatively straightforward, and the resulting value is the coordinate relative to the center sample location. If the intersection point lands somewhere within a pixel in either direction, we have successfully resolved this as a crease. Otherwise, there is no valid intersection point here, indicating that we are dealing with a silhouette edge. If we have a valid crease, we only use it if the intersection point lands within half a pixel. This is because if the intersection point is further away, it is actually within the neighboring pixel's area, and it is that pixel that should do the blending.

Silhouette edges. So far we have only required a standard depth buffer. Unfortunately, when we have a silhouette edge, we do not have an adjacent primitive whose depth values can be used to derive the geometric edge. The background primitive has nothing in particular in common with the foreground primitive that we can take advantage of. In Figure 3.4, from the red dots alone, the only thing we can know is that there is a gap between the second and third sample, so the

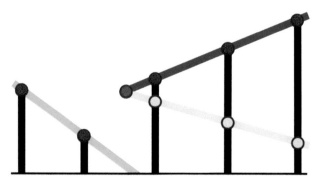

Figure 3.4. Finding the original geometric edge in the silhouette case.

```
if (edge_x)
{
    float k0 = sdx3 - sdx2; // Right second-depth slope
    float k1 = dx3 - dx2; // Right slope
    float k2 = sdx1 - sdx0; // Left second-depth slope
    float k3 = dx1 - dx0; // Left slope

    float m0 = sdx2 - k0; // Right second-depth offset
    float m1 = dx2 - k1; // Right offset
    float m2 = sdx1 + k2; // Left second-depth offset
    float m3 = dx1 + k3; // Left offset
    float offset0 = (m1 - m0) / (k0 - k1); // Right intersection
    float offset1 = (m3 - m2) / (k2 - k3); // Left intersection

    // Pick the closest intersection.
    offset.x = (abs(offset0) < abs(offset1))? offset0 : offset1;
    offset.x = (abs(offset.x) < 0.5f)? offset.x : 0.5f;
}
```

Listing 3.3. Computing horizontal silhouette intersection point.

edge is somewhere in between there, but there is no way for us to know how far that blue primitive stretches over the gap. What we really need here is the depths of the adjacent primitive in the mesh. For the silhouette case, the adjacent primitive will be behind the primitive and back-facing the viewer. We thus need a second layer of depth values for these hidden surfaces, hence the name of this technique: second-depth antialiasing. More on how we generate the second depth layer later in this article. Note though that for this to work we need closed geometry. If no back-face primitive exists, the edge will be left aliased.

Once you have a second layer of depth values, the silhouette case is quite similar to the crease case. However, we need to do a separate test to the left and to the right. Then we select whichever one happened to end up closer to the center pixel. Again, if the edge is determined to be within half a pixel from the center, we can use this edge distance information for blending. (See Listing 3.3.)

Once we have determined the distance to the edge, we need to do the final blending of the color buffer. The distance to the edge can be converted to the coverage of neighboring primitives on this pixel, which can be used for blending with the neighboring pixel. We either blend with a horizontal or vertical neighbor. This can be done in a single sample by simply using a linear texture filter and offsetting the texture coordinate appropriately [Persson 12]. The code for this is presented in Listing 3.4.

Generating second depths. A straightforward way to generate the second depth layer is to render the scene to a depth target with front-face culling. This is the equivalent of a pre-Z pass, except it is only used to generate the second depth texture. An additional geometric pass only for this may seem a bit excessive, though. A better approach is to use this pass instead of a traditional pre-Z pass,

```
// Convert distances to a texture coordinate shift for filtering.
if (abs(offset.x) > abs(offset.y))
{
    offset.x = 0;
    offset.y = ((offset.y >= 0)? 0.5f : -0.5f) - offset.y;
}
else
{
    offset.x = ((offset.x >= 0)? 0.5f : -0.5f) - offset.x;
    offset.y = 0;
}

return BackBuffer.Sample(Linear, TexCoord + offset * PixelSize);
```

Listing 3.4. Final blending.

where we generate this texture and get a full pre-Z at the same time. First we draw the scene to a depth buffer with front-face culling, then copy to the second depth texture, and then proceed with main scene rendering, using back-face culling as usual. The second-depth values in the buffer will in general still be in front of whatever the frontmost surfaces cover, allowing nearly the same culling efficiency in theory. This is the approach the sample code is using by default.

There are two things to note about this approach. First, a second-depth pre-Z pass places the depth values further back than a tradition pre-Z pass. Hierarchical-Z (Hi-Z)) hardware usually stores a low-precision but conservative value of the most distant depth. For things that are very close to the back-face—for instance, things behind the wall that are standing next to the wall—there may be cases where the hardware is unable to cull those pixels because it cannot guarantee it is completely occluded with the low-precision Hi-Z value it has. In those cases a traditional pre-Z pass could be more effective, depending on the hardware. There are also cases where objects intersect, so that the back-facing depth values are actually behind the intersecting object's front faces. In those cases we do lose the Hi-Z culling. The second thing to note, though, is that a second-depth pre-Z pass is generally faster to render, which may or may not result in better performance overall. The reason it is faster is because plenty of geometry does not have anything behind it. The most distant surface never adds anything of value to a pre-Z pass, because there is nothing behind it to cull. For an indoor scene, such as the one in the sample application, the most distant surface is always front-facing. For outdoor scenes this is also the case if you consider the skybox to be a front-facing surface, which is reasonable. This means that if you render front-faces to pre-Z, you will also render walls that have nothing behind them to pre-Z, which is wasteful. On the other hand, realistically there will always be something behind the back-faces. For the kind of closed geometry in the sample application, this is a guarantee. For real game geometry there are exceptions, of course. Terrain is typically not closed geometry per se, i.e., there is no underside of it, so a second-depth pre-Z pass would not cull the skybox behind it if it was drawn immediately after the pre-Z pass. This is, of course, fixable in practice by drawing the terrain before the skybox in the main scene rendering. In that case a second-depth pre-Z pass would provide all the self-occlusion culling the terrain needs while not wasting any precious raster operations on filling large areas of the screen with essentially nothing but skybox behind it.

There are other conceivable approaches for generating a second depth buffer with the potential advantage of not requiring a pre-Z pass or second geometry pass at all. For instance, one method could be to use a geometry shader to send triangles to two different slices in a render target array depending on the facingness. One slice would contain the front-faces and the other the back-faces. Another approach could be to use a DX11-style linked list of fragments [Thibieroz 11]. If this is used for order-independent transparency, we could already have the second layer there ready for use. A full-screen pass could extract the first and second depths from the fragment list and write to a separate buffer. Neither of these methods has been applied to SDAA, so it is unclear if there are any potential issues or how they would compare performance-wise in real-world applications.

3.3 Results

Image quality. Second-depth antialiasing, like other analytical methods such as GBAA [Persson 12], has the advantage that the coverage value is derived analytically rather than reverse-engineered through a set of heuristics—and consequently is very accurately reproduced. This results in a very high-quality antialiasing regardless of edge orientation. However, it should be noted that SDAA is sensitive to depth-buffer precision. For hidden surface removal a 16-bit depth buffer is more than plenty for the simple scene in the accompanying code sample; however, it is insufficient to be useful for computing intersection points for SDAA. For this reason the demo is using the D32F format. However, it should be noted that a 24-bit depth buffer also works.

Figure 3.6 illustrates the antialiasing quality achieved with this method, compared to Figure 3.5 that has the original aliased image.

Figures 3.7 and 3.8 show a standard pixel-zoomed antialiasing comparison. Before applying SDAA we have the regular stair-stepped edge. After applying SDAA the edge is very smooth. Unlike MSAA and many other antialiasing techniques, the number of intermediate gradients is only limited by the precision of the underlying color format.

Performance. The full cost of this technique largely depends on the scene and the state of the engine prior to adding SDAA support. If there was previously no pre-Z pass, or only a partial one, the need for generating the second depth

Figure 3.5. Aliased scene before applying SDAA.

Figure 3.6. Scene antialiased with SDAA.

Figure 3.7. Zoomed pixels before SDAA.

Figure 3.8. Zoomed pixels after SDAA.

buffer may incur a sizeable overhead. The addition of a pre-Z pass may, of course, also improve performance. This is all very dependent on the application, so it is impossible to give a universal statement about performance. However, the sample application was profiled using GPU PerfStudio 2, from the default start position using an AMD Radeon HD5870 at a 1,920 × 1,080 resolution. The results are presented in Table 3.1.

The overhead of SDAA consists of the final resolve pass and the cost of copying the depth buffer after the pre-Z pass. The cost of the depth buffer copy is hard to do much about, but the resolve pass can be optimized. The main bottleneck in the standard DX10 implementation is texture fetches. GPU PerfStudio reports the texture unit being busy 97.5% of the time. Using `Gather()` in DX10.1, we can significantly reduce the number of fetches required, from 17 to 9. This brings the cost of the resolve pass down from 0.33 ms to 0.26 ms, and the total overhead of SDAA down from 0.51 ms to 0.43 ms. The texture unit is now 75% busy.

	DX10	DX10.1
SDAA off	1.736 ms	1.736 ms
SDAA on	2.255 ms	2.180 ms
Depth buffer copy	0.176 ms	0.176 ms
Resolve pass	0.335 ms	0.256 ms

Table 3.1. GPU times on an AMD HD5870 at 1,920 × 1,080.

3.4 Conclusion and Future Work

We have presented an effective analytical antialiasing technique offering high-quality edge antialiasing at a reasonable cost and relatively straightforward engine integration. However, there are several areas on which future work could improve.

The resolve pass is very texture fetch heavy. As shown by the profile and through the gains of DX10.1 optimization, this is a major bottleneck for this technique. Given that all samples are refetched for multiple neighboring pixels, this is a prime candidate for compute shader optimization, trading some increase in ALU for a significant reduction in texture fetches by sharing samples. It is likely that this would result in a moderate performance improvement over the DX10.1 results.

Better ways to generate the second-depth values would be desirable to avoid the need for a complete pre-Z pass. Alternatively, an approach worth studying is combining the crease solution from this technique with other methods for silhouette edges, such as, for instance, geometry post-process antialiasing (GPAA).[2] This would eliminate the need for the second depth buffer. Meanwhile the number of silhouette edges in a typical scene is relatively low, so the line rasterization overhead of GPAA should stay at a reasonable level.

This technique may lose its effectiveness when using very dense geometry where neighboring pixels typically come from different primitives. This is because the implementation presented in this article computes depth slopes from differences between neighboring depth values. A different approach might be to store gradients along with the depth values. This way the resolve shader would not require sampling any neighboring pixels and should be able to cope better with very dense geometry, at the expense of additional storage and output overhead. On the other hand, the resolve shader would likely run faster.

Bibliography

[Reshetov 09] Alexander Reshetov. "Morphological Antialiasing." Preprint, 2009. (Available at http://visual-computing.intel-research.net/publications/papers/2009/mlaa/mlaa.pdf.)

[Jimenez et al. 11] Jorge Jimenez, Belen Masia, Jose I. Echevarria, Fernando Navarro, and Diego Gutierrez. "Practical Morphological Antialiasing." In *GPU Pro 2*, edited by Wolfgang Engel, pp. 95–114. Natick, MA: A K Peters, Ltd., 2011.

---

[2]GPAA works by drawing lines over the edges in the scene and filtering the pixels under the lines. The line equation is used to compute the distance from the pixel center to the line, and this is then converted to a coverage value for the neighboring surface. If the line is mostly horizontal, it will blend pixels with vertical neighbors and vice versa.

[Lottes 11] Timothy Lottes. "FXAA." White paper, NVIDIA, http://developer. download.nvidia.com/assets/gamedev/files/sdk/11/FXAA_WhitePaper.pdf, January 25, 2011.

[Malan 10] Hugh Malan. "Edge Anti-aliasing by Post-Processing." In *GPU Pro*, edited by Wolfgang Engel, pp. 265–290. Natick, MA: A K Peters, Ltd., 2010.

[Persson 12] Emil Persson. "Geometric Antialiasing Methods." In *GPU Pro 3*, edited by Wolfgang Engel, pp. 71–88. Boca Raton, FL: CRC Pres, 2012.

[Thibieroz 11] Nicolas Thibieroz. "Order-Independent Transparency Using Per-Pixel Linked Lists." In *GPU Pro 2*, edited by Wolfgang Engel, pp. 409–432. Natick, MA: A K Peters, Ltd., 2011.

4

III

Practical Framebuffer Compression

Pavlos Mavridis and Georgios Papaioannou

4.1 Introduction

In computer graphics, the creation of realistic images requires multiple samples per pixel, to avoid aliasing artifacts, and floating-point precision, in order to properly represent the high dynamic range (HDR) of the environmental lighting. Both of these requirements vastly increase the storage and bandwidth consumption of the framebuffer. In particular, using a multisample framebuffer with N samples per pixel requires N times more memory. On top of that, the usage of a 16-bit half-float storage format doubles the memory and bandwidth requirements when compared to the 8-bit fixed-point equivalent. As an example, a 1080p framebuffer using $8 \times$ MSAA requires 189 MB of memory when using half-float precision for the color and a 32-bit Z-buffer.

The total framebuffer memory can further increase when using algorithms that store multiple intermediate render buffers, such as deferred rendering or when simply rendering at very high resolutions in order to drive high-density displays, which is a rather recent trend in mobile and desktop computing. The same is also true when driving multiple displays from the same GPU, in order to create immersive setups. All of these factors vastly increase the consumed memory and put an enormous stress on the memory subsystem of the GPU.

This fact was recognized by the hardware manufacturers and most, if not all, of the shipping GPUs today include a form of lossless framebuffer compression. Although the details of these compression schemes are not publicly disclosed, based on the performance characteristics of the GPUs, it is rather safe to assume that these algorithms mostly exploit the fact that a fragment shader can be executed only once per covered primitive and the same color can be assigned to many subpixel samples. It is worth noting that according to the information theory, there is no lossless compression algorithm that can guarantee a fixed-rate encoding, which is needed in order to provide fast random access; therefore, these algorithms can only save bandwidth but not storage.

Figure 4.1. Using our method, color images can be rasterized directly using only two framebuffer channels: original uncompressed framebuffer stored using three color channels (left), and compressed framebuffer using two color channels in the YC_oC_g space (right). The compressed frame appears indistinguishable from the original one. Inset: Heat map visualizing the compression error (47.02 dB PSNR).

In this chapter we describe a practical lossy framebuffer compression scheme, based on chrominance subsampling, suitable for existing commodity GPUs and APIs. Using our method, a color image can be rasterized using only two framebuffer channels, instead of three, thus reducing the storage and, more importantly, the bandwidth requirements of the rasterization process, a fundamental operation in computer graphics. This reduction in memory footprint can be valuable when implementing various rendering pipelines. Our method is compatible with both forward and deferred rendering, it does not affect the effectiveness of any lossless compression by the hardware, and it can be used with other lossy schemes, like the recently proposed surface-based antialiasing (SBAA) [Salvi and Vidimče 12], to further decrease the total storage and bandwidth consumption.

While our method is lossy, it does not result in any visible quality degradation of the final rendered image, as shown in Figure 4.1. Furthermore, our measurements in Section 4.7 indicate that in many cases it provides a rather impressive improvement on the GPU fill rate.

4.2   Color Space Conversion

The human visual system is more sensitive to spatial variations of luminance intensity than chrominance. This fact has been exploited by many image and video coding systems, such as JPEG and MPEG, in order to improve compression rates, without a perceptible loss of quality. This is usually achieved by representing the chrominance components of an image with lower spatial resolution than the luminance one, a process that is commonly referred as *chrominance subsampling*. This process forms the basis of our method.

The color of the rasterized fragments should first be decomposed into luminance and chrominance components. A lot of transforms have been proposed to perform this operation. The RGB to YC_oC_g transform, first introduced in h.264 compression [Malvar and Sullivan 03], has been shown to have better compression properties than other similar transforms, such as YC_bC_r. The actual transform is given by the following equation:

$$\begin{bmatrix} Y \\ C_o \\ C_g \end{bmatrix} = \begin{bmatrix} 1/4 & 1/2 & 1/4 \\ 1/2 & 0 & -1/2 \\ -1/4 & 1/2 & -1/4 \end{bmatrix} \begin{bmatrix} R \\ G \\ B \end{bmatrix}, \tag{4.1}$$

while the original RGB data can be retrieved as

$$R = Y + C_o - C_g, \quad G = Y + C_g, \quad B = Y - C_o - C_g.$$

The chrominance values (C_oC_g) in the YC_oC_g color space can be negative. In particular, when the input RGB range is $[0\ 1]$ the output C_oC_g range is $[-0.5\ 0.5]$. Therefore, when rendering on unsigned 8-bit fixed-point render targets, a bias of 0.5 should be added to these values in order to keep them positive. This bias should be subtracted from the C_oC_g values before converting the compressed render target back to the RGB color space.

It is worth noting that, to avoid any rounding errors during this transform, the YC_oC_g components should be stored with two additional bits of precision compared to the RGB data. When the same precision is used for the YC_oC_g and RGB data, as in our case, we have measured that converting to YC_oC_g and back results in an average peak signal-to-noise ratio (PSNR) of 52.12 dB in the well-known Kodak lossless true color image suite. This loss of precision is insignificant for our purposes and cannot be perceived by the human visual system, but still, this measurement indicates the upper limit in the quality of our compression scheme.

4.3 Chrominance Multiplexing

One option to take advantage of chrominance subsampling is to downsample the render targets after the rendering process has been completed. The problem with this approach is that we can only take advantage of the bandwidth reduction during the subsequent post-processing operations, as described in [White and Barre-Brisebois 11], but not during the actual rasterization.

Instead, our method renders color images directly using two channels. The first channel stores the luminance of each pixel, while the second channel stores

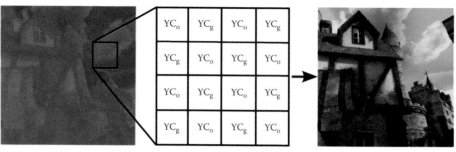

Compact FB/two channels   Resolved FB/three channels

Figure 4.2. Overview of our compact encoding format. The framebuffer is stored in two channels. The first channel stores the luminance of each pixel, while the second channel stores the chrominance interleaved in a checkerboard pattern. A simple and efficient image space reconstruction filter (Section 4.4) is used to uncompress and display the final framebuffer.

either the chroma orange (C_o) or the chroma green (C_g) of the input fragment, interleaved in a checkerboard pattern, as illustrated in Figure 4.2. This particular arrangement corresponds to a luminance-to-chrominance ratio of 2:1 and provides a 3:2 compression ratio, since two color channels are used instead of three. The same luminance-to-chrominance ratio is used by many video compression codecs and is referred as 4:2:2 in the literature, but the details on how the samples are produced and stored are different.

In order to create the compressed framebuffer on the GPU, applications can either request a render buffer with just two color channels, such as GL_RG16F or any similar format exposed by graphics APIs, or use a more traditional format with four color channels and use the free channels to store additional data. The latter case can be particularly useful in deferred rendering pipelines.

The fragments produced by the rasterization phase of the rendering pipeline should be directly emitted in the correct interleaved format. This can be easily done with the code snippet of Listing 4.1. In this code the fragment color is first

```glsl
//Convert the output color to YCoCg space.
vec3 YCoCg = RGB2YCoCg(finalColor.rgb);

//Store the YCo and YCg in a checkerboard pattern.
ivec2 crd = gl_FragCoord.xy;
bool isBlack = ((crd.x&1)==(crd.y&1));
finalColor.rg=(isBlack)? YCoCg.rg:YCoCg.rb;
```

Listing 4.1. Code snippet in GLSL to convert the output color in our compact interleaved format. The RGB2YCoCg function implements Equation (4.1).

converted to the YC_oC_g color space and, depending on the coordinates of the destination pixel, the YC_o or YC_g channels are emitted to the framebuffer.

This approach can also provide some small additional benefits during the fragment shading, where the fragments can be converted to the two-channel interleaved format early in the shader code and then any further processing can be performed only on two channels, instead of three, in the YC_oC_g color space. The actual benefits depend on the exact shading algorithms used in the shader and the underlying GPU architecture (the mix of SIMD and scalar units).

The subsampling of chrominance in our method is performed with point sampling, without using any sophisticated down-sampling filters. In theory this can lead to aliasing of the chrominance components, since we have halved their sampling rate, but in practice we did not observe any severe aliasing issues.

4.4   Chrominance Reconstruction

When reading values of the compressed framebuffer, any missing chrominance information should be reconstructed from the neighboring pixels. The simplest way to do that is to copy the missing chrominance value with one from a neighboring pixel. This *nearest* filter can create some visible mosaic artifacts at the edges of polygons, where strong chrominance transitions occur, as shown in Figure 4.3. Using *bilinear* interpolation of the missing data from the four neighboring pixels mitigates these artifacts but does not completely remove them. Please note that these artifacts are not easily detectable by the human visual system in still im-

Figure 4.3. Quality comparison between the image space reconstruction filters. (a) Original uncompressed framebuffer, (b) nearest reconstruction (43.2 dB), (c) bilinear reconstruction (47.5 dB), (d) edge-directed reconstruction (48.2 dB). Please note that only the edge-directed filter avoids the mosaic artifacts at the edges.

```
//Return the missing chrominance (Co or Cg) of a pixel:
//a1-a4 are the four neighbors of the center pixel a0.
float filter(vec2 a0, vec2 a1, vec2 a2, vec2 a3, vec2 a4)
{
  vec4 lum = vec4(a1.x, a2.x , a3.x, a4.x);
  vec4 w = 1.0-step(THRESH, abs(lum - a0.x));
  float W = w.x + w.y + w.z + w.w;
  //Handle the special case where all the weights are zero.
  W = (W==0.0)? W : 1.0/W;
  return (w.x*a1.y+w.y*a2.y+w.z*a3.y+w.w*a4.y)*W;
}
```

Listing 4.2. GLSL implementation of the edge-directed reconstruction filter.

ages, since the luminance is always correct, but they can become more pronounced when motion is involved.

To eliminate these reconstruction artifacts, we have designed a simple and efficient *edge-directed* filter, where the weights of the four nearest chrominance samples are calculated based on the luminance gradient towards that sample. If the gradient has a value greater than a specific threshold, indicating an edge, then the corresponding chrominance sample has zero weight. Otherwise the weight is one. This is expressed compactly in the following equation:

$$C_0 = \sum_{i=1}^{4} w_i C_i, \qquad w_i = 1.0 - step(T - \mid L_i - L_0 \mid), \qquad (4.2)$$

where C_i and L_i are respectively the chrominance (C_o or C_g) and luminance of pixel i. In our notation, zero denotes the center pixel, while the next four values denote the four neighbors. The step function returns one on positive values and zero otherwise. T is the gradient threshold. Our experiments with framebuffers from real games indicate that our algorithm is not very sensitive to this threshold, and values around 30/255 give similar quality in terms of PSNR. However we have observed that this particular value (30/255) tends to minimize the maximum difference between the original and the compressed framebuffer.

The gradient can be computed as a simple horizontal and vertical difference of the luminance values, as shown in Listing 4.2. The strategy we follow when all the weights are zero, which happens when we cannot find a neighbor with similar luminance, is to set the chrominance to zero. Furthermore, to avoid handling a special case at the edges of the framebuffer, where only pixels inside the frame boundaries should be considered, we are using a "mirrored repeat" wrapping mode when sampling the framebuffer pixels, which is supported natively by the texture hardware. It is also worth noting that the implementation of this filter is using conditional assignments, which are significantly faster than branches on most GPU architectures.

Figure 4.4. Close-ups demonstrating the quality of our edge-directed reconstruction filter in low-dynamic-range sRGB input. As expected, the largest amount of error occurs on edges and areas with noisy content, but it is still low enough to not be visible to the human visual system. The error is measured as the absolute difference in the RGB colors between the original and the compressed data.

The quality of the framebuffer is very important, therefore the reconstruction should be robust enough to handle the most challenging cases, like high-frequency content and strong chrominance transitions, without introducing any visible artifacts. Figure 4.4 demonstrates that these challenging cases are handled without any visual artifacts by the edge-directed filter. High-dynamic-range (HDR) content provides some extra challenges to chroma subsampling schemes, since the HDR of the luminance tends to exaggerate any "chrominance leaking" on edges with high dynamic contrast. The edge-directed nature of the reconstruction in our method prevents the appearance of any chrominance leaks, even on edges with extremely high dynamic contrast, as the one shown in Figure 4.5. For the test in this figure we have integrated our technique to a well-known demo by Emil Persson, combining our compact format with multisample antialiasing (MSAA), HDR render targets, and proper tone mapping before the MSAA resolve.

To test the temporal stability of our method with moving scenes, we have conducted two experiments. In the first experiment we have used the demo of Figure 4.5 and moved the camera around. But since the content of a real game might be more demanding, we have also encoded a sequence of framebuffers from a real game with our method. In both tests our method appears to be temporally stable.

Figure 4.5. An edge with extremely high dynamic range contrast. Places like this naturally draw the attention of the human eye, thus the reconstruction filter needs to deliver best results. The edge-directed filter prevents any chrominance artifacts even in these challenging cases. This particular example combines our compact format with $8\times$ MSAA, HDR render targets, and tone mapping.

4.4.1 Optimizations

A GLSL or HLSL implementation of our method has to perform five fetches, the actual pixel under consideration and four of its neighbors, in order to feed the edge-directed filter of Listing 4.2. Most of these fetches will come from the texture cache, which is very efficient in most GPUs, thus the overhead should be rather small on most architectures. It is worth noting that a GPGPU implementation can completely avoid the redundant fetches, by leveraging the local shared memory of the ALUs. Furthermore, newer architectures, like Nvidia's Kepler, provide intra-warp data exchange instructions, such as SHFL, that can be used to exchange data between threads in the same warp, without touching the shared memory. Nevertheless, since GPGPU capabilities are not available on all platforms, it is very interesting to investigate how the number of fetches can be reduced on a traditional shading language implementation. We focus here on the reduction of memory fetches, instead of ALU instructions, since for years the computational power of graphics hardware has grown at a faster rate than the available memory bandwidth [Owens 05], and this trend will likely continue in the future.

To this end, we can smartly use the built-in partial derivative instructions of the shading language. According to the OpenGL specification, the partial derivatives dFdx and dFdy are computed using local differencing, but the exact accuracy of computations is not specified. Using some carefully chosen test patterns, we have found that for each 2×2 block of pixels that is getting rasterized, the dFdx and dFdy instructions return the same value for pixel blocks of size 2×1 and 1×2, respectively. The same appears to be true for the ddx_fine and ddy_fine functions in HLSL. Assuming C is the chrominance (C_o or C_g) that is stored on each pixel, it is easy to see that we can effectively compute $[C_o \ C_g]$ with the following code snippet:

```
bool isBlack = ((crd.x&1)==(crd.y&1));
vec2 tmp = (isBlack)? vec2(C,0): vec2(0,C);
vec2 CoCg = abs(dFdx(tmp));
```

where crd are the integer coordinates of each pixel. In this case the missing chrominance has beed copied from the horizontal neighbor, but the same principle can be applied in the vertical direction, using the dFdy instruction. Using this approach, we can read the missing chrominance from the two neighbors that fall in the same 2×2 rasterization block, without even touching the memory subsystem of the GPU, thus reducing the total fetches required to implement Equation (4.2) from five to three.

This reduction of fetches did not yield any measurable performance increase in our test cases. The results of course depend on the nature of each particular application and the underlying GPU architecture, therefore we still discuss this low-level optimization because it could be valuable in applications with different workloads or different GPU architectures. Another option is to feed Equation (4.2) with only the two neighbors that fall in the same 2×2 rasterization block, thus completely avoiding any redundant fetches. We have found, however, that the quality of this implementation is not always satisfactory, since in the worst case the required chrominance information will be located in the two missing neighbors.

4.5   Antialiasing

When rendering to a multisample framebuffer with our technique, each pixel will contain either multiple chroma orange (C_o) samples or multiple chroma green (C_g) samples, but never a mixture of both. Therefore, the framebuffer can be resolved as usual, before applying the demosaic filter of Section 4.4. The only restriction is that the reconstruction filter for the resolve should not be wider than one pixel, in order to avoid incorrectly mixing C_o and C_g samples. This means that a custom resolve pass should be used in case the automatic resolve operation of the hardware uses a wider filter. This is hardly objectionable, since custom resolve is also required in order to perform tone mapping on the samples before the resolve, as required for high-quality antialiasing. We should also note that if wider reconstruction filters are desirable, they can be used in the luminance channel only, which is perceptually the most important.

4.6   Blending

Since all operations in the RGB to YC_oC_g transform are linear, blending can be performed directly in the YC_oC_g color space. Therefore, our method directly supports hardware framebuffer blending, without any modification. This is particularly the case when rendering to floating-point render targets, but fixed-point rendering requires some attention.

When rendering to unsigned fixed-point render targets, as noted in Section 4.2, we have added a bias of 0.5 in the chrominance values, in order to keep them positive, since these buffers do not support signed values. This does not create any problems with traditional alpha blending, since the bias will always remain 0.5 and can be easily subtracted when converting back to RGB. Nevertheless, when using other blending modes, such as *additive blending*, the bias will be accumulated and will create clamping artifacts. Furthermore, when additive blending is used to accumulate N fragments, we should subtract $0.5N$ from the chrominance in the framebuffer, but in many cases N is either unknown or difficult to compute. One possible solution is to perform the blending operation inside the shader, in the correct $[-0.5, 0.5]$ range, by reading and writing to the same render target (using the `texture_barrier` extension), but this approach is limited to specific platforms and use cases. However, this limitation only concerns certain blending modes on unsigned 8-bit render targets. High-quality rendering usually requires HDR formats, which are trivially handled by our method.

4.7   Performance

Before providing any GPU measurements, it is worth investigating the theoretical gains from our method. For a visible fragment, the GPU has to read the old 32-bit depth value from the Z-buffer in order to perform the depth test, and then it has to write back the new depth and color information. When blending is enabled, the old color should also be fetched. Based on this theoretical analysis, we can calculate that, for a 16-bit half-float render target, our technique reduces the bandwidth consumption by 25% without blending and by 33% when blending is enabled. We should note that all our measurements and analysis include a depth buffer, since in practice rasterization without a Z-buffer is not very common.

To examine how these theoretical gains translate in practice, we have measured the fill rate during rasterization. The fill rate measures how fast the GPU

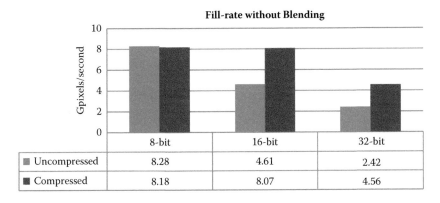

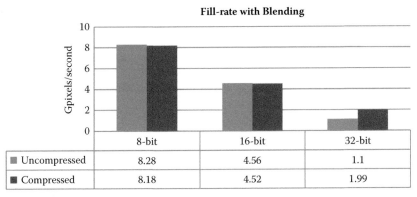

Figure 4.6. Fill-rate measurements (in gigapixels per second) when using the compressed framebuffer to perform forward rendering.

can rasterize pixels, and it is directly proportional to the available framebuffer bandwidth and the number of bits emitted for each pixel. Figure 4.6 shows the actual measurements on an Nvidia GTX 460 with 768 MB of memory (192-bit bus). The compressed framebuffer uses two output channels, while the uncompressed one uses four channels, since three-channel formats are not valid render targets due to memory alignment restrictions.

Our measurements indicate an impressive 75% fill-rate increase when rendering with half-float precision without blending, confirming our theoretical analysis. On the other hand, when blending is enabled on a half-float render target, we could not measure any gain, perhaps indicating some limitation in the flexibility of the render-output units in this specific GPU architecture. When using a 32-bit floating-point render target, our measurements demonstrate the expected increase in the fill rate when blending is both enabled and disabled, but this format is rarely used to store color information. In the 8-bit case we did not measure any

	8-bit	16-bit	32-bit
Uncompressed	0.55 ms	0.75 ms	1.01 ms
Compressed	0.56 ms	0.56 ms	0.78 ms
Speedup	0.98 ×	1.33 ×	1.29 ×

Table 4.1. The time in milliseconds for blitting a 720p render target to the GPU back buffer.

fill-rate increase, indicating that the 8-bit two-channel format (`GL_RG8`) is handled internally as a four-channel format (`GL_RGBA8`).

For the measurements above, we have used a typical fill-rate benchmark application that renders large visible quads on a render target. For the compressed case, the application also performs the compression and decompression of the render target. The results of course will be different on other GPU architectures, but generally we can expect that the performance increase due to the bandwidth reduction outweighs the small increase in the ALU instructions used to encode and decode the color. Although many applications are shader or geometry limited, an increase in the fill rate is always welcomed, especially when rendering particles and other fill-rate-intensive content.

Another operation worth investigating is the time it takes to uncompress and copy (blit) a compressed render buffer to the GPU back buffer. This operation is performed in our tests by rendering a full screen quad that uses the render buffer as a texture. When using a half-float format, resolving a compressed 720p render buffer takes 0.19 ms, which is 25% faster than the uncompressed case. Table 4.1 has the complete measurements for the other precisions too. As noted before, our desktop GPU does not internally support a two-channel 8-bit format, thus in this case our measuements show only the decompression overhead.

Of course, aside from any performance and bandwidth gains, the memory saved by our method can be used to improve other aspects of an application, such as the textures or the meshes. As an example, an uncompressed 1080p render target with 8× MSAA requires 189 MB of storage at 16-bit half-float precision, while with our method it requires only 126 MB. Both numbers include the Z-buffer storage.

4.8   Conclusion and Discussion

In this chapter we have presented a practical framebuffer compression scheme based on the principles of chrominance subsampling. Using our method, color images can be rasterized directly using only two framebuffer channels. The memory footprint of the framebuffer is reduced along with the consumed bandwidth, and as a consequence the fill rate of the GPU rasterizer is significantly increased.

Our solution is simple to implement and can work in commodity hardware, like game consoles. In particular, the memory architecture of the Xbox 360 game console provides a good example of the importance of our method in practice. The Xbox 360 provides 10 MB of extremely fast embedded memory (EDRAM) for the storage of the framebuffer. Every buffer used for rendering, including the intermediate buffers in deferred pipelines and the Z-buffer, should fit in this space. To this end, our technique can be valuable in order to fit more data in this fast memory. Bandwidth savings are also extremely important in mobile platforms, where memory accesses will drain the battery.

Our method was largely influenced by the way most digital cameras capture color images, where a mosaic of color filters is arranged in front of a single layer of monochromatic photo receptors, forming the so-called *Bayer pattern* [Bayer 76]. In fact, in our method we have also tried to use the Bayer pattern, instead of the pattern in Figure 4.2, something that would reduce the storage requirements down to a single channel, but in our experiments we were not satisfied by the robustness and the worst-case quality of this rather aggressive encoding format.

A rather obvious limitation of our method is that it can only be used to store intermediate results and not the final device framebuffer, because the hardware is not aware of our custom format. However, this does not limit the usefulness of our method, since most modern real-time rendering pipelines use many intermediate render buffers before writing to the back buffer.

In the supplemental material of this article, the interested reader can find a complete proof-of-concept implementation of our method in WebGL. Since the method consists of a few lines of code, it should be rather trivial to integrate it on any existing rendering pipeline.

4.9   Acknowledgments

We would like to thank Stephen Hill (Ubisoft Montreal) for his helpful and very insightful comments on the technique. Dimitrios Christopoulos (FHW) was kind enough to proofread our chapter and suggest various improvements. The Citadel dataset, used in many figures of this chapter, is from the publicly available Unreal Development Kit (UDK) from Epic Games. This work was not endorsed by Epic Games. We would also like to thank Emil Persson for providing the source of his HDR demo with a permissive license, allowing very quick testing for our method.

Bibliography

[Bayer 76] Bryce Bayer. "Color Imaging Array." United States Patent 3971065, 1976.

[Malvar and Sullivan 03] Henrique Malvar and Gary Sullivan. "YCoCg-R: A Color Space with RGB Reversibility and Low Dynamic Range." White paper,

Joint Video Team (JVT) of ISO/IEC MPEG & ITU-T VCEG, Document No. JVTI014r3, 2003.

[Owens 05] John Owens. "Streaming Architectures and Technology Trends." In *GPU Gems 2: Programming Techniques, Tips, and Tricks for Real-Time Graphics*, edited by Matt Pharr, pp. 457–470. Reading, MA: Addison-Wesley, 2005.

[Salvi and Vidimče 12] Marco Salvi and Kiril Vidimče. "Surface Based Anti-Aliasing." In *Proccedings of the ACM SIGGRAPH Symposium on Interactive 3D Rendering and Games*, pp. 159–164. New York: ACM, 2012.

[White and Barre-Brisebois 11] John White and Colin Barre-Brisebois. "More Performance! Five Rendering Ideas from *Battlefield 3* and *Need For Speed: The Run*." SIGGRAPH Course: Advances in the Real-Time Rendering in Games, SIGGRAPH 2011, Vacouver, Canada, August 8, 2011.

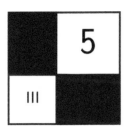

Coherence-Enhancing Filtering on the GPU

Jan Eric Kyprianidis and Henry Kang

5.1 Introduction

Directional features and flow-like structures are pleasant, harmonic, or at least interesting to most humans [Weickert 99]. They are also a highly sought-after property in many of the traditional art forms, such as painting and illustration. Enhancing directional coherence in the image helps to clarify region boundaries and features. As exemplified by Expressionism, it also helps to evoke mood or ideas and even elicit emotional response from the viewer [Wikipedia 12]. Particular examples include the works of van Gogh and Munch, who have emphasized these features in their paintings. This chapter presents an image and video abstraction technique that places emphasis on enhancing the directional coherence of features. It builds upon the idea of combining diffusion with shock filtering for image abstraction, but is, in a sense, contrary to that of [Kang and Lee 08], which is outperformed in terms of speed, temporal coherence, and stability. Instead of simplifying the shape of the image features, the aim is to preserve the shape by using a curvature-preserving smoothing method that enhances coherence. More specifically, smoothing is performed in the direction of the smallest change (Figure 5.1(a)), and sharpening in the orthogonal direction (Figure 5.1(b)). Instead of modeling this process by a partial differential equation (PDE) and solving it, approximations that operate as local filters in a neighborhood of a pixel are used. Therefore, good abstraction results can be achieved in just a few iterations, making it possible to process images and video at real-time rates on a GPU. It also results in a much more stable algorithm that enables temporally-coherent video processing. Compared to conventional abstraction approaches, such as [Winnemöller et al. 06, Kyprianidis et al. 10], the presented method provides a good balance between the enhancement of directional features and the smoothing of isotropic regions. As shown in Figure 5.2, the technique preserves and enhances

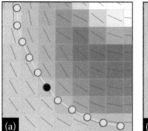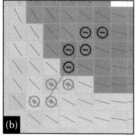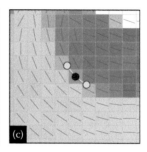

Figure 5.1. Illustration of the different key techniques employed in the presented algorithm. (a) Flow-guided smoothing for simplification and abstraction. (b) Shock filtering to preserve and enhance sharp edge transitions. (c) Edge smoothing for antialiasing.

directional features while increasing contrast, which helps to clarify boundaries and features. This chapter follows up on a technical paper [Kyprianidis and Kang 11] presented at Eurographics 2011 and provides an in-depth discussion of implementation details, including a few enhancements. For a discussion of related work and comparisons with other techniques, the interested reader is referred to the technical paper. The implementation is based on CUDA, and pitch linear memory is used for all image data. This has the advantage that image data is directly accessible on the device for reading and writing but can be bound to textures as well.

A schematic overview of the presented technique is shown in Figure 5.3. Input is given by a grayscale or color image (RGB color space is used for all examples). The algorithm runs iteratively and stops after a user-defined number of iterations,

Figure 5.2. Examples created by the technique described in this chapter.

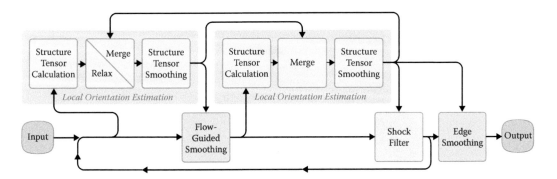

Figure 5.3. Schematic overview of the presented algorithm.

controlling the strength of the abstraction. For each iteration, adaptive flow-guided smoothing (Figure 5.1(a)) and sharpening (Figure 5.1(b)) are performed. Both techniques require information about the local structure, which is obtained by an eigenvalue analysis of the smoothed structure tensor and computed twice for every iteration, once before the smoothing and again before the sharpening. With every iteration, the result becomes closer to a piecewise-constant image, with large smooth or even flat image regions where no distinguished orientation is defined. Since having valid orientations defined for these regions is important for the stability of the algorithm, the structure tensor from the previous calculation is used in this case. For the first calculation, where no result from a previous computation is available, a relaxation of the structure tensor is performed. As a final step, edges are smoothed by flow-guided smoothing with a small filter kernel (Figure 5.1(c)). In the following sections, the different stages of the algorithm are examined in detail.

5.2 Local Orientation Estimation

To guide the smoothing and shock-filtering operations, the dominant local orientation at each pixel must be estimated. For smooth grayscale images with nonvanishing derivative, a reasonable choice are the local orientations given by tangent spaces of the isophote curves (i.e., curves with constant gray value). Since for smooth images the gradient is perpendicular to the isophote curves, the local orientations can easily be derived from the gradient vectors by rotating them 90 degrees (Figure 5.4). Unfortunately, real images are seldom smooth, and computation of the gradient is highly sensitive to noise and other image artifacts. This is illustrated in Figure 5.5(a), where an image with single dominant orientation is shown. Since it is sufficiently smooth, all gradient vectors induce the same orientation. Adding a small amount of Gaussian noise, however, results in noisy gradients and a poor orientation estimation, as shown in Figure 5.4(b).

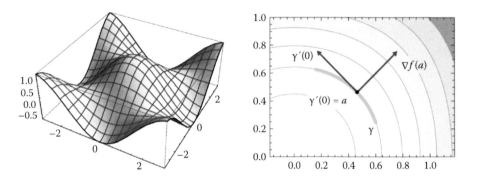

Figure 5.4. Plots of the function $f(x) = \cos(x_1)\cos(x_2)$. On the left, a 3D plot is shown. The contour plot on the right shows various level sets and illustrates that, for regular level sets, the gradient is orthogonal to the tangent of curves locally parameterizing the level set.

A possible solution is to regularize the gradient computation by, for example, smoothing the image prior to derivative computation or using Gaussian derivatives. However, since such approaches also remove high-frequency anisotropic image structures, such as hair, they are generally not suitable for our purpose. Instead, averaged gradient vectors in the least-squares sense will be computed, leading to the structure tensor [Brox et al. 06]—a well-known tool in computer vision.

5.2.1   Smoothed Structure Tensor

For each point x of a grayscale image, let $g(x)$ be the gradient vector at x computed by convolving the image with a suitable derivative operator. As explained earlier, for typical images, these gradients are not sufficiently smooth for our purposes. Simply smoothing the gradient vectors is not an option, since gradient vectors have opposite signs in the neighborhood of extrema and would cancel each other out (Figure 5.5). Hence, a more sophisticated approach is required. For instance, one can seek a vector that approximates the gradient vectors in a neighborhood. To measure how well a unit vector v approximates a gradient vector $g(x)$, the scalar product $\langle g(x), v \rangle$ may be used, which can be interpreted as the length of the projection of $g(x)$ on v. By squaring the scalar product, the measure becomes independent of the sign of the gradient vectors. Moreover, multiplying with a spatially varying weight gives less influence to gradients that are farther away. Hence, the wanted unit vector is a vector whose sum of weighted scalar products is maximal:

$$\mathrm{v}(x) = \operatorname*{arg\,max}_{\|v\|=1} \frac{1}{|G_\rho|} \cdot \sum_{y \in \mathcal{N}(x)} G_\rho(y - x)\, \langle g(y), v \rangle^2. \tag{5.1}$$

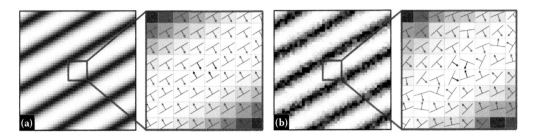

Figure 5.5. For smooth images with strong dominant local orientation, such as the one shown in (a), local orientation may be estimated using the gradient. However, if the image is corrupted by noise, as shown in (b), the gradients are noisy and require further processing. Notice that gradients in the neighborhood of extrema have opposite signs and would cancel each other out if processed with a smoothing filter.

For the spatial weight, a two-dimensional Gaussian function,

$$G_\rho(x) = \frac{1}{2\pi\rho^2} \exp\left(-\frac{\|x\|^2}{2\rho^2}\right),$$

with standard deviation ρ is used. The set $\mathcal{N}(x)$ refers to a local neighborhood of x with reasonable cutoff (e.g., with radius 3ρ), and $|G_\rho| = \sum_{y \in \mathcal{N}(x)} G_\rho(y - x)$ denotes the corresponding normalization term.

Equation (5.1) cannot be solved directly, but rewriting the scalar product $\langle g(y), v \rangle$ in matrix form as $g(y)^T v$ and utilizing the symmetry of the scalar product, yields

$$v(x) = \underset{\|v\|=1}{\arg\max} \; \frac{1}{|G_\rho|} \cdot \sum_{y \in \mathcal{N}(x)} G_\rho(y - x) \, v^T g(y) \, g(y)^T v.$$

Moreover, since v does not depend on y, it follows by linearity that

$$v(x) = \underset{\|v\|=1}{\arg\max} \; v^T J_\rho(x) \, v, \tag{5.2}$$

where

$$J_\rho(x) = \frac{1}{|G_\rho|} \cdot \sum_{y \in \mathcal{N}(x)} G_\rho(y - x) \, g(y) \, g(y)^T. \tag{5.3}$$

The outer product $g(x) \, g(x)^T$ is called the *structure tensor* at x, and $J_\rho(x)$ is called the *smoothed structure tensor* at x. Since it is a sum of outer products weighted by nonnegative coefficients, the smoothed structure tensor is a symmetric positive semidefinite 2×2 matrix. Therefore, from the Rayleigh-Ritz theorem [Horn and Johnson 85, Section 4.2], it follows that the solution of Equation (5.2) is given by the eigenvector associated with the major eigenvalue of

$J_\rho(x)$. The eigenvalues are real, since $J_\rho(x)$ is symmetric, and nonnegative, since $J_\rho(x)$ is positive semidefinite. The major eigenvalue measures the squared rate of change in the direction of the major eigenvector. Its square root can thus be regarded as a generalized gradient strength. The minor eigenvalue, on the other hand, can be regarded as a measure for the error of the approximation.

Up to now, only the case of grayscale images has been considered. The most straightforward way to extend the previous discussion to color images is by solving Equation (5.1) jointly for all color channels, resulting in the following generalization of Equation (5.3):

$$J_\rho(x) = \frac{1}{|G_\rho|} \cdot \sum_{y \in \mathcal{N}(x)} G_\rho(y - x) \sum_{i=1}^{n} g^i(y)\, g^i(y)^T,$$

where n is the number of color channels (i.e., $n = 3$ for RGB images) and $g^i(y)$ denotes the gradient of the ith color channel. Another convenient way to express the sum of outer products is as the scalar product of the partial derivatives:

$$\sum_{i=1}^{n} g^i(y)\, g^i(y)^T = \begin{pmatrix} \sum_{i=1}^{n}(g_1^i)^2 & \sum_{i=1}^{n} g_1^i g_2^i \\ \sum_{i=1}^{n} g_1^i g_2^i & \sum_{i=1}^{n}(g_2^i)^2 \end{pmatrix} = \begin{pmatrix} \langle g_1, g_1 \rangle & \langle g_1, g_2 \rangle \\ \langle g_1, g_2 \rangle & \langle g_2, g_2 \rangle \end{pmatrix}.$$

5.2.2 Eigenanalysis of the Structure Tensor

In this section, the way in which the eigenvalues and eigenvectors of the structure tensor, or more generally of a symmetric positive semidefinite 2×2 matrix

$$J = \begin{pmatrix} E & F \\ F & G \end{pmatrix},$$

can be computed in a numerically stable way will be discussed. Although a straightforward implementation leads to reasonable results, a carefully crafted implementation, as shown in Listing 5.1, is able to achieve much better accuracy by taking care of the numerical subtleties of floating-point calculations [Goldberg 91].

Being positive semidefinite implies that $E, G \geq 0$ and $EG \geq F^2$. Hence, from $E + G = 0$, it follows that $F = 0$, which means that the matrix is zero. Let us now assume that $E + G > 0$. Computation of the eigenvalues requires solving the characteristic polynomial $\det(A - I\lambda) = 0$, which is a quadratic equation, and the solution can be obtained using the monic form of the popular quadratic formula:

$$\lambda_{1,2} = \frac{1}{2}\left(E + G \pm \sqrt{(E + G)^2 - 4(EG - F^2)}\right).$$

The quadratic formula is known to have numerical issues when implemented in a straightforward manner. The subtractions are problematic, as they may result

```
inline __host__ __device__
void solve_eig_psd( float E, float F, float G, float& lambda1,
                    float& lambda2, float2& ev )
{
    float B = (E + G) / 2;
    if (B > 0) {
        float D = (E - G) / 2;
        float FF = F*F;
        float R = sqrtf(D*D + FF);
        lambda1 = B + R;
        lambda2 = fmaxf(0, E*G - FF) / lambda1;

        if (R > 0) {
            if (D >= 0) {
                float nx = D + R;
                ev = make_float2(nx, F) * rsqrtf(nx*nx + FF);
            } else {
                float ny = -D + R;
                ev = make_float2(F, ny) * rsqrtf(FF + ny*ny);
            }
        } else {
            ev = make_float2(1, 0);
        }
    } else {
        lambda1 = lambda2 = 0;
        ev = make_float2(1, 0);
    }
}
```

Listing 5.1. Eigenanalysis of a symmetric positive semidefinite 2×2 matrix.

in loss of accuracy due to cancelation. In case of the major eigenvalue, only the subtractions under the square root are an issue, because of the assumption that $E + G > 0$. The subtractions are best implemented as $(E - G)^2$, since then catastrophic cancelation is avoided and replaced with benign cancelation [Goldberg 91]:

$$\lambda_1 = \frac{E + G}{2} + R, \qquad R = \sqrt{\left(\frac{E - G}{2}\right)^2 + F^2}.$$

For the computation of the minor eigenvalue, we have to take care of the subtraction in front of the square root. A common approach is to use the property that the product of the eigenvalues equals its determinant [Goldberg 91]:

$$\lambda_2 = \frac{\det(J)}{\lambda_1} = \frac{EG - F^2}{\lambda_1}.$$

Notice that $\lambda_1 > 0$, since we assumed $E + G > 0$. Because of rounding errors, $EG - F^2$ may become negative, and therefore it is advisable to compute $\max(0, EG - F^2)$.

Recall that a symmetric matrix has orthogonal eigenvectors. Therefore, it is sufficient to compute only one of the eigenvectors, since the other can be found by rotating the vector 90 degrees. Let us first assume that the eigenvalues are distinct, which can be easily verified by checking that the square root R is nonzero. Under this assumption, we have a well-defined major eigenvector, which can be found by solving the following linear system:

$$(A - \lambda_1 I)v = \begin{pmatrix} E - \lambda_1 & F \\ F & G - \lambda_1 \end{pmatrix} \begin{pmatrix} v_1 \\ v_2 \end{pmatrix} = 0.$$

By construction, $A - \lambda I$ is singular, and therefore the two equations are linearly dependent. Hence, a solution of one equation will also be a solution of the other, providing us with two alternatives to choose from:

$$\eta_1 = \begin{pmatrix} F \\ \lambda_1 - E \end{pmatrix} = \begin{pmatrix} F \\ -\frac{E-G}{2} + R \end{pmatrix}, \qquad \eta_2 = \begin{pmatrix} \lambda_1 - G \\ F \end{pmatrix} = \begin{pmatrix} \frac{E-G}{2} + R \\ F \end{pmatrix}.$$

By choosing η_1 if $E - G < 0$ and η_2 if $E - G \geq 0$, we can kill two birds with one stone. Firstly, subtractive cancelation is avoided, since the first term in the sum is positive. Secondly, if $F = 0$ and, correspondingly, $R = |E - G|/2$, then the computed vector is guaranteed to be nonzero. Finally, if the square root R is zero, we have a single eigenvalue with multiplicity two, and the eigenspace is two-dimensional.

A limitation of the discussed implementation is that computations of the form $\sqrt{a^2 + b^2}$ may underflow or overflow if not computed at higher precision. A common approach to avoid such issues is to exchange a and b if necessary, such that $|a| > |b|$, and compute $|a|\sqrt{1 + (b/a)^2}$.

5.2.3   Structure Tensor Relaxation

In low-contrast regions, the signal-to-noise ratio is low, making the gradient information unreliable. Accordingly, the estimated orientation is almost random and of little value. However, appropriate orientation information is critical for the presented algorithm. Therefore, in this section an approach for replacing unreliable structure tensors will be discussed. As explained earlier, the square root of the major eigenvalue is a generalization of the gradient magnitude and can thus be used to identify points with reliable structure tensors

$$\partial\Omega = \{ \, x \in \Omega \mid \sqrt{\lambda_1} > \tau_r \, \}, \tag{5.4}$$

where τ_r is a control parameter. The idea is now to look for a smooth function s that interpolates the structure tensors S defined on $\partial\Omega$. Such a function is given by the membrane that minimizes

$$\arg\min_s \int_\Omega |\nabla s|^2 \, \mathrm{d}x \quad \text{with} \quad s|_{\partial\Omega} = S|_{\partial\Omega}.$$

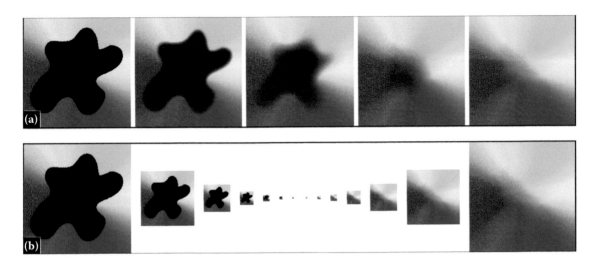

Figure 5.6. Solution of the Laplace equation. (a) Iterative solution using 100, 1,000, 5,000, and 50,000 Jacobi iterations. (b) Multiscale approach.

This problem is known to be equivalent to solving Laplace's equation $\Delta s = 0$ with the corresponding Dirichlet boundary condition $s|_{\partial\Omega} = S|_{\partial\Omega}$. Discretization of the Laplace operator yields a large sparse linear system of equations

$$\Delta s|_{i,j} \approx s_{i+1,j} + s_{i-1,j} + s_{i,j+1} + s_{i,j-1} - 4s_{i,j} = 0,$$

which may be solved using any technique for solving linear systems. One of the simplest approaches is to assume that in the ith equation only the ith parameter is unknown, leaving the other parameters fixed. Solving each of these equations independently and iterating the process converges to the solution and is known as the *Jacobi method*. More specifically, let $s_{i,j}^k$ denote the kth step's structure tensor at pixel (i, j); then a Jacobi relaxation step is given by

$$s_{i,j}^{k+1} = \begin{cases} s_{i,j}^k & \text{if } (i,j) \in \partial\Omega, \\ \dfrac{s_{i+1,j}^k + s_{i-1,j}^k + s_{i,j+1}^k + s_{i,j-1}^k}{4} & \text{otherwise.} \end{cases}$$

Since the computation involves a convex combination, the result is again a positive semidefinite matrix and, thus, is well-defined. Unfortunately, a very large number of iterations is typically required, which is demonstrated in Figure 5.6(a). Obtaining a sufficient approximation of the solution takes approximately 50,000 Jacobi iterations. Even on modern high-end GPUs, this takes several seconds to compute. The implementation of a Jacobi step is shown in Listing 5.2.

```
__global__ void jacobi_step( gpu_plm2<float4> dst ) {
    const int ix = blockDim.x * blockIdx.x + threadIdx.x;
    const int iy = blockDim.y * blockIdx.y + threadIdx.y;
    if (ix >= dst.w || iy >= dst.h) return;

    float4 st = tex2D(texST, ix, iy);
    if (st.w < 1) {
        st = make_float4((
                make_float3(tex2D(texST, ix+1, iy  )) +
                make_float3(tex2D(texST, ix-1, iy  )) +
                make_float3(tex2D(texST, ix,   iy+1)) +
                make_float3(tex2D(texST, ix,   iy-1))) / 4,
                0);
    }
    dst(ix, iy) = st;
}
```

Listing 5.2. Implementation of a Jacobi relaxation step.

Jacobi iterations are effective for removing high-frequency oscillations in the residual, but they perform rather poorly when the residual becomes smooth. Multigrid methods [Briggs et al. 00] address this issue by solving for the residual on a coarser level. A similar approach, which can be regarded as a simplified variant of a multigrid solver, where computation of the residual is avoided, is adopted here. As a first step, which structure tensors should be kept unmodified is determined using Equation (5.4). To this end, the fourth color channel is used, with one indicating a boundary pixel and zero used otherwise.

The reason why convergence of the Jacobi method is slow is illustrated in Figure 5.6(a). One Jacobi iteration computes the average of the neighboring pixels; consequently, it takes a large number of iterations until values on the boundary diffuse into the inner parts. Apparently, a simple way to speed up the diffusion is to compute it on a coarser grid. Since the transfer to a coarser grid can be repeated recursively, this yields a pyramid of images. Moving from a finer to a coarser level is referred to as *restriction*. The pixels on a coarser pyramid level are defined as the average of four pixels on the finer pyramid level, with nonboundary pixels being excluded (Figure 5.7(a)). The left of Figure 5.6(b) exemplifies the pyramid construction. Once the finest pyramid level is reached, the pyramid is processed in a coarse-to-fine manner. On each pyramid level, one to three Jacobi iterations are performed. Nonboundary pixels on the next-finer pyramid level are then replaced by sampling the result using bilinear interpolation. These operations are repeated until the finest pyramid level has been reached, as shown on the right of Figure 5.6(b). The implementations of the restriction and interpolation operations are shown in Listing 5.3 and 5.4.

Nevertheless, performing the relaxation for every computation of the structure tensor is expensive. Therefore, the relaxation is only performed for the first computation of the structure tensor. All subsequent computations substitute the structure tensor of the previous computation.

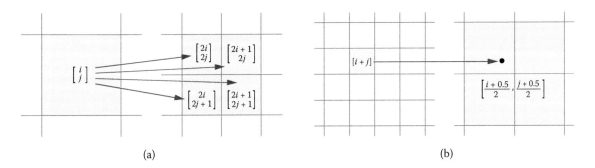

(a)   (b)

Figure 5.7. Illustration of the restriction and interpolation operations. (a) Restriction collapses four pixels into a single pixel by averaging those that are boundary pixels. (b) Interpolation is performed using bilinear interpolation.

```
__global__ void restrict( const gpu_plm2<float4> st,
                          gpu_plm2<float4> dst)
{
    const int ix = blockDim.x * blockIdx.x + threadIdx.x;
    const int iy = blockDim.y * blockIdx.y + threadIdx.y;
    if (ix >= dst.w || iy >= dst.h) return;

    float4 sum = make_float4(0);
    float4 tmp;
    tmp = st(2*ix,   2*iy  ); if (tmp.w > 0) { sum += tmp; }
    tmp = st(2*ix+1, 2*iy  ); if (tmp.w > 0) { sum += tmp; }
    tmp = st(2*ix,   2*iy+1); if (tmp.w > 0) { sum += tmp; }
    tmp = st(2*ix+1, 2*iy+1); if (tmp.w > 0) { sum += tmp; }
    if (sum.w > 0) sum /= sum.w;
    dst(ix, iy) = sum;
}
```

Listing 5.3. Implementation of the restiction operation.

```
__global__ void interpolate( const gpu_plm2<float4> st_fine,
                             gpu_plm2<float4> dst)
{
    const int ix = blockDim.x * blockIdx.x + threadIdx.x;
    const int iy = blockDim.y * blockIdx.y + threadIdx.y;
    if (ix >= dst.w || iy >= dst.h) return;

    float4 st = st_fine(ix, iy);
    if (st.w < 1) {
        st = make_float4(make_float3(
                tex2D(texST, 0.5f * (ix + 0.5f),
                             0.5f * (iy + 0.5f) )), 0);
    }
    dst(ix, iy) = st;
}
```

Listing 5.4. Implementation of the interpolation operation.

5.3   Flow-Guided Smoothing

Let $v\colon \mathbb{R}^2 \to \mathbb{R}^2$ be a vector field, and let (a, b) be an open interval. A curve $\gamma\colon (a, b) \to \mathbb{R}^2$ satisfying $\gamma'(t) = v(\gamma(t))$ for all $t \in (a, b)$ is called an *integral curve* or *stream line* of the vector field v. Taken together, the minor eigenvectors of the smoothed structure tensors at each pixel define a vector field, which is smooth up to a change of sign and closely aligned to image features. The general idea behind the flow-guided smoothing is to perform a filtering operation by following the minor eigenvectors through tracing the corresponding stream line. In contrast to the isophote curves of the image, the stream lines defined by the smoothed structure tensor are much smoother, and smoothing along them results in a regularization of the geometry of the isophote curves. The next section discusses the computation of the stream lines. Then, filtering along them will be examined. Finally, how to adjust adaptively the length of the stream lines used for filtering will be discussed.

5.3.1   Streamline Integration

Formally, finding the stream line $\gamma\colon (a, b) \to \mathbb{R}$ passing through a point x_0 of a vector field v can be described as solving the system of ordinary differential equations $\gamma'(t) = v(\gamma(t))$, $t \in (a, b)$ with initial condition $\gamma(t_0) = x_0$ for $t_0 \in (a, b)$. Several numerical techniques are available to solve such a system. For the presented algorithm, the second-order Runge-Kutta method is used, since it is simple to implement, achieves high-quality results, and has reasonable computational complexity. For pedagogical reasons, the simpler first-order Euler integration method is explained first. Taking the initial condition as a starting point, both methods operate iteratively, adding a new point with every step. Since for the computation of the smoothing operation at a point, a stream line passing through it is required, the integration has to be performed in forward and backward directions, as shown in Figure 5.8.

    If the considered vector field is given by the minor eigenvectors, special attention must be paid to their sign, since the structure tensor defines only orientation but no particular direction. This is due to the quadratic nature of the structure tensor. A straightforward way to define the sign of the minor eigenvectors is to

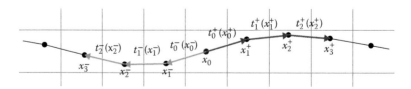

Figure 5.8. Integration of a stream line passing through a point x_0 is performed iteratively in forward and backward directions.

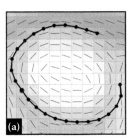 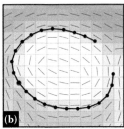 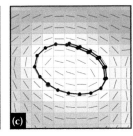 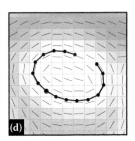

Figure 5.9. Illustrations of different stream line integration methods: (a) first-order Euler integration, (b) second-order Runge-Kutta, (c) second-order Runge-Kutta with fixed length, and (d) second-order Runge-Kutta with adaptive length.

choose the sign that minimizes the curvature of the stream line. This can be achieved by ensuring that the scalar product between the minor eigenvectors of the current and the previous steps is positive. More precisely, let x_0 be the current point, let $+$ and $-$ denote the forward and backward directions, respectively, and let $t_0^{\pm}(x_0) = \pm\xi(x_0)$; then, for $k \geq 0$, the next minor eigenvector is given by

$$t_{k+1}^{\pm}(x) = \mathrm{sign}\,\langle t_k^{\pm}, \xi(x)\rangle \cdot \xi(x),$$

where $\xi(x)$ denotes the minor eigenvector at the point x, computed using Listing 5.1. Let $x_0^{\pm} = x_0$, then for $k \geq 0$, a step with step size h of the Euler method is given by

$$x_{k+1}^{\pm} = x_k^{\pm} + h\,t_k^{\pm}(x_k).$$

At least for long stream lines, which are required by the flow-guided smoothing, the Euler method is comparatively inaccurate. This is illustrated in Figure 5.9(a). The Euler integration method smoothes pixels lying on adjacent isophote curves of the image. This corresponds to smoothing in the direction of the major eigenvector and a loss of information (Figure 5.10(a)). Therefore, instead of using the Euler integration method, the more precise second-order Runge-Kutta method is used, which traces stream lines at a higher accuracy (Figure 5.9(b)), reducing blurring across edges (Figure 5.10(c)). A step with step size h of the second-order Runge-Kutta method is given by

$$x_{k+1}^{\pm} = x_k^{\pm} + h\,t_k^{\pm}\left(x_k^{\pm} + \tfrac{h}{2}\,t_k^{\pm}(x_k)\right).$$

The second-order Runge-Kutta method requires values of the minor eigenvector for arbitrary positions. One option is to calculate these in one pass and then use nearest-neighbor sampling while tracing the stream lines. Bilinear interpolation of the eigenvectors is complicated, since opposite vectors may cancel each other out. A better approach is to sample the structure tensor directly using bilinear interpolation. This is more expensive, since the minor eigenvector has to be computed for every sample, but also provides clearly superior results.

Figure 5.10. Comparison of flow-guided smoothing using first-order Euler versus second-order Runge-Kutta stream line integration with and without shock filtering: (a) Euler, (b) Euler + shock filtering, (c) Runge-Kutta, and (d) Runge-Kutta + shock filtering.

5.3.2   Line Integral Convolution

Let $\gamma\colon (a,b) \to \mathbb{R}^2$ be a smooth curve, and let $f\colon \mathbb{R}^2 \to \mathbb{R}$ be a scalar field. Then the *line integral* of f along γ is defined by

$$\int_\gamma f \, \mathrm{d}s = \int_a^b f(\gamma(t)) \, \|\gamma'(t)\| \, \mathrm{d}t.$$

The factor $\|\gamma'(t)\|$ adjusts for the velocity of the curve's parameter and assures that the line integral is invariant under orientation-preserving reparameterizations. Based on this definition, the convolution of a scalar field with a one-dimensional function $g\colon \mathbb{R} \to \mathbb{R}$ along a curve can be defined:

$$(g *_\gamma f)(t_0) = \int_a^b g(t_0 - t) \, f(\gamma(t)) \, \|\gamma'(t)\| \, \mathrm{d}t. \tag{5.5}$$

If g is normalized, that is, $\int_a^b g(t) \, \mathrm{d}t = 1$, then the convolution above defines a weighted average of the values of f along the curve.

Now, let $v\colon \mathbb{R}^2 \to \mathbb{R}^2$ be a vector field consisting of normalized vectors. Then, for the vector field's stream lines, we have $\|\gamma'(t)\| = \|v(\gamma(t))\| = 1$, which is equivalent to an arc length parameterization. Overlaying the vector field with an image, the convolution along the stream line passing through the pixel can be computed for each pixel. This operation is known as *line integral convolution* and increases the correlation of the image's pixel values along the stream lines. When the convolution is performed over white noise, this yields an effective visualization technique for vector fields [Cabral and Leedom 93]. If the vector field is closely aligned with the image features, such as the minor eigenvector field of the smoothed structure tensor, convolution along stream lines effectively enhances the coherence of image features, while at the same time simplifying the image.

In order to implement line integral convolution, Equation (5.5) must be discretized. For the smoothing function, a one-dimensional Gaussian function G_{σ_s}

with standard deviation σ_s, is chosen. Since the stream lines become less accurate the longer they are, a comparatively short cutoff for the Gaussian function is used. The stream lines are truncated after two times the standard deviation rounded down to the next integer, $L = \lfloor 2\sigma_s \rfloor$, corresponding to approximately 95% of the weights. The integral is approximated by a sum of rectangle functions using the midpoint rule. Sampling of the image is thereby performed using bilinear filtering. Thus, if $x_L^-, \ldots, x_0, \ldots, x_L^+$ denote the stream line points obtained with step size h, as described in the previous section, then the result of the line integral convolution at x_0 is given by

$$\frac{1}{|G_{\sigma_s}|} \left[\sum_{k=1}^{L} G_{\sigma_s}(kh) f(x_k^-) + G_{\sigma_s}(0) f(x_0) + \sum_{k=1}^{L} G_{\sigma_s}(kh) f(x_k^+) \right],$$

where

$$|G_{\sigma_s}| = \sum_{k=1}^{L} G_{\sigma_s}(kh) + G_{\sigma_s}(0) + \sum_{k=1}^{L} G_{\sigma_s}(kh)$$

denotes the corresponding normalization term. The implementation is shown in Listing 5.5.

5.3.3 Adaptive Smoothing

In the previous section, the length of the stream lines used for smoothing was globally defined and proportional to the standard deviation of the Gaussian filter kernel. This may lead to issues in high-curvature regions, as illustrated in Figure 5.9(c). If the stream lines are too long, they may wrap around, resulting in some pixels being sampled more often than others. Moreover, due to rounding errors and inaccuracies in the stream line computation, adjacent isophotes may be sampled, which introduces additional blurring. To avoid these issues, the length of the stream lines and, correspondingly, the size of the Gaussian filter kernel must be controlled adaptively on a per-pixel basis. To this end, in [Kyprianidis and Kang 11] the standard deviation of the filter kernel was adjusted in relation to an anisotropy measure derived from the smoothed structure tensor. While this approach works reasonably well in practice, it is purely heuristic and its exact behavior is difficult to analyze. An alternative and more intuitive approach is therefore presented here.

Instead of adjusting the length of the stream lines in advance, their parameterization is adjusted by slowing down the parameter's velocity if necessary. To this end, the angle between the previous and the current steps' minor eigenvectors is computed:

$$\theta_k = \arccos \left\langle t_{k-1}^\pm(x_{k-1}^\pm), t_k^\pm(x_k^\pm) \right\rangle.$$

Taking the sum $\Theta = \sum_{i=1}^{k} \theta_i$ of the angles measures the cumulated angular change of the stream line. If $\Theta \geq \pi$, the stream line is likely to wrap around or is

```
inline __device__
float3 st_integrate_rk2( float2 p0, float sigma,
                         unsigned w, unsigned h,
                         float step_size, bool adaptive )
{
    float radius = 2 * sigma;
    float twoSigma2 = 2 * sigma * sigma;
    float3 c = make_float3(tex2D(texSRC, p0.x, p0.y));
    float sum = 1;

    float2 v0 = st_minor_ev(tex2D(texST, p0.x, p0.y));
    float sign = -1;
    float dr = radius / CUDART_PI_F;
    do {
        float2 v = v0 * sign;
        float2 p = p0;
        float u = 0;

        for (;;) {
            float2 t = st_minor_ev(tex2D(texST, p.x, p.y));
            if (dot(v, t) < 0) t = -t;

            float2 ph = p + 0.5f * step_size * t;
            t = st_minor_ev(tex2D(texST, ph.x, ph.y));
            float vt = dot(v, t);
            if (vt < 0) {
                t = -t;
                vt = -vt;
            }

            v = t;
            p += step_size * t;

            if (adaptive) {
                float delta_r = dr * acosf(fminf(vt,1));
                u += fmaxf(delta_r, step_size);
            } else
                u += step_size;

            if ((u >= radius) || (p.x < 0) || (p.x >= w) ||
                (p.y < 0) || (p.y >= h)) break;

            float k = __expf(-u * u / twoSigma2);
            c += k * make_float3(tex2D(texSRC, p.x, p.y));
            sum += k;
        }
        sign *= -1;
    } while (sign > 0);
    return c / sum;
}
```

Listing 5.5. Implementation of the flow-guided smoothing using second-order Runge-Kutta stream line integration.

comparatively noisy. In both cases, further extending it in the current direction is undesirable. However, simply stopping the tracing process corresponds to truncating the filtering operation and may introduce sampling artifacts. Instead, a better approach is to modify the stream line's parameter. To this end, the fraction traveled on a half-circle with arc length L can be considered for θ_k:

$$\Delta L_k = \frac{\theta_k}{\pi} L.$$

If ΔL_k is larger than the step size h, this indicates that the parameter of the arc-length parameterized stream line moves too fast, such that a larger step size is required, for which ΔL_k is used:

$$u_{k+1}^{\pm} = u_k^{\pm} + \max(h, \Delta L_k).$$

5.4 Shock Filter

The flow-guided smoothing discussed in the previous section is very aggressive. As shown in Figure 5.10(c), the overall shape of the image features is well preserved, but transitions between color regions are smoothed as well. In order to obtain sharp transitions at edges (Figure 5.10(d)), in this section deblurring by shock filtering will be discussed.

5.4.1 PDE-Based Shock Filter

In image processing, shock filters were first studied by [Osher and Rudin 90]. The classical shock filter evolution equation is given by

$$\frac{\partial u}{\partial t} = -\text{sign}\big(\mathcal{L}(u)\big)|\nabla u|,$$

with initial condition $u(x, 0) = I(x)$ and where $\mathcal{L}$ is a suitable detector, such as the Laplacian Δu or the second derivative in direction of the gradient. In the influence zone of a maximum, $\mathcal{L}(u)$ is negative, and therefore a local dilation with a disc as the structuring element is performed. Similarly, in the influence zone of a minimum, $\mathcal{L}(u)$ is positive, which results in local erosion. This sharpens the edges at the zero-crossings of Δu, as shown in Figure 5.11. Shock filters have the attractive property of satisfying a maximum principle and, in contrast to unsharp masking, therefore do not suffer from ringing artifacts.

Instead of the second derivative in the direction of the gradient, the second derivative in the direction of the major eigenvector of the smoothed structure tensor may be used. This was first proposed by [Weickert 03]. To achieve higher robustness against small-scale image details, the input image can be regularized with a Gaussian filter prior to second-derivative or structure-tensor computation.

Weickert's shock filter achieves excellent results in combination with the flow-guided smoothing, but one limitation is its performance. The filter is typically implemented using an explicit upwind scheme. In order to guarantee stability, the time step size has to be small and multiple iterations have to be performed.

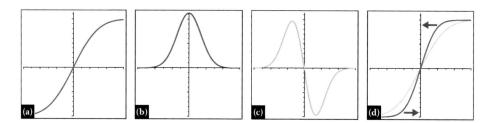

Figure 5.11. Illustration of shock filtering. (a) A smooth step edge. (b) First derivative of the edge. (c) Second derivative of the edge. (d) A shock filter applies a dilation where the second derivative is positive, and an erosion where it is negative, resulting in a sharpening effect.

For each iteration, first- and second-order derivatives, as well as the smoothed structure tensor, have to be calculated. Another limitation is that Weickert's shock filter introduces shocks in almost smooth regions, resulting in maze-like artifacts. The next section discusses an alternative approach.

5.4.2   Gradient-Directed Shock Filter

The idea in obtaining a fast shock filter implementation is to approximate the general working principle discussed earlier and illustrated in Figure 5.11. First, whether a pixel is in the neighborhood of a minimum or maximum is detected. Then, correspondingly, either an erosion or dilation is performed. Both operations are guided by the structure tensor.

Derivative operators are highly sensitive to noise, and sensitivity increases with order. Therefore, the second=derivative operator for the sign computation must be regularized to avoid artifacts. In addition, the regularization allows for artistic control over the resulting line thickness. Two strategies are at hand. First, the image can be isotropically smoothed prior to derivative computation, using a Gaussian filter with standard deviation σ_i. This helps to remove noise and allows for aggressive image simplification. Secondly, the smoothing and derivative operators can be consolidated into a single operator,since convolution and differentiation commute. Inspired by the flow-based difference of Gaussians filter, and its separable implementation [Kyprianidis and Döllner 09], the second-order derivative in direction of the major eigenvector is implemented by convolving the image locally with a one-dimensional (scale-normalized) second-order Gaussian derivative,

$$\sigma_g^2 G_{\sigma_g}''(t) = \sigma_g^2 \frac{\mathrm{d}^2 G_{\sigma_g}(t)}{\mathrm{d}t^2} = \frac{x^2 - \sigma_g^2}{\sqrt{2\pi}\sigma_g^3} \exp\left(-\frac{t^2}{2\sigma_g^2}\right),$$

in the direction of the minor eigenvector. This operation will be referred to as *flow-guided Laplacian of Gaussian* (FLoG). More specifically, let L be the input

```
__global__ void flog( const gpu_plm2<float4> st, float sigma,
                      gpu_plm2<float> dst )
{
    const int ix = blockDim.x * blockIdx.x + threadIdx.x;
    const int iy = blockDim.y * blockIdx.y + threadIdx.y;
    if (ix >= dst.w || iy >= dst.h) return;

    float2 n = st_major_ev(st(ix, iy));
    float2 nabs = fabs(n);
    float ds = 1.0f / ((nabs.x > nabs.y)? nabs.x : nabs.y);
    float2 uv = make_float2(ix + 0.5f, iy + 0.5f);

    float halfWidth = 5 * sigma;
    float sigma2 = sigma * sigma;
    float twoSigma2 = 2 * sigma2;

    float sum = -sigma2 * tex2D(texL, ix + 0.5f, iy + 0.5f);
    for( float d = ds; d <= halfWidth; d += ds ) {
        float k = (d*d - sigma2) * __expf( -d*d / twoSigma2 );
        float2 o = d*n;
        float c = tex2D(texL, uv.x - o.x, uv.y - o.y) +
                  tex2D(texL, uv.x + o.x, uv.y + o.y);
        sum += k * c;
    }

    sum = sum / (sqrtf(2*CUDART_PI_F) * sigma2 * sigma);
    dst(ix, iy) = sum;
}
```

Listing 5.6. Implementation of the FLoG filter.

image converted to grayscale, let $v = G_{\sigma_i} * L$, and let x_0 be the current pixel; then the convolution is computed by

$$z(x_0) = \sigma_g^2 \int G''_{\sigma_g}(t)\, v\big(x_0 + t\,\eta(x_0)\big)\, \mathrm{d}t,$$

where $\eta(x_0)$ denotes the major eigenvector. The implementation is shown in Listing 5.6. Evaluation of the integral is performed using a constant step size that has a unit size, along either the x- or the y-axis (Figure 5.12), and using bilinear

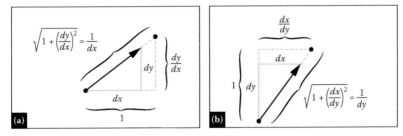

Figure 5.12. Computation of a step vector that has unit size in either horizontal or vertical directions. Two cases must be distinguished: (a) $dx > dy$ and (b) $dy > dx$.

```
__global__ void grad_shock( const gpu_plm2<float4> st,
                            const gpu_plm2<float> sign,
                            float radius,
                            gpu_plm2<float4> dst )
{
    const int ix = blockDim.x * blockIdx.x + threadIdx.x;
    const int iy = blockDim.y * blockIdx.y + threadIdx.y;
    if (ix >= dst.w || iy >= dst.h) return;

    minmax_impl_t mm(make_float2(ix + 0.5f, iy + 0.5f));
    float2 n = st_major_ev(st(ix, iy));
    float s = sign(ix, iy);
    if (s < 0) {
        mm.run<MAX_FLT>(n, radius);
    } else if (s > 0) {
        mm.run<MIN_FLT>(n, radius);
    }
    dst(ix, iy) = tex2D(texSRC, mm.p_.x, mm.p_.y);
}
```

Listing 5.7. Implementation of the gradient-directed shock filter.

interpolation. Due to the unit step size, this results in a linear interpolation of two neighboring pixels and allows for efficient implementation on GPUs using texturing hardware.

The erosion and dilation operations are implemented as directional neighborhood filters as well. Let f denote the input image, and let x_0 be the current point, then the gradient-directed shock filter is defined as

$$
\begin{cases}
\min_{x \in \Lambda_r(x_0)} f(x) & \text{if } z(x_0) > +\tau_s, \\
\max_{x \in \Lambda_r(x_0)} f(x) & \text{if } z(x_0) < -\tau_s, \\
f(x_0) & \text{otherwise.}
\end{cases}
$$

Determination of the minimum and maximum is performed based on the corresponding gray values. The filter neighborhood Λ_r is defined as the set of pixels with a distance less than r from x_0 intersecting the line $\{x_0 + \lambda\,\eta(x_0)\}$ defined by the major eigenvector. The implementation is shown in Listings 5.7 and 5.8. Again, a constant step size with a unit size in either horizontal or vertical direction is used. Bilinear interpolation, however, is not appropriate for the computation of the minimum or maximum; therefore, the two neighboring pixels are sampled explicitly, using nearest-neighbor sampling. Through a small correction of the sampling offset, the correct sampling of horizontal, vertical, and diagonal lines is assured as well.

For the radius, typically $r = 2$ is used. The parameter τ_s controls the sensitivity to noise and is typically set to $\tau_s \in [0, 0.01]$. Since a scale-normalized LoG is used, τ_s does not depend upon σ_g. The threshold effectively prevents

```
enum minmax_t { MIN_FLT, MAX_FLT };

struct minmax_impl_t {
    float2 uv_;
    float2 p_;
    float  v_;

    __device__ minmax_impl_t(float2 uv) {
        uv_ = p_= uv;
        v_ = tex2D(texL, uv.x, uv.y);
    }

    template <minmax_t T>
    __device__ void add(float2 p) {
        float L = tex2D(texL, p.x, p.y);
        if ((T == MAX_FLT) && (L > v_)) {
            p_ = p;
            v_ = L;
        }
        if ((T == MIN_FLT) && (L < v_)) {
            p_ = p;
            v_ = L;
        }
    }

    template <minmax_t T>
    __device__  void run( float2 n, float radius ) {
        float ds;
        float2 dp;

        float2 nabs = fabs(n);
        if (nabs.x > nabs.y) {
            ds = 1.0f / nabs.x;
            dp = make_float2(0, 0.5f - 1e-3);
        } else {
            ds = 1.0f / nabs.y;
            dp = make_float2(0.5f - 1e-3, 0);
        }

        for( float d = ds; d <= radius; d += ds ) {
            float2 o = d*n;
            add<T>(uv_ + o + dp);
            add<T>(uv_ + o - dp);
            add<T>(uv_ - o + dp);
            add<T>(uv_ - o - dp);
        }
    }
};
```

Listing 5.8. Implementation of the gradient-directed minimum and maximum filters.

the creation of shocks in almost smooth regions. The quality of the output is comparable to that of the coherence-enhancing shock filter, but computationally the gradient-directed shock filter is much more efficient. It only requires the smoothed structure tensor and the input image converted to grayscale. For the sake of simplicity, the FLoG and the minimum and maximum filters have been implemented independently, but they obviously could be implemented in a single pass as well. Moreover, the gradient-directed shock filter provides finer artistic control. The parameter σ_g restricts smoothing to the major eigenvector direction. This is especially useful for preserving small image features. To achieve a stronger abstraction, the isotropic smoothing parameter σ_i is useful.

5.5 Conclusion

In this chapter, an automatic technique for image and video abstraction, based on adaptively controlled flow-guided smoothing and directional shock filtering, was presented. It aggressively smoothes out unimportant image regions, but it protects important features by enhancing contrast and directional coherence, providing a good balance between content abstraction and feature enhancement consistently across the image. For abstraction at the level of the anisotropic Kuwahara filter, the GPU implementation processes video in real time and creates temporally coherent output without further processing.

5.6 Acknowledgments

Original photographs from flickr.com kindly provided under Creative Commons license by Tambako the Jaguar (Figure 5.2(a)) and Ivan Mlinaric (Figure 5.10). Original photograph in Figure 5.2(b) courtesy of Phillip Greenspun.

Bibliography

[Briggs et al. 00] W. L. Briggs, V. E. Henson, and S. F. McCormick. "A Multigrid Tutorial." Presentation, SIAM Annual Meeting, Rio Grande, Puerto Rio, July 2000.

[Brox et al. 06] T. Brox, R. van den Boomgaard, F. Lauze, J. van de Weijer, J. Weickert, P. Mrázek, and P. Kornprobst. "Adaptive Structure Tensors and Their Applications." In *Visualization and Processing of Tensor Fields*, edited by Joachim Weickert and Hans Hagen, pp. 17–47. Berlin: Springer, 2006.

[Cabral and Leedom 93] B. Cabral and L. C. Leedom. "Imaging Vector Fields Using Line Integral Convolution." In *Proceedings of the 20th Annual Conference on Computer Graphics and Interactive Techniques*, pp. 263–270. New York: ACM, 1993.

[Goldberg 91] D. Goldberg. "What Every Computer Scientist Should Know about Floating-Point Arithmetic." *ACM Computing Surveys* 23:1 (1991), 5–48.

[Horn and Johnson 85] R. A. Horn and C. R. Johnson. *Matrix Analysis.* Cambridge, UK: Cambridge University Press, 1985.

[Kang and Lee 08] H. Kang and S. Lee. "Shape-Simplifying Image Abstraction." *Computer Graphics Forum* 27:7 (2008), 1773–1780.

[Kyprianidis and Döllner 09] J. E. Kyprianidis and J. Döllner. "Real-Time Image Abstraction by Directed Filtering." In *ShaderX7: Advanced Rendering Techniques*, edited by W. Engel, pp. 285–302. Hingham, MA: Charles River Media, 2009.

[Kyprianidis and Kang 11] J. E. Kyprianidis and H. Kang. "Image and Video Abstraction by Coherence-Enhancing Filtering." *Computer Graphics Forum* 30:2 (2011), 593–602.

[Kyprianidis et al. 10] J. E. Kyprianidis, H. Kang, and J. Döllner. "Anisotropic Kuwahara Filtering on the GPU." In *GPU Pro: Advanced Rendering Techniques*, edited by W. Engel, pp. 247–264. Natick, MA: A K Peters, 2010.

[Osher and Rudin 90] S. Osher and L. I. Rudin. "Feature-Oriented Image Enhancement Using Shock Filters." *SIAM Journal on Numerical Analysis* 27:4 (1990), 919–940.

[Weickert 99] J. Weickert. "Coherence-Enhancing Diffusion of Colour Images." *Image and Vision Computing* 17:3 (1999), 201–212.

[Weickert 03] J. Weickert. "Coherence-Enhancing Shock Filters." In *Pattern Recognition: 25th DAGM Symposium, Magdeburg, Germany, September 10–12, 2003. Proceedings*, Lecture Notes in COmputer Science 2781, pp. 1–8. Berlin: Springer, 2003.

[Wikipedia 12] Wikipedia. "Expressionism". *Wikipedia—The Free Encyclopedia.*, http://en.wikipedia.org/wiki/Expressionism, 2012.

[Winnemöller et al. 06] H. Winnemöller, S. C. Olsen, and B. Gooch. "Real-Time Video Abstraction." *ACM Transactions on Graphics* 25:3 (2006), 1221–1226.

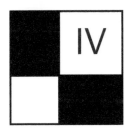

Shadows

Shadows are the dark companions of lights, and although both can exist on their own, they shouldn't exist without each other in games. Achieving good visual results in rendering shadows is considered one of the particularly difficult tasks of graphics programmers.

For this edition of GPU Pro, we accepted only one article for this section. The article "Real-Time Deep Shadow Maps" represents the state of the art in real-time deep shadow maps. The article covers an implementation that only requires a single rendering pass from the light without introducing any approximations. It covers a novel lookup scheme that exploits spatial coherence for efficient filtering of deep shadow maps.

—Wolfgang Engel

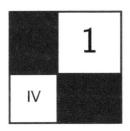

Real-Time Deep Shadow Maps

René Fürst, Oliver Mattausch, and Daniel Scherzer

In offline rendering the algorithm of choice for correctly shadowing transparent objects such as hair or smoke are *deep shadow maps* (DSMs). Algorithms trying to achieve the same effect in *real time* have hitherto always been limited to approximating the solution by depth-peeling techniques. Since the introduction of Direct3D 11, however, it has become feasible to implement the original algorithm using a single rendering pass from the light without introducing any approximations. In this chapter we discuss how to implement a DSM algorithm for rendering complex hair models that runs in real time on Direct3D 11 capable hardware, introducing a novel lookup scheme that exploits spatial coherence for efficient filtering of the deep shadow map.

1.1 Introduction

While real-time (soft) shadows are nowadays routinely used in games, correct shading and rendering of complex hair models, like the ones shown in Figure 1.1, remain nontrivial tasks that are hard to achieve with interactive or even real-time frame rates. The main problem is the complex visibility of hair with super-thin structures that easily creates reconstruction artifacts when using traditional shadow maps. Traditional shadow maps store the distances to the visible front as seen from the light source into each texel of a 2D texture. This means that only the nearest surfaces that block the light are captured. In a second step, a *binary* depth test is performed for each pixel that compares stored texel depth and pixel depth to determine if the pixel is either shadowed or not. While this works well for opaque objects, it has the disadvantage that transparent objects cannot be handled correctly, since every surface behind the visible front is assumed to be fully shadowed.

Shadowing of transparent objects is possible by computing the *percentage of light* that transmits through a material after taking the occlusion of all nearer surfaces along a ray into account. For each texel, a *deep shadow map* (DSM) [Lokovic and Veach 00] stores the transmitted amount of light as a function of

Figure 1.1. Hair models rendered with our real-time DSM algorithm.

depth (shown in Figure 1.2). In reality this amounts to a list of depth values
with associated transmittance stored for each texel. When rendering the scene
from the camera, the current depth value is searched and used as a lookup into
this transmittance function, and the corresponding remaining light is then used

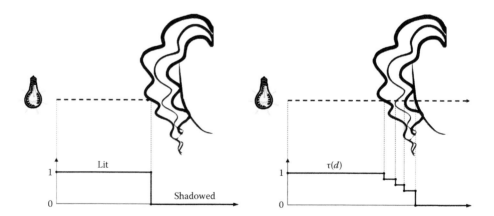

Figure 1.2. Visibility captured for one texel of a shadow map: For traditional shadow
mapping (left) only the visible front is captured, while DSMs (right) also account for
objects behind it. Here the transmittance function $\tau(d)$ stores the visibility along a ray
from the light source.

to correctly shade each pixel. A major part of this article describes how to store and to sort incoming fragments with Direct3D 11 in order to reconstruct the transmittance function and have a suitable representation that allows a fast lookup of the transmittance.

As with most shadow mapping algorithms, deep shadow mapping is also prone to aliasing artifacts. However, most of these artifacts can be overcome by adapting techniques that are also used for traditional shadow maps, e.g., percentage-closer filtering (PCF) [Reeves et al. 87]. We will show how DSMs can be filtered efficiently by exploiting spatial coherence among neighboring pixels. Furthermore, we extend this concept to allow filtering with *exponential shadow maps* (ESMs) [Annen et al. 08].

1.2 Transmittance Function

The major difference between traditional (binary) shadow maps and deep shadow maps is that for each *deep* shadow map test the transmittance function has to be evaluated for the current pixel's depth. Hence this function has to be created and stored first. Creation is made feasible for rasterization hardware by calculating transmittance out of surface opacities. The idea is to rasterize all geometry as seen from the point of view of the light, storing not only the first depth but also all depths (and associated opacities) in a list for each texel. After sorting these lists by depth, the transmittance at a certain depth d at a given texel location can be calculated out of the opacities α_i of all list entries with depth smaller than d (see Figure 1.2) by

$$\tau(d) = \prod_{i=0}^{n(d)} (1 - \alpha_i), \tag{1.1}$$

where $n(d)$ is the number of fragments before depth d. During shadow lookups, the depth of the current fragment can then be used to look up the correct shading value (i.e., percentage of light transmitted) for shadowing the pixels. In the next section we will show how to create and store such a function efficiently on Direct3D 11 hardware.

1.3 Algorithm

Our algorithm can be divided into the following steps:

- Creating list entries. The scene is rendered from the light source. The alpha value and depth value of *all* incoming fragments are stored in a two-dimensional structure of linked lists. Note that the sizes of the linked lists are only limited by video memory, which allows us to store transmittance functions of varying depth complexity.

- **Processing the fragments**. The fragments are sorted, and the transmittance functions are precomputed for the fragment depths from the individual alpha values (using Equation (1.1)) to allow a fast lookup into the transfer function. Finally the transmittance functions are simplified.

- **Neighbor linking**. For each fragment, the neighboring fragments at the same position in the linked lists are also linked, in order to quickly find those neighboring fragments that are nearest in terms of depth to the light source and achieve quicker filtering.

- **Deferred shadowing**. DSM lookups can become quite expensive for complex hair models (i.e., with big depth complexity and transmittance functions with many stored values). Hence, deferred shading is used to render the scene first and then compute the shading value *only once* for each pixel during deferred shading.

- **Spatial filtering**. At this point, we utilize neighbor links to provide fast lookups for large filter kernels. The DSM idea is combined with two well-known filtering methods for binary shadow maps.

The first three steps can be summarized as building up the DSM structure from the light; the last two steps apply the DSM for the final shading from the camera. Each of these steps will be discussed in more detail in the following sections.

1.3.1 Creating List Entries

One of the main issues for implementing DSMs on a modern GPU is that the amount of per-texel data is dependent on the depth complexity of the scene at the texel position and therefore can vary arbitrarily. In Direct3D 11, this problem can be solved by storing the depth and alpha values of *every* incoming fragment along a light ray in a per-texel linked list. In total each linked list element has the format shown in Listing 1.1. There, `next` represents the index of the next element of a linked list, and it contains -1 if the current element is the last element of the linked list. We also store additional links to the previous element links (making it a double-linked list) to fragments from neighboring pixels that come to use later on.

We create a two-level structure to be able to efficiently insert all fragments into these linked lists during a single rendering pass from the light. All fragments in the linked lists are stored in a structure that we denote as the *list element buffer*. For every pixel, we store the index of the first list element in each linked list in a separate buffer that we denote as the *head buffer*, since it points to the first element of a list. If a linked list corresponding to a shadow map texel is empty, the value -1 is stored in the head buffer. An example is shown in Figure 1.3.

```
struct LinkedListEntry
{
  float depth;
  float alpha;

  int next; // next element in linked list
  int prev; // previos element in linked list

  int right; // right neighbor link
  int upper; // upper neighbor link
};
```

Listing 1.1. Linked list entry structure.

In this example the elements 1 and 6 (2 and 5, respectively) form a single linked list, and the first elements 1 and 2 are stored in the head buffer.

Both structures (head buffer and list element buffer) are stored as Direct3D 11 (RW)StructuredBuffers and filled by rendering the geometry once using interlocked operations and the buffer counter in the pixel shader. InterlockedExchange is used to exchange the head of the linked list to ensure that we do not face any problems regarding parallelization. The buffer counter is used to "allocate" linked list

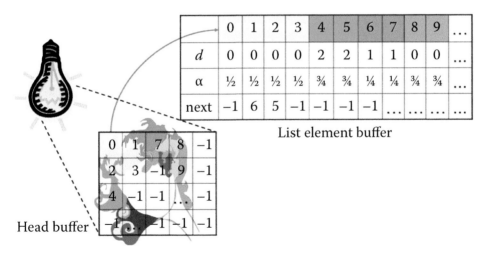

Figure 1.3. We implemented the DSMs as a two-level structure that consists of a per-pixel buffer storing the head of each linked list (head buffer) and the list element buffer for all incoming fragments. For each fragment, we store depth and alpha values, as well as indices of the next and the previous elements, and nearest-depth neighbor links (only the **next** index is shown here for brevity).

```
void ps_main(PS_IN input)
{
  // Allocate a new element in the list element buffer by
  // atomically incrementing the buffer counter.
  int counter = listElementBuffer.IncrementCounter();

  // Store the required information and apply a depth bias.
  listElementBuffer[counter].depth = input.posToShader.z + bias;
  listElementBuffer[counter].alpha = input.alpha;

  //pixel screen coordinate to buffer index
  int index = (int)(input.pos.y * Width + input.pos.x);

  int originalVal;
  // Atomically exchange the element in the head buffer.
  InterlockedExchange(headBuffer[index], counter, originalVal);

  // Create the link to the existing list.
  listElementBuffer[counter].next = originalVal;
}
```

Listing 1.2. Concurrent way of adding a new fragment to the list element buffer and updating the head buffer in a pixel shader.

elements in parallel. The pixel shader for filling both head buffer and list element buffer with a new incoming fragment is shown in Listing 1.2.

1.3.2 Processing the Fragments

Note that up to now the list entries neither are sorted nor contain the final transmittance. These processing tasks are the purpose of this step. The sorting of all fragments with respect to their depth is done in a separate compute shader (executed for every pixel). We load a single linked list per pixel into a local array and do a local sort, which does not require any shared memory. Since neither compute shaders nor OpenCL support recursion yet, a sorting algorithm like quick sort is not very well suited to the GPU architecture. Instead we use *insertion sort* due to its simplicity and because it is known to be very fast on small arrays (as is the case for models with reasonable depth complexity). This fact was confirmed in our experiments, where insertion sort yielded about two times the performance of a nonrecursive version of quick sort. Next we convert the alpha values in the linked list into a transmittance function according to Equation (1.1). This means that we pre-multiply transmittance for each of the depths d_i from the linked list and store the transmittance at each fragment instead of the alpha values. Note that this step is done to accelerate spatial coherent lookups for filtering later on. Here, having to traverse the list from the head to reconstruct the transmittance for each filter sample is exactly what we want to avoid. Furthermore, the `prev` links are stored in this step of the algorithm in order to create a double-linked list.

To accelerate the lookup time, we have to simplify the transmittance function. In the case of volume data, a sophisticated algorithm for handling the inclination of the transmittance function has been proposed in the original DSM paper [Lokovic and Veach 00]. In the case of hair rendering, however, we deal with a simple, piecewise constant version of the transmittance function. Hence, it turned out that a simple but efficient optimization strategy is to merely cut off the transmittance function after its value does not change significantly any more, i.e., if $\prod_{i=0}^{k+1}(1 - \alpha_i) - \epsilon < \prod_{i=0}^{k}(1 - \alpha_i)$. In our experiments the frame time has been improved by approximately 40% using an ϵ of 0.001, which does not visibly compromise the quality of the shadows. Note that a more sophisticated GPU-friendly compression scheme has been proposed by Salvi et al. [Salvi et al. 10] that limits the transmittance functions to a fixed size and works for shadowing both hair and participating media. This method could alternatively be used instead of the simple truncation, and we believe that it would work well in combination with our neighbor-linking approach (possibly further accelerating the lookup time).

1.3.3   Neighbor Linking

In this step we store links with each entry (fragment) of a linked list to those entries (fragments) in the neighboring linked lists that are closest to it in terms of light-space depth. The reasoning behind this step is that for adjacent pixels in screen space, it's very likely that they have approximately the same depth in light space due to spatial coherence. During filtering, the links enable direct access to the depth-nearest neighbors of a fragment in the DSM. Once we found a fragment corresponding to a given light-space depth, the other corresponding fragments of nearby filter samples can be found very quickly. Note that we only create links for the great majority of pixels where the assumption of coherence of depth values holds.

In order to keep the memory overhead as low as possible, *only* links to the left and upper neighbor are stored. This suffices for computing all other filter samples when starting from the lower-left corner of a rectangular filtering window. For creating the links, in each thread (note that there is one thread for each shadow-map texel) we simultaneously traverse the linked list associated with the texel in question as well as the lists associated with the right texel neighbor and the upper texel neighbor. For each fragment, we traverse each neighboring list until we either find a fragment that is farther in depth or encounter the end of the list. Then, either the last traversed or the previously traversed neighboring fragment will be the one that is closest in depth to the current fragment. We link the current fragment to its depth-nearest neighbors by storing their indices, which we denote **right** and **upper** for each list element. The expense of storing three additional integers per list element (the two neighbor links and the **prev** link) increases the overall memory requirements by about 25%, but this pays off during filtering as will become clear in Section 1.3.5.

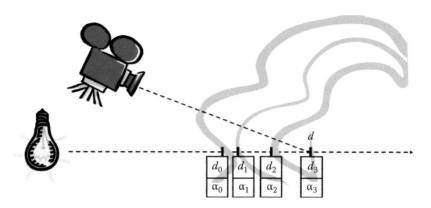

Figure 1.4. To calculate the transmittance for a DSM test evaluation, the opacities α_i of all the surfaces that are nearer than the current pixel's depth d have to be multiplied.

1.3.4   Deferred Shadowing

In the shadowing stage, we search for the depth in the transmittance function, which corresponds to the depth of the current pixel in the eye view (see Figure 1.4). This is done by front-to-back traversal of the linked list corresponding to the current position in the xy-plane. The head of the list is accessed by looking it up in the head buffer. A lookup of the corresponding element in the transmittance function gives the correct transmittance value, which is used to attenuate the shading.

An important point for stabilizing the frame rate and to achieve real-time frame rates is to use a deferred shading pipeline for shadowing. This means that we first render the geometry to store depth and diffuse shading values in render targets before using a single shadow lookup per pixel in the deferred shadowing pass. Consider that with forward rendering, the depth complexity of a hair model potentially requires multiple costly shadow lookups per pixel (and even more when using PCF).

1.3.5   Spatial filtering

Spatial antialiasing is as important for DSM as it is for binary shadow maps in order to achieve high-quality images (see Figure 1.6). Contrary to standard filtering methods for binary shadow maps (e.g., using PCF), we now deal with a list of depth values per pixel. In our case, these depth values are not samples but represent the full transmittance function as it is, which means that we do not need to deal with reconstruction or filtering in z-direction. Therefore we use a 2D filter kernel as in the classical PCF formulation and compare light-space depths of adjacent pixels in screen space.

Initialize 3×3 filter lookups using links

Start traversal with upper link	Start traversal with upper link	Start traversal with upper link
↑	↑	↑
Start traversal with upper link	Start traversal with upper link	Start traversal with upper link
↑	↑	↑
Start traversal with head	→ Start traversal with right link	→ Start traversal with right link

Figure 1.5. We initialize the traversal of the transmittance function using the corresponding link to the closest-depth fragment of the neighboring pixel (going first in y- and then in x-direction).

Since lookup time is slow for DSM, it is essential for DSM filtering to avoid a naive implementation where the overall lookup time grows linearly with the filter size. Searching the whole list of a neighboring pixel for the correct fragment is prohibitively expensive. A binary search would reduce the complexity but is not very suitable for implementation in a compute shader and on linked lists.

Instead we exploit spatial coherence and assume that the neighboring fragment closest in depth has a similar index in its linked list. At this stage we utilize the linking structure from Section 1.3.3, which links list elements closest in depth in order to get a good initial guess for the lookup of a neighboring fragment. This way, the transmittance function has to be traversed from the beginning (the head element) *only once* per pixel, regardless of the used filter size. Once a fragment corresponding to the current depth is found, it is possible to quickly access the neighboring fragments for computing the remaining filter samples.

In our implementation, first the fragment corresponding to the lower-left corner of a filtering window is computed (see Figure 1.5). Next the positions of the fragments linked by `right` and `upper` are used as initial guesses for finding the correct fragment position of a neighboring sample in the DSM (as depicted in Figure 1.4). Then this sample's linked list is traversed by following either `prev` or `next` to determine the correct depth (fragment position in the list). If spatial coherence holds, each traversal only requires a few iterations.

For a filter kernel size of 7×7 and realistic transparency settings, the links speed up the frame times by up to 50% for a frame-buffer resolution of $1{,}280 \times 720$ and up to 100% for a resolution of $1{,}920 \times 1{,}080$ when compared to a brute-force traversal for each filter kernel sample. Note that this technique scales well with the complexity of the hair model (the more complex, the larger the speedup), because the lookup times become roughly constant as long as there is sufficient coherence. Also observe that this technique even scales well with larger filter kernels, since spatial coherence is only required between neighboring pixels. In case of small transmittance functions (e.g., due to high opacity), the gain from the links are minor, which nevertheless only results in a barely noticeable constant overhead due to the links (of about 2%).

Apart from PCF, we also adapted another antialiasing algorithm, exponential shadow mapping, for use with DSM.

Exponential shadow mapping. The standard binary shadow map test causes antialiasing artifacts since it is effectively a step function that jumps between 0 and 1. Hence *exponential shadow mapping* (ESM) [Annen et al. 08] approximates the shadow test with an exponential function (yielding continuous results between [0..1]). This continuous value is subsequently used to attenuate the shading of a pixel.

The DSM algorithm can be combined with ESM in a straightforward fashion, and we denote this combination as *exponential deep shadow mapping* (EDSM). The resulting transmittance is weighted with the continuous shadow test value. As can be seen in Figure 1.6, EDSM performs much better than PCF in terms of visual quality. Note that while the original ESM algorithm supports prefiltering, this feature cannot be used in combination with DSM since the lookup depth along the transmittance function is not known beforehand.

1.4 Results

We computed all our results on an Intel Core i7-2700K Processor (using one core) and using a Geforce GTX 680. All images were rendered in resolution $1,280 \times 720$ and using a deferred rendering pipeline with four 32-bit render targets. The hair model used in our experiments has 10,000 individual strands of hairs and about 87,000 vertices.

SM res	SM	DSM	DSM3	DSM5	EDSM	EDSM3	EDSM5
256	222.8	220.9	192.4	160.3	207.2	166.2	121.6
512	121.2	120.2	111.9	98.4	116.0	99.5	79.9
768	70.7	70.2	66.4	61.4	69.2	60.8	51.0

Table 1.1. This table compares typical FPS values for binary shadow mapping by using only the first fragment of a DSM for shading (SM), our method without filtering (DSM) and with PCF (DSM3 and DSM5), and our EDSM algorithm using different filter kernel footprints. The number after the algorithm's name is the filter kernel size (e.g., a 3×3 kernel for EDSM3).

Figure 1.6. DSMs without filtering (left) exhibit resampling artifacts. Smoother shadows can be achieved with PCF (center), while ESM provides even higher quality (right).

In Table 1.1 we compare the timings for a special version of binary shadow mapping (simulated by using only the first fragment of a DSM for shading), DSMs, and DSMs using a 3×3 and a 5×5 PCF kernel size, respectively, and show the comparison for several shadow map resolutions. The comparison to this version of binary shadow mapping demonstrates the overhead of the DSM lookups (using both optimizations, i.e., neighbor links and truncation of the transmittance function). While the overhead is more pronounced for small shadow maps, it becomes small in relation to the DSM creation for increasing shadow map size.

In Figure 1.6 we compare the quality of DSMs without filtering (left), with PCF (center), and using ESM (right). As can be seen, PCF performs solid antialiasing, while EMS improves the rendering quality even more. Furthermore, while all DSM methods require a depth bias to avoid Z-fighting artifacts, ESM needs significantly less bias for artifact-free rendering than unfiltered and PCF rendering.

1.5 Conclusions

We presented an optimized implementation of deep shadow maps for complex hair models that achieves real-time frame rates by employing new features of current graphics hardware. Note that our implementation requires only Direct3D 11 shader features and compute shaders, which makes our algorithm attractive in environments where GPUs from different vendors are used. In our experiments it turned out that the best DSM quality can be achieved by combining it with ESM. While interactive applications are the main target for this algorithm, we also see applications in the movie industry, where such a real-time DSM implementation could save valuable production time and provide immediate feedback to the artists.

1.6 Acknowledgments

We want to thank Cem Yuksel for the permission to use his hair models and Murat Afsharand for his head model. All models are available at Cem Yuksel's website, www.cemyuksel.com/research/hairmodels.

Bibliography

[Annen et al. 08] Thomas Annen, Tom Mertens, Hans-Peter Seidel, Eddy Flerackers, and Jan Kautz. "Exponential Shadow Maps." In *Proceedings of Graphics Interface 2008*, pp. 155–161. Toronto, Canada: Canadian Information Processing Society, 2008.

[Lokovic and Veach 00] Tom Lokovic and Eric Veach. "Deep Shadow Maps." In *Proceedings of the 27th Annual Conference on Computer Graphics and Interactive Techniques*, pp. 385–392. New York: ACM Press/Addison-Wesley Publishing Co., 2000.

[Reeves et al. 87] William T. Reeves, David H. Salesin, and Robert L. Cook. "Rendering Antialiased Shadows with Depth Maps." *Computer Graphics (SIGGRAPH '87 Proceedings)* 21:4 (1987), 283–291.

[Salvi et al. 10] Marco Salvi, Kiril Vidimče, Andrew Lauritzen, and Aaron Lefohn. "Adaptive Volumetric Shadow Maps." In *Proceedings of the 21st Eurographics Conference on Rendering*, pp. 1289–1296. Aire-la-Ville, Switzerland: Eurographics Association, 2010.

Game Engine Design

Welcome to the Game Engine Design section of this edition of GPU Pro. The selection of articles you will find in here covers various aspects of engine design, such as quality and optimization, in addition to high-level architecture.

First, Donald Revie brings his experience of engine design in his article "An Aspect-Based Engine Architecture." Aspect-based engines apply the principles of component design and object-oriented programming (OOP) on an engine level by constructing the engine using modules. Such architecture is well suited to small or distributed teams who cannot afford to establish a dedicated structure to design and manage all the elements of their engine but would still like to take advantage of the benefits that developing their own technology provides. The highly modular nature allows for changes in development direction or the accommodation of multiple projects with widely varying requirements.

In the article "Kinect Programming with Direct3D 11," Jason Zink provides a walkthrough into this emerging technology by explaining the hardware and software aspects of the Kinect device. The article seeks to provide the theoretical underpinnings needed to use the visual and skeletal data streams of the Kinect, and it also provides practical methods for processing and using this data with the Direct3D 11 API. In addition, it explores how this data can be used in real-time rendering scenarios to provide novel interaction systems.

Finally, Homam Bahnassi and Wessam Bahnassi present a description of a full pipeline for implementing structural damage to characters and other environmental objects in the article "A Pipeline for Authored Structural Damage." The article covers details for a full pipeline from mesh authoring to displaying pixels on the screen, with qualities including artist-friendliness, efficiency, and flexibility.

I would like to thank the authors who contributed to this section for their great work. I would like also to extend these thanks to my wife Suzan, my son Omar, and my brother Homam for their wonderful support.

I hope you find these articles inspiring and enlightening to your rendering and engine development work.

—Wessam Bahnassi

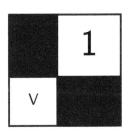

An Aspect-Based
Engine Architecture
Donald Revie

1.1   Introduction

The definition of what constitutes an engine varies across the industry. At its most basic, the term describes a code base that provides common functionality across multiple projects. The aim is to share the cost in resources required to develop this functionality. More advanced engines provide a platform and tools that can have a substantial impact on the game development process. The architecture of an engine determines how flexible, functional, reliable, and extensible that engine is and thus how successfully it can be used across multiple projects.

With an emphasis on modularity and encapsulation to divide large systems into more manageable components, the principles of object-oriented programming (OOP) embody many of these attributes. As games tend to center on a simulation made up of objects, most engines apply these principles on an object level, creating various classes of object, often in an inheritance hierarchy, with progressively complex functionality.

Aspect-based engines instead apply these principles on an engine level. Using aggregation the engine is constructed of modules, called *aspects*, each of which supplies a strict subset of the required functionality such as rendering, audio, or physics simulation. These aspects share a common interface allowing them to communicate with the core of the engine and access shared data describing the current game state. In theory each aspect is a separate engine with a very specific task, interpreting the shared data in the core via a narrow viewpoint that best fits the functionality it provides.

1.2   Rationale

Engine design and development is not just a problem of programming, it is also one of management. For developers who have limited resources in both staff and time, the approach taken to developing their engine will have a vast impact on everyone involved in developing and using it. This means that any such engine is unlikely to be developed by a dedicated team with months of time to plan and execute; instead, it will have to be written rapidly with the immediate needs of projects in mind.

An aspect-based engine architecture reduces this burden of management by creating a simple interface and set of rules to which all aspects must be written. Once the core and its interface to the aspects are defined, work on the aspects themselves can be carried out by individuals or teams with a considerable amount of autonomy. Interactions between the aspects and thus their authors remain informal, being implemented entirely through manipulating the core of the engine via the aspect interface.

As such, this architecture is well suited to small or distributed teams who cannot afford to establish a dedicated structure to design and manage all the elements of their engine but would still like to take advantage of the benefits that developing their own technology provides. The highly modular nature also allows for changes in development direction or the accommodation of multiple projects with widely varying requirements.

Next, we describe details of the architecture of the engine that can be summarized by the engine's core, the aspects, and their interactions.

1.3   Engine Core

The core is the most important element of the engine; all the aspects can be replaced or altered at any time but each one is highly dependent on the interface and functionality provided by the core, making it vital that the core remains stable throughout development. The function of the engine core is to store the structure and state of the game or simulation upon which the aspects will act. As the name suggests, the core is the very center and foundation upon which the rest of the engine is constructed (Figure 1.1).

1.3.1   Scene Graph

One component at the core of the engine design is a representation of the game's simulated environment, the actual logical representation of objects and concepts that interact to create everything within the game. This representation is stored as a scene graph of sorts, a tree structure where each node represents a point of interest within the simulation. However, its function is not as strictly defined as the term *scene graph* might suggest. This tree does not necessarily represent a single physical space; one branch, or subgraph, might store the information for a 3D scene while another might store a 2D GUI and another purely abstract data (Figure 1.2).

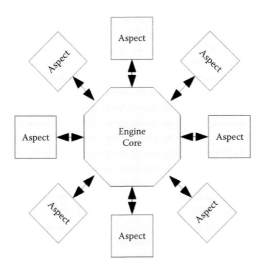

Figure 1.1. The core of the engine is the common link between its many aspects.

1.3.2 Scene Nodes

Because the scene graph does not impose specific meanings upon its subgraphs, the structure of the simulation is defined purely via data. This information is stored within the nodes of the scene graph and must be interpreted by the aspects. To facilitate this level of flexibility, the nodes of the scene graph are not defined using an inheritance hierarchy, as might usually be the case, but are instead constructed using aggregation at runtime.

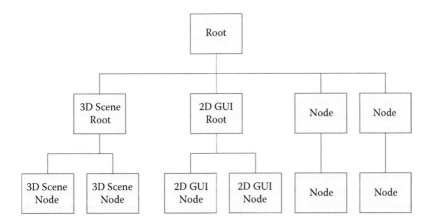

Figure 1.2. Scene graph layout.

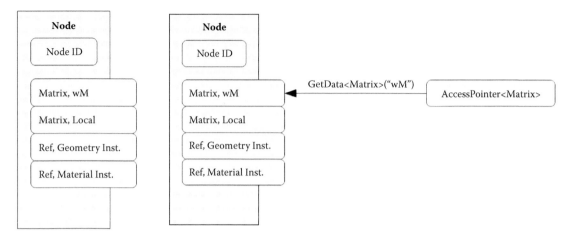

Figure 1.3. Node composition.   **Figure 1.4.** Data access request

Each node within the scene graph stores a list of data attributes, identified by name and type (Figure 1.3). The meaning of a node and the makeup of its attributes are not restricted or defined by the engine design, allowing for any number of meanings to be expressed as required.

A node might describe a physical object, such as a light or camera from a 3D scene. Likewise it might describe a bone from a character's animation rig or a mouse cursor. It may even represent an abstract concept, such as a victory condition, within the rules of the game. The meaning of each node is determined by its relative position in the graph, its attributes, and how those things are interpreted by the aspects that make up the rest of the engine.

1.3.3   Data Access

One consequence of implementing nodes using aggregation is that there is no interface providing a direct means of accessing the data contained within a node. Instead access must be requested, the calling code querying the node to see if it contains an attribute with the desired name and type. The node then returns an access pointer templated to the correct type and increments a reference count (Figure 1.4).

In a multithreaded environment, safe access through these pointers, and to the rest of the core elements, requires a mutual exclusion (mutex) to be acquired by the calling thread. In this circumstance it is often more efficient for aspects to duplicate any relevant data and operate on an internal representation of the object that can be synchronized with the core scene graph at defined points.

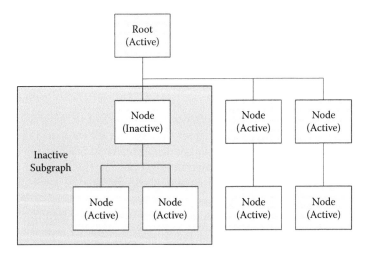

Figure 1.5. Deactivation being propagated from the root node of a subgraph.

1.3.4 Subgraph State

Nodes within the scene graph can be in one of several states that impact all the child nodes in the subgraph rooted at that node (Figure 1.5):

- Active. When a node is active it means that all interested aspects are able to process it and update any data or internal resources associated with it.

- Inactive. Subgraphs can be deactivated at any time. Once inactive the nodes should be treated by the aspects as if they don't exist but can retain any resources. Subgraphs are appended to the scene in an inactive state to allow aspects to initialize any associated resources before updating begins.

- Pending deletion. All nodes within the subgraph are inactive and will shortly be deleted. Aspects should prepare for this by cleaning up any associated resources.

As with all node attributes, the exact definition of subgraph states can be defined by the users of the engine. However, additional care should be taken due to the wide impact of such states and how various aspects might interpret them.

1.3.5 Event Queue

The scene graph and its constituent nodes describe the current structure and state of the simulation. This simulation, however, will not remain static. It will be characterized by changes to the structure of the scene and the contents of the nodes as the logic of the simulation is played out.

The engine aspects must be aware of and react to such changes in the simulation state. While this could be performed by aspects continuously inspecting elements of the scene for change, it would be prohibitively slow. A more efficient solution is to maintain a queue of events describing such changes that each aspect can review during its update, ignoring any events that are not relevant to its function.

Events use a similarly flexible definition to the rest of the engine. Each event has an identifier describing the nature of the event and can provide two pointers to either nodes or data within specific nodes. This is sufficient to describe most events within the simulation, flagging either a change in the status of a node, and thus the subgraph rooted in it, a change in a specific attribute within the node, or an interaction between two nodes.

More complex events can be described using additional attributes within the referenced node or by creating a node within the scene to represent the event itself. Thus a collision between two nodes that results in a sound and particle effect could spawn a new subgraph containing these elements, rather than an event describing them.

1.4   Aspects

The engine core stores the current state of the simulation and any changes that have occurred recently. It is not concerned with the contents of the simulation or how it might work. Instead, all operations carried out by the engine occur within the aspects.

An aspect is an engine module that exists to provide a limited subset of engine functionality. This might include rendering, animation, physics, audio, and even the logic of the game. As such, aspects are often used to wrap the functionality of individual APIs for tasks such as physics, synchronizing the API's internal simulation with the corresponding objects within the engine core. The scope of each aspect is completely arbitrary, a single aspect could be used to encapsulate all the functionality provided by an existing third-party engine, framework, or group of related APIs. Similarly a single API may have its functionality subdivided between multiple aspects if that best fits their purpose.

One restriction of this architecture is that aspects should adhere to strict dependency rules: they can share knowledge of base engine libraries, the engine core, and shared libraries but should not know about one another (Figure 1.6). This means that all access to shared resources should be performed through the interfaces supplied by the engine core, thus preventing any coupling or interdependencies forming between aspects. Thus if two aspects share a base library with specific classes, this data can be embedded into entities like data of any other type. As it is only relevant to the interested aspects, it remains opaque to the rest of the engine.

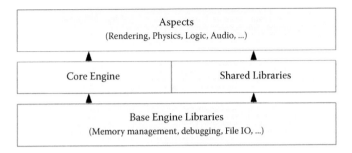

Figure 1.6. Dependency layers.

Aspects should be designed to keep this kind of sharing to a minimum. Static resources like the current graphics device/context or window handle should not be shared between aspects, though where sharing is unavoidable, these should provide a mutex to control access.

By maintaining these rules, aspects will operate independently and be much easier to maintain and replace. An audio aspect using one API will be interchangeable with an aspect using another API. Each aspect can therefore be developed and tested independently, interacting with each other by manipulating the engine core.

The engine manages all aspects through a single interface, initializing, updating, and shutting down aspects in an order specified by the user of the engine. This could in theory be performed through data, allowing the engine to construct itself from dynamically linked libraries at runtime.

1.4.1 Scene Interpretation

Each aspect should maintain an internal structure of references to nodes in which it is interested. Interest is determined by querying the node's attributes looking for specific patterns. For instance, a node with an identifier matching a rigid body would be of interest to the physics aspect, whereas one that referenced a geometry and material instance would be of interest to the render aspect. The nature of this structure and the way it references the nodes can be tailored to the aspect, allowing the most efficient solution for the functionality it provides. This could be a spatial tree for operations based on the relative position of nodes, such as frustum culling visible nodes against a camera node, or a simple linked list of nodes that can be iterated over once per frame (Figure 1.7).

When an aspect is registered with the engine core, it parses the whole of the existing scene graph and registers interest in any nodes. From then on it will receive events regarding changes to nodes and to the structure of the scene graph, allowing it to synchronize its own internal structures.

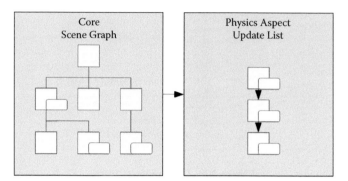

Figure 1.7. Aspects reinterpret the scene structure as required.

1.4.2   Node Interfaces

When presented with a new subgraph, an aspect inspects the nodes within, querying for patterns of data that would indicate that the node represents a concept that the aspect recognizes. This pattern of attributes can be thought of as an interface that the node exports via a subset of its attributes (Figure 1.8).

In most cases these interfaces will be predefined by the aspect, mapping directly to objects within their functional domain. An audio aspect might interpret nodes as potential sound emitters, receivers, or environmental modifiers. While an animation aspect will be interested in nodes representing bones or skinned mesh segments.

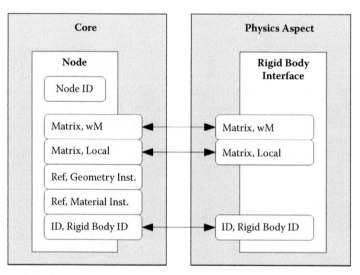

Figure 1.8. Aspects reinterpret nodes based on the attributes they exhibit.

In some cases interfaces will be defined via data loaded into the aspect. In this way the engine can request access to arbitrary attributes, usually after ascertaining that the node represents the desired object using a separate predefined interface. This allows the engine to map attributes of a node to the inputs of a script or shader automatically without needing to understand the contents of either the node or the intended target.

It is usually preferable for the aspect to use the interface to synchronize its own internal objects with the scene graph rather than perform operations directly on the shared data. In the case of aspects that wrap APIs, these objects will likely already be provided and indeed be required to use the desired functionality. This allows aspects to perform operations in parallel; they are only required to lock the core of the engine at set points to synchronize their internal data with the central simulation.

1.5   Common Aspects

1.5.1   Render Aspect

The article "Designing a Data-Driven Renderer" in *GPU Pro 3* [Revie 12] describes in detail the key elements of a render aspect. The design illustrates the flexibility of the core scene representation in defining objects with a wide range of concepts, from concrete entities such as cameras or lights to the abstract elements of the frame graph, used to control the order of rendering. It also describes the process of interrogating objects to retrieve arbitrary input for shaders.

1.5.2   Logic Aspect

The logic aspect is where any game-specific functionality should be added. This is the aspect that will interpret objects in the scene graph as the entities they represent in the game, such as players, enemies, weapons, and power-ups. It will update the scene using the rules of the game provided.

The way in which the logic aspect is implemented can vary greatly and should be subject to the needs of the project and the makeup of the team. A programmer-centric team might want to handle a lot of the logic through code, hiding the interface to the engine core behind their own entity classes and structures. Alternatively the logic aspect can be completely data-driven, executing script files attached to the individual nodes and exposing the contents of the attached nodes as parameters or objects within the script language.

1.5.3   Data Instrumentation Aspect

By implementing an aspect that simply exposes the components of the core through a simple GUI, users of the engine can directly observe the internal state of the engine and even edit the values of individual node attributes. Depending on the level to which such an aspect is developed, it could vary in functionality from a simple debugging tool displaying attribute values as formatted strings to an in-game editor capable of manipulating the structure of the scene graph and rendering complex widgets for editing node attributes.

1.5.4   File Aspect

Notable by its absence from the engine core is any ability to load data from files into the engine. That is because this functionality also is supplied by an aspect. The loading of the scene data into the core is controlled by the file aspect, an aspect that looks for nodes with attributes that reference filenames. Once found these names are submitted to a factory system.

Factories. This factory system itself follows a modular structure. Each file type is associated with a factory module that processes the file, constructing a subgraph from its contents. This subgraph is then passed back to the factory aspect, which can then replace the file-referencing node with the subgraph that it represented. Once inserted into the scene, the new subgraph will be parsed by all the aspects, including the file aspect, ensuring that any file references contained within the subgraph will also be processed.

As such factory modules exist above the aspects in the dependency rules, it is possible for them to have knowledge of individual aspects. If a file contains resources only pertinent to a single aspect, then the factory can communicate directly with the aspect or even be a part of the aspect itself, bypassing the need to insert this data into the scene graph.

Scene conditioners. When a scene is constructed from a variety of file types and by recursively dereferencing nodes, in this fashion it can result in a structure with many redundant nodes and various other inefficiencies. To counteract this, a further system of modules is used to iterate over sections of the scene graph, analyzing and optimizing its structure. These conditioning modules can also be used to add further attributes to entities required by an aspect, thus acting as a preprocessing stage for the aspects.

When a subgraph is constructed by the factory system, it is processed by pre-insertion conditioners. Then, once it has been inserted into the scene graph, it can be processed by a set of post-insertion conditioners to perform further operations based on the context of its position within the graph. The tasks carried out by these conditioners are specific to the engine, the design of the aspects, and the types of files being loaded. Their modular nature makes it simple to construct a small, highly specialized conditioner for each task.

Pre-insertion conditioners are often used to optimize scene data that may be needed during the authoring of the assets but not required in the specific game. Doing so in the conditioning stages reduces the complexity of the factories, allowing for a finer grained control. These might include tasks such as

- the removal of collision geometry that has been exported to matching API-specific files earlier in the asset pipeline but still exists in the source file;

- the removal of editor-specific nodes representing cameras and other UI elements that exist within the scene.

Post-insertion conditioners, on the other hand, perform tasks that require knowledge of the context into which a file's contents is dereferenced. Such tasks might include

- generating unique IDs with which to reference each node;

- propagating transforms to the dereferenced subgraph so that the nodes are positioned and oriented relative to the subgraph's immediate parent in the scene;

- collapsing long columns of redundant nodes that contain no data beyond transforms and only a single child. These are often created during the dereferencing process and artificially increase the depth of the scene.

Offline processing. The flexibility of the architecture allows it to be used in constructing not just various engine configurations but also tools that work upon the same data set. Such tools can be used to process or analyze scene data offline using a very different set of aspects and conditioners from those involved in the game itself.

These can be built into the asset pipeline to automatically process data exported from authoring programs and create files optimized for loading directly into the game on a range of target platforms.

1.6 Implementation

One of the key principles of this engine design is the construction of scene nodes through data aggregation rather than explicit classes within the engine's code. Much of the interaction between the aspects and the core scene will be informed by the implementation of this principle. It is therefore worthy of more in-depth discussion.

Nodes are in essence containers that associate a description of each attribute, a name and a type identifier, with a pointer to the relevant data. The Standard Template Library (STL) provides a variety of containers with different properties and a shared interface (see Listing 1.1), making it relatively simple to choose one to fit any given situation [SGI 11]. In this instance an associative container like a map or set (or multimap/multiset if you want to allow duplicate attribute names) would be an obvious choice because it features easy searching of content and does not require elements to be stored in contiguous memory, which can cause excessive fragmentation when inserting/deleting contents.

```
std::map<std::pair<attribute name, attribute type>, attribute data>
```

Listing 1.1. Using a map to store attributes.

In reality, all searching, insertion, and removal of data should ideally be restricted to the initialization and shutdown of objects, making the choice of container less vital. Custom allocators can be written to further reduce the impact
of memory reallocation from containers, although their implementation is beyond
the scope of this article.

The attribute data can be of any type. However, a container may only hold
objects of a single type. Therefore, a layer of indirection must be introduced by
storing a set of uniform pointers to the nonuniform set of attribute data. Data
could be constructed on the heap and then the pointer returned cast to void.
This has the notable drawback of discarding any type information regarding the
data and the possibility of calling its destructor without being able to cast it back
to the original type.

Another solution is to construct an attribute interface class from which a
templated class can be automatically derived for each attribute type. This will
allow information about the type to be accessible via the interface class as well
as provide the appropriate virtual destructor to clean up the attribute data.
Through the use of compile time features, generally provided as part of runtime
type information (RTTI), it is possible to retrieve a simple type information
object that represents the type of data being stored, allowing it to be identified
and compared against other types. (See Listing 1.2.) Such an implementation
will allow the attribute objects to not only store correctly typed pointers to their
respective data, but also to store the identifying name of the attribute and provide
access to a type info object. As such, a separate key is not required to identify
the attribute when searching, and the contents of the node can be stored using
a set constructed with a custom sorting algorithm that interrogates the interface
pointer for the name and type of the attribute.

1.7   Aspect Interactions

Aspects are deliberately independent of one another, and the core of the engine
interacts with them all through a generic interface. The only code that knows
about the composition of the engine will be the project-specific code used to
assemble all the relevant modules, aspects, factories, and conditioners, though
even this could theoretically be performed through data.

During the course of a session, the core of the engine will be initialized, then
each aspect will be initialized in turn before being registered with the core to
receive events and be provided with access to the scene representation. Once

```
class iAttribute
{
public:
    virtual                           ~iAttribute()=0;

    virtual type_info                 GetTypeID()     const=0;
    virtual const std::string&        GetName()       const=0;
};

template<typename _tAttribute>
class cAttribute : public iAttribute
{
public:
    cAttribute(): m_name(), m_pData(NULL) {}
    ~cAttribute()                     { if(m_pData) delete m_pData; }

    type_info         GetTypeID()  const { return typeid(_tAttribute); }
    const std::string& GetName()   const { return  m_name; }

    _tAttribute*      GetPointer()      { return  m_pData; }

private:
    std::string    m_name;
    _tAttribute*   m_pData;
};
```

Listing 1.2. Attribute classes.

this occurs the engine can start one or more threads and from these execute any update loops that the aspects may require. It is here that any aspect precedence should be resolved; correct functioning of the engine may be dependent on the order of updates, and there will usually be an optimal order and frequency with which aspects should be updated.

1.7.1 Aspect Update

As each aspect is autonomous, being in effect a *vertical slice* of engine functionality, each has its own update loop performing all the operations needed to manage both the core scene and its own internal resources in respect to its subset of functionality (Figure 1.9).

When it is time for the aspect to update, it must acquire a lock on the core of the engine, then process any new events that have occurred since the last update, parsing subgraphs that have been added to the scene or removing aspects for nodes that will soon be deleted. It will also need to synchronize the values in its own internal objects with those of the corresponding scene nodes before releasing the lock. At this point the aspect is potentially updating in parallel with the rest of the engine, performing any internal logic. Once its internal state is fully updated, the aspect reacquires the lock upon the core of the engine, synchronizes the core entities with any relevant data, and generates new events before again

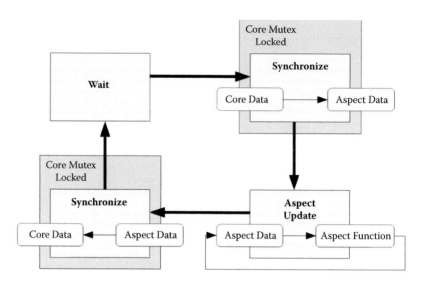

Figure 1.9. Aspect update loop.

releasing the lock. It must now wait for a period of time until the next update step can be performed.

1.7.2   Example: Entity Changing Color Upon Taking Damage

This simple example describes a possible set of operations that might occur in an aspect-driven engine when a bullet strikes a character in the game causing the target's material values to change.

1. During the update of the physics aspect, a bullet object intersects the collision hull of a character. This generates an internal event in the physics API. Upon synchronizing with the core at the end of its update, the physics aspect pushes a collision event referencing the bullet and the character onto the event queue.

2. When the logic aspect next updates, it retrieves the collision event from the queue. It recognizes the event type "Collision" and is observing both of the referenced nodes. It calls the collision handler script functions for both the bullet and the character. The collision handler for the bullet requests that the subgraph representing the bullet be removed from the scene. That of the character changes the character's internal state to "damaged," subtracts the bullet's damage attribute from the character's health attribute, and modifies the character's color attribute from white to red.

3. Once the logic aspect releases its lock on the core, the render aspect is able to start updating. It notices the pending removal state change on the

bullet subgraph and cleans up the internal entity that it uses to represent the bullet. It then proceeds to synchronize the shader inputs for all the currently visible entities with the attributes of their respective nodes. In doing so it pulls the new color value from the character's attribute, and when the relevant batch is rendered, the character is now tinted red.

1.8 Praetorian: The Brief History of Aspects

Praetorian, Cohort Studios' proprietary engine, was developed using the aspect-based architecture described. The engine's purpose was to enable the company to quickly develop prototypes of games within a wide range of genres and then to rapidly bring the most promising projects to full production.

Initially it was planned to develop these games using middleware to save development time; however, while evaluating third-party engines, it became clear that they were often better suited to one genre or another or they placed restrictions on the features that could be added. Therefore it was decided to allow a small group with limited resources to begin work on an internally developed engine that could be used across the wide range of projects envisaged.

An alternative agile-themed approach might have been to develop engine functionality directly within projects, refactoring the code as the project developed until any common functionality fell out into modules that could be shared. However, such an approach might take far longer to produce an engine that could be used as the foundation for a wide range of games with several projects needing to reach completion.

The first goal of the new engine was to reduce the amount of new code that needed to be written, reusing existing technology or incorporating third-party APIs wherever possible. In that light, it made sense to create a core scene representation onto which these disparate modules could be attached.

The term *aspect* was originally encountered in research regarding multithreaded access to a single scene graph in OpenSG [Voss et al. 02], indicating that each thread or remote client would maintain a specific viewpoint on the contents of the scene graph. This diverged from simple multithreaded access into the idea of such viewpoints differing based on the task required and then into the concept of aspects as described in this article.

Further research suggested that adopting an aggregation-based approach to entities over inheritance would further increase the flexibility of the system [Cafrelli 01]. This would neatly sidestep the issue of developing a hierarchy of entities that could meet the needs of all the aspects without creating dependencies between them.

The last component of the core to be implemented was the event system. Although it was in the initial design, it had been dropped to help speed up the development of the aspects that depended on the core interface being complete.

Event management was later implemented though not as a central part of the core. Events were used within the transform aspect to correctly propagate updates of node positions to their children, then used in relation to collision events between physics objects, and finally were implemented within the scene graph to facilitate asynchronous operations on the structure of the scene graph, processing insertions and removals. In hindsight it would have been more efficient to implement event handling from the outset even if it meant proceeding with a less efficient design.

Development of the aspects progressively added functionality to this core. The first usable build of the engine simply consisted of the render aspect and a simple file loading module that could parse Collada data and push it into the core (later formalized as the Collada factory used by the file aspect). This allowed assets to be exported from model-editing software and imported directly into the engine. Shortly after this the first pass of the physics aspect allowed the objects exported with additional data to be updated by a physics simulation. This was followed by a scripting aspect that updated objects with associated Lua scripts to perform game logic.

Within a relatively short period of time, project teams were able to start building games on a simple but functional data-driven engine that grew in functionality as it was required.

1.9 Analysis

As with all designs, there are benefits and limitations to building an engine based upon aspects. The characteristics of the aspect-based architecture predominantly benefit the development process through modularity and flexibility of data, but the rigid structure and indirection create limits on efficiency.

Benefits. The benefits of building an engine based upon aspects include the following:

- Promoting a data-driven development philosophy helps to engage asset creators and designers.

- The highly modular drop in/drop out architecture allows quick changes to the engine.

- The modular nature allows quicker tracking and debugging of errors.

- Encapsulation accelerates the integration of third-party APIs.

- The direct connection of shader and script inputs makes developing new graphics techniques and prototype game features easier and quicker.

- Decentralizing the knowledge and management of functionality increases the autonomy of the programmers of different aspects.

Limitations. The following are some of the limitations:

- The creation of duplicate or redundant data within the aspects and the aggregate structure used to store data in the core can significantly reduce memory efficiency.

- The asynchronous nature of aspects can be difficult for programmers to work with as cause and effect are rarely directly adjacent in the code.

- Trying to maintain complete autonomy between aspects across multiple threads of execution requires additional mechanisms to coordinate the order of updates.

1.10   Conclusion

There are as many ways to write an engine as there are programmers. The aspect-based architecture is as much a concession to the individuality of developers and the needs of their projects as it is an engine design in itself. At the same time, while the strict rules regarding encapsulation of aspects and accessing shared data inevitably limit optimization, they help to structure and inform the design of functionality, making it quicker to implement what is required.

The intention is to provide developers with a simple, easy-to-follow framework that helps accelerate engine development but leaves them with the freedom to explore structures and techniques where desired.

The use of this engine architecture has been observed across a wide range of projects, and it appears, on the whole, to meet these goals. There will always be situations that stretch the abilities of an engine, but none so far have proved insurmountable within the limits of this design.

1.11   Acknowledgments

Thanks to everyone who worked at Cohort Studios and in particular those whose work had an impact on Praetorian and its design. Thanks to Andrew Collinson who worked on Praetorian from the very beginning and Bruce McNeish for having the foresight to let us start building it, despite being straight out of university. Also, thanks to Gordon Bell for showing a lot of faith when I told him things "should just work" and to Peter Walsh for lending his many years of experience and a truly comprehensive range of anecdotes. Thanks to Shaun Simpson for helping to push the engine design so much further in so many ways and to Dave Sowerby for the scripting aspect and his tireless work in actually making a game, which is after all the reason behind all this.

Bibliography

[Cafrelli 01] C. Cafrelli. "A Property Class for Generic C++ Member Access." In *Game Programming Gems 2*, edited by Mark DeLoura, pp. 46–50. Hingham, MA: Charles River Media, 2001.

[Revie 12] D. Revie, "Designing a Data-Driven Renderer." In *GPU Pro 3*, edited by Wolfgang Engel, pp. 291–319. Boca Raton, FL: CRC Press, 2012.

[SGI 11] Silicon Graphics International. *Standard Template Library.* http://www.sgi.com/tech/stl/, 2011.

[Voss et al. 02] G. Voss, J. Behr, D. Reiners, and M. Roth. "A Multi-Thread Safe Foundation for Scene Graphs and Its Extension to Clusters." In *Proceedings of the Fourth Eurographics Workshop on Parallel Graphics and Visualization*, pp. 33–37. Aire-la-Ville, Switzerland: Eurographics Association, 2002.

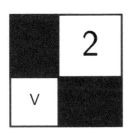

Kinect Programming
with Direct3D 11

Jason Zink

2.1 Introduction

The Microsoft Kinect is a sensor peripheral originally released for use with the Xbox 360 and later on the PC. The sensor includes a variety of different inputs, including a microphone array, color image acquisition, and a special depth image-acquisition system. With these diverse inputs, Microsoft has developed a number of algorithms that can be used to sense and track the position, pose, and voice status of one or more users—which can subsequently be used by a game or application as input. This allows for a number of new ways for a user to interact with their computers—instead of using a gamepad, the user interacts with the application in a very natural way.

Applications that wish to utilize the Kinect and the data streams that it produces can do so with the Kinect for Windows software development kit (SDK) [Microsoft 12]. To properly obtain and interpret these data streams, a developer must understand the mechanics of how the device operates and also have a clear understanding of what can and can't be done with it. This article seeks to provide the theoretical underpinnings needed to use the visual and skeletal data streams of the Kinect, and it also provides practical methods for processing and using this data with the Direct3D 11 API. In addition, we will explore how this data can be used in real-time rendering scenarios to provide novel interaction systems.

2.2 Meet the Kinect

We will begin our investigation of the Kinect by examining how its camera systems function. The camera system is essentially composed of a color (RGB) camera, an infrared (IR) projector, and an IR camera. These three elements are shown in Figure 2.1. These sensors, when used together, provide a form of a vision

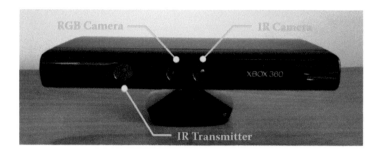

Figure 2.1. The Kinect sensor and its individual camera system components.

system that can be used to track and inspect the scene in front of them. We will investigate each of these devices in more detail in the following sections.

2.2.1   Color Camera

We begin with the color camera, as this is probably the most familiar device for most developers (and consumers in general for that matter). This camera functions more or less the same as a traditional web cam does. Visible light from the scene enters into the camera lens and eventually strikes a sensing element inside of the camera. With a large array of sensing elements arranged in a rectangular grid, the camera can determine the amount of visible light in the scene over a predefined area at a particular moment in time. This general concept is used to synthesize a camera image at regular time intervals, which ultimately produces a video stream. The geometry involved in this process is depicted in Figure 2.2.

With this in mind, we can consider the geometric interpretations of the scene that are used in such an imaging system. It is quite common to utilize a pinhole

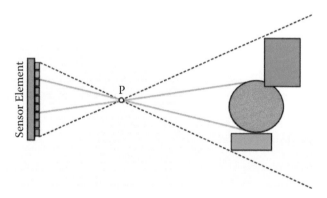

Figure 2.2. The geometry of the Kinect color camera.

camera model, in which we make the assumption that all light that enters the camera and strikes the sensing element does so through a single point, the pinhole. This point is referred to as the center of projection, and it is essentially the same concept as the camera location when rendering a scene. We will examine the mathematical properties of this camera configuration in Section 2.3, "Mathematics of the Kinect," but for now we can simply accept that we are able to capture the projected 2D image of the 3D world being viewed by the camera.

The color images obtained by the Kinect are made available to the developer at a variety of frame rates and data formats. At the time of writing this article, the available resolutions span from $1,280 \times 960$ all the way down to 80×60. This selectable resolution allows the developer to only receive the size of data that is most relevant for them, reducing bandwidth if a full size image isn't needed. The available data formats include an sRGB and a YUV format, which again allow the data to be provided to the program in the most suitable format for a given application. Not all resolutions are valid for all formats, so please consult the Kinect for Windows SDK documentation [Microsoft 12] for more details about which combinations can be used.

2.2.2 Depth Camera

The Kinect's depth-sensing system is much more unique than its color-based brother. As mentioned above, the depth-sensing system actually uses two devices in conjunction with one another: an infrared projector and an infrared camera. The IR projector applies a pattern to the scene being viewed, producing an effect similar to that shown in Figure 2.3. The infrared camera then produces an image that captures the pattern as it interacts with the current scene around the Kinect. By analyzing the pattern distortions that are present in the image, the distance from the Kinect to the point in the scene at each pixel of the infrared image can be inferred. This is the basic mechanism used to generate a secondary image that represents the depth of the objects in the scene.

Figure 2.3. Sample infrared and depth images produced by the Kinect depth-sensing system.

Figure 2.4. Blind spots in the depth image caused by the offset of the IR transmitter and receiver.

It is worth noting the location of the IR transmitter and receiver with respect to one another, as well as the color camera. The IR transmitter is located at the far side of the Kinect, with the color and IR cameras located in the center of the device. The relative locations of these components on the Kinect have a significant effect on their respective operations. For example, since the IR transmitter is offset from the IR camera, the portions of the scene that can be "viewed" by each of them are slightly different. This effect is depicted in Figure 2.4, where it can be seen that there are portions of the scene where no depth information is available.

In a real-time rendering context, you could imagine a very similar configuration with a camera and a spotlight light source that are oriented in a similar fashion as the IR transmitter and receiver are. The blind spot corresponds to the "shadow" produced by the spot light, and the camera is still able to "see" a portion of the shadow. This same effect applies to the relationship between the depth camera and the color camera as well. There will be portions of the scene that are visible in the color image that aren't visible in the depth image and vice versa. In addition, this also means that a scene point within one image may or may not be at the same pixel location within the other image. Since the two cameras are close together these discrepancies are usually minimal, but they still exist and must be taken into consideration. We will consider how to handle these effects in Section, 2.3, "Mathematics of the Kinect."

Similar to the color-image stream, the depth data is made available to the application in a variety of resolutions and data formats. The depth data itself provides a 13-bit value representing the camera space Z-coordinate of the object being sensed at each pixel. This value provides a millimeter precision value, with a valid data range of either 800 mm to 4,000 mm or 400 mm to 3,000 mm depending on the operational mode selected. In addition, the remaining 3 bits per pixel can be used to provide a player ID produced by the Kinect skeletal system. The available resolutions are 640×480, 320×240, or 80×60. Once again, please check the SDK documentation for full details about the possible combinations of these options.

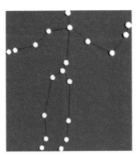

Figure 2.5. A visualization of the skeletal information available from the Kinect.

2.2.3 Skeletal Tracking

As discussed earlier in the chapter, one of the biggest advances that the Kinect provides is the ability to view a user with the sensing systems we have just described and to discern where they are within the scene and what pose they are holding. This is made possible by the Kinect by analyzing each pixel of the depth frame and applying a decision tree algorithm to determine to which part of a human body that pixel is most likely to belong [Shotton et al. 11]. All of this work is largely hidden from the developer—we simply receive the benefit that we know what the user's pose is in any give frame.

In general, the skeletal information that is available is quite similar to the skeletal information that one would expect when rendering a skinned model [Fernando and Kilgard 03]. (See Figure 2.5.) Each joint is represented by an absolute position and optionally an orientation that describes that portion of the model. In recent releases of the Kinect for Windows SDK, there is even support for different types of skeletons. For example, when a user is standing, it is possible to obtain a full 20 joint skeleton. However, when a user is sitting it is also possible to obtain a smaller skeleton that only includes a reduced subset of 10 joints corresponding to the upper body. This allows for a wide variety of usage scenarios and gives the developer freedom to choose how to interact with the user.

2.3 Mathematics of the Kinect

In this section we will look at the mathematics required to interpret the various camera spaces in the Kinect and to develop the needed concepts for matching objects in each space together. As we have just seen, the Kinect has two different camera systems, producing color and depth images. Both of these cameras can be handled in the same manner, using the pinhole camera model. Understanding this model will provide the necessary background to take an object found in one of the camera images and then determine to what that object correlates in the other image.

As a brief aside, conceptually the acquisition of an image with a camera uses the same geometric concepts as rendering an image, except that the two operations are effectively inverses of one another. In rendering we have a geometric model of the objects in the scene, and then we project them to an image plane. With a camera, the 2D image is generated for us by the real world, and we are trying to convert back to a 3D geometric representation of the objects in the scene. Keeping this in mind during the following discussion should provide some familiarity to the concepts being discussed.

2.3.1   Pinhole Camera Model

The simplest camera model is typically referred to as a *pinhole camera*. This name comes from the fact that we assume that all light that enters the camera to create the image enters through only a single point and is then striking an image sensor inside the camera. An example of this type of camera configuration is depicted in Figure 2.6, which only considers the y- and z-axes for the sake of simplicity.

Using this image as a reference, we can develop the equations that govern the projection of 3D objects to 2D representations of those objects in an image. On the right side of the diagram, we can see an example point P that we want to project onto our image plane. The light that is reflected off of point P travels toward the camera, and only some small amount of the light is able to enter the camera through the pinhole. That light then strikes the image sensor, which we will simply refer to as the image plane.

The path along which this light travels defines two triangles: one outside of the camera and one inside of the camera. Since the interior angles of both of the

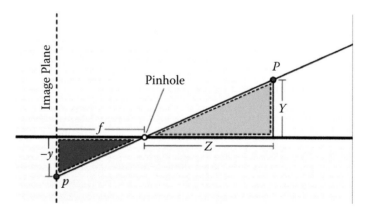

Figure 2.6. The pinhole camera model.

triangles are the same, we can use similar triangles to determine where the point P will project to:

$$\frac{y}{f} = \frac{Y}{Z},$$

$$y = \frac{yY}{Z}.$$

Here we denote world coordinates in 3D space as capital letters, while the image space coordinates are denoted with lowercase letters. The same relationship can be used to show the mapping of P in the x-direction as well:

$$x = \frac{fX}{Z}.$$

With these two simple relationships, it is possible to project a point in the scene to a point in the image. However, to go the other direction and take an image point and unproject it back into the world, we can only determine a ray along which the point must lay. This is because a traditional camera only produces an intensity value at each pixel—you no longer have any information about how deep into the scene the point was when the image was taken. Fortunately for us, the Kinect has two different camera systems—one of which produces a depth value at each pixel. The next section discusses how to take advantage of this fact and find a mapping between the 2D depth and color images we are given and the 3D objects that appear in them.

2.3.2 Kinect Coordinate Systems

When we are given a depth image from the Kinect, we are essentially given three pieces of data for each pixel. The first two are the x and y image coordinates where that particular pixel is located. In addition, the value stored at that pixel provides the world-space distance from the depth camera. This is precisely the Z distance that we used from Figure 2.6 when projecting a point onto the image. Given this additional piece of data, we can easily determine the world-space point that every pixel in the depth image represents by changing around our previous equations:

$$X = \frac{xZ}{f},$$

$$Y = \frac{yZ}{f}.$$

This allows us to utilize the Kinect to produce 3D representations of the scene that it is viewing. That is already an interesting capability, but we also want to be able to map the color-image stream to this 3D representation so that we can produce a colored surface and take full advantage of the Kinect's abilities. The process for doing this requires us to know how to take a depth pixel, convert it to world space, and then determine where that point would project to in the color image. This is more or less converting from the depth camera's coordinate system to the color camera's coordinate system.

We have already discussed most of the required concepts to do this. The conversion from depth-image pixel to world space is already described above. We also know the final step in the process, which is to project from world coordinates to the color-image coordinates. However, we need to know what is different about how the world space is perceived by each of the cameras. In Figure 2.1 we can see that the depth and color cameras are offset from one another. This means that an object that appears in the center of the depth-image stream will appear off-center in the color-image stream. Our mapping process requires us to know how to compensate for this offset—we want to know where in the color image our depth pixels will end up!

This process is actually quite common in computer vision, and it is typically referred to as *stereo calibration* [Bradski and Kaehler 08] and is used to find corresponding points in two cameras. The process itself can be somewhat complex, although there are fairly good examples available in open-source libraries. However, the hard work of performing this calibration is already performed for us by the Kinect SDK. A set of functions are provided to map between depth-image coordinates and color-image coordinates that uses the factory calibration of the Kinect. This is a very useful set of tools that can handle most of the heavy lifting for us. We will use these functions in our example application later in this article.

2.4   Programming with the Kinect SDK

At this point, we are now ready to see in more detail how we can acquire the Kinect data streams and use them in an example application. This section will cover how to initialize the runtime and start acquiring data. Next we will discuss how to map that data into a Direct3D 11 resource and finally how to use and interpret those resources for a visualization of the Kinect data. The example program has been written with the Hieroglyph 3 [Hieroglyph 3 12] open-source Direct3D 11 framework. The framework, along with the example program and utility code, is available for download from its Codeplex project page. The general interfacing to the Kinect is available in the GlyphKinect project, while the example application is available in the KinectPlayground project.

To enable your application to receive information from the Kinect, you must first install the Kinect for Windows SDK. This SDK is freely available from Microsoft [Microsoft 12] and is provided with an installer that takes care of setting up the drivers and the build environment for the Kinect (there are good installation instructions available with the SDK, so we won't repeat them here).

```
hr = NuiInitialize(
    NUI_INITIALIZE_FLAG_USES_DEPTH_AND_PLAYER_INDEX |
    NUI_INITIALIZE_FLAG_USES_SKELETON |
    NUI_INITIALIZE_FLAG_USES_COLOR );
```

Listing 2.1. Initializing the Kinect runtime.

Once the SDK is installed, we must build the connection between the Kinect API and our target application. This is actually a fairly painless process, but it requires some thought to be put into how the Kinect data is received and stored for later use. There are two options provided by the runtime for getting access to the data. The user can either poll the runtime to find out if new data is available, or an event system can be used in which the runtime signals to the application when new data is ready for processing. We will discuss the event-based model since it is more efficient, and we will describe its implementation here.

2.4.1 Initialization and Acquisition

The first step in getting access to the Kinect data is to initialize the runtime. This is done with a single function, `NuiInitialize`, whose arguments allow you to specify which data streams you are interested in receiving. In Listing 2.1 we request the three data streams that have been discussed earlier in this article: the color-image stream, the depth-image stream with player index, and also the skeletal player data stream.

After we tell the runtime what data we want, then we simply need to provide a mechanism for the runtime to signal that the data is available for reading. This is performed with a set of events, each of which is used to indicate that data is available from one of the data streams. The application creates an event and then passes it to the runtime when opening each data stream. In return we receive a handle with which to identify the data stream. The resolution and format of the data stream is configured during the opening of the stream. This process is shown in Listing 2.2 for the depth-image stream.

```
m_hNextDepthFrameEvent = CreateEvent( NULL, TRUE, FALSE, NULL );

hr = NuiImageStreamOpen(
    NUI_IMAGE_TYPE_DEPTH_AND_PLAYER_INDEX,
    NUI_IMAGE_RESOLUTION_320x240,
    0,
    2,
    m_hNextDepthFrameEvent,
    &m_pDepthStreamHandle );
```

Listing 2.2. Opening a data stream.

```
HRESULT hr = NuiImageStreamGetNextFrame(
    m_pDepthStreamHandle,
    0,
    &pImageFrame );

INuiFrameTexture * pTexture = pImageFrame->pFrameTexture;
NUI_LOCKED_RECT LockedRect;
pTexture->LockRect( 0, &LockedRect, NULL, 0 );

if( LockedRect.Pitch != 0 ) {

    BYTE * pBuffer = (BYTE*) LockedRect.pBits;

    if ( m_pSysMemDepthBuffer != NULL ) {

        USHORT * pBufferRun = (USHORT*) pBuffer;

        for( int y = 0 ; y < 240 ; y++ ) {
            for( int x = 0 ; x < 320 ; x++ ) {

                USHORT s = *pBufferRun;
                USHORT RealDepth = (s & 0xfff8) >> 3;
                USHORT Player = s & 7;


                pBufferRun++;
                USHORT* pDestBuff =
                 (USHORT*)(&(m_pSysMemDepthBuffer[(x+320*y)*2]));
                *pDestBuff = RealDepth;
            }
        }

        m_DepthFrameTimer.Update();
        m_pSysMemDepthBuffer = NULL;
    }
}

NuiImageStreamReleaseFrame( m_pDepthStreamHandle, pImageFrame );
```

Listing 2.3. Acquiring a depth frame from the Kinect runtime.

What we have set up here is the mechanism for the runtime to let us know when the next depth image frame is ready. The passed-in event will be triggered when the frame is ready, and the handle is used to refer to the depth frame later on. Once the runtime signals that a frame is ready for reading, the application must acquire access to it using runtime methods. To complete this event-based system, we utilize a separate processing thread that simply waits for the event to be signaled and then copies the frame data as necessary. This process is depicted in Listing 2.3, once again for the depth data stream.

Getting the data from the runtime consists of four general steps. First, we acquire the frame using the `NuiImageStreamGetNextFrame` function. This returns a structure that contains an `INuiFrameTexture` pointer, which holds the actual frame data. Next we lock this texture interface, read the raw frame data out, and finally release the frame after we are finished with it. The actual bit format for each image or data stream will vary based on the data formats that you have configured during initialization, but this general process allows the developer to easily access all of the stream-based data that the Kinect runtime makes available. For example, instead of receiving an `INuiFrameTexture` pointer, when working with the skeletal information the application will access an `NUI_SKELETON_FRAME` structure. Further examples of reading out each type of data can be found in the example program.

2.4.2 Direct3D 11 Resource Selection

Once the data streams of the Kinect are accessible to our application, we have to do something with the data that they carry. In order to use this data with Direct3D 11, we must first select an appropriate Direct3D 11 resource to house the data streams for us. In general, Direct3D 11 requires us to follow a particular sequence when updating a resource with data from the CPU. Resources must be created with the specification of their intended "usage." This usage indicates how the resource will be read from and/or written to by the application. Since the resources will be written to by the CPU and read by the GPU, this means that we need to perform a two-step update process. First the CPU will update a staging resource, which is then followed by copying the contents of the staging resource to an additional default usage resource. (See Figure 2.7.) This second resource is then accessible for reading within the programmable pipeline stages of the GPU.

In addition to choosing the usage options of our resources, we also need to decide what type of resource would make the most sense for holding the desired data. In general, the type of resource will be dictated by the way that an application will be using the Kinect data. For our two image-based data streams, a natural first choice for holding each frame would be a texture resource. These textures would be created with their own appropriate formats for the data that they are holding, but accessing their contents would be fairly intuitive.

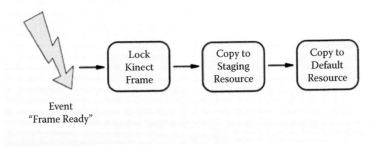

Figure 2.7. The process of acquiring data from the Kinect runtime and using it in the GPU.

However, we should also consider which programmable pipeline stage will be using these resources before finally deciding on a resource type. If the resources will be used within the compute-shader stage, then there is a choice of using either a buffer or a texture resource—whichever fits better with the threading model to be used in the compute shader. If the resources will be used directly to perform some rendering in the graphics pipeline, then the choice is based more upon which pipeline stage will be used to read the data. When the pixel shader will be consuming the data, then a texture resource probably makes the most sense due to the similarity of pixel to texel orientation. However, if the data will be read elsewhere in the pipeline, then either a buffer or a texture may make more sense. In each of these examples, the key factor ends up being the availability of addressing mechanisms to access the resources.

With these considerations in mind, we have chosen to utilize the `Texture2D` resource type for the color, depth, and depth-to-color offset data in the sample application since we are performing the manipulation of the frame-based data streams in the graphics pipeline. You may have noticed the mention of the depth-to-color offset data, which hasn't been described up to this point. This is a resource used to map from a depth pixel to the corresponding coordinates in the color pixel, using the Kinect API functions to fill in the data with each depth frame that is acquired. This essentially gives a direct mapping for each pixel that can be used to find the correspondence points between the depth and color frames.

We have also chosen to acquire the color data stream at a resolution of 640 × 480, with the sRGB format. The depth data stream will use a resolution of 320 × 240 and will contain both the depth data and the player index data. Finally, the skeletal data is only used on the CPU in this application, so we simply keep a system memory copy of the data for use later on.

2.4.3   Rendering with the Kinect

After selecting our resource types, and after configuring the methods for filling those resources with data, we are now ready to perform some rendering operations with them. For our sample application, we will be rendering a 3D reconstruction of the depth data that is colored according to the color camera frame that is acquired with it. In addition, a visualization of the skeletal joint information is also rendered on top of this 3D reconstruction to allow the comparison of the actual scene with the pose information generated by the Kinect.

The first step in the rendering process is to determine what we will use as our input geometry to the graphics pipeline. Since we are rendering a 3D representation of the depth frame, we would like to utilize a single vertex to represent each texel of the depth texture. This will allow us to displace the vertices according to the depth data and effectively recreate the desired surface. Thus we create a grid of indexed vertices that will be passed into the pipeline. Each vertex is

```
VS_OUTPUT VSMAIN( in VS_INPUT v)
{
    VS_OUTPUT o;

    // Multiplying the retrieved depth by 0.001 is done
    // to convert to meters.
    float fDepth =
        ((float)KinectDepthBuffer[
            int2( v.coords.x, 240-v.coords.y ) ]) * 0.001f;

    uint2 uiOffsets =
        KinectOffsetBuffer[ int2( v.coords.x, 240-v.coords.y ) ];

    o.colorOffset =
        float2( (float)uiOffsets.x / 640.0f,
                (float)uiOffsets.y / 480.0f );

    float3 normal =
        ComputeNormal( int2( v.coords.x, 240-v.coords.y ) );

    float diffuse =
        max( dot( normal, normalize(float3( 1.0f, 0.0f, 1.0f )) ),
            0.0f );

    // x_meters = (x_pixelcoord - 160) * z_meters *
    // NUI_CAMERA_DEPTH_IMAGE_TO_SKELETON_MULTIPLIER_320x240

    // y_meters = (y_pixelcoord - 120) * z_meters *
    // NUI_CAMERA_DEPTH_IMAGE_TO_SKELETON_MULTIPLIER_320x240

    float x_meters = (v.coords.x-160) * 0.003501f * fDepth;
    float y_meters = (v.coords.y-120) * 0.003501f * fDepth;
    float4 DepthCamViewSpace =
        float4( x_meters, y_meters, fDepth, 1.0f );

    o.position = mul( DepthCamViewSpace, WorldViewProjMatrix );
    o.height = fDepth;

    return o;
}
```

Listing 2.4. The vertex shader for rendering a 3D reconstruction of a depth frame.

given its integer coordinates of the pixel in the depth texture that it should be representing.

Next we will consider the pipeline configuration that we will use to render the geometry. In total, we will use the vertex shader, the geometry shader, and the pixel shader stages. We will consider the vertex shader first, which is shown in Listing 2.4. It starts out by reading the depth data and the offset for the depth-to-color mapping frame texture. This offset is supplied in pixels, so we scale it accordingly to produce texture coordinate offsets out of them. Next we calculate a normal vector from the depth texture by using a Sobel filter. The normal vector is not strictly needed, but it can be used to perform lighting operations on the reconstructed surface if desired.

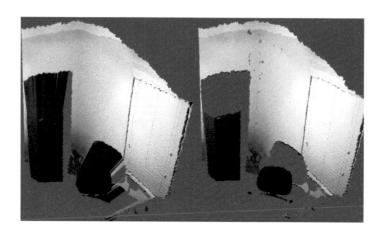

Figure 2.8. Removal of unwanted triangles from our surface reconstruction.

Now we take the depth pixel data and convert it to a 3D position in the depth camera's view space. This is performed using the relationships we provided earlier, where the focal length and camera parameters are baked into constants (the values of the constants are taken from the Kinect for Windows SDK header files). After this we project the depth-camera view-space coordinates to clip space for rasterization and also keep a copy of the original depth value for use later on.

Each of these vertices is then assembled into a triangle by the graphics pipeline and passed to the geometry shader. The main reason for using the geometry shader is to detect and remove triangles that have excessively long edges. If there is a long edge on a triangle, it would typically mean that the triangle spans a discontinuity in the depth frame and it doesn't represent a real surface. In that case we can skip the passing of the triangle into the output stream. Figure 2.8 demonstrates the removal of these unwanted features, and the geometry shader to perform this operation is shown in Listing 2.5.

After the geometry passes the geometry shader, it is rasterized and passed to the pixel shader. In the pixel shader we can simply sample the color frame texture with our offset coordinates. This performs the mapping from depth space to color space for us and allows us to minimize the amount of work needed to be performed at the pixel level. The pixel shader code is provided in Listing 2.6.

The end result of this rendering is a reconstructed 3D representation of what is visible in front of the Kinect. The final step in our sample application is to visualize the skeletal data and how it corresponds to the reconstructed surface. We receive the complete skeletal data from the Kinect runtime and simply create a sphere at each joint to show where it lies. Since the joint positions are provided in the depth-camera view space, there is no need for further manipulations of the data. The overall results of our sample application can be seen in Figure 2.9.

```
[maxvertexcount(3)]
void GSMAIN( triangle VS_OUTPUT input[3],

            inout TriangleStream<VS_OUTPUT> OutputStream )
{
    float minHeight = min( input[0].height, input[1].height );
    minHeight = min( minHeight, input[2].height );

    float maxLength =
        max( length( abs(input[0].height - input[1].height) ),
             length( abs(input[1].height - input[2].height) ) );

    maxLength =
        max( maxLenth,
             length( abs(input[2].height - input[0].height) ) );

    if (( minHeight > 0.1f ) && ( maxLength < 0.075f )) {
        for ( int i = 0; i < 3; i++ ) {
            OutputStream.Append(input[i]);
        }
    }

    OutputStream.RestartStrip();
}
```

Listing 2.5. The geometry shader for expelling elongated triangles.

```
float4 PSMAIN( in VS_OUTPUT input ) : SV_Target
{
    float4 vValues = KinectColorBuffer.Sample(
        LinearSampler, input.colorOffset );

    return ( vValues );
}
```

Listing 2.6. The pixel shader for sampling the color frame data.

Figure 2.9. The final output from the sample application.

2.5 Applications of the Kinect

Now that we have seen the Kinect data streams used in a live application, we should have a feel for what types of data are available to us for use in an application. We can now take a moment and consider several potential types of applications that can be built around it. As described in the introduction, this data is very unique and allows the developer to interact with their users in very new and novel ways. This section will briefly describe several uses for the Kinect to get the reader thinking about the possibilities—and hopefully lead to more ideas for uses of this intriguing device.

2.5.1 3D Scanning

At first thought, it is very common to see the Kinect as a very inexpensive 3D scanner. Certainly, having the ability to generate a 3D model of a real-world object would have many potential practical uses. However, in practice this isn't quite as straightforward as initially thought. The depth data that is received in each depth frame is not a complete surface mapping due to the blind spots that we discussed earlier. In addition, the depth data that is available within the frame is typically somewhat noisy over time. These restrictions introduce complications to the implementation of such a scanner system.

However, even with these limitations in mind, it is indeed possible to perform a 3D scanning function with a fairly high fidelity. The Kinect Fusion algorithm [Izadi et al. 11] utilizes computer vision algorithms that track the location and orientation of a handheld Kinect device. By knowing its own position relative to the object being scanned, multiple depth frames can be taken over time to build a volumetric model of that object. Using multiple frames allows the blind spots from one frame to be filled in by the data introduced in a subsequent frame. This process is repeatedly performed, and over time a complete model can be built. The final generated volumetric model can then be either converted to a renderable mesh or stored in whatever desired output format for later use. Thus for the cost of a computer and a Kinect, you can produce a 3D scanner!

2.5.2 Interactive Augmented Reality

If we have the ability to generate models of a particular object, then by extension it should also be possible to generate a model of the complete environment that is surrounding the Kinect as well. With a fairly accurate model of the surroundings around a user, it becomes possible to use this information within a rendered scene that combines the physically acquired Kinect data with simulation-based data. For example, after acquiring a model of the area surrounding your desk, you could then produce a particle system simulation that interacts with the model. Each particle can interact with objects in the scene, such as bouncing off of your desk.

The resulting combined scene can then be rendered and presented to the user in real time from the perspective of the Kinect. Since the volumetric model of the environment really is actually volumetric, the rendering of the particle system will properly occlude rendered objects if a physical object obstructs the view of it from the Kinect. This provides a very powerful mechanism for incorporating game elements into a realistic scene.

2.5.3 User Pose and Gesture Tracking

The production of the user pose information is perhaps the most widely known application of the Kinect data streams. This is essentially provided to the developer for free, with a stream of skeletal frames being provided by the Kinect runtime. With skeletal information available for the user in the scene, it becomes quite easy to render an avatar that appears in the pose in which the user is currently. For example, the user could move around their living room and see a rendered representation of their favorite character onscreen that is moving in the same manner. This effect is not only a novelty. This mechanism can be used as the input method for a game or simulation. In such a scenario, the avatar could interact with a game environment and replicate the user's actions in the game, letting them interact with a virtual scene around them.

However, since the virtual scene is likely not going to match exactly the physical scene surrounding the user, this method will quickly become limited in what interactions can be modeled. Instead, the user's movements can be translated into the detection of gestures as they move over time. These gestures can then be used as the input mechanism for the game or simulation. This breaks the direct dependency between the virtual and physical scenes and allows the developer to both interact with their users directly and also provide them with a large scene to interact with as well. This is the typical method employed by games that currently use the Kinect.

2.5.4 Rendering Scenes Based on User Pose

Another interesting area that the Kinect can be used for is to manipulate rendering parameters by monitoring the user. A prime example of this is to modify the view and projection matrices of a rendered scene based on the location and proximity of a user's head to the output display. For example, when a user is standing directly in front of a monitor, the typical view and projection matrices are more or less physically correct. However, when the user moves to stand to the right of the display, the view and projection matrices used to project the scene onto the monitor are no longer correct.

The Kinect can be used to detect the user's head location and gaze and modify these matrix parameters accordingly to make the rendered scene change correctly as the user moves. The effect of this is that a display serves as a type of window into a virtual scene, which is only visible by looking "through" the display. This introduces many new potential uses and interactions that can be integrated into an application. For example, in an adventure game the user can move around and gain a better view of the scene around them, potentially finding new items that aren't visible by standing directly in front of the display.

2.6   Conclusion

We have taken a brief tour of the Kinect device and studied what it can do, how we as developers connect to and use its data streams, and also some of the interesting and novel applications that could arise from its use. There is a vibrant development community building around the Kinect, with significant support from Microsoft for this popular device. It remains to be seen what the next fantastic application of the Kinect will be, but I hope that this article has helped put the reader into the position that they can start building it!

Bibliography

[Bradski and Kaehler 08] Gary Bradski and Adrian Kaehler. *Learning OpenCV: Computer Vision with the OpenCV Library*. Sebastopol, CA: O'Reilly Media, 2009.

[Fernando and Kilgard 03] Randima Fernando and Mark Kilgard. *The Cg Tutorial: The Definitive Guide to Programmable Real-Time Graphics*. Boston: Addison-Wesley Professional, 2003.

[Hieroglyph 3 12] Hieroglyph 3 Rendering Library. http://hieroglyph3.codeplex. com, last accessed August 27, 2012.

[Izadi et al. 11] Shahram Izadi, David Kim, Otmar Hilliges, David Molyneaux, Richard Newcombe, Pushmeet Kohli, Jamie Shotton, Steve Hodges, Dustin Freeman, Andrew Davison, and Andrew Fitzgibbon. "KinectFusion: Real-Time 3D Reconstruction and Interaction Using a Moving Depth Camera." In *Proceedings of the 24th Annual ACM Symposium on User Interface Software and Technology*, pp. 559–568. New York: ACM, 2011.

[Microsoft 12] Microsoft Corporation. Kinect for Windows homepage. http:// www.microsoft.com/en-us/kinectforwindows/, last accessed August 27, 2012.

[Shotton et al. 11] Jamie Shotton, Andrew Fitzgibbon, Mat Cook, Toby Sharp, Mark Finocchio, Richard Moore, Alex Kipman, and Andrew Blake. "Real-Time Human Pose Recognition in Parts from Single Depth Images." In *Proccedings og the 2011 IEEE conference on Computer Vision and Pattern Recognition*, pp. 1297–1304. Los Alamitos, CA: IEEE Press, 2011.

A Pipeline for
Authored Structural Damage
Homam Bahnassi and Wessam Bahnassi

3.1 Introduction

There are scenarios in which a game needs to show damage and injuries to characters and buildings. Severe damage cannot be conveyed acceptably by classic decal approaches, as the structure of the object itself changes. For example, a character might have holes in its body, or severed limbs, or a building façade might take rocket damage in various locations causing holes in the structure.

In this article, we present a description of a full pipeline for implementing structural damage to characters and other environmental objects that is comparable to previous work in the field. We cover details for a full pipeline from mesh authoring to displaying pixels on the screen, with qualities including artist-friendliness, efficiency, and flexibility.

3.2 The Addressed Problem

True structural damage often requires change in shape. The modeling of the 3D object may differ in the damaged parts. There are tools and methods that automatically calculate fracture and damage on objects, but these methods generally work in cases where damage detail is not important and the structure of the object is generally uniform (e.g., concrete columns or wood planks). The other possibility is to add damage detail manually according to an artistic vision. We call this *authored damage*, and it has the capability of revealing any details the artist finds interesting (e.g., rebars in concrete walls or internals of a space alien). It is true that authored damage can lack in variety when compared to an automatic method due to the latter being able to generate virtually unlimited possibilities of fracture and damage, but even nowadays the automatic methods tend to "bake" their fracture calculations to avoid performance issues at runtime, thus reducing variety in a similar way as authored damage does. In this article, we concentrate on authored damage techniques.

We aim in this article to find a solution to the problem that fulfills the following goals as much as possible:

- **Artist-friendliness.** The technique should not add complexities to the authoring process or requirements that interfere with common authoring techniques.

- **Flexibility.** It should be able to support an unrestricted number of damage areas on a single object in unrestricted locations.

- **Rendering efficiency.** It should have a predictable rational cost and avoid taxing the original object rendering with expensive shader costs or reducing overall efficiency.

In the next few sections we review previous work and compare it against the goals above, then we describe our own technique and compare it also to the same set of goals.

3.3   Challenges and Previous Work

Previous work addressing the issue exists with varying capabilities and features [Vlachos 10, Reis 10, Kihl 10]. In all of these works, it is clear that the main difficulty is in hiding the original undamaged mesh geometry in order to make a clean location for the damage geometry to replace it. This step is necessary because, in most cases, the damage shape "eats away" from the original structure, thus some parts of the original 3D object need to be removed.

There are a number of existing techniques for hiding geometry from a 3D object in real time. The list below shows a selection of these techniques. It also includes some of the shortcomings of each of them.

- Modeling the original object in separate pieces that can be shown/hidden selectively at runtime: Although this is simple, it suffers from a few issues. First, it can be inconvenient for artists to build objects in separate pieces (particularly animated characters). Second, rendering of such an object might require several draw calls, which can cause performance issues in some cases.

- Collapsing bones to hide geometry by forcing triangles to become degenerate around a certain point [Reis 10]: This is effective and easy to implement; however, it is limited to skinned meshes only and cannot handle arbitrary geometry-hiding locations (i.e., only terminal limbs can be hidden).

- Using alpha-testing to kill pixels of the geometry to be hidden [Vlachos 10]: This technique offers flexible per-pixel geometry hiding. However, it has the following disadvantages (most are already listed in [Vlachos 10]):

  - It is not very efficient as the hidden pixels will execute their pixel shader even though alpha-testing might kill them, and pixel processing cost is not saved for hidden pixels.

  - The use of alpha-testing may interfere with early-Z optimization on some GPU architectures (e.g., Playstation 3 RSX) and thus results in reduced depth-testing efficiency for the entire rendered object.

  - The technique evaluates a parametric ellipsoid for each damage area in the shader. This puts a practical limitation on the number of evaluated ellipsoids, which in turn limits the number of damaged areas that may appear on a single object at once (only two were allowed in [Vlachos 10]).

  - Killing pixels in the shape of an ellipsoid results in curved cuts that are difficult to fill accurately with replacement damage geometry. The workaround (which our artists found inconvenient) is to add a thick edge or "lip" around the actual damage geometry to cover the empty areas between the ellipsoid and the damage geometry.

The second part of the problem is the rendering of damage geometry in an optimal manner. Although this part of the problem is not as challenging as the first part, it can still benefit from some optimizations that we will cover in this article.

3.4 Implementation Description and Details

From the previous section one can conclude that finding an optimal solution for the problem is not a straightforward task, but there are a few lessons that can be learned to reach better results:

- It is more efficient to hide geometry by triangle culling than per-pixel culling.

- Per-pixel culling makes it difficult for artists to fill the gaps.

- If support for an unrestricted number of damage areas is needed, then the calculations must be independent of the number of damage areas; otherwise, performance will increasingly suffer the more damage areas are supported.

On a high level, the approach we propose can be summarized by the following steps:

1. **Authoring step**. An artist paints groups of polygons on the mesh with vertex colors to mark them as "hide-able."

2. Pipeline step. The content pipeline processes each colored polygon group and assigns it an ID.

3. Runtime step. At runtime, the programmer decides to hide all polygons belonging to a certain ID, so he passes the ID in a bit field to the vertex shader. The vertex shader collapses the marked polygons, effectively preventing them from rasterizing any pixels. The programmer then renders fill geometry in place of the hidden polygons.

Next, we delve into the details of each of the above mentioned steps. Then we will analyze the technique and see if it achieves the goals mentioned in Section 3.2.

3.4.1   Authoring Step

The first step is to decide what damage will appear on the 3D object. For each enumerated damage area, we assign it a unique color code. This color will be used to mark polygons of the 3D object to be hidden when the respective damage is to appear at runtime. Table 3.1 shows an example for a hypothetical character object.

Once the table is set, the artists use the color-coding scheme to paint *polygons* of the 3D object belonging to each supported damage area using per-vertex coloring techniques (see Figure 3.1). This is necessary to later allow the programmer to hide the polygons at runtime before he renders the replacement damage geometry.

It is important to note that even though we are using per-vertex colors, the artist should restrict the painting to entire polygons, not individual vertices. This is key to allow proper polygon hiding, otherwise rendering artifacts will appear (see Figure 3.2).

In Maya, this can be achieved by selecting the polygons that belong to a particular damage area and applying the corresponding color code value using the "Apply Color" command. In Maya 2012, this command can be accessed from the "Polygons" module under the "Color" menu. In the command options, the

Damage	Color Value	Color Sample	Color Name	Color ID
Head	255/0/0		Red	1
Left shoulder	0/0/255		Blue	2
Left arm	0/255/0		Green	3
Left palm	255/255/0		Yellow	4
Chest	255/0/255		Pink	5
Stomach	0/255/255		Cyan	6
...	...	...	...	...

Table 3.1. Damage-area color-code table for a hypothetical character object.

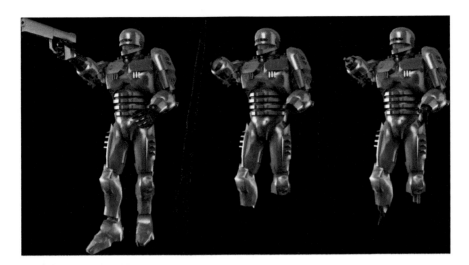

Figure 3.1. Painting polygons to mark them as "hide-able" at runtime (left). The model with marked polygons hidden, leaving gaps to be filled by damage geometry (center). Filling the gaps with damage geometry (right).

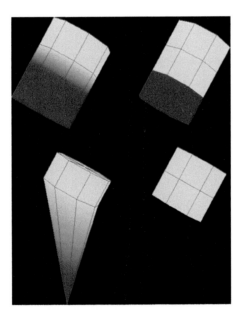

Figure 3.2. Incorrect painting (top left) results in stretching polygons when applying the technique at runtime (bottom left). Proper painting is applied to whole polygons (top right), resulting in proper hiding at runtime (bottom right).

Figure 3.3. Recommended settings for the "Apply Color" command in Maya.

"Operation" should be set to "Replace color" or else the applied color may not be the same as the one selected in the option box (see Figure 3.3).

In Softimage, the same result can be achieved by using the "Paint Vertex Color Tool" under "Property\Map Paint Tools." Color and other painting options can be set through the "Brush Properties" under the same menu (see Figure 3.4). The following recommended options can be set under the "Vertex Color" tab in the brush property page:

- Color Paint Method to Raycast.

- Bleeding to Polygon.

These values allow the artist to paint colors on polygons quickly without being afraid of bleeding on vertices of adjacent polygons.

Finally, in 3dsMax, one can add the "VertexPaint" modifier to the object. This will open a floating window where the artist can control brush options. The "Opacity" value should be set to 100 to get the exact selected color. Then the

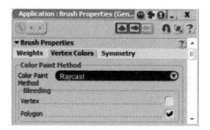

Figure 3.4. Recommended settings for "Brush Properties" in Softimage.

Figure 3.5. A custom toolbar in Softimage with three commands for applying vertex colors for each damage area, in addition to other commands for visualizing the damage effects.

artist can either apply the color using the "Paint All" button on the selected polygons, or he can use the brush tool to paint the colors on vertices directly.

To avoid applying incorrect colors and to minimize painting time, a custom tool can be developed to store the color codes for each damage area. The artist can use this tool to apply the correct colors without needing to memorize their values or mappings. (See Figure 3.5.)

Once the polygons are marked, the artist can then hide them in the 3D authoring tool and build the replacement damage geometry to fit their place accurately.

The main 3D object is then exported along with its per-vertex color channel and the accompanying damage meshes for processing in the pipeline step.

3.4.2 Pipeline Step

The goal of the pipeline step is to transform the marked damage areas into data that can be easily and effectively used at runtime. Table 3.1 shows the color coding scheme used for an object. The last column assigns a single integer value (*color ID*) to each color code entry. This is the value that will be used at runtime to identify each damage area. We use the data-processing pipeline to detect the color coding of each polygon and assign it its matching ID instead. Later, we will see how this ID is used in the runtime step.

The data-processing pipeline usually performs tasks such as reading mesh data from source files, cleaning the mesh and optimizing it, compressing its data, and checking it for validity. We add one more step that does the following:

1. Validate the presence of vertex color information in meshes that support damage, otherwise consider this an export error (missing required information).

2. For each vertex, compare its color with the colors in the damage areas table. If the color was not found, then return an error (unknown color code used for marking a damage area).

3. Obtain the ID of the color found from the table, and store the ID in the final mesh vertex information. If the vertex does not belong to any damage area, set the ID to zero.

   It is possible to store this number in its own vertex attribute or to try to compress it. For example, we can store the ID in the vertex normal by adding 1 to the ID value then multiply it by the vertex normal value. To extract the value in the shader, simply take the vertex normal length and subtract 1 from it. The original vertex normal can be reclaimed by standard normalization. This trick requires no additional space of per-vertex data, but it might not work if the vertex normal is already compressed by some form.

This color ID is all that is needed to support hiding the polygons at runtime. The damage geometry exported with the main object can be processed using the standard mesh-processing pipeline.

3.4.3   Runtime Step

The final step of the process is to actually use the data to control the visibility of damage on the object at runtime. For each object supporting damage, we prepare a bit field that holds flags representing the visibility of each damage area on the object, where the first bit represents the damage area with ID 1 from the damage table, and so on. To hide the polygons of the object associated with a particular color code, we raise the bit matching the ID to 1. Notice that multiple bits may be set to 1 simultaneously, resulting in the ability to show/hide different damage area polygons freely. Damage areas that are not "damaged" yet should set their respective bits in the bit field to 0.

When the time comes to render the object, the damage bit field is set as a vertex-shader constant. The vertex shader then checks if the damage ID value of the vertex has its respective bit set to 1 in the bit field. If so, the position of the vertex is set to $(0, 0, 0)$; otherwise it is left untouched.

Note that this bit-check operation is an integer computation that is not supported by all shader models and current-generation console GPUs. Thus, we will describe a way to achieve the same result with floating-point mathematics only for such cases.

```
// Return 1 if bit at zero-based index is 1 in the bit field;
// otherwise return 0.
float checkBit(float bitField, float bitIndex)
{
    float bitValue = pow(2,bitIndex);
    bitField = fmod(bitField,bitValue*2);
    return (bitField - bitValue) >= 0.0f ? 1.0f : 0.0f;
}
```

Listing 3.1. Code for the `checkBit()` function.

Bit-field check using floating-point mathematics. The damage bit-field value is stored on the CPU as an integer variable. However, current-generation shader models do not support useful integer operations, so we have to do the work with floating-point mathematics. First, store the bit-field value in a vertex shader constant. We store the value "logically." That is, if our bit-field is 010110, then this translates to 22 in decimal, so we set the constant value to 22.0f for the vertex shader. Then, in the vertex shade,r we can pass this value to the function `checkBit()` in Listing 3.1.

Listing 3.2 shows an example of how to use the `checkBit()` function to detect whether the vertex belongs to a damaged area or not.

It is important to note that using floating-point mathematics to do the bit check cannot benefit from all bits available in the floating-point variable. If we were doing integer mathematics, then a standard 32-bit integer can represent 32

```
extern float damageBitField;
VS_OUTPUT VS_Main(VS_INPUT In)
{
    .
    .
    .
    // Check whether this vertex belongs to a "damaged" area.
    // Damage ID is compressed with vertex normal.
    float damageID = round(length(In.normal))-1;
    if (damageID > 0)
    {
        float damaged = checkBit(damageBitField, damageID-1);
        In.position *= 1.0f-damaged; // Collapse vertex if damaged
    }
    .
    .
    .
}
```

Listing 3.2. Sample code of a vertex shader that supports damage.

damaged areas, but due to how floating-point numbers work, we are limited to 24 damaged areas per single-precision floating-point variable.[1]

One might note that this effectively limits us to 32 or 24 damaged areas at most (depending on whether we use integer or floating-point mathematics). But, in fact, it is still possible to support more bits at a fixed cost by utilizing more than one variable to store the bit field. The only reason we have limited ourselves to a single variable for the bit field so far is for ease of explanation and that it is expected that not many objects exceed that number of damage areas. Thus, the code given in Listings 3.1 and 3.2 is a simpler and faster version than the more general case we are going to show next.

Expanding the bit field into a bit array. To support an unrestricted number of damage areas, we have to modify the above method slightly. First, the bit field is now turned into a bit array on the CPU side. At render time, the bit array must be converted into an array of floating-point vectors of enough size to hold all bits in the array in the same way we did in the single variable case. Next, in the shader, based on the damage ID, we calculate the array index of the floating-point variable that holds the bit value. That variable is then passed to `checkBit()` and everything else remains unchanged. Listing 3.3 adds this operation to the same sample code in Listing 3.2.

Rendering replacement damage geometry. Now that we have managed to hide polygons of a damaged area in an effective manner, all that remains is to fill the gaps with replacement geometry that depicts the damage shapes. There are a few ways to do this, each having its pros and cons:

1. Rendering damage geometry in the same draw call as the main object: The benefit of this way is that no additional draw calls are ever needed for the damaged object. The disadvantage is that if the damage geometry is dense then rendering power may be wasted on processing vertices that remain hidden for quite some time (depending on gameplay circumstances). On some platforms this might be OK, as vertex processing power is often underused. However, this is not always the case (e.g., the Playstation 3 RSX is relatively slow in vertex processing).

   To implement this method, the damage-geometry vertices must be identified uniquely from the main-object vertices. This can be represented by one single bit in the vertex attributes (e.g., the sign of UV coordinate x). Then, depending on whether the vertex belongs to the main object or not, the condition for collapsing the vertex based on its damage ID is reversed.

---

[1]You can safely represent integer numbers in a 32-bit floating-point variable to a value up to 16,777,215 (0xFFFFFF) that is 24-bits wide. Higher numbers can still be represented, but discontinuities occur (e.g., 16,777,217 cannot be represented), thus going to such limits is not reliable.

```
extern float damageBitArray[16]; // Set to maximum size needed.

VS_OUTPUT VS_Main(VS_INPUT In)
{
    .
    .
    .
    // Check whether this vertex belongs to a "damaged" area.
    // Damage ID is compressed with vertex normal.
    float damageID = round(length(In.normal))-1;
    if (damageID > 0)
    {
        // Assume a single-precision floating-point number
        // can represent an integer number of about 24 bits.
        float bitArrayIndex;
        damageID = modf((damageID-1)/24, bitArrayIndex) * 24;
        float damageBitField = damageBitArray[bitArrayIndex];
        float damaged = checkBit(damageBitField, damageID);
        In.position *= 1.0f-damaged; // Collapse vertex if damaged
    }
    .
    .
    .
}
```

Listing 3.3. Sample code of the more complex case of supporting an unrestricted number of damage areas in the vertex shader.

2. Rendering each damage geometry in a separate draw call: This is the direct method, but it suffers from increased draw-call count per damaged object. For certain platforms, this can be more efficient than wasting time processing hidden damage-geometry vertices all the time.

3.5 Level of Detail

One important aspect to 3D objects is that they might be authored in multiple levels of detail (LODs), which are used to increase rendering efficiency at runtime by reducing the geometric detail of a 3D object as it covers smaller area of the screen. Since our technique is tightly bound to the topology of the 3D object, any change in this topology requires adjusting the marked damage polygons and their replacement damage geometry. This requires that when the artist builds additional LODs for a certain 3D object, he must remember to mark the damage polygons in those additional LODs in a similar way to the main LOD. The replacement geometry could also benefit from having LODs of their own, but in some cases authoring LODs for those pieces of geometry is not necessary, and the main LOD version can be reused as is with lower main-object LODs. It really depends on the type of 3D object and how it was modeled.

3.6   Discussion

If we compare our proposed technique with the goals we set in Section 3.2, we can find that it manages to largely achieve all of the three aspects together:

- Artist-friendliness. Artists can easily mark hidden polygons and can accurately model replacement damage geometry. Supporting LODs requires a little bit of rework, but unfortunately that is how LODs are done.

- Flexibility. The technique supports an unrestricted number of damage areas on a single object in unrestricted locations. The only limitation is that damage areas cannot overlap (a vertex may belong to only one damage area at a time).

- Rendering efficiency. The only cost added is a few conditional vertex-shader instructions. The cost is irrespective of the number of damage areas on the object. Additionally, we do not require any changes to the object's pixel shader nor its rendering states. There is no need for alpha-testing nor other tricks that might hinder hardware optimizations.

There are many damage effects that can benefit from this technique. However, some games might have different requirements that are not compatible with this technique. In that case, we hope at least that we have succeeded in giving some ideas to build upon when developing new techniques for damage effects.

3.7   Conclusion

In this chapter, we have studied the possible approaches of rendering authored structural damage on 3D objects. A review of previous work is made with a description of the advantages and drawbacks of each technique mentioned. A high-level description of a new artist-friendly, efficient, and flexible technique for rendering authored damage is presented, followed by detailed implementation steps covering the entire pipeline from content authoring to rendering at runtime, including a few tricks for simulating bit-testing with floating-point mathematics on shader profiles that do not support native integer operations. The matter of supporting LODs is highlighted, followed finally by a discussion that compares the new technique to the ideal-case goals.

There is potential for further expansion of the technique so that it supports the complex case of overlapping damage areas.

3.8   Acknowledgments

We would like to thank Abdulrahman Al-lahham for his help and time reviewing this chapter.

Bibliography

[Kihl 10] Robert Kihl. "Destruction Masking in Frostbite 2 Using Volume Distance Fields." SIGGRAPH Course: Advances in Real-Time Rendering in 3D Graphics and Games, Los Angeles, CA, July 2010. (Available at http://advances.realtimerendering.com/s2010/Kihl-Destruction%20in%20 Frostbite(SIGGRAPH%202010%20Advanced%20RealTime%20Rendering%20 Course).pdf.)

[Reis 10] Aurelio Reis. "Real-Time Character Dismemberment." In *Game Engine Gems 1*, edited by Eric Lengyel, Chapter 19. Burlington, MA: Jones and Bartlett Publishers, 2010.

[Vlachos 10] Alex Vlachos. "Rendering Wounds in Left 4 Dead 2." Presentation, Game Developers Conference 2010, San Francisco, CA, March 9, 2010. (Available at http://www.valvesoftware.com/publications/2010/gdc2010_ vlachos_l4d2wounds.pdf.)

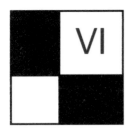

GPGPU

Today, the use of GPGPU is prevalent on most modern architectures. With the parallel nature of the GPU, any algorithm that can process data in parallel can generally run orders of magnitudes faster than their CPU counterparts. Therefore it makes sense to take advantage of this power, considering that suitable hardware can now be found on most common hardware configurations. This section will covers articles that present techniques that go beyond the normal pixel and triangle scope of GPUs and take advantage of the parallelism of modern graphic processors to accomplish such tasks.

The first article, "Bit-Trail Traversal for Stackless LBVH on DirectCompute" by Sergio Murguía, Francisco Ávila, Leo Reyes, and Arturo García, describes an improvement to existing stackless bounding volume hierarchy (BVH) methods that enables the fast construction of the structure while maintaining traversal performance sufficient for real-time ray tracing. The algorithm can be used for basic ray tracing but can also be extended for use in global illumination and other algorithms that can depend on rapid BVH traversal on the GPU. The article covers an implementation of the stackless linear BVH running solely on the GPU as well as the various traversal algorithms that may be needed.

And finally, in "Real-Time JPEG Compression Using DirectCompute," Stefan Petersson describes a complete JPEG encoder implementation on the GPU using DirectCompute. This allows for the real-time storage and encoding of not only image data but also video sequences. With the close integration of the encoder with the application, the latency and compression cost is reduced, making real-time video streaming from 3D applications more feasible. In the article, he covers all aspects from color quantization to color-space conversions and entropy coding—and how each of the different elements can be implemented on the GPU.

—Sébastien St-Laurent

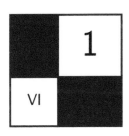

1

Bit-Trail Traversal for Stackless LBVH on DirectCompute
Sergio Murguía, Francisco Ávila, Leo Reyes, and Arturo García

1.1 Introduction

Rendering dynamic scenes with ray tracing is a major challenge on current hardware and software implementations. Fast construction algorithms are usually needed to rebuild acceleration structures from scratch on each frame in current state-of-the-art implementations. However, these algorithms tend to have poor traversal performance.

This article describes an improvement to the stackless linear bounding volume hierarchy (SLBVH) presented in [Murguia et al. 11], which is a new way for traversing and constructing a linear bounding volume hierarchy (LBVH). The SLBVH enables dynamic scenes relying on a fast construction algorithm while maintaining traversal performance for real-time ray tracing. Furthermore, a naive Monte Carlo algorithm allows the framework to produce high-quality global illumination effects.

The current implementation is the continuation of the chapter "Interactive Ray Tracing Using the Compute Shader on DirectX 11" published in *GPU Pro 3* [Garcia et al. 12]. The core of this new chapter is the heap-based structure. The main contributions of the article are

1. a tutorial on how to implement a SLBVH running solely on the GPU using DirectCompute and DirectX 11;

2. a stackless binary heap as an LBVH, reducing memory accesses while maintaining traversal performance;

3. four arithmetic operations that compute the left, right, parent, and next-to-visit nodes (which depend on the direction of the ray);

4. a traversal that can restart from the last node hit instead of the root using a bit trail (intersections for secondary rays are computed faster).

1.2   Ray Tracing Rendering

The SLBVH implementation adds a new stage to the original work of [Garcia et al. 12]. Instead of preloading a stack-based BVH from the CPU, an SLBVH is built from scratch on each frame using the available mesh data on the GPU. The process is the following:

1. Initialize the application on the CPU.

2. Send data to the GPU.

3. Build a SLBVH from scratch.

4. Render:

    (a) Throw primary rays.

    (b) Compute intersections.

    (c) Throw secondary rays.

    (d) Compute color.

5. Repeat Steps 3–4.

The coloring process includes phong shading, flat shading, texturing, normal mapping, gloss mapping, reflections, environment mapping, and shadows. These algorithms are common on rasterization implementations and introductory computer graphics topics.

During the primary ray stage, one ray is thrown through each pixel. The origin is located at the current camera position, and the direction is given by the destination pixel. Each ray, either primary or secondary, travels the structure's tree searching for the closest intersection on the camera space. The ID of the *best intersection* is stored on a buffer in order to calculate the color of the current pixel using the properties of the intersected triangle. The coloring of the pixel takes place on the last stage.

1.3   Global Illumination

In order to generate global illumination effects, the framework uses a Monte Carlo approach. It generates multiple images and renders the average of all of them. The way it presents the images is incremental. First, only one image is generated and displayed. Then, a second image is generated, combined with the previous one, and displayed on the screen. This is repeated until the camera position

```
if (Pdiff >= randomDir.w){
    // Take diffuse reflection.
    g_uRays[index].vfReflectiveFactor *= tx_TextureColor.xyz;
    g_uRays[index].vfDirection = normalize(randomDir.xyz);
}
  else
  {
    // Take specular reflection.
    g_uRays[index].vfReflectiveFactor *= tx_SpecularColor.xyz;
    g_uRays[index].vfDirection =
        normalize(reflect(g_uRays[index].vfDirection, vfNormal));
}
```

Listing 1.1. Reflection in global illumination.

changes or the shaders are reloaded. When the nth image is generated, every pixel p_a in the accumulated image is updated following the formula

$$p_a = \frac{n-1}{n} p_a + \frac{1}{n} p_n.$$

The main difference from conventional ray tracing is that each time a ray hits a primitive, the reflected direction is generated from a random distribution based on the properties of the material. Under global illumination, the reflected ray can be either a diffuse or a specular reflection. When it is reflected in a diffuse way, the new direction is sampled from a unitary sphere; while in the specular reflection, it is computed by taking the reflection around the normal at the hit point. The decision on whether to follow a diffuse reflection over the specular reflection is based on a material parameter called *Pdiff*, which is a number between 0 and 1 that represents the probability of doing a diffuse reflection. The code in Listing 1.1 shows the details on how it is implemented.

Since there are no explicit functions for computing random values in the compute shaders, all the random values are computed in the CPU and sent to the compute shader using a texture. Updating that texture on every frame would be very expensive and could cause the application to slow down. To prevent this, only a two-dimensional offset is updated in every frame and the texture is sampled using that offset combined with the *thread ID*, causing different threads to use a different pixel of the random texture on the same dispatch. Also, since the offset is updated every time a random value is going to be used, the pixel used by an specific thread will be different every time.

Once Monte Carlo is used, it can also be extended to handle other effects; for example, to reduce aliasing, the ray direction can be computed using a point around the center of the pixel causing a subsampling on the pixel. Another effect is depth of field; instead of taking the ray origin as the same point for all the rays as in a pinhole model, the ray origin is taken as a random point around a circle centered at the camera position. Figure 1.1 demonstrates the use of those effects.

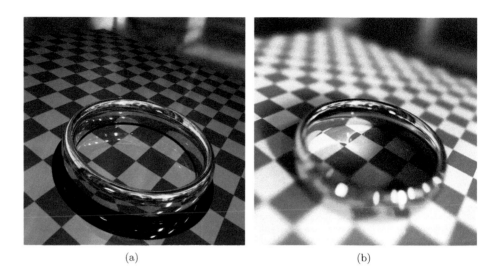

(a)   (b)

Figure 1.1. Comparison of the same scene using (a) Whitted-style ray tracing and (b) Monte Carlo for global illumination. Notice how other effects such as caustics, soft shadows, depth of field, and antialiasing are present when using Monte Carlo.

The current implementation is not fully optimized for global illumination. It produces a high-quality render in 15–30 minutes on large scenes such as the Welsh Dragon and Thai Statue. However, this approach can be used as a starting point for optimized algorithms, as demonstrated in [Ernest and Woop 11], to yield better performance.

1.4   Stackless LBVH

The SLBVH is a stackless and pointerless binary heap that uses a middle split approach based on the Morton code of primitives [Lauterbach et al. 09]. While traversing, the next node to be visited is computed using arithmetic operations. One 32-bit integer is used to store the trail of each ray, which allows restarting the traversal from the last node hit instead of the root [Laine 10]. Also, using the split axis and the direction of the ray, the trail can be used to decide whether the left or right child must be visited first.

The resulting tree is a *heap*. In a heap, the left child of node n is located at $2n$ and the right child is at $2n + 1$. The tree representation assumes that the depth of the tree D will be constant, thus the number of nodes will also remain fixed (regardless of the scene complexity). In this approach, a heap with depth D requires an array of $2^D - 1$ elements. The scene could have either 1 or 1,000,000 primitives, yet the number of nodes remains the same. This introduces some disadvantages since empty nodes must be stored (yet are never visited) in order to satisfy the arithmetic operations that relate the nodes in the heap. On the other hand, the memory footprint of the SLBVH is lower than other stackless approaches [Popov et al. 07] since no extra information is stored in the tree; at the same time, SLBVH has more advantages than similar BVH algorithms [Laine 10] using a bit trail.

Besides the common properties of a heap, the SLBVH possesses the following characteristics:

- The root node is at position $i = 1$. The node at position $i = 0$ is invalid. In this way, the arithmetic operations to traverse the tree are simpler.

- The first right ancestor of node n is found by removing all the least significant bits that are 0 in the binary notation of n.

- The binary notation of an auxiliary 32-bit integer (the "trail") can be used to substitute the stack (commonly used to store the visited nodes during ray traversal). Each bit represents one level in the tree. A 0 means that the level still has unvisited nodes, while a 1 means that all nodes in that level have already been visited.

The tree uses a breadth-first scheme. A depth-first construction scheme was also considered, but the traversal formula becomes more complex and an extra variable is needed to keep track of which side of the subtree is being traversed.

1.4.1 Construction

The size of each node is 32 bytes. Six 32-bit floats are stored per node representing an axis-aligned bounding box (AABB), two 32-bit integers storing the number of primitives (`PrimCount`), and a primitive offset (`PrimPos`). Additionally, `PrimCount` stores the split axis and whether the node is leaf or internal, as shown in Figure 1.2. The axis is stored on the two least-significant bits of `PrimCount`, and the node flag (leaf = 1, internal = 0) is stored on its third least-significant bit. Two bits are enough to store the axis and the flag, but this would increase the number of comparisons when traversing the structure.

Figure 1.2. Binary breakdown of the `PrimCount` variable. The two least-significant bits are used to store the axis: $x = 00$, $y = 01$, and $z = 10$. The third least-significant bit is used to mark a node as leaf. The rest of the bits store the number of primitives in that node.

The construction stage is divided in four steps:

1. Generate AABBs and 32-bit Morton codes for each primitive.

2. Sort primitives using their Morton codes as their keys.

3. Build the tree.

4. Generate AABBs for each node.

Generate AABBs and Morton codes for each primitive. The first step is straight-forward. Each thread computes the Morton code of one primitive. This process assumes that the bounding box for the whole model is known. Since we know the boundaries of the bounding box of the root, it is possible to initialize node 0 (which is invalid) and node 1, which "contains" the whole model. The output of this stage is the input of the sorting algorithm. Each primitive is represented by a Morton code in order to take advantage of its space coherence. The code used is shown in Listing 1.2.

```
// The centroid is not divided by 3
// so we have to adjust the points of the box.
float3 bbMin = (3*g_vfMin);
float3 bbMax = (3*g_vfMax);

// inverse of the boundaries (size of the grid)
float3 invBox = 1024.0f / (bbMin - bbMax);

// Set initial bits according to the position of the primitive.
int3 primComp = int3((vfCentroid - bbMin) * invBox);
uint zComp = (primComp.z & 1);
uint yComp = ((primComp.y & 1) << 1);
uint xComp = ((primComp.x & 1) << 2);

// Initialize Morton code's components.
uint mCode = zComp | yComp | xComp;

int shift3 = 2;
int shift = 2;

// 30 bits for the Morton code (xyz=3 shifts*10)
for (int j = 1; j < 10; j++)
{
  mCode |= (tmp.z & shift) << (shift3++);
  mCode |= (tmp.y & shift) << (shift3++);
  mCode |= (tmp.x & shift) << (shift3);
  shift <<= 1;
}

// Copy to global memory.
g_uMortonCode[index].primitiveId = index;
g_uMortonCode[index].code = mCode;
```

Listing 1.2. Computation of the Morton code for each primitive.

Sort primitives. Our current implementation uses a modified version of the bitonic sort included in the DirectX 11 software development kit (SDK) [Microsoft 10]. According to [Satish et al. 09], radix sort currently seems to be the fastest sorting algorithm on GPU platforms. However, it is not within the scope of the current chapter to discuss the advantages of radix sort against bitonic sort. Bitonic sort allows the current application to build models as big as 2^{18} (262,144) primitives.

A proper sorting implementation would allow the building of bigger models from scratch every frame. The algorithm sorts the primitives in ascending order based on the Morton code computed on the previous stage. For bigger models, the framework uses a CPU-based BVH.

Build the tree. On the third step, the tree is built in a top-down fashion. Each thread computes the data of two nodes, left and right. Since two children share the same parent, race conditions are avoided. The number of passes is equal to the depth of the tree because each pass computes the nodes of one level. It is easy to see that the first levels are poorly parallelized, which represents a serious issue on hierarchical structures. The algorithm stores three types of nodes: invalid, leaf, and internal nodes. For invalid nodes, the algorithm checks the parent of the current nodes. If `PrimCount` is negative, it means that the parent is invalid. Since an invalid node cannot contain valid nodes underneath it, both children are marked as invalid. When the ith node is less than 2^{D-1}, the node is internal. If it is greater than that, then it is a leaf node (as shown in Listing 1.3). There are exceptions to this rule. Internal nodes may be marked as leaf nodes and their children would be marked as invalid (which will never be visited) when

1. a branch finishes all possible geometry partitions before reaching the maximum depth of the tree, D (in this case, the primitives are stored in an internal node, and the node is marked as a leaf node);

2. two or more primitives have the same Morton code (in this case, all primitives with the same Morton code are stored in the same node; if the node is an internal node, then the same process described previously is followed).

The first exception improves traversal performance by 20% because it avoids unnecessary comparisons on deeper branches. In this way, the SLBVH emulates an adaptive BVH by storing primitives in internal nodes. These internal nodes have all the properties of a leaf node. The second exception has the same advantage. If two primitives have the same Morton code, then in the end, they will be stored on the same node. Instead of waiting until the last level of the tree, the primitives are stored on a node as soon as possible.

Leaf nodes are also created when computing the nodes on the last level of the tree, as shown in Listing 1.3. All remaining primitives are stored on either the left or the right child. This is a disadvantage due to memory constraints. On large models, in order to decrease the number of comparisons per ray, the depth

```
int isLeaf = 0;

// If the index corresponds to the lastLevel -1, it is leaf .
if( index >= ( 1 << (g_Depth -1)) )
{
  // Set flag for leaf as true.
  isLeaf = 4;
}

// Check if the node should be leaf.
int primCount = (g_uNodes[parent].iPrimCount >> 3) - 1;
int a = g_uNodes[parent].iPrimPos;
int b = g_uNodes[parent].iPrimPos + primCount;
int mask = g_uMortonCode[a].iCode ^ g_uMortonCode[b].iCode;

// It is  leaf .
if( mask == 0 )
{
  // Make both children invalid.
  // left child
  g_uNodes[index].iPrimPos = -MAX_INT;
  g_uNodes[index].iPrimCount = -MAX_INT;
  // right child
  g_uNodes[index+1].iPrimPos = -MAX_INT;
  g_uNodes[index+1].iPrimCount = -MAX_INT;

  // Set the node as leaf.
  g_uNodes[parent].iPrimCount |= 4;
  return;
}
[...]
```

Listing 1.3. Check for if a node is a leaf node.

of the tree is increased. However, the depth is constrained by GPU memory. Most practical implementations will store more data besides the structure (like the model itself and the textures), which limits the size of the SLBVH built on the GPU. Although increasing the depth of the tree improves the traversal performance, it increases construction time as well. On dynamic scenes, a tradeoff between construction and traversal times is needed. After a certain depth, the traversal performance barely increases.

The cut is done on the longest axis, which improves traversal performance on heterogeneous models such as the Sponza model. On models with uniform primitive size, the gain is minimal. A round-robin approach is also an option, and it works almost as fast as using the longest axis. The axis is stored in the two least-significant bits of `PrimCount` where $x = 00$, $y = 01$, and $z = 10$ in binary notation. If nodes are neither invalid nor leaf, then both nodes are considered internal. The boxes will be computed on the next step of construction. Therefore, this step must store the primitives' offset `PrimPos` and the number of primitives `PrimCount`.

Generate AABBs for each node. Finally, after the tree is completely built, the AABBs for each node are computed. Contrary to the previous step, the tree is now traversed in a bottom-up fashion. This step considers two type of nodes: internal nodes and leaf nodes. If the node is leaf, then the box is built using the box of each primitive. If the node is internal, then the thread takes the boxes of both left and right nodes to create a new box. Using this approach, race conditions are avoided and no synchronization barriers are needed.

1.4.2 Traversal

The traversal algorithm has two important characteristics: it uses a bit trail instead of a stack, and ray traversal restarts on the last node hit (instead of the root). As far as the authors know, the SLBVH is the first algorithm that uses a heap representation and arithmetic operations in order to avoid the use of stacks and pointers. The traversal is similar to a classical BVH. A ray is casted through the scene. The ray performs ray-box intersection tests until it reaches a node marked as leaf. At that point, the ray performs ray-primitive intersection tests and stores the closest intersection to the camera. The difference relies on how the ray visits the next node and on how the ray comes back to a previous nonvisited node. The algorithm stops if the ray comes back to the root. This means that the ray cannot find more intersections.

The trail, which is a "hidden" stack, is a 32-bit integer. Each bit in the trail represents a level on the tree. Each bit in the trail has the following meanings:

- bit = 0. The level on the current subtree contains unvisited nodes. They might be on either the left or the right branches.

- bit = 1. All nodes in the current level of the subtree have been visited.

The initial value of `trail` is 1 << firstbithigh(nodeNum).

- The `firstbithigh` function is an intrinsic DirectX function available in Shader Model 5. It returns the location of the first bit set starting from the highest-order bit and working downwards.

- The output of the `firstbithigh` function returns the depth of the current node.

- If a function similar to `firstbithigh` is not available, the following formula can be used instead:
$$\frac{n+1}{((n+1) \oplus n) \& (n+1)},$$
where n is `nodeNum` and $\&$ is the bitwise AND operator.

- `nodeNum` is the last hit node. It is initially set to 1 (the root).

After the first intersection is found, the traversal stores the intersected `nodeNum` and it is passed to the next traversal iteration. The trail *pushes* nodes when an internal node is intersected (just as a classical BVH) and *pops* nodes when either an intersection was not found or when a leaf node is intersected. A `push` is computed using a bitwise shift-left operation and a `pop` using a bitwise shift-right operation.

The algorithm starts with both `nodeNum` and `trail` set to 1. When going down the tree, the algorithm checks the ray's sign along the current split axis. If the ray is positive, it appends a 0 to `nodeNum` and 1 otherwise. In this case, it also appends a 0 to `trail` (because if the ray goes down the tree, that means that there was an intersection, which is a push). It is also possible to check which of the boxes is hit first by the ray (in case an intersection exists). If the left node is hit first, a 0 should be "pushed" into `nodeNum` and a 1 otherwise.

When going up the tree, `trail = trail + 1`; and then the number `n` of consecutive 0's starting from the least significant bit (LSB) in `trail` is counted. Next, the algorithm sets `trail = trail >> n` (which corresponds to a pop) and `nodeNum = nodeNum >> n`. Finally, `nodeNum`'s LSB is inverted (to mark the other branch as visited). The regular BVH traversal checks are also performed. At each internal node, the ray is intersected with the current box. If there is an intersection, we go "down" the tree. If there is no intersection, we go "up" the tree. Traversal ends when `nodeNum = 1`, which means that the ray returns to the root and no intersections were found.

To illustrate the algorithm, let us walk through an example. Figure 1.3 shows an SLBVH built with 3-bit codes. Each node in the tree is labeled with its index (in binary notation) and, for internal nodes, the split axis is also specified. Note, for instance, that the root is labeled 001 so the left child is $1 \times 2 = 2$ (010_2) and the right child is $1 \times 2 + 1 = 3$ (011_2). Figure 1.3 also shows the signs of an example ray across each axis. In this case, we have a ray that is positive on the x-axis and negative on the y- and z-axes. Positive signs for the ray map to 0 and negative signs to 1. In order to illustrate a full traversal, we will assume that no primitive intersections are found along the ray but all internal nodes intersect the ray. In this way, we are forced to visit all the nodes.

Let n and t stand for the current node and the trail, respectively. Initially, $n = 001_2$ and $t = 001_2$ (Figure 1.3(a)). The current node is the root and its split axis is the x-axis (positive sign $= 0$), so the traversal appends a 0 to n (n is now 010_2). The trail is always appended with a 0 when going down. Thus, we end up with $n = 010_2$ and $t = 010_2$ (which means we went down the left child, see Figure 1.3(b)). For the current node ($n = 010_2$), the split was done along the z-axis (negative sign $= 1$), so we append a 1 to the current node (n is now 101_2) and a 0 to the trail (t is now 100_2). We now have $n = 101_2$ and $t = 100_2$ (1.3(c)). Node $n = 101_2$ is leaf, so we test the primitives contained in it for an intersection. Assuming no intersection was found, we need to "backtrack" to the next sibling.

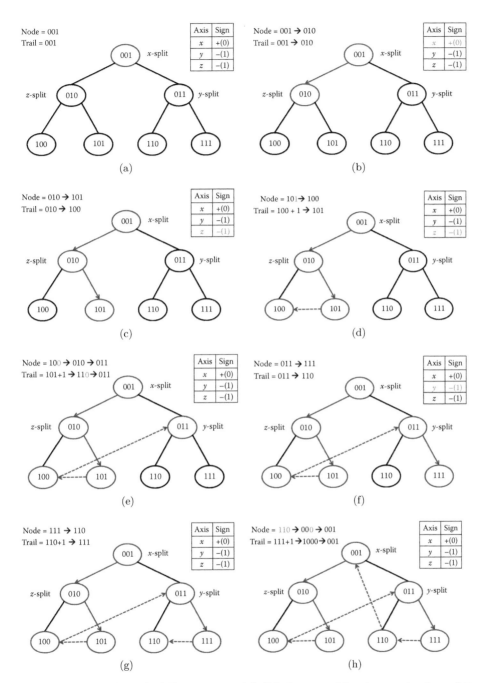

Figure 1.3. Walkthrough, following steps (a)–(h), for a stackless traversal using a bit trail.

```
bool isLeaf = (g_uNodes[nodeNum].iPrimCount & 4);
// Traverse the tree until we find a leaf node.
[allow_uav_condition]
while( !isLeaf )
{
  hit = intersectBox(ray.vfOrigin, invDir, nodeNum);
  p = firstbitlow(trail + 1);

  // Intersection is better than the current one
  // and it's not behind the camera.
  if ((hit[0] > bestIntersection.t) ||
  (hit[1] < 0.0f))
  {
    // does not intersect
    // "Pop" node from trail.
    trail = (trail >> p) + 1;
    // Change to next node.
    nodeNum = (nodeNum >> p) ^ 1;
  }
  else
  {
    // "Push" node to trail.
    trail = trail << 1;
    int axis = g_uNodes[nodeNum].iPrimCount&3;
    int direction = dirIsNeg[axis];
    // Set next node to visit.
    nodeNum = (nodeNum << 1) | direction );
  }
  // If we finish on the root, stop traversal.
  if(trail <= 1) break;
}
```

Listing 1.4. Setting the next node.

To find the next sibling, we add 1 to the trail, yielding $t = 101_2$, and we count the number of 0's starting from the LSB until we find a 1. In this case, there are no trailing zeros, so we simply invert the node's LSB, yielding $n = 100_2$ and $t = 101_2$ (Figure 1.3(d)). Node $n = 100_2$ is another leaf node. Assuming no intersections, we again must find the next sibling. We add 1 to the trail yielding $t = 110_2$. In this case, we get 1 trailing 0, so we remove one bit from the node and the trail and then invert the node's LSB, yielding $n = 011_2$ and $t = 011_2$ (Figure 1.3(e)). Node $n = 011_2$ is internal with a split along the y-axis (negative sign $= 1$). We append 1 to the node and 0 to the trail, yielding $n = 111_2$ and $t = 110_2$ (Figure 1.3(f)). Node $n = 111_2$ is leaf. Assuming no intersections, we add 1 to the trail to yield $t = 111_2$. Since there are no trailing 0's, we invert the node's LSB to yield $n = 110_2$ and $t = 111_2$ (Figure 1.3(g)). Node $n = 110_2$ is leaf. Assuming no intersections, we again need to find the next sibling. Adding 1 to the trail yields $t = 000_2$ with three trailing 0's. Removing three bits from the node and the trail, and inverting the node's LSB, yields $n = 001_2$ and $t = 000_2$ (Figure 1.3(h)). We have returned to the root, so this is the end of the algorithm. Listing 1.4 is the code for the walkthrough of Figure 1.3.

Figure 1.4. The Stanford Bunny (left, 94 fps), Welsh Dragon (center, 31 fps), and Happy Buddha (right, 49 fps) models rendered in real time using the SLBVH. The application uses gloss mapping, phong shading, and one ray for shadows with one light source.

1.5 The SLBVH in Action

The tests were executed on an NVIDIA GTX 590 but using just one of its GPUs. The models compared are the Stanford Bunny (69,451 primitives), Crytek Sponza (279,163 primitives), Conference Room (282,759 primitives), and Welsh Dragon (2,097,152 primitives). The data is normalized and scaled to fit within a sphere of radius 0.8. An average of six different camera positions are used to measure performance.

The grid size is $64 \times 64 \times 1$, and the group size is $16 \times 16 \times 1$ to launch a total of 1,048,576 threads in the compute shader. The resolution is set to $1,024 \times 1,024$ pixels where each thread computes the color of one pixel. The tests shown in Figure 1.5 were executed using shadows, phong shading, and gloss mapping. Reflections were not activated on benchmarks. Shadow rays are not coherent, which heavily impacts on performance. When deactivating shadows, the frame is computed up to two times faster. However, a ray reordering [Garanzha and Loop 10] scheme could improve rendering times.

A BVH using a surface area heuristic (SAH-BVH) is used to compare traversal performance with our SLBVH. The BVH is based on the one provided on the PBRT framework [Pharr and Humphreys 04] and it is built on the CPU.

1.5.1 Traversal Frame Rate

The rendering times are shown in Figure 1.5. Three models are traversed using an SLBVH and a stack-based SAH-BVH. On small models with constant primitive sizes, the SLBVH is as fast as a stack-based SAH-BVH. Since the algorithm is not using a stack, cache memory usage is significantly lower than a BVH with higher tree quality. However, on larger models such as the Welsh Dragon, a high number of primitives occupy the same leaf node, which decreases rendering time.

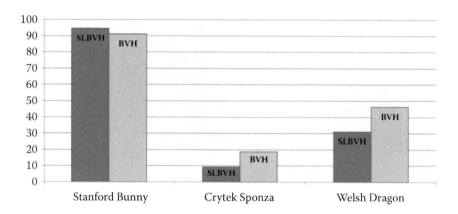

Figure 1.5. Three different-sized models are compared (frames per second) using SLBVH and regular stack-based BVH traversal: Stanford Bunny (depth = 18), Crytek Sponza (depth = 21), and Welsh Dragon (depth = 23).

Two options might yield better results: building a two-level SLBVH or using the surface area heuristic (SAH) as a partition scheme. The first one would produce a "deeper" tree and primitives would disperse on more nodes. The second one would increase tree quality and should be less complex to introduce in the current construction algorithm.

The SLBVH suffers with heterogeneous models such as the Conference Room and Crytek Sponza. Hundreds of small triangles are stored in leaf nodes, which impacts enormously on traversal times. One interesting option would be using the DirectX tessellator in order to partition large triangles into small ones. The number of primitives would increase, but as shown with large models, the traversal performance allows real-time frame rates.

1.5.2 Memory Footprint

The SLBVH is a stackless structure with less memory overhead than the ropes scheme for the stackless kd-trees [Popov et al. 07]. For example, the Stanford Bunny occupies 23 MB in Popov's SKD-Tree. As shown in Figure 1.6, an SLBVH of depth 18 uses only 8 MB of memory, which is enough to store this model due to its small size. This is just one third of the SKD-Tree size. The Conference Room and the Crytek Sponza models have similar characteristics. In the SKD-Tree, the Conference Room occupies 85 MB, while the SLBVH just needs 64 MB. Just as on the Bunny Model, SLBVH shows a better utilization of memory on a stackless approach. However, the SLBVH has a bigger memory footprint than a regular BVH. We are currently working on ways to lower this footprint for the SLBVH.

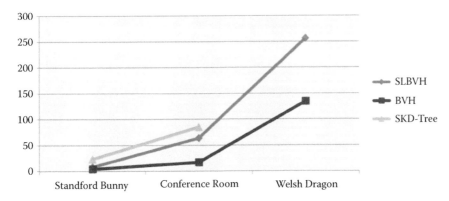

Figure 1.6. Memory footprint (MB) for different structures: SLBVH with varying depth, SAH-based BVH, and SKD-Tree.

1.5.3 Empty Nodes

Contrary to common structures, the SLBVH stores empty nodes in order to satisfy the arithmetic operations (which allow us to traverse the heap without a stack). The percentage of occupied nodes versus empty nodes is considerably low, as shown in Figure 1.7. However, the geometry is not well partitioned given that the middle-split scheme based on Morton codes is not optimal for balanced distributions. On the other hand, using SAH for all levels (or perhaps just the first few levels) of the structure might improve the tree quality. Yet, a tradeoff between construction time and traversal performance must be accomplished. A faster traversal does not mean a more efficient structure on dynamic scenes.

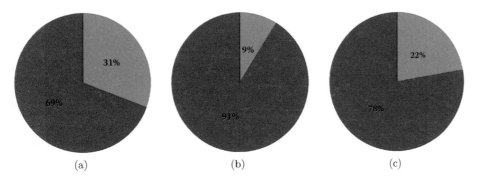

Figure 1.7. SLBVH nodes distribution. The red and blue colors represent empty nodes and occupied nodes, respectively on the (a) Stanford Bunny (depth = 18), (b) Crytek Sponza (depth = 21), and (c) Welsh Dragon (depth=23) models. The primitive-per-leaf ratio is 1.72, 2.98, and 2.35, respectively.

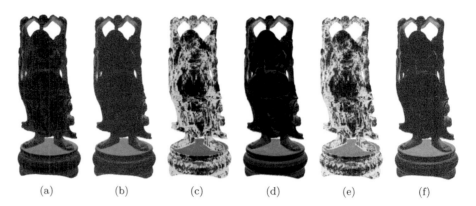

(a)   (b)   (c)   (d)   (e)   (f)

Figure 1.8. Number of intersections per box (a–b, red) and per primitive (c–d, green).
The images show the differences between the SLBVH (a,c,e) and the BVH (b,d,f). The
last two images (e–f) combine the intersections of both boxes and primitives.

Intersections per box and per primitive. Besides the memory waste occasioned by
the heap's scheme, the nonuniform primitives' distribution is not handled opti-
mally by the partition algorithm. Many primitives end up sharing the same leaf
node, leading to an unbalanced tree. As a result, rays intersect few boxes but a
lot of primitives. As shown in Figure 1.8, the BVH does a better job traversing
the structure than the SLBVH, though the comparison is a little unfair since they
are using different partitioning schemes. By decreasing the number of intersected
primitives, the overall performance of the structure should improve. One of the
options to decrease the number of intersected primitives per pixel is using the
SAH algorithm instead of a middle split.

1.6   Conclusion

As far as the authors know, the SLBVH traversal is the first heap-based structure
used for real-time ray tracing. In this approach, traversing the tree can be done
easily with bit-wise operations, removing the need for additional information like
a stack or the "ropes" in the SKD-Tree. This scheme has the additional advantage
that the traversal can be restarted at any point in the tree, which is useful when
computing reflections or refractions.

Even though the memory usage for the SLBVH is higher than the regular LBVH, its memory footprint is lower when compared with other stackless
approaches—even when storing empty nodes. The weakest part of the algorithm
it its poor partition on complex scenes. This is due to the fixed partition scheme
we used (the Morton codes) that ends up with big boxes for a wide range of primitive sizes. However, using a better partition scheme (like SAH) could conceivably
solve this problem.

Besides the partition issue, the memory consumption could be optimized by decreasing or removing the empty space on the structure. However, doing this might lead to having an extra look-up table or to a lack of simple arithmetic operations to traverse the tree. We are currently looking for ways to remove the empty nodes in the SLBVH while retaining the simple stackless traversal scheme.

We have also shown a very simple way to extend the framework to do global illumination. Although naive, this implementation could also serve as a starting point to create more optimized global illumination algorithms.

Even though the SLBVH was used on a ray-tracing environment, the data structure may be used in other, more generic geometric search problems where performance relies on efficiently traversing a uniform set of data tokens represented in a heap. For instance, fast geometric search algorithms are widely used in video games for collision detection and scene culling.

1.7 Acknowledgments

The authors would like to thank the Stanford Computer Graphics Laboratory for the Happy Buddha and the Stanford Bunny models, the Bangor University for the Welsh Dragon model (released for Eurographics 2011), and Crytek for its modified version of the Sponza model.

Bibliography

[Ernest and Woop 11] Manfred Ernest and Sven Woop. "Embree—Photo-Realistic Ray Tracing Kernels." *Intel Software*, http://software.intel.com/en-us/articles/embree-photo-realistic-ray-tracing-kernels/, 2011.

[Garanzha and Loop 10] Kirill Garanzha and Charles Loop. "Fast Ray Sorting and Breadth-First Packet Traversal for GPU Ray Tracing." *Computer Graphics Forum* 29:2 (2010), 289–298.

[Garcia et al. 12] Arturo Garcia, Francisco Avila, Sergio Murguia, and Leo Reyes. "Interactive Ray Tracing Using DirectX11 on the Compute Shader." In *GPU Pro 3*, edited by Wolfgang Engel, pp. 353–376. Boca Raton, FL: CRC Press, 2012.

[Laine 10] Samuli Laine. "Restart Trail for Stackless BVH Traversal." In *Proceedings of the Conference on High Performance Graphics*, pp. 107–111. Aire-la-Ville, Switzerland: Eurographics Association, 2010.

[Lauterbach et al. 09] Christian Lauterbach, Michael Garland, Shubhabrata Sengupta, David Luebke, and Dinesh Manocha. "Fast BVH Construction on GPUs." *Computer Graphics Forum* 28:2 (2009), 375–384.

[Microsoft 10] Microsoft. "DirectX Software Development Kit." *Microsft Download Center*, http://www.microsoft.com/en-us/download/details.aspx?id=6812, June 2010.

[Murguia et al. 11] Sergio Murguia, Arturo Garcia, Francisco Avila, and Leo Reyes. "Stackless LBVH Traversal for Real-Time Ray Tracing." Short paper, Computer Graphics International 2011, Ottawa, Canada, June 15, 2011. (Available at https://docs.google.com/file/d/0BxcYFN7UTqwWeWQ4MWh1WXhKdTQ/edit?usp=sharing.)

[Pharr and Humphreys 04] Matt Pharr and Greg Humphreys. *Physically Based Rendering: From Theory to Implementation*. San Francisco: Morgan Kaufmann Publishers Inc., 2004.

[Popov et al. 07] Stefan Popov, Johannes Günther, Hans-Peter Seidel, and Philipp Slusallek. "Stackless KD-Tree Traversal for High Performance GPU Ray Tracing." *Computer Graphics Forum* 26:3 (2007), 415–424.

[Satish et al. 09] Nadathur Satish, Mark Harris, and Michael Garland. "Designing Efficient Sorting Algorithms for Manycore GPUs." In *Proceedings of the 2009 IEEE International Symposium on Parallel and Distributed Processing*, pp. 1–10. Washington, DC: IEEE Computer Society, 2009.

Real-Time JPEG Compression Using DirectCompute

Stefan Petersson

Transporting frames within a DirectX application to a target destination is a nontrivial task. For example, both low latency and available bandwidth are important factors when streaming image frames via a network connection. By using the technique presented in this chapter, JPEG image data can be encoded in real time. The resulting data may thereafter be streamed to a network destination, saved as an image file, or appended to a movie sequence.

2.1 Introduction

Since the advent of DirectCompute, it is possible to execute more general algorithms using Direct3D with full cross-vendor support. In this chapter a technique is presented that uses DirectCompute to encode baseline JPEG images. The technique is implemented using C++ and Direct3D 11.0, which ease integration into existing rendering systems. By using standard quantization and Huffman tables, a majority of encoding steps can be computed in the GPU and encoded images may be stored as still image JPEG files or appended to a motion-JPEG (MJPEG) movie sequence file. This technique has advantages when source images are generated by the GPU, for example, taking a screenshot or recording gameplay video. GPU encoding can outperform CPU encoding when modern hardware is used.

2.1.1 Baseline JPEG Encoding

JPEG is a digital image compression standard created by the Joint Photographic Experts Group. The standard was accepted in 1992 and supports both lossless and lossy compression modes. Lossy versions are frequently used in, for example, digital cameras and web pages. The image compression method is used in multiple data formats such as the JPEG file interchange format (JFIF) [Hamilton 92]. Files with JFIF information are often referred to as "jpg-files." This section describes

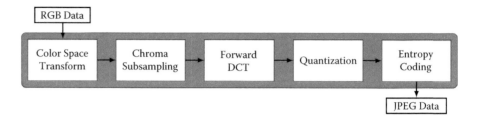

Figure 2.1. Baseline JPEG compression scheme.

the process of encoding uncompressed RGB data into compressed JPEG data. The sequential baseline is the codec implemented in the presented GPU technique. The JPEG codec is widely used and sufficient for most applications. Several encoding steps are required and a brief introduction to each step is presented. Figure 2.1 outlines the main steps that are applied to 8×8 blocks of pixels independently in each color-space component plane. Images with dimensions that are not multiples of 8 have border pixels padded by repeating the edge color. Processed blocks are appended to a final JPEG bit stream.

2.1.2   Color-Space Transform

This first step in the encoding process is optional as the JPEG algorithm is not bound to any specific color space, such as RGB or YC_bC_r. Encoders often sample and convert source-image RGB data into YC_bC_r color-space data, where luminance and chrominance information are separated. Luminance data is stored in the Y component and chrominance data in the C_b and C_r components. RGB to YC_bC_r conversion—see Equation (2.1)—is defined in the *ITU-R BT.601* standard:

$$
\begin{aligned}
Y   &= & & & 0.299R & + & 0.587G & + & 0.114B, \\
C_b &= & 128 & - & 0.168736R & - & 0.331264G & + & 0.5B, \\
C_r &= & 128 & + & 0.5R & - & 0.418688G & - & 0.081312B.
\end{aligned}
\tag{2.1}
$$

2.1.3   Chroma Subsampling

Chroma subsampling describes different sampling patterns used to lower resolution of the C_bC_r planes. Chroma resolution can be reduced because human vision is more sensitive to luminance variations than to chrominance variations [Pennebaker and Mitchell 93]. Luminance information is rarely modified, normally maintaining source-image resolution. One common approach to lower chrominance resolution is by averaging adjacent chroma components together [Kerr 12]. Sampling patterns are described as $W : H : V$, where W represents sampling width, H represents the number of horizontal samples, and V represents the

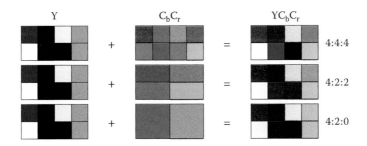

Figure 2.2. Chroma subsampling patterns.

number of vertical samples. Example results of chroma subsampling are illustrated in Figure 2.2, where decoded samples are shown by combining luminance and chrominance information.

2.1.4 Forward Discrete Cosine Transform

After chroma subsampling, a forward discrete cosine transform (FDCT) is applied to each 8×8 block. Before applying FDCT, color components are level shifted to the range $[-128, 127]$. The level shift is applied by subtracting 128 from each component. Subsampled and level-shifted components are grouped into an 8×8 matrix referred to as M. The FDCT is calculated by matrix multiplications, seen in Equation (2.3), where matrices F and F^{T} are defined using Equation (2.2):

$$
F_{i,j} = \begin{cases} \dfrac{1}{\sqrt{8}} & \text{if } i = 0, \\[2ex] \sqrt{\dfrac{2}{8}}\, \cos\left[\dfrac{(2j+1)i\pi}{16}\right] & \text{if } i > 0, \end{cases} \tag{2.2}
$$

$$
D = FMF^{\mathrm{T}}. \tag{2.3}
$$

FDCT converts color information to a frequency domain where more efficient encoding schemes can be used. When applying FDCT, components are divided into differing intensity frequencies. The frequency values are referred to as *DCT coefficients*. Coefficients are usually grouped in a 8×8 matrix, which is referred to as D. The coefficient D_{00} is called the *DC coefficient*, which has zero frequency in both dimensions. The remaining 63 coefficients are called *AC coefficients*, which have nonzero frequency information. FDCT concentrates most signal information in the lower spatial frequencies, which often results in multiple coefficients with zero or near-zero amplitude. Frequency amplitudes that are zero or near-zero are ignored in the following steps.

$$
\begin{bmatrix}
16 & 11 & 10 & 16 & 24 & 40 & 51 & 61 \\
12 & 12 & 14 & 19 & 26 & 58 & 60 & 55 \\
14 & 13 & 16 & 24 & 40 & 57 & 69 & 56 \\
14 & 17 & 22 & 29 & 51 & 87 & 80 & 62 \\
18 & 22 & 37 & 56 & 68 & 109 & 103 & 77 \\
24 & 35 & 55 & 64 & 81 & 104 & 113 & 92 \\
49 & 64 & 78 & 87 & 103 & 121 & 120 & 101 \\
72 & 92 & 95 & 98 & 112 & 100 & 103 & 99
\end{bmatrix}
\qquad
\begin{bmatrix}
17 & 18 & 24 & 47 & 99 & 99 & 99 & 99 \\
18 & 21 & 26 & 66 & 99 & 99 & 99 & 99 \\
24 & 26 & 56 & 99 & 99 & 99 & 99 & 99 \\
47 & 66 & 99 & 99 & 99 & 99 & 99 & 99 \\
99 & 99 & 99 & 99 & 99 & 99 & 99 & 99 \\
99 & 99 & 99 & 99 & 99 & 99 & 99 & 99 \\
99 & 99 & 99 & 99 & 99 & 99 & 99 & 99 \\
99 & 99 & 99 & 99 & 99 & 99 & 99 & 99
\end{bmatrix}
$$

(a) Luminance Q_{50} (b) Chrominance Q_{50}

Figure 2.3. Standard quantization tables for (a) luminance and (b) chrominance.

2.1.5   Quantization

Small changes in high-frequency intensity are not perceived by human vision [Pennebaker and Mitchell 93]. Some DCT coefficient precision may therefore be discarded without major impact in the perception of a decoded image for a viewer. Each DCT coefficient is divided by a corresponding factor in a precalculated quantization table, where each table entry is an integer ranging from 1 to 255. The resulting value is thereafter rounded to the nearest integer. This quantization process loses information and will affect the JPEG data size output. Luminance and chrominance components are quantized using different tables because of the differences explained in Section 2.1.3. The JPEG standard provides optional standard quantization tables—see Figure 2.3—for both luminance and chrominance components. In Equation (2.4), standard table Q_{50} is used to derive tables of different quality levels:

$$
Q_{\text{quality}} =
\begin{cases}
Q_{50}\dfrac{(100 - \text{quality})}{50} & \text{if quality} > 50, \\[3mm]
Q_{50}\dfrac{50}{\text{quality}} & \text{if quality} < 50.
\end{cases}
\tag{2.4}
$$

After quantization all coefficients are ordered in a zigzag sequence; see Figure 2.4. The zigzag ordering is used to place low-frequency coefficients, which have higher probability to be nonzero, before high-frequency coefficients.

2.1.6   Entropy Coding

After quantization the coefficients are entropy-coded to compact coefficient information into a bit stream. Each nonzero coefficient is encoded as the concatenation of two symbols, wherein the first symbol is Huffman coded. Huffman tables may be computed per image before compression or predefined and used for all images. In this chapter two predefined, JPEG standard, Huffman coding tables are used. There is one DC coefficient code table and one AC coefficient code table. DC coefficients are coded as deltas from the previous block in that color plane. The

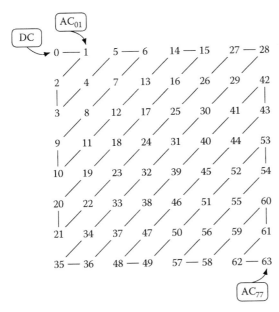

Figure 2.4. Zigzag sequence order.

first DC symbol includes the bit count and the second symbol includes the amplitude information. The first AC symbol contains preceding zeros and the number of bits needed to represent the second AC symbol, in which amplitude information is stored. Figure 2.5 illustrates how symbols are represented in memory,

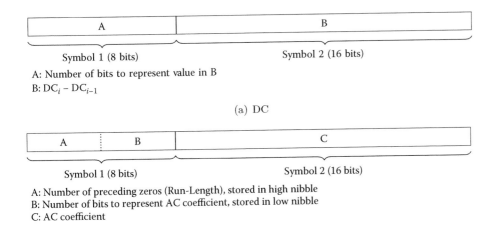

Figure 2.5. Code symbol structure for (a) DC and (b) AC coefficients.

before Huffman coding is applied. Coefficient symbols are sequentially variable length encoded (VLE) and concatenated into a JPEG bit stream. Special marker symbols are used in the following conditions:

1. for every preceding 16 zeros of an AC coefficient,

2. when an additional 0x00 byte is appended directly after bytes that equals 0xFF,

3. to indicate end of block (EOB) or end of image (EOI).

Further entropy coding details are beyond the scope of this chapter.

2.2   Implementation

Based on the description in Section 2.1.1, this section describes the implementation of a baseline JPEG encoder using DirectX 11.0 and Shader Model 5.0. The encoder is designed and implemented using C++ and the Direct3D 11.0 API, making it trivial to use in an existing DirectX 11.0-based renderer. Shader preprocessor directives are used in the example implementation to control the output index and texture sampling behavior: this makes it possible to use the same shader program for all YC_bC_r components. Each thread group consists of 8×8 threads—see Listing 2.3—and the number of dispatched thread groups is based on the source-image dimensions and chroma subsampling mode. The following features of Direct3D are beneficial to encoding JPEG data:

- full interoperability with all Direct3D resources,

- execution of group threads synchronization,

- computations' access to group shared memory,

- read and write capabilities on resources via *unordered access views*,

- automatic bounds check when reading from or writing to *shader resource views* and unordered access views,

- atomic intrinsic functions,

- source texture rescaling by hardware.

2.2.1   Performance Considerations

This encoder technique is designed and implemented to minimize global memory accesses. Global accesses may considerably lower performance if overused, for example, when the same data is processed in multiple dispatch calls. Therefore only one dispatch call per color plane is invoked. Loops accessing memory are manually unrolled to help the compiler. To maintain computation performance, shared memory registers are reused. The total size of shared members is 32 KB for data. Group shared memory is smaller in size than 16 KB and may therefore make it possible for a multiprocessor to execute two thread groups simultaneously [Fung 10]. Global memory accesses are, whenever possible, coalesced to avoid multiple transactions.

2.2.2 Challenges

Source-image data is stored in `Texture2D` resource objects. To encode `Texture2D` resource data, three technical problems may arise. Also challenges may occur, for example, if the output-image dimensions differ from the source-image dimensions.

No shader resource. When creating a texture resource in Direct3D, different *bind flags* are set. Bind flags tell how a resource is bound to the pipeline. After resource creation, it is no longer possible to modify any bind flag settings. This means that a nonshader resource texture has to be copied to a resource with the flag set. Compatible resources can copy data to and from each other using the device method `CopyResource`. Swap-chain buffers (back buffer) can be created with the `DXGI_USAGE_SHADER_INPUT` flag that maps to `D3D11_BIND_SHADER_RESOURCE`. Back-buffer data can then be sampled directly without copying to another resource. It is not possible to sample textures that are currently bound to the output merger stage, and therefore the back buffer has to be unbound before encoding starts.

Multisampling enabled. Texture resources with multisampling enabled have to be processed before encoding starts. A multisampled resource, of same dimensions and compatible format, is copied into a nonmultisampled resource by using the device context method `ResolveSubresource`. The target resource may thereafter be encoded.

Image dimensions not multiples of 8 or 16. Depending on the chroma subsampling mode, image dimensions have to be multiples of either 8 or 16. One solution to the problem is to repeat edge pixels until evenly divisible values are met. In this technique edge pixels are repeated by dispatching threads outside texture boundaries. Threads sample source-texture color data using the `D3D11_TEXTURE_ADDRESS_CLAMP` address mode. The sampling mode automatically repeats border-color values, avoiding the need for conditional behavior in the shader. Texture coordinates are calculated from `SV_DispatchThreadID` values; see Listing 2.1. Border-pixel data is also entropy coded and actual image dimensions are specified in the JFIF header. Padded image dimensions are now referred to as *computation dimensions*.

```
float2 GetTexCoord(uint3 DispatchThreadID)
{
    return float2(DispatchThreadID.x / ImageWidth,
                  DispatchThreadID.y / ImageHeight);
}
```

Listing 2.1. Texture coordinate calculation used with chroma subsampling 4:4:4.

Element	Resource Type
Image dimensions	Constant buffer
Computation dimensions	Constant buffer
Output block size	Constant buffer
Source texture	Shader resource view
Quantization table	Shader resource view
AC Huffman table	Shader resource view
GPU output result	Unordered access view

Table 2.1. Shader resources used in different instances.

2.2.3   GPU Initialization

Some Direct3D resources can be created at encoding system initialization, while others have to be created based on encoding parameters. The necessary resource types used are either textures, *constant buffers*, or *structured buffers* that utilize cache functionality. Constant buffers are used when multiple threads read the same data. Structured buffers are used when multiple threads read different data. The output buffer size is calculated based on the JPEG quality and the chroma subsampling mode, since lower chroma resolution results in fewer computation blocks and less memory to be copied from the GPU to the CPU. Textures and structured buffers are accessed as shader resource views, and the output buffer is accessed as an unordered access view. One compute shader instance is created per color plane, and the shader resources in Table 2.1 are used in each instance.

2.2.4   Execution

Figure 2.1 illustrates a generic encoding process where only some of the steps are suited for GPU processing. The execution path used in this technique involves both GPU and CPU processing. The GPU is used to compute a majority of encoding steps, and the CPU is used to stitch together final JPEG data. Encoding can take place when all required resources are created. The input data to each encode invocation includes image width, image height, source-image resource, data block size, and JPEG quality. Quantization tables are calculated based on JPEG quality, while computation dimensions are calculated from image dimensions and subsampling mode. Figure 2.6 illustrates an execution of a single thread group, where the final output is one DC coefficient, a bit-stream of entropy coded AC coefficients, and the number of bits occupied by the AC data.

Dispatch thread groups. For each color plane, thread groups are spawned by calling the device context method `Dispatch`; see the C++ code in Listing 2.2. The method takes three input parameters that specify how many thread groups to spawn in each dimension. Each thread group consists of 64 threads, 8 threads

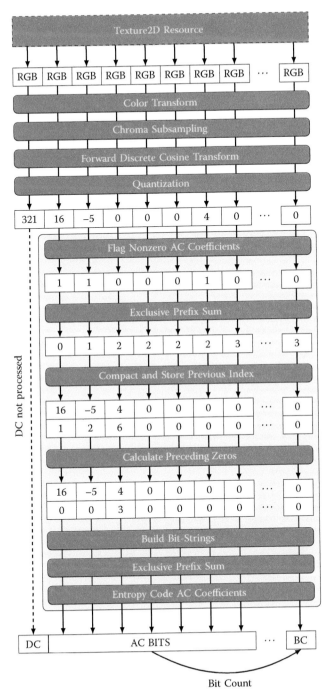

Figure 2.6. Thread group execution flow example.

```
void Dispatch()
{
    ...
    d3dContext->Dispatch(numBlocksY_x, numBlocksY_y, 1);
    ...
    d3dContext->Dispatch(numBlocksCb_x, numBlocksCb_y, 1);
    ...
    d3dContext->Dispatch(numBlocksCr_x, numBlocksCr_y, 1);
}
```

Listing 2.2. Dispatching of thread groups.

per x- and y-dimension, as the main HLSL function in Listing 2.3 shows. The group thread count is a multiple of 32, which is recommended to maximize hardware occupancy [Bilodeau 11, Fung 10]. The number of spawned thread groups equals the precalculated computation dimensions described in Section 2.2.2. Af-

```
[numthreads(8, 8, 1)]
void ComputeJPEG(
   uint3 DispatchThreadID  : SV_DispatchThreadID,
   uint3 GroupThreadID     : SV_GroupThreadID,
   uint3 GroupID           : SV_GroupID,
   uint GroupIndex         : SV_GroupIndex)
{
   InitSharedMemory(GroupIndex);

   //RGB -> YCbCr component and level shift
   ComputeColorTransform(GroupIndex, DispatchThreadID);

   //Apply forward discrete cosine transform.
   ComputeFDCT(GroupIndex, GroupThreadID);

   //Quantize DCT coefficients.
   ComputeQuantization(GroupIndex);

   //Move nonzero quantized values to
   //beginning of shared memory array
   //to be able to calculate preceding zeros.
   StreamCompactQuantizedData(GroupIndex);

   //Initiate bitstrings, calculate number of
   //bits to occupy, and identify if thread represents EOB.
   BSResult result = BuildBitStrings(GroupIndex);

   //Do entropy coding to shared memory
   //using atomic operation.
   EntropyCodeAC(GroupIndex, result);

   //Move result from shared memory to device memory.
   CopyToDeviceMemory(GroupIndex, GroupID, result);
}
```

Listing 2.3. Main compute shader function.

```
float Get_YCbCr_Component_From_RGB(float3 RGB)
{
#ifdef COMPONENT_Y
  return dot(RGB,float3(0.299,0.587,0.114)) * 255.0f;
#elif COMPONENT_CB
  return dot(RGB,float3(-0.168736,-0.331264,0.5)) * 255.0f + 128.0f;
#elif COMPONENT_CR
  return dot(RGB,float3(0.5,-0.418688,-0.081312)) * 255.0f + 128.0f;
#endif
}
```

Listing 2.4. RGB to YC_bC_r conversion.

ter finished execution, each group has computed one 8×8 block of partial JPEG data that is later processed by the CPU. One `Dispatch` method call per color plane is invoked. All relevant shader resources are set before each invocation.

Compute color transform and chroma subsampling. Source texture data is sampled using the clamp addressing mode; see details in Section 2.2.2. Depending on the chroma subsampling mode, each thread group may simulate a different group size by sampling multiple texture elements per thread. When encoding using, for example, 4:2:0 subsampling, each thread block acts over a 16×16 pixel block by having each thread sample four pixels each. Sampled RGB color values are converted to YC_bC_r color space using Equation (2.1). Listing 2.4 shows how this conversion is done using HLSL, where defines are used to differentiate between the shaders for the different color planes. Converted values are averaged and finally rescaled to the range $[0, 255]$.

Compute forward discrete cosine transform. Before DCT is applied, color values are level shifted and grouped in an 8×8 color matrix M. The DCT matrix multiplications, as in Equation (2.3), are computed in parallel [Kirk and Hwu 10]. Each thread calculates a matrix element result by adding corresponding row and column element multiplications together. To avoid data dependency errors, threads are synchronized before the second multiplication takes place. The HLSL implementation is listed in Listing 2.5.

Compute quantization. After DCT computation, the resulting matrix is quantized. Quantization is computed by dividing each DCT coefficient by a corresponding quantization table element. The resulting floating-point value is rounded to the nearest integer and copied in the zigzag order, shown in Figure 2.4, to an integer array. See the quantization HLSL code in Listing 2.6.

Calculation of preceding zeros. AC coefficients are, for any chroma subsampling and quality level, entropy coded as described in Section 2.1.6. To comply with the JPEG standard, run-length zeros are counted. Scan primitives provide a method

```
void ComputeFDCT(uint GroupIndex, uint3 GroupThreadID)
{
  DCT_MatrixTmp[GroupIndex] = 0;
  [unroll] for(int k = 0; k < 8; k++)
    DCT_MatrixTmp[GroupIndex] += DCT_matrix[GroupThreadID.y*8+k] *
            TransformedPixelData[k*8+GroupThreadID.x];

  GroupMemoryBarrierWithGroupSync();

  DCT_Coefficients[GroupIndex] = 0;
  [unroll] for(int k = 0; k < 8; k++)
    DCT_Coefficients[GroupIndex] += DCT_MatrixTmp[GroupThreadID.y*8+k] *
            DCT_matrix_transpose[k*8+GroupThreadID.x];

  GroupMemoryBarrierWithGroupSync();
}
```

Listing 2.5. Forward cosine transform computed in parallel.

```
void ComputeQuantization(uint GroupIndex)
{
  //Divide and round to nearest integer.
  QuantizedComponents[GroupIndex] =
      round( DCT_Coefficients[ZigZagIndices[GroupIndex]] /
              Quantization_Table[GroupIndex]);
}
```

Listing 2.6. Quantization code.

```
void StreamCompactQuantizedData(uint GroupIndex)
{
  //Set to 0 when a DC component or AC == 0.
  if(GroupIndex > 0 && QuantizedComponents[GroupIndex] != 0)
    ScanArray[GroupIndex] = 1;
  else
    ScanArray[GroupIndex] = 0;

  GroupMemoryBarrierWithGroupSync();

  Scan(GroupIndex);

  if(GroupIndex > 0 && QuantizedComponents[GroupIndex] != 0)
  {
    RemappedValues[ScanArray[GroupIndex]] = QuantizedComponents[GroupIndex];
    PrevIndex[ScanArray[GroupIndex]] = GroupIndex;
  }

  GroupMemoryBarrierWithGroupSync();
}
```

Listing 2.7. Calculate run-length zeros and stream compact AC coefficients.

for performing stream compaction in parallel, which is used in the counting process [Harris et al. 07]. First the DC coefficient and all nonzero AC coefficients are flagged and copied to a separate array in shared memory. The collected values are accumulated by computing an exclusive scan. Each nonzero AC coefficient is, together with its current index position, copied to a new array where the destination index position is equal to the corresponding scan result value; see the HLSL implementation in Listing 2.7.

Build bit strings. After stream compaction, entropy bit strings are constructed. Here each thread group is responsible for generating a bit stream of encoded AC coefficients that complies to the JPEG standard. Each thread identifies which, if any, bit strings to construct and append to the thread-group bit stream. Threads also keep track of the total bit count of all constructed bit strings. Bit count is retrieved by using the Shader Model 5.0 intrinsic function firstbithigh. Total bit count is used when calculating output positions, to calculate where bit strings should be concatenated. The bit-string construction HLSL code is in Listing 2.8.

```
typedef int BitString; // <-- numbits stored in high 16 bits

struct BSResult
{
  int NumEntropyBits;
  BitString BS[6];
};

BSResult BuildBitStrings(uint GroupIndex)
{
  BSResult result = (BSResult)0;

  static const uint mask[] = {1,2,4,8,16,32,64,128,256,
              512,1024,2048,4096,8192,16384,32768};

  //special marker symbols
  BitString M_16Z = AC_Huffman[0xF0];
  BitString M_EOB = AC_Huffman[0x00];

  if(GroupIndex == 0 && RemappedValues[0] == 0)
  {
    result.BS[5] = M_EOB;
  }
  else if(RemappedValues[GroupIndex] != 0)
  {
    uint PrecedingZeros = (PrevIndex[GroupIndex] -
            PrevIndex[GroupIndex-1] - 1);

    //Append 16 zeros markers.
    for(int i = 0; i < PrecedingZeros / 16; i++)
    {
      result.BS[i] = M_16Z;
    }

    int tmp = RemappedValues[GroupIndex];

    //Get number of bits to represent number.
    uint nbits = firstbithigh(abs(tmp)) + 1;
```

```
//AC symbol 1
result.BS[3] = AC_Huffman[((PrecedingZeros % 16) << 4) + nbits];

//AC symbol 2
if(tmp < 0) tmp--;
result.BS[4] = (nbits << 16) | (tmp & (mask[nbits] - 1));

//Insert end of block (EOB) symbol?
if(PrevIndex[GroupIndex] != 63 && RemappedValues[GroupIndex+1] == 0)
{
  result.BS[5] = M_EOB;
}
}

//Calculate total bit count.
[unroll] for(int i = 0; i < 6; i++)
{
  if(result.BS[i] != 0)
  {
    result.NumEntropyBits += (result.BS[i] >> 16);
  }
}

return result;
}
```

Listing 2.8. Construction of bit strings.

Entropy code AC coefficients. When using precomputed Huffman tables, VLE on GPU hardware has previously been shown to be efficient [Balevic 09]. Each constructed bit string is appended to a bit stream in shared memory. Bits are appended using the atomic intrinsic function `InterlockedOr`. When all threads have finished entropy coding, as seen in Listing 2.9, the final block output is copied to device memory. The last group thread is also responsible for outputting the bit count of the AC entropy data.

```
void EntropyCodeAC(uint GroupIndex, BSResult result)
{
  ScanArray[GroupIndex] = result.NumEntropyBits;

  Scan(GroupIndex);

  uint bitpos = ScanArray[GroupIndex];
  [unroll] for(int i = 0; i < 6; i++)
  {
    if(result.BS[i] != 0)
    {
      Write(result.BS[i], bitpos);
      bitpos += result.BS[i] >> 16;
    }
  }

  GroupMemoryBarrierWithGroupSync();
}
```

Listing 2.9. Entropy coding of group AC coefficients.

```
void CopyToDeviceMemory(uint GroupIndex, uint3 GroupID, BSResult result)
{
  uint outIndex = GetOutputIndex(GroupIndex, GroupID);

  if(GroupIndex > 0 && GroupIndex < EntropyBlockSize -1)
    EntropyOut[outIndex] = ConvertEndian(EntropyResult[GroupIndex -1]);

  else if(GroupIndex == 0)
    EntropyOut[outIndex] = QuantizedComponents[0];
  else if(GroupIndex == 63)
    EntropyOut[outIndex - 64 + EntropyBlockSize] = ScanArray[63];
}
```

Listing 2.10. Copying group result to device memory.

Copy to device memory. Each thread that has valid output data is responsible for copying that data to device memory, as shown in Listing 2.10. Endianness conversion is applied to optimize the final CPU coding step where each byte is treated separately. Block data copied to the output buffer is ordered in a pattern based on the chroma subsampling mode used. Figure 2.7 illustrates how YC_bC_r blocks are copied to device memory at different chroma subsampling modes.

Final CPU coding. After GPU computation, the data is copied to a staging buffer resource for final CPU processing. Each GPU generated block is processed by coding delta DC values and appending to the final JPEG bit stream, as described in Section 2.1.6. No modifications are done to already entropy-coded AC data. The CPU process is briefly illustrated in Figure 2.7. The GPU is not suited to do this concatenation because of challenges with delta DC calculations and special cases when an appended byte equals 0xFF. Every 0xFF byte has to be directly followed by a 0x00 byte, otherwise it would be confused with a JPEG marker symbol. After all blocks have been appended to the stream, an end of image (EOI) marker is appended and the JPEG data is complete.

The CPU is also creating the corresponding JFIF header, which is used when decoding generated baseline JPEG data [Hamilton 92]. The following, relevant encoding data is stored in the JFIF header structure:

- quantization tables,

- Huffman tables,

- chroma subsampling factors,

- image dimensions,

- number of color components,

- sample precision (8 bits).

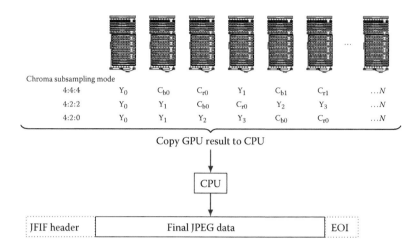

Figure 2.7. GPU to CPU process showing thread group output order based on chroma subsampling mode.

2.3   Performance

Performance tests were performed by compressing back-buffer data into JPEG data. Two source images, of dimensions $2,268 \times 1,512$ pixels, were encoded with different settings using the presented technique and libjpeg-turbo version 1.2.0.[1] The back buffer has the relevant flags to be treated as a shader resource. The source `Texture2D` resource is created by loading RGB data from a file. This texture is mapped to a full screen quad, which is rendered to the back buffer in each test run. For libjpeg-turbo tests, back-buffer data is copied to a CPU-accessible staging resource and thereafter encoded. The DirectCompute tests are done by sampling back-buffer data directly. Resulting JPEG data size was always smaller when encoding using the DirectCompute encoder. Encoded images, with chroma subsampling disabled and JPEG quality 100, were decoded and thereafter compared to source-image data. The comparison showed that the decoded version was almost identical to the source image; details are presented in the following sections for each benchmark scenario.

The 32-bit test application was executed using a computer equipped with Microsoft Windows 7 Professional x64, Intel i7 860 CPU at 2.8 GHz, 8 GB RAM, and AMD Radeon 7970 GPU. Each run was executed 50 times, in which each run was performance timed. The test results show that the presented technique outperforms libjpeg-turbo in all test cases.

---

[1]libjpeg-turbo 1.2.0 uses SIMD instructions to encode baseline JPEG image data and is one of the fastest CPU encoders available today.

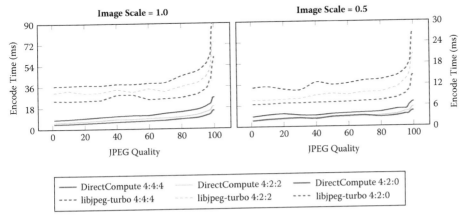

Figure 2.8. Benchmark Scenario 1 results.

2.3.1 Benchmark Scenario 1

The source image[2] used was selected to benchmark how the technique performs when encoding nonartificial image data, such as a photograph. Benchmark results are presented in Figure 2.8. Resulting data sizes at JPEG quality 100 and chroma subsampling 4:4:4 were 1,973 KiB when encoding using DirectCompute and 2,602 KiB when encoding using libjpeg-turbo. A comparison between encoded results and source-image data is presented in Table 2.2.

	Color Channel Difference Tolerance				
	0	1	2	3	4
DirectCompute	56.99%	97.52%	99.98%	100.00%	100.00%
libjpeg-turbo	59.30%	95.72%	99.54%	99.98%	100.00%

Table 2.2. Decoded Scenario 1 data compared to source-image data. JPEG data was encoded with chroma subsampling 4:4:4 and quality 100. The cell values represent the match percentages at different tolerance levels in the range $[0, 255]$.

---

[2]The source image was taken from www.imagecompression.info, where images have been "carefully selected to aid in image compression research and algorithm evaluation."

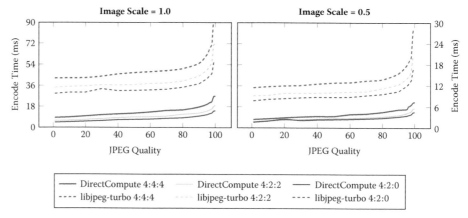

Figure 2.9. Benchmark Scenario 2 results.

2.3.2 Benchmark Scenario 2

The source image[3] used was selected to benchmark how the technique performs when encoding artificial image data, such as a game screenshot. Benchmark results are presented in Figure 2.9. Resulting data sizes at JPEG quality 100 and chroma subsampling 4:4:4 were 1,926 KiB when encoding using DirectCompute and 2,519 KiB when encoding using libjpeg-turbo. A comparison between encoded results and source-image data is presented in Table 2.3.

| | Color Channel Difference Tolerance | | | | |
	0	1	2	3	4
DirectCompute	63.58%	98.62%	99.99%	100.00%	100.00%
libjpeg-turbo	66.84%	97.27%	99.77%	99.99%	100.00%

Table 2.3. Decoded Scenario 2 data compared to source-image data. JPEG data was encoded with chroma subsampling 4:4:4 and quality 100. The cell values represent the match percentages at different tolerance levels in the range [0, 255].

[3]The source image was taken from a game called *Screen Space Combat*, which has been developed by the author.

2.4   Conclusion

This chapter demonstrates how to encode JPEG standard compliant images using DirectCompute. The technique supports both chroma subsampling and varying quality settings, which broadens usage scenarios. Benchmark scenarios show that this GPU-based encoder is well suited, compared to using a CPU encoder, when transforming uncompressed back-buffer data into JPEG image data. A demo application is supplied that can be trivially adapted and integrated into existing Direct3D 11.0-based renderers.

2.5   Acknowledgments

I would like to thank Andrew Moss, Francisco Lopez Luro, Håkan Grahn, and Jonas Petersson for their valuable input and support.

Bibliography

[Balevic 09] Ana Balevic. "Parallel Variable-Length Encoding on GPGPUs." In *Euro-Par'09: Proceedings of the International Conference on Parallel Processing*, pp. 26–35. Berlin: Springer-Verlag, 2009.

[Bilodeau 11] Bill Bilodeau. "Efficient Compute Shader Programming." Presentation, Game Developers Conference, San Francisco, CA, 2011.

[Fung 10] James Fung. "DirectCompute Lecture Series 210: GPU Optimizations and Performance." http://channel9.msdn.com/Blogs/gclassy/DirectCompute-Lecture-Series-210-GPU-Optimizations-and-Performance, 2010.

[Hamilton 92] Eric Hamilton. "JPEG File Interchange Format: Version 1.02." *JPEG*, http://www.jpeg.org/public/jfif.pdf, September 1, 1992.

[Harris et al. 07] Mark Harris, Shubhabrata Sengupta, and John D. Owens. "Parallel Prefix Sum (Scan) with CUDA." In *GPU Gems 3*, edited by Hubert Nguyen, Chapter 39. Reading, MA: Addison-Wesley Professional, 2007.

[Kerr 12] Douglas A. Kerr. "Chrominance Subsampling in Digital Images." http://dougkerr.net/pumpkin/articles/Subsampling.pdf, January 19, 2012.

[Kirk and Hwu 10] David Kirk and Wen-mei Hwu. *Programming Massively Parallel Processors: A Hands-on Approach*. San Francisco: Morgan Kaufmann, 2010.

[Pennebaker and Mitchell 93] William B. Pennebaker and Joan L. Mitchell. *JPEG Still Image Data Compression Standard*. Norwell, MA: Kluwer Academic Publishers, 1993.

About the Editors

Wessam Bahnassi is a software engineer with a background in building architecture. This combination is believed to be the reason behind Wessam's passion for 3D engine design. He has written and dealt with a variety of engines throughout a decade of game development. Currently, he is a lead rendering engineer at Electronic Arts Inc., and a supervisor of the Arabic Game Developer Network. Although a bit out of context here, his heart beats for the Syrian revolution, as well as the other Arabic revolutions in general, to which he dedicates this work.

Carsten Dachsbacher is a full professor at the Karlsruhe Institute of Technology. Prior to joining KIT, he was an assistant professor at the Visualization Research Center (VISUS) of the University of Stuttgart, Germany, and postdoctoral fellow at REVES/INRIA Sophia-Antipolis, France. He received a MS in computer science from the University of Erlangen-Nuremberg, Germany, in 2002 and a PhD in computer science in 2006. His research focuses on real-time computer graphics, interactive global illumination, and perceptual rendering, on which he has published several articles at various conferences, including SIGGRAPH, I3D, EG, and EGSR. He has been a tutorial speaker at Eurographics, SIGGRAPH, and the Game Developers Conference and a reviewer for various conferences and journals.

Wolfgang Engel is the CTO/CEO and cofounder of Confetti Special Effects Inc. (www.conffx.com), a think tank for advanced real-time graphics research for the video game and movie industry. Previously he worked for more than four years in Rockstar's core technology group as the lead graphics programmer. His game credits can be found at http://www.mobygames.com/developer/sheet/view/developerId,158706/. He is the editor of the *ShaderX* and *GPU Pro* book series, the author of several other books, and speaks on graphics programming at conferences worldwide. He has been a DirectX MVP since July 2006 and is active in several advisory boards in the industry. He also teaches "GPU Programming" at UCSD. You can find him on twitter at @wolfgangengel.

Christopher Oat is Lead Graphics Programmer at Rockstar New England where he works on real-time rendering techniques used in Rockstar's latest games. Previously, he was the Demo Team Lead for AMD's Game Computing Applications Group. Christopher has published his work in various books and journals and has presented at graphics and game developer conferences worldwide. Many of the projects that he has worked on can be found on his website: www.chrisoat.com.

Sebastien St-Laurent holds a degree in computer engineering from Sherbrooke University in Quebec (Canada) where he graduated at the top of his class in 1999. Since then, he has worked at many video game companies, including Z-Axis, Microsoft, and Neversoft. His interest, focus, and passion has always been computer graphics. Sebastien St-Laurent is also a published author who has written *Shaders for Game Programmers and Artists* and *The COMPLETE Effect and HLSL Guide.*

Michal Valient leads the technology team at Guerrilla in Amsterdam. He spends his time working on the core engine technology powering the highly acclaimed games such as *Killzone 2* and *Killzone 3* as well as some yet unreleased projects. Previously he worked as a programmer and a lead at Caligari where he developed the shader-based real-time rendering engine for Caligari trueSpace7. His interests include many aspects of light transfer, shadows and parallel processing in general. He believes in sharing the knowledge and he gave talks at GDC and Siggraph and wrote graphics papers published in ShaderX books and conference journals.

About the Contributors

Ulf Assarsson is an associate professor at Chalmers University of Technology. His main research interests are real-time shading, hard and soft shadows—including shadows in hair, fur, smoke, and volumetric participating media—GPGPU algorithms, GPU ray tracing, and real-time global illumination. He is also coauthor of the book *Real-Time Shadows* (2011).

Francisco Ávila is a research engineer at the King Abdullah University of Science and Technology (KAUST), Saudi Arabia, where he works on lightweight visualization techniques for the web. Before joining KAUST, he was a research intern at Intel working on ray-tracing techniques, data structures, and GPU programming. He received a BS in computer science from ITESM, Mexico, in 2011.

Daniel Bagnell is a software developer at Analytical Graphics, Inc., where he is working on Cesium, a WebGL virtual globe. He received his BS degrees in mathematics and computer science from Drexel University.

Homam Bahnassi has multi-disciplinary experience backed up by ten years of 3D knowledge and has made several contributions in both academic and professional areas. During his research for his master's degree, he developed a motion-planning framework for simulating autonomous construction equipment. On the professional side, he is working on designing and developing tools for 3D game artists. Currently, he works at EA Montreal as a technical artist.

Markus Billeter holds an MSc degree in physics and complex adaptive systems. He is currently completing his PhD in the computer graphics research group at Chalmers University of Technology (Gothenburg, Sweden), where he participates in research in real-time rendering and high-performance and highly-parallel algorithms for GPGPU applications. In late 2012 and early 2013, he interned at the Robert Bosch Research and Technology Center in Palo Alto, California.

Michael Bukowski graduated magna cum laude with a BS in computer systems engineering from Rensselaer Polytechnic Institute. After a brief stint with IBM as a hardware designer, he jumped head first into the games industry. He has spent the last ten-plus years in game development, where he has shipped six-plus titles working as a lead engineer and as a production engineer in a range of areas such as audio, systems, and graphics. He has handled IPs such as *Doom 3*, *Marvel Ultimate Alliance*, and *Guitar Hero*. He also has a number of publications at conferences such as SIGGRAPH, I3D, and HPG. Currently he is an engineering specialist at Vicarious Visions where he leads the Visual Alchemy Team, a research and development group focused on creating and supporting industry-leading graphics technologies for a variety of gaming platforms.

Patrick Cozzi is coauthor of *3D Engine Design for Virtual Globes* (2011) and coeditor of *OpenGL Insights* (2012). At Analytical Graphics, Inc., he leads the graphics development of Cesium, a WebGL virtual globe. He teaches "GPU Programming and Architecture" at the University of Pennsylvania, where he received a master's degree in computer science. At Khronos, he is part of the COLLADA working group.

Hawar Doghramachi studied dental medicine at the Semmelweis University in Budapest, Hungary, and in 2003 received the Doctor of Dental Medicine (DMD) title. After working for a while as a dentist, he decided to turn his lifetime passion for programming into his profession. He studied 3D programming at the Games Academy in Frankfurt, Germany. Since September 2010, he has been working as an engine programmer in the Vision Team of Havok. He is particularly interested in finding solutions for common real-time rendering problems in modern computer games, using DirectX 11 as well as modern OpenGL—thus trying to take advantage of features introduced in modern graphics hardware.

René Fürst is a graduate student of visual computing at Vienna University of Technology. He is interested in various GPGPU topics, for example, shadowing, global illumination, and fluid simulation in real time.

Athanasios Gaitatzes received his PhD in 2012 from the University of Cyprus. He received his master of science in computer science, with a specialization in computer graphics, in 1989 from Purdue University. He has developed virtual reality exhibits at the cultural center of the Foundation of the Hellenic World (FHW) in Greece, worked as a project manager of the virtual reality stereoscopic production "The Battle of Chaeronia," and worked as a software engineer at the Advanced Systems Division of IBM. Based on his extensive experience in the design and development of software, he has taken part in several European research projects. His research interests include real-time computer graphics, photorealistic visualization, and real-time rendering techniques.

Arturo García holds a BS degree in computer sciences from the University of Guadalajara. He received an MS degree in computer science from CINVESTAV and an MBA degree from ITESO. He is currently Engineering Manager at Intel.

Takahiro Harada is a researcher in AMD's office of the CTO, where he is exploring the possibility of GPU computing, mainly focusing on applications to physics simulation. Before joining AMD, he engaged in research and development on real-time physics simulation on PC and game consoles at Havok. Before coming to industry, he was in academics as an assistant professor at the University of Tokyo, where he also earned his PhD in engineering.

Padraic Hennessy is a senior graphics engineer at Vicarious Visions, an Activision Blizzard Studio. He is a primary member of the Studio's Visual Alchemy Team. Work from this team has been published at SIGGRAPH, I3D, and HPG. The team has also worked on AAA franchises such as *Skylanders*, *Doom*, *Marvel Ultimate Alliance*, and *Guitar Hero*. While graphics is his main focus at the studio, he has contributed as a core engine architect, tools engineer, network engineer, and gameplay systems engineer. When not working on developing new graphics techniques, he strives to improve artist workflow and to help artists understand complex graphics techniques through training seminars. He received a BS in computer engineering from Binghamton University in 2006.

Karl Hillesland creates GPU product demos and graphics research for AMD. Prior to AMD, Karl worked in physics middleware (Pixelux's Digital Molecular Matter or DMM) and game development (Maxis, Electronic Arts). His PhD in computer science is from the University of North Carolina at Chapel Hill.

Henry Kang received a BS in computer science from Yonsei University, Korea, in 1994 and his MS and PhD degrees in computer science from the Korea Advanced Institute of Science and Technology (KAIST) in 1996 and 2002, respectively. He is currently an associate professor of computer science at the University of Missouri St. Louis. His research interests include nonphotorealistic rendering and animation, illustrative visualization, image and video processing, image-based modeling and rendering, and facial expression animation.

Jan Eric Kyprianidis graduated in mathematics from the University of Hamburg, Germany, and received his doctoral degree in computer science from the University of Potsdam, Germany. Previously, he held positions as senior software engineer at Adobe Systems and as research scientist at the Hasso-Plattner-Institut. He is currently a post-doctoral researcher with the computer graphics group at TU Berlin, Germany. His research interests include differential geometry, geometry processing, nonphotorealistic rendering, and digital image processing.

Sébastien Lagarde is a senior engine/graphics programmer who has been in the game industry for ten years. He has been credited on several games including casual and AAA titles on different platforms (PS2, GameCube, Nintendo DS, Xbox 360, PS3, PC), and he developed the 3D stereoscopic Trioviz SDK technology that has been integrated in several games (*Batman Arkham Asylum*, *Batman Arkham City*, *Assassin's Creed 2* and *3*, *Gear of War 3*, etc.). He has worked for several companies—Neko entertainment (video game), DarkWorks (video game), Piranese (architecture), Trioviz (stereoscopy middleware)—and now, he is using his expertise at DONTNOD entertainment in France on *Remember Me*, edited by Capcom. Passionate about rendering technologies, he has a blog (http://seblagarde.wordpress.com/) where he publishes some graphics articles.

Gabor Liktor is a PhD student at the Karlsruhe Institute of Technology (KIT), Germany. He received his diploma in computer science from the Budapest University of Technology and Economics (BUTE), Hungary. As a member of the computer graphics research group first at VISUS, University of Stuttgart, then at KIT, he is working in collaboration with Crytek GmbH. His primary areas of interest are real-time rendering architectures, volume rendering, adaptive shading, and geometry subdivision.

Sean Lilley is a senior studying digital media design at the University of Pennsylvania. He has interned at Electronic Arts and AMD, which reflects his passion for both video games and 3D graphics. Currently he is building a game engine with his brother Ian as part of their senior design project. He hopes to join the game industry after graduation.

Oliver Mattausch is currently employed as a post doctorate in the VMML Lab of the University of Zurich, working on processing and visualizing large datasets. Previously he worked as a computer graphics researcher at the Vienna University of Technology and at the University of Tokyo/ERATO. He received his MSc in 2004 and his PhD in 2010 from Vienna University of Technology. His research interests are real-time rendering, visibility and shadows, global illumination, and geometry processing.

Pavlos Mavridis is a software engineer at the Foundation of the Hellenic World, where he is working on the design and implementation of real-time rendering techniques for virtual reality installations. He received his BSc and MSc degrees in computer science from the University of Athens, Greece. He is currently pursuing his PhD in real-time computer graphics at the Department of Informatics of the Athens University of Economics and Business. His current research interests include real-time photorealistic rendering, global illumination algorithms, texture compression, and texture filtering techniques.

Morgan McGuire teaches game design and computer graphics at Williams College and works on new products in the games industry. His industry work includes *Skylanders: SWAP Force* and *Marvel Ultimate Alliance 2* at Vicarious Visions, *Titan Quest* at Iron Lore, the EInk display for the Amazon Kindle, and designs for recent GPUs at NVIDIA. His academic publications include *The Graphics Codex for iOS* (2012), *Creating Games: Mechanics, Content, and Technology* (2008), *Computer Graphics: Principles and Practice* (Third Edition, 2013), and SIGGRAPH papers on video and GPU ray tracing. He received his PhD from Brown University.

Jay McKee is a senior engineer in the Advanced Technology Initiatives group at AMD. There he conducts research on real-time rendering techniques and develops graphics-related tools and demos. He was the technical lead for AMD's 2012 "Leo" demo. He received a BS in computer science from the University of West Florida.

Benjamin Mistal graduated with a degree in computer science from the University of Victoria in 1998, and he spent a number of years developing industrial software applications utilizing 2D and 3D laser cloud data. After joining the 3D Application Research Group at ATI (now part of AMD), he helped develop, and later lead the development of, the popular RenderMonkey shader development tool. He has been involved with Right Hemisphere's Deep Exploration and Deep Creator products, and he cofounded Esperient Corporation to further develop the Deep Creator (renamed to Esperient Creator) product. He is currently researching and developing programming languages and web-related graphics technologies for Mistal Research, Inc. (www.mistal-research.com) and is also developing products for Qualcomm Technologies Inc., highlighting their next generation of mobile graphics hardware. Often found in various places throughout the Rocky Mountains, he is an avid hiker, rock climber, and runner.

Sergio Murguía received a BSc from the University of Guanajuato in 2005 and an MSc from the Center of Research in Mathematics (CIMAT) in Mexico. In 2009, he joined Intel to work on software validation of DirectX and OpenGL drivers. He is currently working as a software validation engineer for high performance products. His areas of interest include computer graphics and photorealistic rendering.

Ola Olsson is currently a PhD student at Chalmers University of Technology in Gothenburg, Sweden. He's a member of the computer graphics group and spends most of his time these days forcing pixels into boxes of various shapes and sizes. His primary research focus is algorithms for managing and shading thousands of lights in real time, resulting in several influential publications on tiled and, later, clustered shading. Before becoming a PhD student, Ola was a game programmer for around ten years with roles ranging from game-play programmer on *Ty the Tasmanian Tiger* to lead rendering programmer on *Race Pro*.

Brian Osman is a senior software engineer at Vicarious Visions, where he specializes in rendering and engine technology. He has spent over ten years working on games in a variety of genres and for a wide range of platforms. He received his BS and MS in computer science from Rensselaer Polytechnic Institute.

Georgios Papaioannou is currently an assistant professor of computer graphics at the Department of Informatics of the Athens University of Economics and Business. He received a BSc in computer science and a PhD in computer graphics and pattern recognition, both from the University of Athens, Greece. In the past, he has worked as a research fellow in many research and development projects, and as a virtual reality software engineer at the Foundation of the Hellenic World. His research is focused on real-time computer graphics algorithms, photorealistic rendering, virtual reality systems, and three-dimensional pattern recognition. He has contributed many scientific papers in the above fields and has coauthored one international and two Greek computer graphics textbooks. He is also a member of IEEE, ACM, SIGGRAPH, and Eurographics Association and has been a member of the program committees of many computer graphics conferences.

Emil Persson is the head of research at Avalanche Studios, where he is conducting forward-looking research, with the aim to be relevant and practical for game development, as well as setting the future direction for the Avalanche Engine. Previously, he was an ISV engineer in the Developer Relations team at ATI/AMD. He assisted tier-one game developers with the latest rendering techniques, identifying performance problems and applying optimizations. He also made major contributions to SDK samples and technical papers. He also runs the website http://www.humus.name, where he blogs about graphics technology and posts demo applications and photographic skyboxes.

Stefan Petersson received a BSc and an MSc in computer science from Blekinge Institute of Technology (BTH), Sweden. He is currently a lecturer and PhD student in the School of Computing, where he is part of the GSIL Computer Graphics group. Stefan is also a program manager for the Master of Science in Game and Software Engineering program at BTH. His current research and teaching interests include computer graphics and GPGPU.

Donald Revie graduated from the University of Abertay with a BSc (Hons) in computer games technology before joining Cohort Studios in late 2006. He worked on Cohort's Praetorian Tech platform from its inception, designing and implementing much of its renderer and core scene representation. He also worked individually and with others to develop shaders and graphics techniques across many of the company's projects. Since leaving Cohort Studios in early 2011 he has continued refining his ideas on engine architecture and pursuing his wider interests in game design and writing.

Leo Reyes studied computer engineering at the University of Guadalajara, Mexico. He received his MS and PhD degrees in computer vision from the Center of Research and Advanced Studies (CINVESTAV). His research interests include computer vision, computer graphics, image processing, and artificial intelligence. He is currently working at Intel Labs in Guadalajara.

Christophe Riccio is a graphics programmer with a background in digital content creation tools, game programming, and GPU design research. He is also a keen supporter of real-time rendering as a new medium for art. He has an MSc degree in computer game programming from the University of Teesside. He joined e-on software to study terrain editing and to design a multi-threaded graphics renderer. He worked for Imagination Technologies on the PowerVR series 6 architecture. He is currently working for AMD doing some OpenGL gardening. For the past ten years, Christophe has been an active OpenGL community contributor, including contributions to the OpenGL specifications. Through G-Truc Creation, he writes articles to promote modern OpenGL programming. He develops tools, GLM and the OpenGL Samples Pack, which are part of the official OpenGL SDK.

David C. Schedl received his master's degree in the program of Interactive Media at the University of Applied Sciences Upper Austria Campus Hagenberg in 2011. He worked as a scientific researcher at the Institute of Computer Graphics and Algorithms at the Vienna University of Technology until 2012. He is currently a project assistant at the Institute of Computer Graphics at the Johannes Kepler University Linz. His research interests include real-time rendering, image processing, and light fields.

Daniel Scherzer is professor of visual computing at the University of Applied Sciences Ravensburg-Weingarten. He has also worked at MPI, KAUST, the University of Applied Sciences Hagenberg, the Ludwig Boltzmann Institute for Archaeological Prospection and Virtual Archaeology, and the Institute of Computer Graphics and Algorithms of the Vienna University of Technology, where he received an MSc in 2005, an MSocEcSc in 2008, and a PhD in 2009. His current research interests include global illumination, temporal coherence methods, shadow algorithms, modeling, and level-of-detail approaches for real-time rendering. He has authored and coauthored several papers in these fields.

Michael Wimmer is an associate professor at the Institute of Computer Graphics and Algorithms of the Vienna University of Technology, where he received an MSc in 1997 and a PhD in 2001. His current research interests are real-time rendering, computer games, real-time visualization of urban environments, point-based rendering, and procedural modeling. He has coauthored many papers in these fields, was papers cochair of EGSR 2008 and of Pacific Graphics 2012, and is associate editor of the journal *Computers & Graphics*.

Jason C. Yang is senior manager of the Advanced Technology Initiatives group at AMD, which develops new graphics algorithms, real-time physics technologies, and GPU demos. He received his BS and PhD in electrical engineering and computer science from MIT.

Antoine Zanuttini works for DONTNOD Entertainment as a software engineer. He received his PhD in 2012 from the Arts and Technologies of Image Department of Université Paris 8. His research interests include material lighting, fluids simulation, depth of field, and expressive rendering.

Jason Zink is a senior engineer and software developer currently working in the automotive industry. He holds a bachelor's degree in electrical engineering and a master's degree in computer science. He has received a Microsoft MVP award for XNA/DirectX for the past four years running. Jason is also an active writer, coauthoring the book *Practical Rendering and Computation with Direct3D 11* (2011) and the online book *Programming Vertex, Geometry, and Pixel Shaders* (2008–2011), and he has contributed to the *ShaderX* series, the *Game Programming Gems* series, and the GameDev.net collection. He also actively maintains and develops the open source rendering framework Hieroglyph 3 (http://hieroglyph3. codeplex.com/) and can be found on the GameDev.net forums as "Jason Z," where he maintains a regularly updated developer journal.